Persian Gulf 2014

Persian Gulf 2014

India's Relations with the Region

Edited by
P. R. Kumaraswamy

SAGE   www.sagepublications.com
Los Angeles • London • New Delhi • Singapore • Washington DC

First published in 2014 by

 SAGE Publications India Pvt Ltd
B1/I-1 Mohan Cooperative Industrial Area
Mathura Road, New Delhi 110 044, India
www.sagepub.in

SAGE Publications Inc
2455 Teller Road
Thousand Oaks, California 91320, USA

SAGE Publications Ltd
1 Oliver's Yard, 55 City Road
London EC1Y 1SP, United Kingdom

SAGE Publications Asia-Pacific Pte Ltd
3 Church Street
#10-04 Samsung Hub
Singapore 049483

Published by Vivek Mehra for SAGE Publications India Pvt Ltd, Phototypeset in
10/13pt Berkeley by Diligent Typesetter, Delhi and printed at Saurabh Printers
Pvt Ltd, New Delhi.

Library of Congress Cataloging-in-Publication Data

Persian Gulf 2014 : India's relations with the region / edited by P.R. Kumaraswamy.
    pages cm
  Includes bibliographical references and index.
  1. India—Relations—Persian Gulf Region. 2. Persian Gulf Region—Relations—
India. 3. Persian Gulf States—Politics and government—21st century. 4. Persian
Gulf States—Economic conditions—21st century. I. Kumaraswamy, P. R.
DS326.P436   303.48'254053—dc23   2014   2014030091

ISBN: 978-93-515-0077-3 (HB)

The SAGE Team: Rudra Narayan, Alekha Chandra Jena, Anju Saxena and
Rajinder Kaur

To
Atul and Atul
For making MEI@ND a virtual reality

Contents

List of Tables and Figures   ix
List of Abbreviations   xiii

CHAPTER 1
Introduction   1
P. R. Kumaraswamy

CHAPTER 2
Bahrain   34
Melissa M. Cyrill

CHAPTER 3
Iran   54
Alvite Singh Ningthoujam

CHAPTER 4
Iraq   99
Anjani Kumar Singh

CHAPTER 5
Kuwait   118
Paulami Sanyal

CHAPTER 6
Oman   143
Marimuthu Ulaganathan

CHAPTER 7
Qatar   166
Manjari Singh

CHAPTER 8
Saudi Arabia   191
Md. Muddassir Quamar

CHAPTER 9
UAE   223
Jatung Raja Philemon Chiru

CHAPTER 10
Yemen   253
Dipanwita Chakravortty

CHAPTER 11
Gulf Cooperation Council (GCC)   277
Priyanka Mittal

CHAPTER 12
Policy Options for India   290
MEI@ND

About the Editor and Contributors   294
About MEI@ND   296
Index   297

List of Tables and Figures

TABLES

1.1	Place of Persian Gulf Countries among the Top 25 Trading Partners of India during 2012–13	9
1.2	Persian Gulf's Share in India's Total Imports (in US$ Million)	10
1.3	Persian Gulf's Share in India's Total Exports (in US$ Million)	12
1.4	India's Five Largest Trading Partners in 2012–13 (in US$ Million)	13
1.5	India's Trade Deficit–Oil Import Linkages	15
1.6	India's Energy Imports from the Persian Gulf Region (in US$ Million)	17
1.7	Top Five Energy Suppliers of India	19
1.8	Share of Oil-related Exports to Iran (in US$ Million)	19
1.9	Share of Oil Products in India's Exports (in US$ Million)	21
1.10	Share of Energy in India's Total Foreign Trade (in US$ Million)	22
1.11	Oil Reserves	24
1.12	Gas Reserves	25
1.13	List of Countries Requiring ECR for Indian Migrant Labourers	26
1.14	Number of ECR Issued	27
1.15	Size of the Expatriate Population in Saudi Arabia	29
2.1	India–Bahrain Bilateral Trade (in US$ Million)	42
2.2	Share of Oil in India's Imports from Bahrain (in US$ Million)	44
2.3	India's Energy Imports from Bahrain (in US$ Million)	45
3.1	Iranian Presidential Elections, June 2013	57
3.2	India–Iran Bilateral Trade (in US$ Million)	64
3.3	Share of Oil in India's Imports from Iran (in US$ Million)	65
3.4	India's Energy Imports from Iran (in US$ Million)	71

4.1   India–Iraq Bilateral Trade (in US$ Million)   105
4.2   Share of Oil in India's Imports from Iraq (in US$ Million)   107
4.3   India's Energy Imports from Iraq (in US$ Million)   108
5.1   Kuwaiti Parliamentary Elections, July 2013   120
5.2   India–Kuwait Bilateral Trade (in US$ Million)   126
5.3   Share of Oil in India's Imports from Kuwait (in US$ Million) 127
5.4   India's Energy Imports from Kuwait (in US$ Million)   129
6.1   India–Oman Bilateral Trade (in US$ Million)   151
6.2   Share of Oil in India's Imports from Oman (in US$ Million) 152
6.3   India's Energy Imports from Oman (in US$ Million)   156
7.1   India–Qatar Bilateral Trade (in US$ Million)   174
7.2   Share of Oil in India's Imports from Qatar (in US$ Million) 175
7.3   India's Energy Imports from Qatar (in US$ Million)   178
8.1   India–Saudi Arabia Bilateral Trade (in US$ Million)   200
8.2   Share of Oil in India's Imports from Saudi Arabia
        (in US$ Million)   201
8.3   India's Energy Imports from Saudi Arabia (in US$ Million)   205
9.1   India's Five Largest Trading Partners in 2012–13
        (in US$ Million)   231
9.2   India–UAE Bilateral Trade (in US$ Million)   231
9.3   Share of Oil in India's Imports from the UAE (in US$ Million) 232
9.4   India's Energy Imports from the UAE (in US$ Million)   236
10.1 Composition of the National Dialogue Conference (NDC)
        in Yemen   255
10.2 India–Yemen Bilateral Trade (in US$ Million)   262
10.3 Share of Oil in India's Imports from Yemen
        (in US$ Million)   263
10.4 India's Energy Imports from Yemen (in US$ Million)   265
11.1 India–GCC Bilateral Trade (in US$ Million)   280
11.2 India's Energy Imports from GCC (in US$ Million)   281

FIGURES

1.1   Exports, Imports and Ranking of Persian Gulf Countries
        in India's Total Trade (2012–13)   9
1.2   Persian Gulf's Share in India's Total Imports   11
1.3   Persian Gulf's Share in India's Total Exports   13

1.4   Exports and Imports with the Five Largest Trading
      Partners (2012–13) of India   14
1.5   Trade Balance with India's Top Five Trading Partners
      in 2012–13   14
1.6   India's Trade Deficit–Oil Import Linkages   16
1.7   India's Energy Imports from the Persian Gulf Region   18
1.8   Share of India's Oil-related Exports to Iran (in US$ Million) 20
1.9   Share of Oil Products in India's Exports   22
1.10 Share of Energy in India's Total Foreign Trade   23
1.11 Persian Gulf's Share of Oil   24
1.12 Persian Gulf's Share of Gas   25
1.13 Number of ECR Issued   28
1.14 Per Cent of ECR Issued to Persian Gulf Countries in 2012   28
1.15 Size of Expatriate Population in Saudi Arabia   29
2.1   India–Bahrain Bilateral Trade   43
2.2   Share of Oil in India's Total Imports from Bahrain   44
3.1   Iranian Presidential Elections, June 2013   58
3.2   India–Iran Bilateral Trade   65
3.3   Share of Oil in India's Total Imports from Iran   66
4.1   India–Iraq Bilateral Trade   105
4.2   Share of Oil in India's Total Imports from Iraq   108
5.1   Kuwaiti Parliamentary Elections, July 2013   121
5.2   India–Kuwait Bilateral Trade   126
5.3   Share of Oil in India's Imports from Kuwait   127
6.1   India–Oman Bilateral Trade   151
6.2   Share of Oil in India's Imports from Oman   152
7.1   India–Qatar Bilateral Trade   175
7.2   Share of Oil in India's Imports from Qatar   176
8.1   India–Saudi Arabia Bilateral Trade   201
8.2   Share of Oil in India's Imports from Saudi Arabia   202
8.3   Share of Saudi Arabia in India's Oil Imports   206
9.1   India–UAE Bilateral Trade   232
9.2   Share of Oil in India's Imports from UAE   233
10.1 Composition of the National Dialogue Conference in Yemen   256
10.2 India–Yemen Bilateral Trade   262
10.3 Share of Oil in India's Imports from Yemen   263
11.1 India–GCC Bilateral Trade   280
11.2 India's Energy Imports from GCC   282

List of Abbreviations

ACPRA	Saudi Civil and Political Rights Association
ADACH	Abu Dhabi Authority for Culture and Heritage
ADIA	Abu Dhabi Investment Authority
AIFVs	Armoured Infantry Fighting Vehicles
APIs	Active Pharmaceutical Ingredients
AQAP	Al-Qaeda in the Arabian Peninsula
AQI	Al-Qaeda in Iraq
ASSOCHAM	Associated Chambers of Commerce and Industry of India
BAFA	Federal Office of Economics and Export Control (Germany)
bcf	billion cubic feet
BICI	Bahrain Independent Commission of Inquiry
BIIP	Bahrain International Investment Park
BIPA	Bilateral Investment Promotion and Protection Agreement
BIS	Bahrain-India Society
BITEX	Bahrain International Technology Exhibition
BITS	Birla Institute of Technology and Science
BJP	Bharatiya Janata Party
BORL	Bharat Oman Refineries Limited
bpd	barrels per day
BOP	balance of plant
CAGR	compound annual growth rate
CAPEXIL	Chemical and Allied Export Promotion Council of India
CCITP	Chamber of Commerce for Iran Trade Promotion
CEC	Chief Election Commissioner
CENTCOM	US Central Command

CIDS	Chief of Integrated Defence Staff (India)
CIFF	Chennai International Film Festival
CII	Confederation of Indian Industry
CISC	Chairman Chiefs of Staff Committee (UAE)
CNS	Chief of Naval Staff (India)
CPCL	Chennai Petroleum Corporation Limited
CPI-M	Communist Party of India (Marxist)
CPPCC	Chinese People's Political Consultative Conference
CSIS	Center for Strategic and International Studies (Washington, D.C.)
DEA	Department of Economic Affairs (India)
DFTP	Duty Free Tariff Preference (India)
DMIC	Delhi–Mumbai Industrial Corridor
EAM	External Affairs Minister (India)
ECR	emigration check required; enhanced oil recovery
EDB	Economic Development Board (Bahrain)
EEP	Educational Exchange Programme
EEPC	Engineering Export Promotion Council (India)
EIP	Energy Insurance Pool
EPC	Engineering, Procurement and Construction
ESPD	Essar Steel Processing and Distribution
FAPCCI	Federation of Andhra Pradesh Chamber of Commerce and Industry
FDI	foreign direct investment
FICCI	Federation of Indian Chambers of Commerce and Industry
FIFA	Fédération Internationale de Football Association
FTA	Free Trade Agreement
FTZ	Free Trade Zone
GCC	Gulf Cooperation Council
GDP	gross domestic product
GIA	General Investment Authority
GNFC	Gujarat Narmada Valley Fertilisers and Chemicals
GSFCL	Gujarat State Fertilizers and Chemicals Limited
HLTFI	India–UAE High Level Task Force on Investments
HPCL	Hindustan Petroleum Corporation Limited

HSBC	Hongkong and Shanghai Banking Corporation
IAEA	International Atomic Energy Agency
IBPN	Indian Business and Professional Network (Qatar)
ICBF	Indian Community Benevolent Forum (Qatar)
ICC	Indian Cultural Centre (Qatar)
ICCR	Indian Council of Cultural Relations
ICRC	International Committee of the Red Cross
IDEX	International Defence Exhibition and Conference (UAE)
IDPs	internally displaced persons
IFFK	International Film Festival of Kerela
IGIC	India–GCC Industrial Conference
IISS	International Institute for Strategic Studies (London)
IL&FS	Infrastructure Leasing & Financial Services Limited (India)
IMF	International Monetary Fund
INS	Indian Naval Ships
IOC	Indian Oil Corporation
IOJIF	India–Oman Joint Investment Fund
IONS	Indian Ocean Naval Symposium
IOOC	Iranian Offshore Oil Company
IOR-ARC	Indian Ocean Rim Association for Regional Cooperation
IOSCG	India–Oman Strategic Consultative Group Meetings
IPI	Iran–Pakistan–India gas pipeline
IRGC	Iranian Revolutionary Guard Corps
ISCC	Indian Social and Cultural Centre
ISIL	Islamic State of Iraq and the Levant
ISIRI	Institute of Standards and Industrial Research of Islamic Republic of Iran
ITA	Iran Tea Association
ITEC	Indian Technical and Economic Cooperation Programme
ITUC	International Trade Union Confederation
IUML	Indian Union Muslim League
JBC	Joint Business Council
JCDC	Joint Committee of the Defence Co-operation
JCM	Joint Commission Meeting

JCSM	Joint Committee on Security Matters
JDCC	Joint Defence Cooperation Committee
JSPL	Jindal Steel and Power Limited
JWG	Joint Working Group
KDI	Kuwait Diplomatic Institute
KIA	Kuwait Investment Authority
KISR	Kuwait Institute for Scientific Research
KRG	Kurdish Regional Government (Iraq)
KUNA	Kuwaiti News Agency
L&T	Larsen & Toubro
LC	Letters of Credit
LIFF	Ladakh International Film Festival
LNG	Liquefied Natural Gas
MEA	Ministry of External Affairs (India)
MEI	Middle East Institute
MENA	Middle East and North Africa
MLFPS	Market Linked Focus Product Scheme
mmcfd	million cubic feet per day
MMTPA	million metric tonnes per annum
MOIA	Ministry of Overseas Indian Affairs
MOLSA	Ministry of Labour and Social Affairs (Qatar)
MoPIC	Minister of Planning & International Cooperation (Yemen)
MoU	Memorandum of Understanding
MRPL	Mangalore Refinery and Petrochemicals Limited
MTPA	million tonnes per annum
NAC	National Audit Court (Bahrain)
NBT	National Book Trust, India
NCDEX	National Commodity and Derivatives Exchange
NCERT	National Council of Educational Research and Training (India)
NCSM	National Council of Science Museums (India)
NDA	National Democratic Alliance (India)
NDC	National Dialogue Conference (Yemen)
NIGEC	National Iranian Gas Exports Company
NIOC	National Iranian Oil Corporation

NITC	National Iranian Tanker Company
NPT	Nuclear Non-Proliferation Treaty
NSA	National Security Advisor (India)
OCCI	Omani Chamber of Commerce and Industry
OETC	Oman Electricity Transmission Company
OIC	Organisation of Islamic Cooperation
OICC	Indian Overseas Cultural Congress
OIDB	Oil Industry Development Board
OITE	Oman International Trade and Exhibition
OMIFCO	Oman India Fertilizer Company
ONGC	Oil and Natural Gas Corporation (India)
OPEC	Organization of Petroleum Exporting Countries
OVL	ONGC Videsh Limited (India)
P&I	Protection and Indemnity
PAIPED	Public Authority for Investment Promotion of Export Development, Oman
PAM	Public Authority for Manpower (Kuwait)
PBD	Pravasi Bharatiya Divas (India)
PCLD	Petroleum Contracts and Licensing Directorate (Iraq)
PDO	Petroleum Development Oman
PNZ	Partitioned Neutral Zone (Saudi Arabia–Kuwait)
QIA	Qatar Investment Authority
QIMC	Qatar Industrial Manufacturing Company
QSTec	Qatar Solar Technologies
RBI	Reserve Bank of India
RCF	Rashtriya Chemicals and Fertilizers (India)
RNOV	Royal Navy of Oman Vessels
SABIC	Saudi Basic Industries Corporation
SAGIA	Saudi Arabian General Investment Authority
SCER	Supreme Commission for Elections and Referendum (Yemen)
SEZ	Special Economic Zones
SFA	Strategic Framework Agreement (US–Iraq)
SLOC	Sea Line of Communication
SMEs	Small and Medium Enterprises
THAAD	Thermal High Altitude Area Defence

UAE	United Arab Emirates
UAVs	Unmanned Aerial Vehicles
UNSC	United Nations Security Council
UPA	United Progressive Alliance (India)
WFP	World Food Programme
WMD	weapon of mass destruction
YIBC	Yemen–India Business Council

1
Introduction

P. R. Kumaraswamy

The year 2013 was eventful for the Middle East, especially the Persian Gulf region. The problems of the previous years, especially popular unrest, difficulties of the Arabization of the labour force, succession uncertainties, Arab–Persian tensions and unclear American policy continued to haunt the region. Though none of the issues that dominated the region's landscape were resolved, there were significant movements with mixed outcomes. Some of the regional problems have become more intense, violent and destabilizing. The situation is not different in other parts of the Arab world. A meaningful road map to stability continues to elude many Arab countries that are under the grip of popular unrest. Tunisia[1] and Yemen[2] witnessed significant progress towards constitutional processes but these were contrasted by intensification of violence, unrest and political upheavals in other parts of the Middle East.

The post-Tahrir Square democratic experiment in Egypt did not survive. Within a year of his election as President, in July 2013, Mohammed Morsi was overthrown by the military. This, however, did not go down well with a powerful section of Egyptians, especially the supporters of the Muslim Brotherhood, who protested and challenged the return of the military in Egyptian politics. The limited public space that was available after the February 2011 overthrowing of President Hosni Mubarak ended on 25 December 2013 when the Muslim Brotherhood was declared a terrorist organization.[3] This was following the Egyptian military court sentencing hundreds of Muslim activists, supporters and sympathizers to death. Having freed Mubarak in August 2013, the military charged Morsi with treason. The military, which has dominated the political scene since the Free Officers Revolution of 1952, came to occupy a much greater role in Egypt since Morsi was overthrown.

The civil situation has worsened in Syria. The active involvement of external players, especially the resourceful Qatar and Saudi Arabia, has only moved the crisis away from a possible political compromise and accommodation.[4] Backed by Doha, Syria, a founding member of the Arab League, was suspended from it; in March 2013, the Syrian seat was given to the Syrian opposition. By the end of 2013, over 100,000 persons had been killed in the Syrian conflict, with over four million becoming refugees or internally displaced. Neither the government nor the opposition could secure a definite victory; nor were they prepared for a political compromise. The human suffering continues unabated in Syria. The Russia-mediated chemical disarmament did not progress smoothly as internal situation and Syrian reluctance prevented the removal of all chemical weapons from Syria by the February 2014 deadline set by United Nations Security Council (UNSC) Resolution 2118.[5]

The Persian Gulf region witnessed some developments during 2013 that would have far-reaching consequences. The most important one was the surprise and decisive election of Hassan Rouhani in June 2013 as President of Iran. Rouhani's election ended the eight-year long presidency of Mahmoud Ahmadinejad, which was marked by controversies surrounding Iranian nuclear ambitions, belligerent approach towards neighbours and Holocaust denial rhetoric. Rouhani's conciliatory approach and his willingness to engage with the US towards resolving the nuclear issue considerably relaxed regional tension. This was followed by the Geneva deal that was concluded on 24 November between Iran and the P5+1. Through this interim deal, Iran and the US signalled their willingness to avoid confrontation and resolve the issue peacefully. Even though final and mutually acceptable agreement still remains elusive, the deal was a positive development.

At the same time, the Geneva deal also exposed and spurred regional tensions and rivalry. Despite uncertainties and misgivings in resolving the nuclear controversy, the deal was seen in Riyadh as an attempt to ignore and marginalize Saudi concerns vis-à-vis Iran. There were fears of a resumption of Iran–West bonhomie of the past. Under such a situation,

Saudi importance to the West is in doubt. These concerns over the weakening of American determination to challenge and reverse the Iranian nuclear ambitions ironically brought Riyadh closer to the Jewish State. Though much of the contacts have remained clandestine,[6] the emerging Israeli–Saudi understanding is a reversal of the peripheral diplomacy. In the 1950s, shared concerns vis-à-vis Arab countries brought the two non-Arab powers, Jewish Israel and Persian Iran, into closer ties. Now the shared concerns vis-à-vis Iran, especially its nuclear programme and the ineffective American policy, have brought the erstwhile enemies to seek a common ground. Their mutual doubt over American dependability is an added incentive.

Ageing leadership is a concern for some Arab countries in the region. Octogenarian King Abdullah has been struggling to set in motion a process whereby the grandsons of founder King Ibn Saud could take over the reins of the most important Islamic country in the world. The passing away of Crown Princes Sultan (1928–2011) and Nayef (1934–2012), and marginalization of potential challengers, such as Prince Ahmed, had smoothened the process. The selection of crown prince by the next ruler will determine the future course of al-Saud rule. By all indications, Prince Muqrin—current second deputy Prime Minister and Abdullah's half-brother—could be the last son of the founder to be the ruler. Moving the line of succession to the next generation would not be easy as there are far too many contenders and potential rulers. The Allegiance Council, comprising senior members of the al-Saud or their sons, would have a bigger say in the 'selection' of the next Saudi King.

There are concerns about other key positions in the Saudi government. Despite speculations, the ageing and ailing Prince Saud al-Faisal continues to hold the position of Foreign Minister, which he assumed in 1975. However, since the death of Prince Nayef, who held the ministry during 1975 and 2012, the powerful Interior Ministry has seen two incumbents; first Prince Ahmed and then Prince Muhammad bin Nayef. This is partly due to internal struggle within the al-Saud.

The Qatari situation was different. Indirectly citing health reasons, al-Thani, who overthrew his father and took over the reign in June 1995, voluntarily abdicated the throne in June 2013. He was succeeded by his fourth son Tamim bin Hamad al-Thani, who became crown prince in August 2003, and this generational transfer was accompanied by the departure of Hamad bin Jassim al-Thani, who was Qatari Prime Minister since 3 April 2007.

Far from reducing regional problems, the succession has intensified the Qatari problem vis-à-vis Egypt where Doha and Riyadh backed rival factions in the post-Mubarak era. The military decision to overthrow President Mohammed Morsi, the first democratically elected Egyptian leader in history in July 2013, increased the tension not only between Doha and Cairo but also between Qatar and its Arab neighbours in the Gulf. The proscription of the Muslim Brotherhood as a terrorist organization by the Egyptian military was followed by a series of court cases levelled against journalists working for al-Jazeera, the most visible manifestation of Qatari soft power. Though in the past many Arab leaders had problems with the freewheeling nature of al-Jazeera, Morsi's overthrowing marked a new low.[7]

In Syria, Qatar and Saudi Arabia are supporting the opposition and demanding the removal of President Bashar al-Assad as the precondition for political settlement; yet, their political and financial support is channelled to different opposition groups.

In recent years, Qatar has emerged as the principal player in the Middle Eastern politics and sought to mediate in a number of issues and problems. Using its financial clout, it has sought to arbitrate a number of disputes and problems, such as Hamas–Fatah differences, election of Lebanese president in November 2007 and Hamas–Jordan differences in 1999.

The growing Qatari diplomatic involvement in region's trouble zones is also a reflection of the weakening Saudi involvement in these issues and the reversals it has suffered. Despite much publicity, the Mecca accord between Hamas and Fatah mediated personally by King Abdullah in March 2007 collapsed within weeks. The much publicized Arab peace initiative unveiled by the then Crown Prince Abdullah in February 2002 was bogged down in inter-Arab differences and Israeli indifference. The failure of Saudi efforts in Lebanon was partly due to its excessive identification with Saad Hariri, whose father and former Prime Minister Rafik Hariri made his fortunes in Saudi Arabia.

The recent Saudi failures in Lebanon, Palestine, Syria and Arab–Israeli conflict were overshadowed by its decision on 18 October 2013 to not assume the non-permanent seat in the UNSC. For the first time since the founding of the UN, on 17 October 2013, Saudi Arabia unanimously secured the two-year term for 2014–15. Its unanimous election from the Asian group was a testimony to its political and financial clout. However, in a sudden and unexpected move, citing American unwillingness, Saudi Arabia refused to assume UNSC membership. Though the seat was eventually filled by Jordan, the incident raises doubts not only about the compelling reasons for the Saudi decision but also its ability and willingness to shoulder international responsibilities commensurate to its position and aspirations.

Tensions with the US over a host of issues are seen as the principal reason for the Saudi move. The US–Saudi table is crowded with unresolved issues and tensions. Despite public efforts and pronouncements, the erstwhile Saudi–US bonhomie was irreversibly damaged by the September 2011 attacks, where 15 out of 19 terrorists carried Saudi passports. Prolonged Western indifferences towards Saudi funding of various extremist groups came to an abrupt end. The American inability to resolve the decade-long controversy over the Iranian nuclear programme also undermined the Saudi trust and confidence in American security guarantees. Both in pubic and in private, Saudi and other Gulf leaders have expressed their concern over the nuclear ambitions of Iran and its hegemonic designs in the region.[8]

The Saudi uncertainty over American commitments was marked by two recent developments. Much to the constraint and displeasure of Riyadh, President Barack Obama was prepared to abandon Hosni Mubarak who had been a most trusted friend of the US since the assassination of Anwar Sadat. Riyadh saw the American nudging of the military, more than the Tahrir Square protest, responsible for the fall of Mubarak.[9] The Saudi willingness to back the military over Morsi was partly due to this calculation, especially when the West, including the US, was prepared to accept the Muslim Brotherhood. Secondly, the ascendance of Obama coincided with more public American spat and disagreements with Israel. While American pressure did not yield flexibility or concessions from Prime Minister Benjamin Netanyahu, it exposed Israeli doubts and concerns vis-à-vis the US. Both these issues raised doubts about American commitments to its long-time allies in the Middle East.

Not long ago, the Gulf Cooperation Council (GCC) was positively inclined to accept the membership of Jordan and Morocco and expand its membership beyond the narrow confines of the Persian Gulf. There were even efforts by Saudi Arabia for a political union of the GCC and a visa-regime modelled on the European Union. However, 2013 exposed deep divisions within the GCC, especially the growing competition, rivalry and tension between Qatar and Saudi Arabia over a number of regional issues and larger political differences.

Like other countries, India would not be able to remain indifferent to these tensions, competition and upheavals in the Persian Gulf region and beyond.

INDIA AND THE PERSIAN GULF

For India, the wider Middle East, stretching from Morocco in the West to Iran in the East, is perhaps the most important region, even though this fact is less commonly recognized. The region not only provides opportunities but also poses challenges for India's political ambitions and diplomatic skills. India's willingness to shoulder wider responsibilities would be tested by its ability to handle some of the sensitive issues concerning the Middle East. The region occupies a pivotal place in India's political, economic, cultural, religious and, above all, strategic interests and policies. The primacy of the Middle East is not reflected in New Delhi's attitudes and policies towards it. The region continues to remain marginal to Indian interest and draws wider attention only for controversies and conflicts; violent political upheavals; external intervention; terrorism and other forms of political violence; resurgent piracy and threats against international shipping; civil war situations in Iraq, Yemen and Syria; marginalization of ethnic and religious minorities; intensifying competition between Iran and Saudi Arabia over leadership of the Islamic world; concerns over weapons of mass destruction; nascent fears over the political ascendance of Islamist parties; and the prolonged and futile Middle East peace processes.

As a result, India's historical, political, cultural, economic, civilizational and energy links with the Middle East, especially the Persian Gulf region, continue to be ignored or do not receive adequate attention.[10]

Political Issues

The Persian Gulf received scant attention in India and the Congress party-led United Progressive Alliance (UPA) government, which was in power until May 2014, was indifferent towards the region. Tied down by what was widely described as policy paralysis due to electoral reversals and widespread corruption, it could maintain very few high-level political contacts with the region. The last major political visits took place in March 2010 when Prime Minister Manmohan Singh visited Saudi Arabia and when he attended the non-aligned summit meeting in Tehran in 2012. Indeed, no Indian president, vice-president or prime minister has visited the Arab world since the outbreak of the Arab Spring. This represents continuation of the historical neglect, which is evident in the fact that no Indian prime minister has visited Bahrain and Yemen since the British departure from these countries.

During 2013, there was only one state-level visit from the region when Kuwait Prime Minister Jaber bin Mubarak al-Sabah visited India towards the end of the year. From India, with the exception of Vice-President Hamid Ansari's visit to Iran for the inauguration of President Mohammed Rouhani in August, no other visits to the Gulf took place. Even at the level of Foreign Minister, there were minimal contacts between India and the Persian Gulf region.

Countries of the region are not members of various summit meets attended by Prime Ministers, such as G-8, Asian Regional Forum and Brazil, Russia, India, China and South Africa (BRICS), and, hence, personal contacts with leaders of the Gulf region have to happen only through bilateral visits. Thus, the absence of state visits or less frequent Foreign Minister–level visits are an impediment to improving bilateral relations.

Despite the region being India's largest trading partner, supplier of about two-thirds of oil and gas imports and home to about six-million strong expatriate labour force, the Indo-Gulf relations primarily remain commercial without any political or strategic dimension. The Persian Gulf region, accounting for 23.7 per cent of the Indian trade, has not scaled up to its political importance and interactions. Depicting Indo-Gulf energy ties as 'strategic' has become a self-satisfying mirage. With minor exceptions, energy imports are carried out on ad hoc basis and are rarely transformed into political capital.

India's failure to build upon the growing trade relations with the Persian Gulf can be attributed to three distinct factors. One, trade relations continue to remain mercantile transactions devoid of larger political or strategic vision. Two, decisions in the Persian Gulf region, especially in the Arab countries, are taken at the highest level, often by the ruler or his close aides. Hence, sending officials or junior ministers of Ministry of External Affairs (MEA) inherently suffers from hierarchical deficiencies. In the eyes of the Arab interlocutors, the low-level Indian delegations lack the necessary mandate to make, commit or execute sensitive decisions.

Domestic political preoccupation and bureaucratic nature of the MEA have inhibited Indian leaders from establishing close personal rapport with foreign leaders. During her four-year tenure as US Secretary of State, Hillary Clinton personally met and interacted with leaders of over 112 countries. Her rapport with leaders of a number of key countries had enabled her to contact them in person when the situation demanded. Indian leaders continue to shy from such personal diplomacy in furtherance of Indian interests. Formal meetings appear to be the only occasions for much of the political interaction between India and the outside world, including the Persian Gulf.

Third, much of the attention and resources of India's Foreign Minister is consumed by domestic considerations and controversies. This was more so for Salman Khurshid, who became Minister of External Affairs in October 2012. As a senior member of the UPA, he had to divide his attention between the party and the government and in the process could not improve prospects of either. The Minister of State for External Affairs, E. Ahamed, continued to be the principal person for the Middle East. Given the hierarchy consciousness of the region, his junior position was an impediment. Furthermore, as has been highlighted elsewhere, his continued refusal to engage with Israel raised concerns that Ahamed was pursuing a parochial policy of the Indian Union Muslim League (IUML) towards Middle East.[11]

On the economic arena, the relations have flourished considerably.

Economic Relations

The Persian Gulf region continues to dominate India's foreign trade and during 2012–13 six countries in the region were among India's top 25 trading partners (Table 1.1 and Figure 1.1). Except for smaller economies,

Table 1.1
Place of Persian Gulf Countries among the Top 25 Trading Partners of India during 2012–13

Country	Ranking	Imports from	Exports to	Total trade	Total trade (in per cent)
UAE	1	39,138.36	36,316.65	75,455.01	9.54
Saudi Arabia	4	33,998.11	9,785.78	43,783.89	5.53
Iraq	8	19,247.31	1,278.13	20,525.44	2.59
Kuwait	12	16,588.13	1,601.08	17,649.21	2.23
Qatar	14	15,693.08	687.18	16,380.26	2.07
Iran	17	11,594.46	3,351.07	14,945.53	1.89

Source: Adapted from Directorate General of Foreign Trade, New Delhi, available at: www.dgft.gov.in/.

Figure 1.1
Exports, Imports and Ranking of Persian Gulf Countries in India's Total Trade (2012–13)

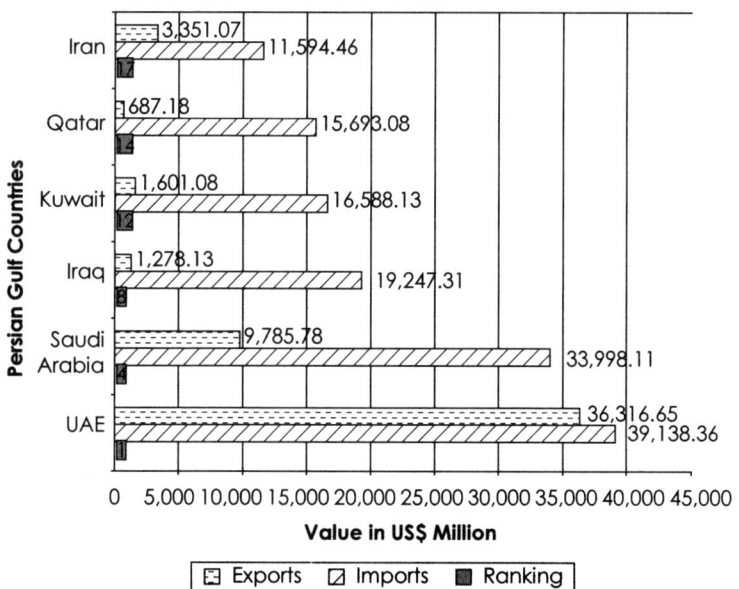

Source: Adapted from Directorate General of Foreign Trade, New Delhi, available at: www.dgft.gov.in/.

such as Bahrain, Oman and Yemen, rest of the countries in the region are its principal trade partners. Overtaking China, the United Arab Emirates (UAE) regained its number one slot and accounted for close to 10 per cent of India's total trade. The war-torn Iraq has emerged as India's eighth largest trading partner in the world. Reduced oil imports due to American sanctions did not diminish Iran's status as a major trade partner. Indeed, during 2012–13, Iran was India's third largest export destination in the Persian Gulf.

During 2012–13, India imported close to US$140 billion worth of goods from the Persian Gulf. This is over 28 per cent of India's total imports during this period (Table 1.2 and Figure 1.2). India's exports

Table 1.2
Persian Gulf's Share in India's Total Imports (in US$ Million)

Year	Total imports	Imports from persian gulf	Share (in per cent)
1996–97	39,132.41	5,225.60	13.35
1997–98	41,484.49	5,182.19	12.49
1998–99	42,388.71	6,252.67	14.75
1999–2000	49,738.06	7,708.73	15.50
2000–01	50,536.45	1,914.12	3.79
2001–02	51,413.28	2,018.62	3.93
2002–03	61,412.14	2,189.82	3.57
2003–04	78,149.11	3,549.26	4.54
2004–05	111,517.43	7,505.67	6.73
2005–06	149,165.73	8,519.55	5.71
2006–07	185,735.24	46,131.24	24.84
2007–08	251,654.01	64,328.98	25.56
2008–09	303,696.31	80,292.24	26.44
2009–10	288,372.88	73,640.76	25.54
2010–11	369,769.13	96,595.68	26.12
2011–12	489,319.49	133,825.28	27.35
2012–13	490,736.65	139,892.75	28.51

Source: Adapted from Directorate General of Foreign Trade, New Delhi, available at: www.dgft.gov.in/.

Figure 1.2
Persian Gulf's Share in India's Total Imports

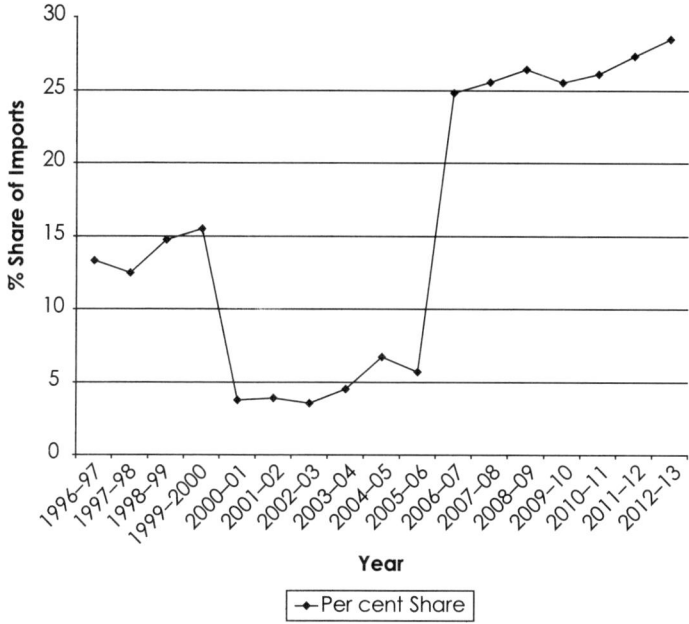

Source: Adapted from Directorate General of Foreign Trade, New Delhi, available at: www.dgft.gov.in/.

to this region are comparatively smaller. During the same period, its exports to the Persian Gulf rose significantly from US$48.8 billion in 2011–12 to just over US$57 billion the following year. This is about 19 per cent of India's total exports (Table 1.3 and Figure 1.3). During the same period, its imports from the Persian Gulf grew from US$133.8 billion to US$139.8 billion.

Indeed, two out of India's top five trading nations are to be found in the Persian Gulf. These are the UAE, which occupied the top slot, and Saudi Arabia, which occupied the fourth slot during 2012–13 (Table 1.4 and Figures 1.4 and 1.5). Its trade deficit with the UAE is marginal and stood at US$2.8 billion whereas it reached an astronomical US$38.7 billion vis-à-vis China, India's second largest trading partner during the year.

Table 1.3
Persian Gulf's Share in India's Total Exports (in US$ Million)

Year	Total exports	Exports to persian gulf	Share (in per cent)
1996–97	33,469.95	2,720.03	8.13
1997–98	34,784.98	2,952.81	8.49
1998–99	33,218.72	3,280.56	9.88
1999–2000	36,822.49	3,539.78	9.61
2000–01	44,560.29	4,376.42	9.82
2001–02	43,826.72	4,405.61	10.05
2002–03	52,719.43	5,946.79	11.28
2003–04	63,842.55	8,277.87	12.97
2004–05	83,535.94	11,423.92	13.68
2005–06	103,090.53	13,398.41	13.00
2006–07	126,414.05	19,209.10	15.20
2007–08	163,132.18	25,997.08	15.94
2008–09	185,295.36	35,104.98	18.95
2009–10	178,751.43	33,537.55	18.76
2010–11	251,136.19	50,076.90	19.94
2011–12	305,963.92	48,882.30	15.98
2012–13	300,400.68	57,160.12	19.03

Source: Adapted from Directorate General of Foreign Trade, New Delhi, available at: www.dgft.gov.in/.

The overall trade balance is heavily loaded against India. As Commerce Minister Anand Sharma told Lok Sabha in August 2013, during 2012–13, India had a trade deficit with as many as 80 countries of the world and the top 10 countries included four from the Gulf region, namely, Saudi Arabia, Iraq, Kuwait and Qatar.[12] This is largely due to the excessive domination of fossil fuel in Indo-Gulf trade and India's inability to diversify its exports to the region. Indeed, despite the rupee payment arrangement, India has not been able to expand the basket of its exports to Iran. Such a heavy trade imbalance is unsustainable in the

Figure 1.3
Persian Gulf's Share in India's Total Exports

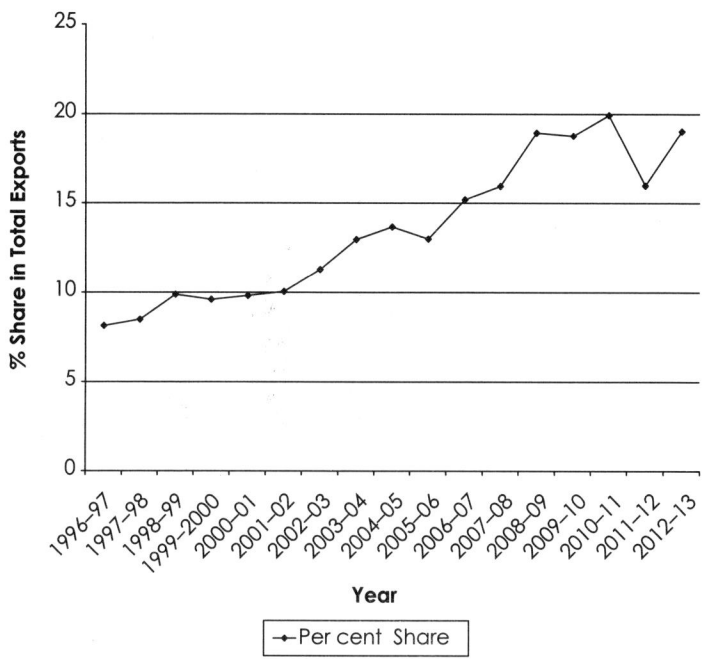

Year

→ Per cent Share

Source: Adapted from Directorate General of Foreign Trade, New Delhi, available at: www.dgft.gov.in/.

Table 1.4
India's Five Largest Trading Partners in 2012–13 (in US$ Million)

Country	Exports	Imports	Total trade	Trade balance
UAE	36,316.65	39,138.36	75,455.01	–2,821.72
China	13,534.88	52,248.33	65,783.21	–38,713.45
US	36,155.22	25,204.73	61,359.95	10,950.4
Saudi Arabia	9,785.78	33,998.11	43,783.89	–24,212.33
Switzerland	1,117.28	32,166.54	33,283.82	–31,049.25

Source: Adapted from Directorate General of Foreign Trade, New Delhi, available at: http://commerce.nic.in/eidb/iecnttopn.asp/.

Figure 1.4

Exports and Imports with the Five Largest Trading Partners (2012–13) of India

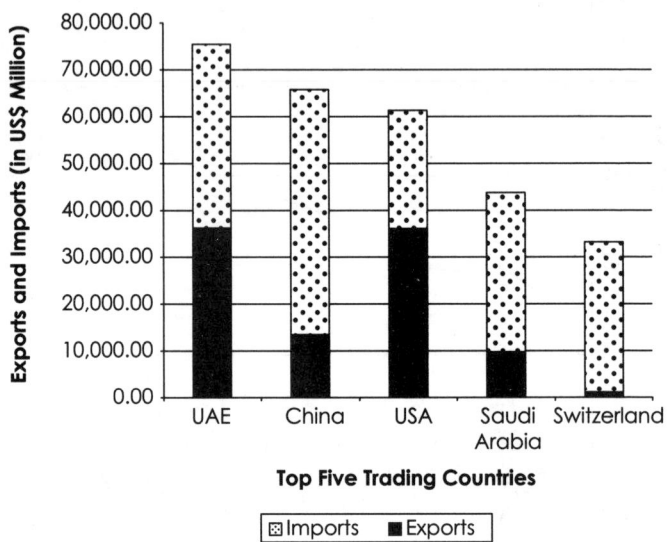

Top Five Trading Countries

☒ Imports   ■ Exports

Source: Adapted from Directorate General of Foreign Trade, New Delhi, available at: http://commerce.nic.in/eidb/iecnttopn.asp/.

Figure 1.5

Trade Balance with India's Top Five Trading Partners in 2012–13

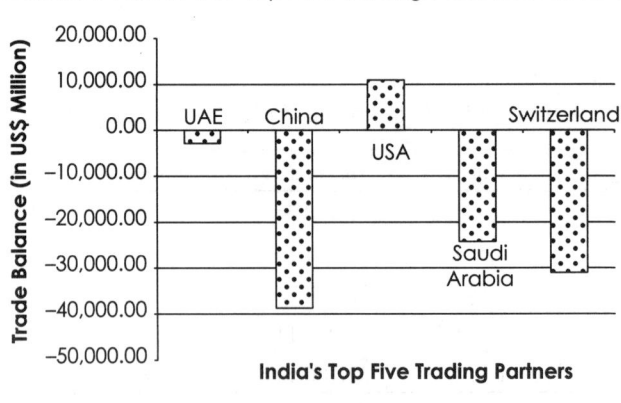

India's Top Five Trading Partners

☒ Trade Balance

Source: Adapted from Directorate General of Foreign Trade, New Delhi, available at: http://commerce.nic.in/eidb/iecnttopn.asp/.

long run and would hamper India's political options and undermine its influence in the Persian Gulf.

Moreover, the increasing energy dependency for its oil and gas demands has an adverse effect upon India's trade deficit and for long its oil bill has exceeded its total trade deficit. In 2006–07, its trade deficit stood at US$59.3 billion whereas its oil bill was over US$61 billion (Table 1.5 and Figure 1.6). In other words, energy imports were 104 per cent of its trade deficit. Since then, there has been a slight drop in the

Table 1.5
India's Trade Deficit–Oil Import Linkages

Year	Total exports	Total imports	Trade deficit	Energy imports	Per cent of oil imports to trade deficit
1996–97	33,469.95	39,132.41	5,662.46	11,464.60	202.47
1997–98	34,784.98	41,484.49	6,669.51	10,067.75	150.95
1998–99	33,218.72	42,388.71	9,169.99	8,043.19	87.71
1999–2000	36,822.49	49,738.06	12,915.57	14,350.19	111.11
2000–01	44,560.29	50,536.45	5,976.16	17,545.14	293.59
2001–02	43,826.72	51,413.28	7,586.56	15,771.75	207.89
2002–03	52,719.43	61,412.14	8,692.71	19,680.60	226.40
2003–04	63,842.55	78,149.11	14,306.56	22,700.20	158.67
2004–05	83,535.94	111,517.43	27,981.49	34,818.66	124.43
2005–06	103,090.53	149,165.73	46,075.20	50,310.06	109.19
2006–07	126,414.05	185,735.24	59,323.19	61,778.90	104.14
2007–08	163,132.18	251,654.01	88,521.83	86,384.07	97.59
2008–09	185,295.36	303,696.31	118,397.95	103,933.81	87.78
2009–10	178,751.43	288,372.88	109,621.45	96,321.16	87.87
2010–11	251,136.19	369,769.13	118,633.24	115,929.02	97.72
2011–12	305,963.92	489,319.49	183,355.57	172,753.97	94.22
2012–13	300,400.68	490,736.65	190,335.97	181,344.67	95.28

Source: Adapted from Directorate General of Foreign Trade, New Delhi, available at: www.dgft.gov.in/.

Figure 1.6
India's Trade Deficit–Oil Import Linkages

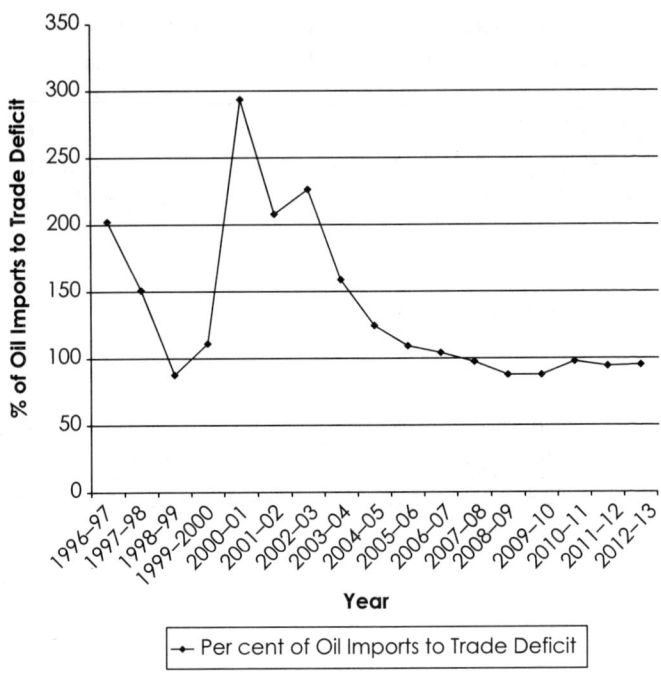

Source: Adapted from Directorate General of Foreign Trade, New Delhi, available at: www.dgft.gov.in/.

ratio share and during 2012–13 its trade deficit was US$190.3 billion whereas its energy bill was US$181.3 billion or 95.28 per cent of its deficit. Bulk of this asymmetric situation is directly linked to the India's trade imbalance with the Persian Gulf countries. For example, during 2012–13, India's trade deficit with the Persian Gulf region alone stood at over US$80 billion.

This widening trade deficit is primarily because of the nature of Indo-Persian Gulf trade, especially India's import of huge quantities of oil and gas from this region. About 60 per cent of India's imports come from the Persian Gulf countries. In recent years, depleting resources have considerably reduced the share of Bahrain and Oman but resurgent Iraq has

Table 1.6
India's Energy Imports from the Persian Gulf Region (in US$ Million)

Country	2007–08	2008–09	2009–10	2010–11	2011–12	2012–13
Bahrain	599.46	1,215.37	248.34	219.19	605.89	329.85
Iran	10,048,97	11,248.63	10,362.04	9,377.88	11,764.01	9,716.39
Iraq	6,834.57	7,660.78	6,981.32	8,954.66	18,826.19	19,166.06
Kuwait	7,289.51	9,193.78	7,909.80	9,729.09	15,718.33	15,737.46
Oman	688.68	624.70	2,904.41	3,293.14	2,083.84	507.88
Qatar	1,897.18	2,890.14	4,101.68	6,060.95	11,697.83	14,578.34
Saudi Arabia	17,755.00	18,386.52	15,390.04	17,932.31	28,302.37	29,896.53
UAE	7,806.25	10,317.90	6,443.36	9,398.23	15,102.54	14,984.68
Yemen	1,445.39	745.07	1,563.15	1,722.95	955.26	942.00
Total Persian Gulf	54,365.01	62,282.89	55,904.14	66,688.4	105,056.26	105,859.19
Total Imports	86,384.04	103,933.77	96,321.16	115,929.06	172,753.97	181,344.67
Percentage of Persian Gulf Imports to Total Imports	62.93	59.93	58.04	57.53	60.81	58.37

Source: Adapted from Directorate General of Foreign Trade, New Delhi, available at: www.dgft.gov.in/.

Figure 1.7

India's Energy Imports from the Persian Gulf Region

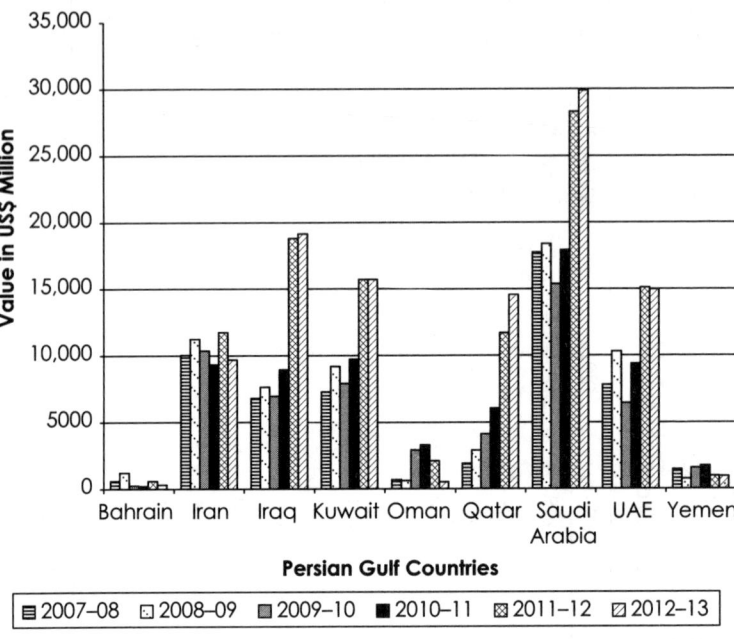

Source: Adapted from Directorate General of Foreign Trade, New Delhi, available at: www.dgft.gov.in/.

emerged as the second largest energy supplier to India during the year under review (Table 1.6 and Figure 1.7).

In terms of India's overall energy imports, the Persian Gulf plays a significant role. Besides supplying a large chunk of oil and gas, the region also occupies an important place in the basket of suppliers. Since 1996–97, the Persian Gulf countries were among the top five energy suppliers to India (Table 1.7). During the current year, the Persian Gulf countries have occupied all the top five positions, overtaking Nigeria, which at times was the largest supplier of oil to India. The Western sanctions have pushed Iran to the seventh position in terms of its share in India's energy imports during this year. During 2007–08, the Islamic Republic was the second major supplier after Saudi Arabia and during 2012–13, dropped out of the top five slots. Because of the civil war situation, oil imports from Yemen have dropped for the second year in a row. The Western sanctions have also

Table 1.7
Top Five Energy Suppliers of India

Year	First	Second	Third	Fourth	Fifth
1996–97	Nigeria	Saudi Arabia	UAE	Kuwait	Australia
1997–98	Saudi Arabia	Nigeria	Australia	Kuwait	UAE
1998–99	Saudi Arabia	Kuwait	Nigeria	UAE	Australia
1999–2000	Nigeria	Saudi Arabia	UAE	Kuwait	Iran
2006–07	Saudi Arabia	Nigeria	Iran	Kuwait	Iraq
2007–08	Saudi Arabia	Iran	UAE	Nigeria	Kuwait
2008–09	Saudi Arabia	Iran	UAE	Kuwait	Nigeria
2009–10	Saudi Arabia	Iran	Kuwait	Nigeria	Iraq
2010–11	Saudi Arabia	Nigeria	Kuwait	UAE	Iran
2011–12	Saudi Arabia	Iraq	Kuwait	UAE	Nigeria
2012–13	Saudi Arabia	Iraq	Kuwait	UAE	Qatar

Source: Adapted from Directorate General of Foreign Trade, New Delhi, available at: www.dgft.gov.in/.
Note: Non-Gulf suppliers are identified in italics.

curtailed India's exports of oil products to Iran. During 2008–09, India exported over a billion dollar worth of oil products to Iran but it dropped to a meagre US$42 million during 2012–13 (Table 1.8 and Figure 1.8).

Table 1.8
Share of Oil-related Exports to Iran (in US$ Million)

Year	Oil exports to Iran	Total oil exports	Iran's share in total oil exports	Exports to Iran	Per cent of oil in exports to Iran
2007–08	845.12	29,085.48	2.91	1,943.92	43.48
2008–09	1,056.17	28,437.14	3.71	2,534.01	41.68
2009–10	180.80	29,036.29	0.62	1,853.17	9.76
2010–11	31.04	42,610.74	0.07	2,492.90	1.25
2011–12	49.77	57,391.93	0.09	2,411.33	2.06
2012–13	42.40	62,105.50	0.07	3,351.07	1.27

Source: Adapted from Directorate General of Foreign Trade, New Delhi, available at: www.dgft.gov.in/.

Figure 1.8
Share of India's Oil-related Exports to Iran (in US$ Million)

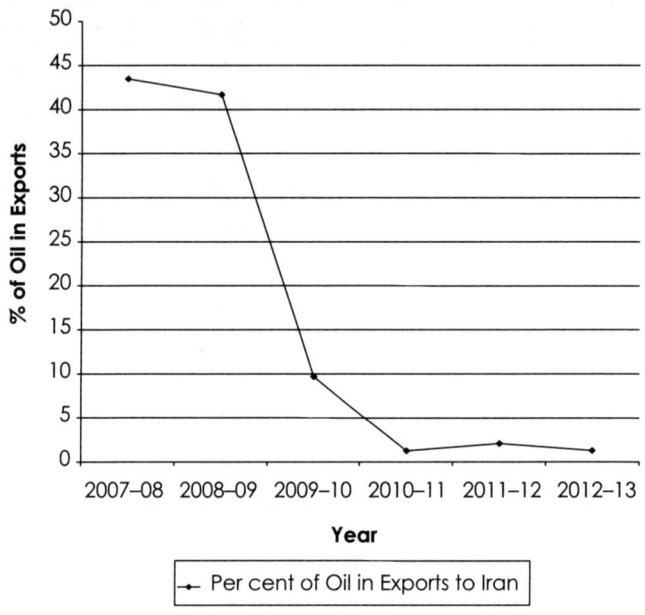

Source: Adapted from Directorate General of Foreign Trade, New Delhi, available at: www.dgft.gov.in/.

It is essential to recognize that oil imports not only cater to growing domestic demand but also play a key role in India's export trade. A significant portion of crude oil is processed and re-exported as different types of oil products. Thus, since 2000, the export of oil products has been on the rise and it crossed US$11 billion during 2005–06. Oil exports have overtaken other export commodities and during 2012–13, more than one-fifth of India's exports were oil-related and stood at over US$62 billion (Table 1.9 and Figure 1.9). Interestingly, during 2012–13, India's overall exports to the Persian Gulf were US$57 billion whereas its total oil exports were US$62 billion.

As a result of its pre-eminent role both in India's imports as well as exports, trade in oil and gas has increasingly dominated India's foreign trade. Since 2007–08, it accounts for over US$100 billion worth of foreign trade and, thereby, makes up the largest sector. During 2011–12,

Table 1.9
Share of Oil Products in India's Exports (in US$ Million)

Year	Total exports	Energy exports	Share (in per cent)
1996–97	33,469.95	516.43	1.54
1997–98	34,784.98	394.52	1.13
1998–99	33,218.72	141.08	0.42
1999–2000	36,822.49	90.87	0.25
2000–01	44,560.29	1,930.99	4.33
2001–02	43,826.72	2,182.94	4.98
2002–03	52,719.43	2,707.24	5.13
2003–04	63,842.55	3,734.32	5.85
2004–05	83,535.94	7,140.39	8.55
2005–06	103,090.53	11,866.60	11.51
2006–07	126,414.05	18,859.48	14.92
2007–08	163,132.18	29,085.48	17.83
2008–09	185,295.36	28,437.14	15.35
2009–10	178,751.43	29,036.29	16.24
2010–11	251,136.19	42,610.74	16.97
2011–12	305,963.92	57,391.93	18.76
2012–13	300,400.68	62,105.50	20.67

Source: Adapted from Directorate General of Foreign Trade, New Delhi, available at: www.dgft.gov.in/.

India's oil-related external trade stood at over US$230 billion or close to 29 per cent of its foreign trade. In the current financial year, the figure rose to US$243.4 billion or over 30 per cent (Table 1.10 and Figure 1.10). As result, even to maintain its export profile and, thereby, bridge the trade deficit, India would continue to rely on the energy imports from the Persian Gulf region.

As highlighted by Tables 1.11 and 1.12 and Figures 1.11 and 1.12, a large portion of the known oil and gas reserves of the world are to be found in the Persian Gulf region. This would demand India seeking and maintaining close political and economic relations with the region

Figure 1.9
Share of Oil Products in India's Exports

Source: Adapted from Directorate General of Foreign Trade, New Delhi, available at: www.dgft.gov.in/.

Table 1.10
Share of Energy in India's Total Foreign Trade (in US$ Million)

Year	Total trade	Energy exports	Energy imports	Total oil	Percentage of oil trade
1996–97	72,602.36	516.43	11,464.60	11,981.03	6.06
1997–98	76,269.47	394.52	10,067.75	10,462.27	13.74
1998–99	75,607.43	141.08	8,043.19	8,184.27	10.85
1999–2000	86,560.55	90.87	14,350.19	14,441.06	16.70
2000–01	95,096.74	1,930.99	17,545.14	19,476.13	20.50
2001–02	95,240.00	2,182.94	15,771.75	17,954.69	18.87
2002–03	114,131.57	2,707.24	19,680.60	22,387.84	19.63
2003–04	141,991.66	3,734.32	22,700.20	26,434.52	18.63
2004–05	195,053.37	7,140.39	34,818.66	41,959.05	22.00
2005–06	252,256.26	11,866.60	50,310.06	62,176.66	26.71

(Table 1.10 continued)

(*Table 1.10 continued*)

Year	Total trade	Energy exports	Energy imports	Total oil	Percentage of oil trade
2006–07	312,149.29	18,859.48	61,778.90	80,638.38	25.83
2007–08	414,786.19	29,085.48	86,384.07	115,469.55	27.84
2008–09	488,991.67	28,437.14	103,933.81	132,370.95	27.07
2009–10	467,124.31	29,036.29	96,321.16	125,357.45	26.84
2010–11	620,905.32	42,610.74	115,929.02	158,419.95	25.51
2011–12	795,283.41	57,391.93	172,753.97	230,145.90	28.94
2012–13	791,137.33	62,105.50	181,344.67	243,450.17	30.77

Source: Adapted from Directorate General of Foreign Trade, New Delhi, available at: www.dgft.gov.in/.

Figure 1.10
Share of Energy in India's Total Foreign Trade

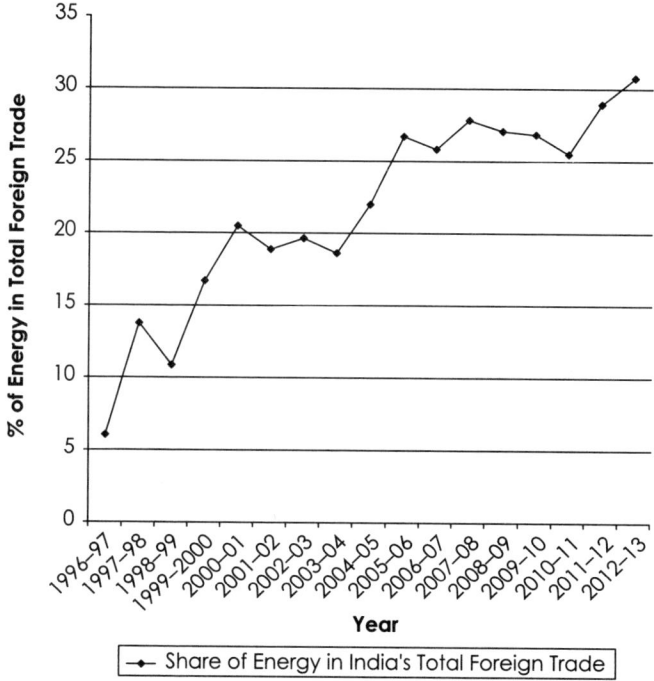

Source: Adapted from Directorate General of Foreign Trade, New Delhi, available at: www.dgft.gov.in/.

Table 1.11
Oil Reserves

Country	Thousand million barrels (at the end of 2012)	Share of global total (in per cent)	R/P ratio
Iran	157.0	9.4	More than 100 years
Iraq	150.0	9.0	More than 100 years
Kuwait	101.5	6.1	88.7
Oman	5.5	0.3	16.3
Qatar	23.9	1.4	33.2
Saudi Arabia	265.9	15.9	63.0
UAE	97.8	5.9	79.1
Yemen	3.0	0.2	45.4

Source: Adapted from BP Statistical Review of World Energy, June 2013.

Figure 1.11
Persian Gulf's Share of Oil

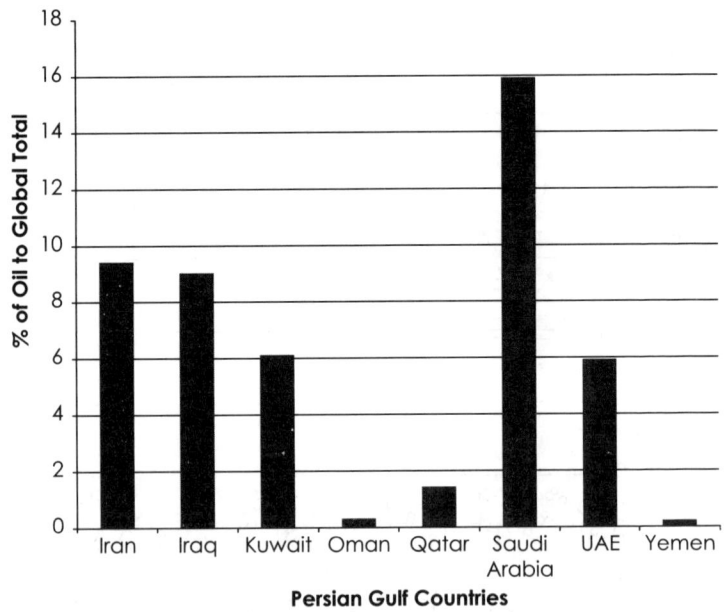

Source: Adapted from BP Statistical Review of World Energy, June 2013.

Table 1.12
Gas Reserves

Country	Trillion cubic feet (at the end of 2012)	Share of global total (in per cent)	R/P ratio
Bahrain	7.0	0.1	14.0
Iran	1187.3	18.0	More than 100 years
Iraq	126.7	1.9	More than 100 years
Kuwait	63.0	1.0	More than 100 years
Oman	33.5	0.5	32.8
Qatar	885.1	13.4	More than 100 years
Saudi Arabia	290.8	4.4	80.1
UAE	215.1	3.3	More than 100 years
Yemen	16.9	0.3	63.1

Source: Adapted from BP Statistical Review of World Energy, June 2013.

Figure 1.12
Persian Gulf's Share of Gas

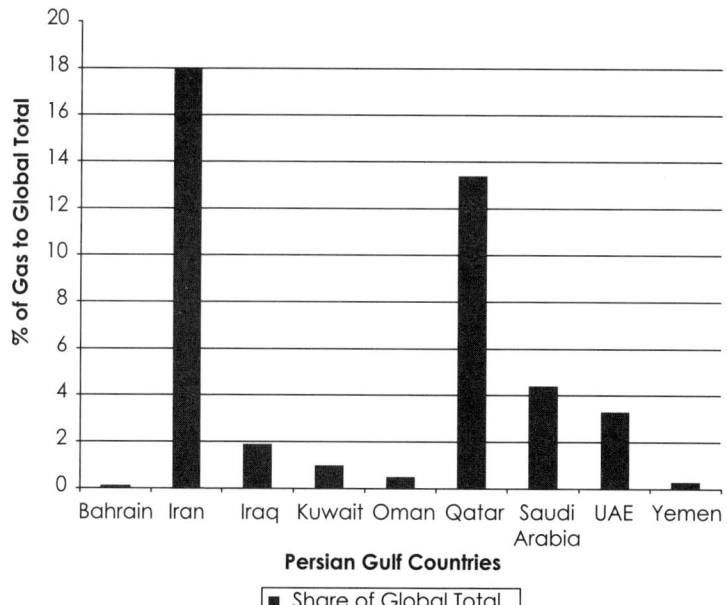

Source: Adapted from BP Statistical Review of World Energy, June 2013.

that not only plays an important role in its energy security calculations but also in providing employment to significant number of its citizens. In short, as long as its energy demands are heavily dependent upon imports, the Persian Gulf would continue to occupy an important position in India's foreign trade, energy security concerns and, hence, strategic calculations.

The only reliable data concerning India's labour migration is the Emigration Check Required (ECR) category or those who require emigration clearance certificate issued by the Ministry of Overseas Indian Affairs (MOIA). According to the liberalized norm, the ECR is mandatory 'only to those possessing educational qualification below Class-X'.[13] This category of workers could, hence, be classified as semi-literates and are employed as unskilled and semi-skilled labourers in the Gulf countries. Until 2006, such ECR was required for labour migrants to 153 countries but the number was drastically reduced and as of August 2008, migrants only to 17 countries require ECR; out of them, 13 are located in the Middle East, including eight countries along the Persian Gulf.[14] Only Iran is missing in this category as it is not the destination for Gulf migration from India (Table 1.13). In 2012, the eight Arab countries accounted for over 97 per cent of total ECR-category émigrés from India (Table 1.14).

Despite the Arabization of the workforce, the number of ECR category workers has been on the rise. Even though it is still below the

Table 1.13
List of Countries Requiring ECR for Indian Migrant Labourers

Global	Middle east countries	Persian gulf countries
Afghanistan	Jordan	Bahrain
Indonesia	Lebanon	Iraq
Malaysia	Libya	Kuwait
Thailand	Sudan	Oman
	Syria	Qatar
		Saudi Arabia
		UAE
		Yemen

Source: Adapted from MOIA, *Annual Report 2011–12.*

Table 1.14
Number of ECR Issued

Country	2008	2009	2010	2011	2012
Bahrain	31,924	17,541	15,101	14,323	20,150
Iraq	—	—	390	1,177	917
Kuwait	35,562	42,091	37,667	45,149	55,868
Oman	89,659	74,963	105,807	73,819	84,384
Qatar	82,937	46,292	45,752	41,710	63,096
Saudi Arabia	228,406	281,110	275,172	289,297	357,503
UAE	349,827	130,302	130,910	138,861	141,138
Yemen	492	421	208	29	0
Total Gulf	786,883	592,720	611,007	604,365	725,068
Total Gulf as Per Cent	92.79	97.13	95.27	96.46	97.06
Total ECR	847,994	610,270	641,355	626,565	747,041

Source: Adapted from MOIA, Annual Report 2012–13, p. 58.

peak reached in 2008, there was a 20 per cent jump from 2011 to 2012 (Table 1.14 and Figure 1.13). Saudi Arabia continues to be the principal destination for this type of emigration and was followed by the UAE and Oman (Figure 1.14). Although internal turmoil prevented ECR being granted to Yemen, the figures indicate a similar situation has not dampened those seeking a better fortune in Bahrain.

The guess estimates put the number of Indian workers in the Gulf region between 5.0 and 6.5 million. Even official estimates tend to present a varying picture. For example, the MEA gives a figure of 6.5 million, while the MOIA projects a figure of 5.8 million as of June 2012. Thus, ECR category makes up just over 10 per cent of estimated Indian labourers in the Gulf.

It is widely accepted that Indians constitute a major and in some cases the largest expatriate population in the Gulf countries. Official estimates put the number of Indians at about 30 per cent of the total resident population in the UAE. Another estimate puts Indians overtaking Egyptians as the largest expatriate population in Saudi Arabia (Table 1.15 and Figure 1.15).

Figure 1.13
Number of ECR Issued

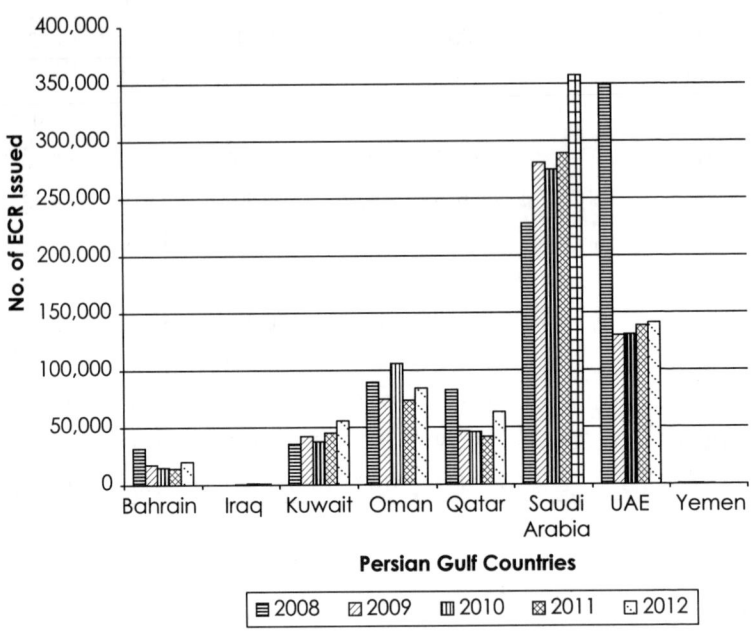

Source: Adapted from MOIA, *Annual Report 2012–13*, p. 58.

Figure 1.14
Per Cent of ECR Issued to Persian Gulf Countries in 2012

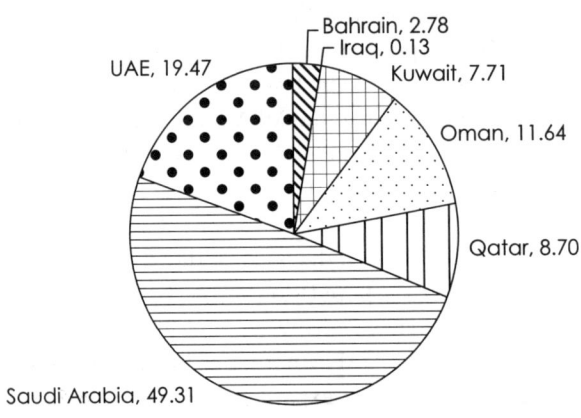

Source: Adapted from MOIA, *Annual Report 2012–13*, p. 58.

Table 1.15
Size of the Expatriate Population in Saudi Arabia

Nationality	Size (in millions)
Indians	1.42
Egyptians	1.00
Pakistanis	0.90
Bangladeshis	0.70
Filipinos	0.45
Indonesians	0.24

Source: Adapted from MOIA, Country Brief, Saudi Arabia. The report estimates the number of expatriate workers in Saudi Arabia at seven million, p. 2.

Figure 1.15
Size of Expatriate Population in Saudi Arabia

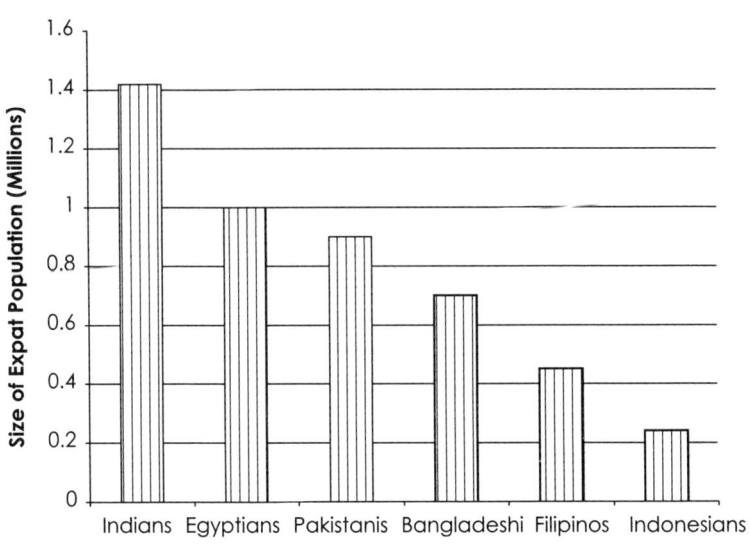

Source: Adapted from MOIA, Country Brief, Saudi Arabia.

Likewise, there are no accurate figures for the Gulf remittances. According to the World Bank, during 2012–13, India received US$68.8 billion in the form of overseas remittances from its expatriate population.[15] According to the same source, at least US$32.6 billion, accounting for 47 per cent of total inflow of remittances, came from the expatriate labour force in the Gulf.[16]

India's long-term economic ties with the Gulf countries, however, would be affected by two interrelated developments. A number of countries have been actively pursuing the policy of Arabization of their labour force. The process would be long, slow and often would fall short of the stated objective of domestic labourers replacing the expatriate workers. Social tensions manifested through the Arab Spring and depleting oil resources of Bahrain and Oman are the principal reasons behind this path. The introduction of Nitaqat policy by Saudi Arabia has caused tension and anxiety among thousands of Indian workers in the Kingdom. The practice of overstaying and other forms of visa violations have been the principal reason for the return of over 140,000 during 2013.[17] The Gulf returnees cause social and economic hardships to states such as Kerala whose residents are employed as workers in large numbers in Saudi Arabia.

In addition to Arabization, there is a growing demand in some of the Arab countries for women empowerment. Granting of political and social rights to women would naturally expand to education and employment rights. These, in turn, would pose a challenge to expatriate employment, especially those in the professional sector.

The Geneva deal and the relaxation of US–Iran tension have not eased the sanction pressures and India's ability to increase its oil imports from Iran continues to remain uncertain. Moreover, without finding a permanent solution to the payment issue, India would not be able to contemplate any long-term energy arrangement with Iran.

Looking Forward

Despite its vast importance, the Persian Gulf did not receive adequate importance in India during 2013 and the region continues to be ignored in favour of the immediate South Asian neighbourhood and its myriad problems. The strategic importance of the Middle East for

India is inversely proportionate to the expertise within the country. However, there is a greater openness in the official circles to the more common expression *Middle East* than the traditional Indian nomenclature, West Asia. The inauguration of Israel Studies as part of Centre for Middle East Studies in the private institution, the O. P. Jindal Global University, marked a new beginning in the expansion of Middle East scholarship in India.

Towards furthering a serious, nuanced and non-partisan understanding of the Middle East and its complexities, the Middle East Institute at New Delhi (MEI@ND) has undertaken a number of academic and outreach activities. *Persian Gulf Series*, inaugurated in 2012, is one such endeavour. Because the core Indian interests lie in the region, the MEI@ND seeks to focus on India's bilateral relations with the Gulf region. Given the region's political, strategic, economic, energy, cultural and social importance, the MEI@ND has initiated this Series to closely follow, detail and assess bilateral relations annually. The current volume focuses on the bilateral developments of 2013.

On terminologies, the MEI@ND prefers Persian Gulf to other nomenclature because of its historic nature. If there can be an Arabian Sea, none should object to the Persian Gulf; moreover, the term Persian Gulf does not denote Iranian ownership of the said waters.

A note of caution is needed for trade figures put out by the Directorate General of Foreign Trade in India. The trade figures for a current year are often revised in the following year and, hence, there could be a slight discrepancy. For example, the trade figures for 2011–12 would be different in 2012 and 2013.

The *Persian Gulf Series* has become possible because of the active support of Vivek Mehra of SAGE, with whom the MEI has established a long-term partnership. We are grateful to R. Chandra Sekhar and Rudra Narayan Sharma for successfully seeing the volume through.

Persian Gulf 2014 is the result of a team of young researchers who are associated with the MEI@ND. As the editor of this Series and as the Honorary Director of the MEI@ND, I register my sincere gratitude to them. Special thanks are reserved for Md. Muddassir Quamar and Dipanwita for their delicate skills in improving the earlier drafts. Figures and diagrams are the handiwork of Manjari Singh.

With great personal gratitude, I am dedicating our third volume in the Series and the second print version to Atul Kumar and Atul Mishra who made the MEI@ND a virtual reality. All omissions and commissions are mine. And mine alone.

P. R. Kumaraswamy
20 May 2014

NOTES

1. The new Constitution was adopted on 26 January 2014; Tristan Dreisbach, 'New Tunisian Constitution Adopted', *Tunisia Live*, 26 January 2014, available at: http://www.tunisia-live.net/2014/01/26/new-tunisian-constitution-adopted/.

2. President Abd Rabbuh Mansur Hadi was expected to work towards drafting a new Constitution during 2012–14; no development as yet has taken place.

3. 'Egypt government declares Muslim Brotherhood "terrorist group"', *Ahram Online*, 26 December 2013, available at: http://english.ahram.org.eg/News-Content/1/64/90037/Egypt/Politics-/Egypt-government-declares-Muslim-Brotherhood-terro.aspx/.

4. While Saudi Arabia has backed the military and pledged millions in aid, Qatar has supported the Muslim Brotherhood.

5. 'As deadline passes, UN joint mission urges Syria to complete chemical weapons removal', *UN News Centre*, 27 April 2014, available at: http://www.un.org/apps/news/story.asp?NewsID=47663#.U310ONKSySp/.

6. Israeli Foreign Minister Avigdor Lieberman in an interview to Hebrew daily *Yedioth Ahronoth* had claimed that Israel has made secret contacts with Gulf States. Saudi Arabia and Kuwait, however, denied having any contacts with the Jewish State. See 'Kuwait, Saudi Arabia Deny Ties with Israel', *The Times of Israel*, 16 April 2014, available at: http://www.timesofisrael.com/kuwait-saudi-arabia-deny-ties-with-israel-burgeoning/.

7. Al Jazeera was accused of partisan reporting by the Egyptian military government and three of its journalists were detained for their involvement with the banned Muslim Brotherhood. This has been criticized by international human rights organizations, such as Amnesty International; see Amnesty International, 'Egypt Must End 'Vindictive' Detention of Al Jazeera Journalists', 9 April 2014, available at: http://www.amnesty.org/en/news/egypt-s-must-end-vindictive-detention-al-jazeera-journalists-2014-04-09.

8. For example, see 'Saudi Prince Says Gulf States Must Balance Threat from Iran', *Reuters*, 23 April 2014, available at: http://www.reuters.com/article/2014/04/23/us-saudi-security-idUSBREA3M1BJ20140423/.

9. For further reading on US–Saudi tensions, see F. Gregory Gause III, *Saudi Arabia in the New Middle East: Council Special Report No. 63* (Washington, D.C.: Council on Foreign Relations, 2011).

10. For a detailed discussion, see the Introduction of P. R. Kumaraswamy (ed.) *Persian Gulf 2013: India's Engagement with the Region* (New Delhi: SAGE, 2013), pp. 1–40.

11. P. R. Kumaraswamy, 'Krishna Goes to Jerusalem', *The Pioneer*, 12 January 2012.

12. 'India has trade deficits with 80 countries: Sharma', *The Economic Times*, 5 August 2013, available at: http://articles.economictimes.indiatimes.com/2013-08-05/news/41093401_1_trade-deficit-industry-minister-anand-sharma-countries/.

13. *Annual Report 2011–12*, MOIA, p. 25.

14. Ibid., p. 36.

15. The World Bank, *Migration and Remittances Data, Annual Remittance Data Inflows and Outflows*, available at: http://go.worldbank.org/092X1CHHD0/.

16. Ibid.

17. 'Nitaqat in Saudi Arabia had no major impact on Indian workers', *The Economic Times*, 11 December 2013, available at: http://economictimes.indiatimes.com/news/nri/visa-and-immigration/nitaqat-in-saudi-arabia-had-no-major-impact-on-indian-workers/articleshow/27220473.cms/.

2

Bahrain

Melissa M. Cyrill

Key Information

Area: 760 sq km; **Population:** 1.34 million (2014); **Native:** 46 per cent; **Expats:** 54 per cent; **Youth:** 15.9 per cent; **Population growth rate:** 2.49 per cent; **Life expectancy at birth:** 78.58 years; **Major population groups:** Bahraini 46 per cent, Asian 45.5 per cent, other Arabs 4.7 per cent, African 1.6 per cent, European 1 per cent, others 1.2 per cent (2010); **Religious groups:** Shia 60–65 per cent, Sunni 30–35 per cent, others 1–2 per cent; **GDP:** US$34.96 billion; **Per capita income:** US$29,800; **Foreign trade:** US$35.1 billion; **Oil reserves:** 124.6 million bbl (2013); **Gas reserves:** 92.03 billion m³; **Ruling family:** al-Khalifa; **Ruler:** King Hamad bin Isa al-Khalifa (since 6 March 1999); **Crown Prince:** Prince Salman bin Hamad bin Isa al-Khalifa (since 9 March 1999); **National Day:** 16 December; **Defence budget:** 3.14 per cent of GDP; **HDI rank:** 48; **Literacy rate:** 94.6 per cent; **UN Education index:** 0.748; **Gender inequality index:** 0.258; **Labour force:** 716,500; **Unemployment rate:** 15 per cent; **External debt:** US$28.82 billion (December 2013); **Sovereign wealth fund:** US$7.1 billion; **Infant mortality rate:** 9.68 deaths out of 1,000; **Last national census:** 2010; **Parliament:** 40-member Nominated Consultative Council and 40-member Elected Chamber of Deputies; **Last parliamentary election:** October 2010; **Number of Indians:** 350,000; **Last Indian prime minister to visit:** None since 1947.

Sources: CIA, *The World Factbook*, available at: https://www.cia.gov/library/publications/the-world-factbook/; *UN Human Development Report*, Statistics, available at: http://hdr.undp.org/en/statistics/; *United States Commission on Religious Freedom*, US Department of State; *Annual Report 2013*; *Briefs on Foreign Relations*, Ministry of External Affairs, Government of India and *Centre for Arms Control and Proliferation* (Washington, D.C.).
Note: All figures for 2013.

The continuing popular protests and the active involvement of two of its bigger neighbours, namely Iran and Saudi Arabia, have contributed to the persistent political instability in Bahrain. The efforts to secure a political settlement through national dialogue remained elusive. Though it managed to post an impressive economic growth, Bahrain's problems are far from over as the Arab Spring continues to be a sectarian struggle. Diminishing oil reserves has compounded its difficulties. The much hyped political union of the Gulf Cooperation Council (GCC) did not materialize and in 2013, Bahrain's dependence upon Saudi Arabia increased considerably.

These situations compel India to closely observe the turn of events in the country. The important socio-economic linkages of a large Indian expatriate population in Bahrain, at the backdrop of such sustained discontent in the kingdom, have meant that India has had to sensitively navigate its relationship through the maintenance of an enduring bilateral framework.

DOMESTIC DEVELOPMENTS

Responding to severe international criticisms and with a view towards pacifying the protestors, on 29 June 2011, the King had established the Bahrain Independent Commission of Inquiry (BICI)[1] whose report and recommendations were accepted. The report was a scathing indictment of the government's handling of the protest movement. It confirmed torture and physical and psychological abuse of detainees[2] and made a series of recommendations towards ensuring transparency and accountability. Parallel to this, the government initiated a 'National Consensus Dialogue'. Initially considered a positive step towards engagement, the opposition parties were assigned only 25 out of 300 seats. As a result, on 17 July 2011, the main opposition party, al-Wefaq, pulled out from the dialogue, which subsequently collapsed due to the government's attempt to frame the dialogue towards preserving partisan interests than addressing the political crisis. The national dialogue remains in stalemate.[3]

Thus, frustrations following the regime's rhetoric, on the one hand, and lack of meaningful implementation of reforms outlined in the BICI report,[4] on the other, have escalated discontent. The failure to secure judicial and legislative reforms to conduct fair trials, end torture and establish criminal accountability for human rights violation has led to sharpening sectarian divides, increase in violence and the polarization of opinion. According to Amnesty International, the Bahraini authorities have defaulted on their assurances to pursue reform, severely weakening the state of civil and human rights in the kingdom.[5]

Meanwhile, on 28 July, the Bahraini parliament proposed an amendment to the 2006 Protection of Society from Acts of Terrorism law that criminalizes public demonstration and free speech, ascribes the increasing of detention period and revocation of citizenship of those found guilty of committing or inciting an act of terrorism. These have further heightened the atmosphere of mistrust and suspicion. On 29 July, the King welcomed the recommendation and ordered immediate implementation. However, Amnesty International raised doubts about the proposed changes arguing that it 'would pose further risk to human rights' in Bahrain.[6] Importantly, the intermittent media coverage of the situation in Bahrain has not resulted in foreign governments pushing for a change of behaviour—possibly favouring stability over accountability—thereby reinforcing a sense of international impunity.

Pressures to achieve stability have inevitably led Western allies seeking more from the Bahraini regime. In an address to his weekly cabinet meeting in late December, King Hamad stressed on the values of moderation and mutual acceptance as critical to overcoming sectarianism and promoting tolerance.[7] These goals would require the adoption of effective strategies to prevent and punish attempts to spread animosity, sectarian polarization and fanaticism. Additionally, he referred to the need to ensure that issues raised from religious and public platforms were in consonance with the national values enshrined in the National Action Charter. However, in a move to suppress criticism, the regime sought to prosecute anyone found guilty of insulting the king. On 18 November, the Shura Council set a one-to-seven-year sentence, aside from fines, as punishment for those violating Article 214 of Penal Law, severely limiting the country's freedom of expression.[8] Such policies tend to be self-defeating as they exacerbate division and tension. This is ironical since policies instituting the regime's fiat have consistently been explained by the royal establishment as necessary to foster cohesion and peace. Regardless, the domestic discontent has continued to foment, interfering with the country's economic, security and political goals.

In the socio-religious realm, the government has continued a differentiated system of respect for the freedom of worship, a right not explicitly enshrined in the 2002 Constitution. Sunni Muslim citizens continue to enjoy a favoured status over their Shia counterpart.[9] Shia groups conducted regular demonstrations and protests demanding political reform and were subjected to increasing scrutiny and use of force, if not arrest, by government officials. On the other hand, the government permitted the transfer of the Roman Catholic Vicariate of Northern Arabia from Kuwait to Bahrain and donated land for the building of its religious complex.

According to the 2010 Census, which does not detail a sectarian breakdown, Muslims constitute 99 per cent of the citizenry while Jews, Christians, Hindus and Bahais make up the remaining 1 per cent. There are approximately 350 licensed Sunni mosques and those licensed as Shia places of worship count for about 863 mosques and 589 *matams* or religious cultural centres. However, newer residential developments with mixed Shia and Sunni populations, such as Hamad and Isa Town, consist of a larger number of Sunni mosques. Foreigners, mostly from South Asia and other Arab states, comprise about 54 per cent of the resident population. Nearly half the foreign residents are non-Muslims and are Hindus, Buddhists, Christians (primarily Roman Catholic, Protestant, Syrian Orthodox and the South Indian Mar Thoma (Syrian Church of Malabar), Bahais and Sikhs. These groups enjoy a relatively free religious environment.[10]

On the security front, the ninth Manama Dialogue was held during 6–8 December. It provided a platform for national security leaders from Asia, North America and Europe to consult and interact on key security and foreign policy challenges facing the Gulf and wider Middle Eastern region. They focus on issues such as challenges in Syria and Egypt, management of political Islam and sectarianism, expanding security relationships of the GCC and the geopolitics of energy security. Bahrain has also repeatedly underlined security and strategic reasons for its support to the establishment of a Gulf Union[11] of the GCC countries, though this has been met with internal GCC resistance.[12]

Bahrain has been focusing on developing services and manufacturing sectors for over a decade. Though it was the first Arab state in the Gulf region to discover oil, oil industry accounts for barely 20 per cent of its economy. However, oil accounts for close to 70 per cent of the government revenue—a steep challenge in the wake of rising socio-political discontent, on the one hand, and depleting indigenous energy reserves, on the other. Nonetheless, Bahrain's economic performance continued to register positive growth rates and in 2013 the oil and gas sector rebounded in addition to strengthening of the non-oil sector.[13] The Economic Development Board (EDB) report indicated the renewed momentum as a contributing factor to expanding Bahraini trade and has, thus, set targets for higher foreign direct investment (FDI) in 2014.[14]

Key sectors for investment in Bahrain include financial services, professional and industrial services, logistics, education and training, manufacturing and information and communications technology (ICT).[15] The global investment climate and its domestic troubles notwithstanding, Bahrain is still proving to attract foreign investors in the manufacturing sector and a special economic zone—the Bahrain International Investment Park (BIIP)—has been established in the area between the international airport and the seaport in 2005. By the end of 2012, 89 projects had been approved by BIIP at a value of US$1.5 billion, much of which has been overseas investment.[16] Of these, 43 were operational in 2012, 15 were under construction, eight had signed leases and 22 were either approved or were at the pre-lease stage. As a key growth facilitator, BIIP—ranked the best investment park in the Middle East and North Africa (MENA) for its FDI promotion strategies by *fDi Magazine* and second best in terms of incentivization—will continue to generate much required high-quality jobs.

Further, the relatively robust growth in the region's economies contributed to Bahrain's gross domestic product (GDP) growth, which was at about 5 per cent in 2013.[17] This was enhanced by the eventual adoption of the budget halfway through the year that lent a stimulus to economic activity, pushing the annual pace of non-oil growth from 2.5 per cent in Q2, 2013 to 3 per cent in Q3, 2013.[18]

Bahrain's overall growth has been projected to be around 5 per cent and the EDB forecasts an increase in the contributing strength of the non-oil sector due to the proposed injection of investment in project spending, either from local funds or from the GCC Development Fund.[19] In the energy sector, consultancy work for the planned offshore liquefied natural gas (LNG) import terminal to become operational in 2016 has begun and the modernization and expansion of the Sitra Refinery is scheduled to be completed by 2017.[20] Further, Saudi Arabia and Bahrain have agreed to replace the existing 230,000 bpd-capacity oil pipeline with a 350,000 bpd-capacity pipeline.[21] There are also plans for drilling exploratory deep gas well in 2014.[22]

However, while the economic performance presents a story of growth, the regime has simultaneously been tied down with allegations of corruption and Bahrain's ranking in the Corruption Perception Index worsened by six places to 57 in 2013.[23] The annual report of the National Audit Court (NAC), an independent institution established by the King in 2002, has been unable to redress public grievance due to its limited mandate and the absence of a credible enforcement mechanism.[24] Moreover, it cannot investigate major cases of corruption dated prior to the agency's creation, that is, 2002. One such instance is the multi-billion dollar Alba corruption scandal that negatively implicated the regime through the payment of kickbacks to highly placed government officials, receiving intense public coverage and fuelling the debate on the need for transparency.[25]

Towards addressing unemployment, the Labour Ministry proposed an amendment to the nationalization of workforce, favouring a qualitative-based system over the existing percentage quota in the private sector.[26] This is to target the gap between the expectations of job-seekers and job opportunities. Under the new system, companies offering higher grade jobs to locals, such as managerial positions, would receive greater benefits from the government in exchange. Professional sectors that are either unattractive to Bahrainis or hold requirements that are not met by Bahraini abilities will see their respective percentages re-evaluated.[27]

Unlike its cancellation in 2011, Bahrain hosted its ninth Formula One Grand Prix in Sakhir on 21 April 2013 amidst continuing protests in the country.[28] This was aimed at projecting an international image that spoke of 'business as usual'. Bahrain also held its annual World Islamic Banking Conference in December[29] for the 20th year in a row.[30] It saw a gathering of international Islamic finance industry leaders and focused on creating an environment that could fast-track growth opportunities both for regional and international investors. The Energy Management Exhibition,[31] the first to be held in the country, provided a key platform for equipment, materials and service providers to display and demonstrate their products and services towards sustainable energy production. In another first of its kind, the Bahrain International Technology Exhibition (BITEX), held from 10 to 12 December, provided an opportunity for all information, technology and communications companies to interact and display their progress. The International Design Week organized from 5 to 7 December focused on the display and promotion of new innovative design trends and approaches in the arts and creative industry.

BILATERAL RELATIONS

India and Bahrain have shared historic ties going back to the Dilmun and Harappan civilizations, illustrated by the discovery of ancient trading seals and artefacts in various archaeological sites.[32] In modern times when Bahrain was a British protectorate in the nineteenth and the early twentieth centuries, the Bahraini currency was minted in India and Bahrain enjoyed a robust pearl trade with India's princely states. Since the oil boom of the 1970s, Indians along with other migrants have benefitted from the Gulf region's policies of inviting foreign labour to offset the mismatch between the availability of human resources and the requirements of rapid modernization. At present, Indians constitute about 32 per cent of the population—about 400,000 out of a total of 1.2 million residents in Bahrain—making India the largest foreign supplier of workforce to Bahrain. According to 2011 estimates, the remittances sent to India from Bahrain amounted to US$690 million. It underscores the importance of Indo-Bahraini relations that have largely been cordial across political, economic and cultural spheres with the leaderships of the two countries investing considerable energy and interest in developing these relations.

Political Relations

The two countries established diplomatic relationships at the ambassadorial level on 12 October 1971[33] and the Indian embassy in Bahrain was established in 1973.[34] India has since enjoyed good relations with Bahrain marked by close people-to-people contacts. Though the high-level visits have been limited, political relations have been marked by regular ministerial-level visits. This bilateral relationship will receive a boost with the official visit of King Hamad bin Isa al-Khalifa in February 2014.[35] Further, the two countries have signed, over the past decade, various memorandums of understandings (MoUs) covering critical issues as labour, extradition, aviation, media and culture, thereby maintaining a healthy bilateral relationship. India agreed to support Bahrain's candidacy for the non-permanent membership to the United Nations Security Council (UNSC) during 2026–27 and latter had supported India's earlier non-permanent membership during 2011–12. Additionally, Bahrain has also expressed support for India's bid for the permanent membership of the UNSC.[36]

In keeping with this steady engagement, the Indian Minister of State for External Affairs E. Ahamed paid a two-day visit to Bahrain during 4–5 June.[37] The discussion centred on the matters related to the protection and welfare of the Indian labour migrant community and other areas of mutual concern. Earlier, Crown Prince Salman Bin Hamad al-Khalifa visited Kerala during 17–18 March accompanied by a large delegation. He held meetings with several state-level ministers and officials and expressed 'keenness to further bolster economic and trade ties.'[38] India also participated in the 12th Asia Cooperation Dialogue themed on Promoting Intra-Asian Tourism hosted by Manama on 25 November. Addressing the meeting, E. Ahamed praised Bahrain's concept of the Asian Tourism City and acknowledged India's support towards this enterprise.[39] He also conveyed India's initiative to compile an anthology of poetry written by eminent writers of the region which would enhance cross-regional understanding and better facilitate cultural exchange.

Economic Relations

Although India and Bahrain have enjoyed historic economic and trade relations, these have become meaningful engagement only in the recent past, beginning with the oil boom of the early 1970s. The increase in prosperity and standards of living throughout the Gulf region allowed countries, such as Bahrain, to widen their import of goods and services, including from India. The Bahraini government's policy of economic diversification and industrial growth and development enhanced the scope of economic relations between the two countries, which included new job opportunities across sectors. Today, Bahrain rivals Malaysia as a global centre for Islamic banking,[40] though its reputation as the financial hub of the Gulf has been damaged due to its resurgent domestic unrest and the emergence of other booming regional financial centres, such as Dubai and Doha. Bahrain stands amongst the most diversified economies of all the Gulf States as 75 per cent of its GDP is accounted for by the aluminium, financial and tourism sectors.[41] However, petroleum production and refining remains its most important source of revenue accounting for more than 60 per cent of Bahrain's export receipts, 70 per cent of government revenues and 11 per cent of its GDP (exclusive of allied industries). The kingdom is looking to seek new natural gas supplies to support its expanding petrochemical and aluminium industries.

India's trade with Bahrain, though important in its own right, constitutes a small fraction of the total Indian trade with the GCC. During 2012–13 bilateral trade stood at US$1,268.13 million witnessing a slight decline of 0.01 per cent (Table 2.1). Out of this value, India's non-oil trade stood at US$854.50 million. India's oil import bill from Bahrain was worth US$329.85 (Table 2.2), while India exported US$83.78 million worth of oil products to Bahrain during 2012–13. India's top five non-oil exports to the kingdom comprise some of the following: inorganic chemicals, organic or inorganic compounds of precious metals, electrical machinery and equipment, cereals and vehicles. India's non-oil imports from Bahrain included: aluminium salt, sulphur and fertilizers.[42] India's bilateral trade with Bahrain is, thus, significant and fluctuates at around a billion dollars (Table 2.1 and Figure 2.1).

Table 2.1
India–Bahrain Bilateral Trade (in US$ Million)

	2009–10	2010–11	2011–12	2012–13
India's Exports to Bahrain	250.21	651.83	439.99	603.47
India's Imports from Bahrain	502.86	641.25	905.98	664.66
Total Bilateral Trade	753.07	1,293.08	1,345.97	1,268.93
Share of Bahrain in India's Total Trade	0.16	0.21	0.17	0.16

Source: Adapted from Directorate General of Foreign Trade, New Delhi, available at: www.dgft.gov.in/.

Figure 2.1
India–Bahrain Bilateral Trade

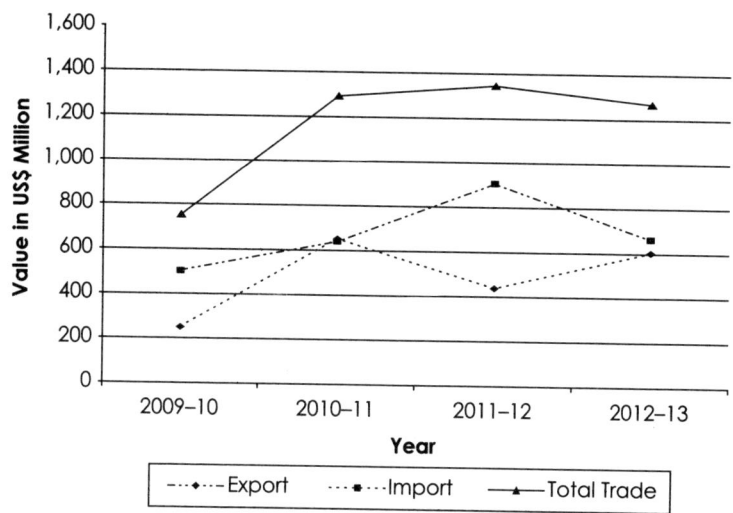

Source: Adapted from Directorate General of Foreign Trade, New Delhi, available at: www.dgft.gov.in/.

With a view to bolstering economic and trade ties, Crown Prince Salman bin Hamad al-Khalifa, who is also Deputy Supreme Commander and First Deputy Prime Minister, visited the Indian state of Kerala in March.[43] During 22–24 October, Bahrain–India Exhibition and Conference was held in Manama as part of Bahrain's look east approach towards promotion of trade and investment.[44] It saw a high-level delegation from India led by the Confederation of Indian Industry (CII) consisting of ministers, government officials and industry leaders.[45] Minister of State for External Affairs E. Ahamed delivered the key note address and lauded the Bahraini initiative.[46] Indian Ambassador to Bahrain, Mohan Kumar, urged players in the private sector to take advantage of Bahrain's friendly economic climate and nourish business-to-business contacts.[47] Appreciating the fact that 123 Indian companies and businesses are based in Bahrain, he spoke of the need to overturn the perception that Bahrain is too small an economy for Indian investment whilst India is too huge a country for Bahrainis.

The exhibition-cum-conference was held ahead of the visit to India of a senior Bahraini economic and business delegation[48] and was spread

Table 2.2
Share of Oil in India's Imports from Bahrain (in US$ Million)

Year	Oil imports from Bahrain	Total oil imports	Bahraini share in total oil imports	Imports from Bahrain	Per cent of oil in imports from Bahrain
2009–10	248.34	96,321.12	0.26	502.86	49.39
2010–11	219.19	115,929.02	0.19	641.25	34.18
2011–12	605.89	172,753.97	0.35	905.98	67.53
2010–13	329.85	181,344.67	0.18	664.66	49.63

Source: Adapted from Directorate General of Foreign Trade, New Delhi, available at: www.dgft.gov.in/.

Figure 2.2
Share of Oil in India's Total Imports from Bahrain

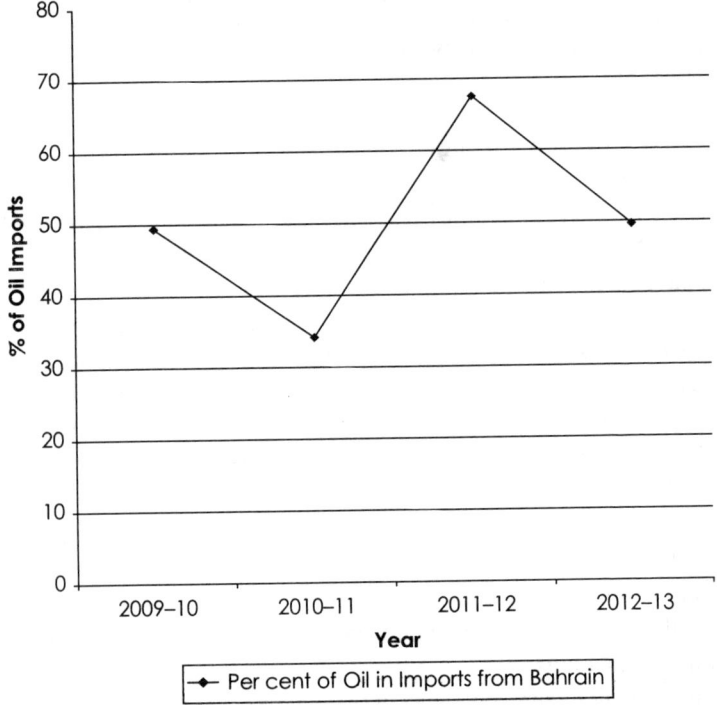

Source: Adapted from Directorate General of Foreign Trade, New Delhi, available at: www.dgft.gov.in/.

across a range of sectors including investment, finance, banking, insurance, tourism, ICT, industrial products, consumer goods, handicrafts, real estate, hotels, catering, health tourism, law firms, software development, consultancy, IT parks, etc. Since Bahrain has a vast Indian community, Ahamed reiterated the importance of the welfare and well-being of the Indian residents to the bilateral relationship.[49]

The year also saw an increase in remittances from Bahrain as Indian expatriates remitted more cash back home as the Rupee value experienced a long slump. The Bahraini dinar, being pegged to the US dollar, displayed a strong showing against most international currencies. According to Bahrain–India International Exchange the amount of remittance payments to India would have been up by about 50 per cent of the rate in 2012.[50]

Energy Relations

Despite its relatively limited energy reserves, oil forms a significant portion of the trade with Bahrain in terms of value. India's crude oil import from Bahrain was US$591 million during 2011–12 and fell to about US$329.85 million in 2010–13 (Table 2.2 and Figure 2.2). India's total oil import bill for 2012–13 was US$181,344.67 million and from the Gulf region was US$105,859.15 (Table 2.3).

Table 2.3
India's Energy Imports from Bahrain (in US$ Million)

	2009–10	*2010–11*	*2011–12*	*2012–13*
Energy Imports from Bahrain	248.34	219.19	605.89	329.85
Total Energy Imports	96,321.12	115,929.02	172,753.97	181,344.67
Total Energy Imports from Persian Gulf	55,904.14	66,688.4	105,056.26	105,859.15
Share of Bahrain in Total Imports	0.26	0.19	0.35	0.18
Share of Bahrain in Imports from Persian Gulf	0.44	0.33	0.58	0.31

Source: Adapted from Directorate General of Foreign Trade, New Delhi, available at: www.dgft.gov.in/.

Cultural Relations

Although a small country with a national population of 1.34 million, Bahrain has a large and thriving Indian expatriate community.[51] The appeal of Bahrain as a favoured destination for Indian labour migrants may be ascertained from the jump in the Indian population from about 90,000 in 2000 to around 400,000 in 2013.[52] Indians form a key component of the Bahraini workforce and contribute significantly to the economic life of the kingdom. *Bahraini India Society* was launched in December 2007 in a move to nurture ties between the countries in social affairs, science, politics and culture as well as to develop business links. The apolitical nature of the Indian workforce and their strong work ethic, serve interests of the regime and are a key source of remittance to India. Though the vast majority of them are employed as unskilled labourers, those working in skilled professions occupy roles in the banking, medicine and management sectors.[53]

External Players

The US: Bahrain is an important security partner to the US as it hosts the headquarters of the Fifth Fleet and contributes to US-led military coalitions, including the International Security Assistance Force in Afghanistan. Bahrain has actively supported the counter-piracy missions and has been the first Arab state to lead a Coalition Task Force patrolling the Gulf. Given this key role in the security architecture in the Persian Gulf region, in 2002 the US designated Bahrain as a major non-NATO ally. This enabled Bahrain to receive defence assistance despite the ongoing political unrest and violence. While the US suspended the sale of most arms and licences in 2011–12, it has continued the supply of those on a case-by-case basis to ensure Bahrain's external defence capabilities lest American national security objectives are compromised. The uneasiness between the two explains the absence of any direct reference to the US as an important actor during the recent Manama Dialogue. In 2013, the US has staunchly, albeit discreetly, pushed for reconciliation between the regime and the opposition. Nevertheless, the two countries have been long-term allies and Bahrain has maintained vital defence relationships to avoid undue dependence on its GCC partners. Further, bilateral trade between the two countries has continued to flourish, reaching close to US$2 billion in 2012, up from about US$1.1 billion in 2006 when Bahrain became the first GCC country to conclude a Free Trade Agreement (FTA) with the US.

China: The last few years have witnessed China expanding its relationships with the Persian Gulf region. Bilateral relations between Bahrain and China have developed since the exchange of diplomatic relations in 1988. Currently, Bahrain and China enjoy a robust trade relationship and the bilateral trade reached over US$1.5 billion in 2012[54] with a forecast of US$1.9 billion in 2013.[55] This bilateral relationship has been further deepened with visit of King Hamad bin Isa al-Khalifa during 14–16 September. The three-day visit saw official meetings with top leaders from both sides also in Shanghai and the King's visit to Ningxia where the first China–Arab State Expo will be held.[56] The trip resulted in a number of cooperation agreements in the fields of culture, health, finance, energy, taxation and education and agreement to enhance cooperation in economics, commerce, infrastructure, tourism, media and sports. Both countries supported each other's efforts at securing national stability and unity, affirmed respect for each other's sovereignty and rejected external interference in their internal affairs. Bahrain is the current chairman of the GCC and has pledged to boost relations between China and the GCC through a strategic dialogue and expansion of mutual cooperation. The two countries also acknowledged their role in the Gulf and the Middle East towards maintaining peace and stability and the importance of peaceful dialogue and consultation to resolve any disputes. King Hamad extended an invitation to Chinese President Xi Jinping to visit Bahrain.

Pakistan: The bilateral relationship between Bahrain and Pakistan continues to be strong and cordial and the two are committed to strengthening their cooperative equation.[57] Prime Minister Nawaz Sharif highlighted 'special relations' during his meeting with the Commander of the National Guard of Bahrain Lieutenant General Sheikh Mohammad bin Isa Bin Salman al-Khalifa.[58] According to official data, about 45,000 Pakistanis[59] (expatriates and those of Pakistani origin) live and work in Bahrain and other estimates put the number at 60,000.[60] In terms of trade, the value is small and stands at US$394.7 million but is projected to double in the next five years following an agreement between the Bahrain Chamber of Commerce and Industry and the Karachi Chamber of Commerce.[61] However, fundamental to their ties has been the close defence and security cooperation. Since 1971, Pakistani military assistance to Bahrain has covered the fields of military training and provision of deputations for the Bahrain Defence Forces on a contractual basis.[62] Pakistan has assisted Bahrain in setting up its naval forces and Pakistani personnel comprise 18 per cent of the Bahraini air force. In the aftermath of the outbreak of popular protests in Bahrain in February 2011, the Pakistani army provided several thousand soldiers to the Bahrain National Guard.[63] Pakistan has a significant presence in the Bahraini security services, which has been a source of tension as protesters of the regime have demanded their removal.

Saudi Arabia: Saudi Arabia has been a key influence in the political economy and foreign policy of Bahrain given its geographical proximity and Bahrain's energy dependence. Further, the oil-rich Eastern Province of the Saudi Arabia has a significant Shia population and the causeway linking it with Bahrain figures prominently in the Saudi security calculations. Thus, Saudi Arabia was quick to respond to the protests that erupted in Bahrain in 2011, which received little international criticism. However, 2013 saw a positive change in the Saudi policy from erstwhile confrontation to favouring conciliation as a more organic solution to a long-standing problem. In a significant diplomatic move, a Saudi politician has for the first time, established direct and informal contact with the Shia opposition party, al-Wefaq.[64] Behind the scenes, the US, the UK and Saudi Arabia have begun to push for a political settlement with the disaffected Shia populace to limit and prevent further radicalization that could foment protests in the region.[65] Coming months would also see construction of a rail line linking all GCC states.[66] The proposed railway network, to be functional in 2017, will cover 2,117 km, starting from Kuwait and passing through Saudi Arabia, Bahrain, Qatar and the United Arab Emirates (UAE) to end up in Oman; Saudi Arabia and Bahrain have meanwhile begun discussions with private companies to build a US$4.5 billion, 90 km rail line that will connect the two kingdoms.

CONCLUSION

India's ties with Bahrain have grown steadily in the past decade, and Bahrain has seen a significant rise in the Indian expatriate population. The relationship has expanded across economic and cultural spheres with key MoUs establishing a bilateral framework. Due to its fast-depleting energy reserves and objectives towards sustaining a healthy diversified economy, Bahrain has prioritized attracting investments. Forming mutually beneficial economic partnerships, particularly with rising economies, such as India, is fundamental to its foreign policy. Whilst the resurgence of political discontent posed worries for the safety of Indian expatriates in Bahrain, the Bahraini authorities have been able to positively reassure the Indian government. High-level contacts will be further boosted by the Bahraini King's visit to New Delhi in 2014.

NOTES

1. The Report of the Bahrain Independent Commission of Inquiry, November 2011, available at: http://www.bici.org.bh/.
2. 'Government Inaction in Implementing the Bahrain Independent Commission of Inquiry', *Bahrain Watch*, available at: https://bahrainwatch.org/bici/.
3. 'Bahrain Profile', *BBC*, 19 September 2013, available at: http://www.bbc.co.uk/news/world-middle-east-14540571/.
4. 'Tracker of Government Inaction in Implementing the Bahrain Independent Commission of Inquiry', *Bahrain Watch*, available at: https://bahrainwatch.org/bici/tracker.php/. Also see, 'The Outlook for Bahrain', *Middle East and North Africa Programme Roundtable Summary*, Chatham House, November 2012, available at: http://www.chathamhouse.org/sites/default/files/public/Research/Middle%20East/1112bahrain_summary.pdf/.
5. Amnesty International, 'Bahrain: Promises of Reform Broken, Repression Unleashed', 21 November 2012, available at: http://www.amnesty.org/en/news/bahrain-promises-reform-broken-repression-unleashed-2012-11-21-0/.
6. Amnesty International, 'Bahrain: New Anti-Terrorism Powers Would Pose Further Risk to Human Rights', 31 July 2013, available at: https://www.amnesty.org/en/library/asset/MDE11/026/2013/en/d9eef74e-866e-45b1-961f-bd53aeab8839/mde110262013en.html/.
7. 'HM King Hamad Chairs Weekly Cabinet Meeting', *Bahrain News Agency*, 29 December 2013, available at: http://www.bna.bh/portal/en/news/595313/.

8. Elliot Abrams, 'Bahrain: Insulting the King Means Jail', *Pressure Points*, Council on Foreign Relations, 30 December 2013, available at: http://blogs. cfr.org/abrams/2013/12/30/bahrain-insulting-the-king-means-jail/.

9. Minority-related data are taken from *International Religious Freedom Report for 2011*, US Department of State, available at: http://www.state.gov/j/drl/rls/irf/2011religiousfreedom/index.htm?dlid=192697#wrapper/.

10. See, SPIEGEL Interview with the King of Bahrain: 'Arab Spring? That's the Business of Other Countries', *Der Spiegel*, 13 February 2012, available at: http://www.spiegel.de/international/world/spiegel-interview-with-the-king-of-bahrain-arab-spring-that-s-the-business-of-other-countries-a-814915.html/.

11. 'Bahrain PM Reiterates Full Support to Gulf Union', *Gulf News*, 24 December 2013, available at: http://gulfnews.com/news/gulf/bahrain/bahrain-pm-reiterates-full-support-to-gulf-union-1.1270442/.

12. 'Gulf Security: A Risky New US-Saudi Blueprint', *Middle East Online*, 10 December 2013, available at: http://www.middle-east-online.com/english/?id=63116/.

13. 'Bahrain Economic Quarterly—December 2013', *Bahrain Economic Development Board*, available at: http://www.bahrainedb.com/en/EDBDocuments/BEQ-December-2013.pdf/.

14. Ibid.

15. 'India–Bahrain Economic Relations', *FICCI*, available at: http://www.ficci.com/international/75181/Project_docs/India-Bahrain-Economic-Relations.pdf/.

16. 'FDI Flame Still Burns Brightly', *The Gulf Online*, March 2013, available at: http://www.thegulfonline.com/Print.aspx?ArtID=5243/.

17. 'Bahrain Economic Quarterly—December 2013'.

18. 'Bahrain's Nonoil Growth Set to Accelerate in 2014', *Arab News*, 1 January 2014, available at: http://www.arabnews.com/news/501581/.

19. Ibid.

20. 'Bahrain's GDP Growth Set to Hit Five Per Cent', *Gulf Daily News*, 30 December 2013, available at: http://www.gulf-daily-news.com/NewsDetails.aspx?storyid=367762/.

21. 'Saudi Arabia, Bahrain Approve New Oil Pipeline', *Arab News*, 19 September 2013, available at: http://www.arabnews.com/news/465069/.

22. 'Bahrain's GDP Growth Set to Hit Five Per Cent'.

23. 'This Week's Window on the Middle East—January 17, 2014', *Open Democracy*, 17 January 2014, available at: http://www.opendemocracy.net/arab-awakening/arab-awakening/this-weeks-window-on-middle-east-january-17-2014/.

24. Ibid.

25. Ibid.

26. 'New Bahrain Employment Plan to Focus on Quality', *Gulf News*, 21 June 2012, available at: http://m.gulfnews.com/new-bahrain-employment-plan-to-focus-on-quality-1.1038631/. Also see, 'GCC Demographic Shift', *Markaz*,

Kuwait Financial Center 'Markaz' Research, June 2012, available at: http://www.markaz.com/DesktopModules/CRD/Attachments/DemographicsResearch-MarkazResearch-June%202012.pdf/.

27. 'Committee Reviews Bahrainisation Rates', *Gulf Daily News*, 31 January 2013, available at: http://www.gulf-daily-news.com/NewsDetails.aspx?storyid=346525/.

28. 'Bahrain Hosts a Second Formula One Grand Prix amidst Nationwide Protests', *Skift*, 22 April 2013, available at: http://skift.com/2013/04/22/bahrain-hosts-a-second-formula-one-grand-prix-amidst-nationwide-protests/.

29. 'Bahrain: 2013 and 2014 Events Calendar', *Bahrain.com*, available at: http://www.bahrain.com/en/events/Pages/default.aspx?year=2013&month=12&Category=Business+Events#.UwJja4X9b8c/.

30. 'Bahrain to Host Leading Islamic Banking Conference For 20th Year in a Row', *Bahrain Economic Development Board*, 3 December 2013, available at: http://www.2030.bh/edbpress/en/index.php/news/item/211-bahrain-to-host-leading-islamic-banking-conference-for-20th-year-in-a-row/.

31. 'Bahrain Hosts a Second Formula One Grand Prix amidst Nationwide Protests'.

32. Alsho'ala, Abdulnabi, 'Cooperation on the Western Flank: Possibilities of Indian Engagement with the GCC', in Sudhir T. Devare, Swaran Singh and Reena Marwah (eds), *India and GCC Countries Iran and Iraq: Emerging Security Perspectives* (New Delhi: Pentagon Press, 2013), pp. 238–259.

33. 'Bahrain-Indo Relations', The Embassy of the Kingdom of Bahrain, India, New Delhi, available at: http://www.bahrainembassyindia.com/relation-with-india.html/.

34. About the Embassy, Embassy of India, available at: http://www.indianembassybahrain.com/embassy_bahrain.html/.

35. 'Bahrain MOIC and EDB Coordinate Business Delegation Visit to India in Preparation for His Majesty's Visit', *Bahrain Economic Development Board*, 18 February 2014, available at: http://www.bahrain.com/en/media-centre/Pages/BAHRAIN-MOIC-AND-EDB-COORDINATE-BUSINESS-DELEGATION-VISIT-TO-INDIA-IN-PREPERATION-FOR-HIS-MAJESTY%E2%80%99S-VISIT.aspx#.UwSSSLRfSrw/.

36. Mushtaq Hussain, 'Bahrain', in P. R. Kumaraswamy (ed.), *Persian Gulf 2013: India's Relations with the Region* (New Delhi: SAGE, 2014), p. 47.

37. *India Speaks* No. 48, July 2013, available at: http://www.mei.org.in/documentsettings/pdf/684_pdf.pdf/.

38. 'Visit of His Royal Highness Prince Salman bin Hamad Al Khalifa, Crown Prince, Deputy Supreme Commander and First Deputy Prime Minister of the Kingdom of Bahrain to Indian State of Kerala', Embassy of India, Kingdom of Bahrain, 17–18 March 2013, available at: http://www.indianemcom/cp_bah_visits_india_mar2013.html.

39. *India Speaks*, No. 53, December 2013, available at: http://www.mei.org.in/documentsettings/pdf/778_pdf.pdf/.

40. 'Bahrain Economic Profile 2013', *Index Mundi*, available at: http://www.indexmundi.com/bahrain/economy_profile.html/.
41. 'Bahrain Economic Quarterly—December 2013'; 'India—Bahrain Economic Relations'.
42. 'India—Bahrain Bilateral Relations', Embassy of India, Kingdom of Bahrain, available at: http://www.indianembassybahrain.com/india_bahrain_bilateral_relations.html/.
43. *India Speaks*, No. 45, April 2013, available at: http://www.mei.org.in/front/cms/resourcesDetail.php?id=NjM5/.
44. 'India Rivets Eyes on Bahrain's Look East Approach', *24x7 News*, 20 October 2013, available at: http://www.twentyfoursevennews.com/headline/india-rivets-eyes-on-bahrains-look-east-approach/.
45. 'The Bahrain—India Exhibition and Conference', October 2013, available at: http://www.bahind.com/.
46. *India Speaks*, No. 52, November 2013, available at: http://www.mei.org.in/front/cms/resourcesDetail.php?id=Nzc0/.
47. *India Speaks*, No. 45, April 2013; 'India Rivets Eyes on Bahrain's Look East Approach'.
48. 'Bahrain—India Conference Opens in Manama', *Bahrain.com*, 22 October 2013, available at: http://www.bahrain.com/en/media-centre/Pages/BAHRAIN-%E2%80%93-INDIA-CONFERENCE-OPENS-IN-MANAMA.aspx#.UwSSd7RfSrw/.
49. 'The Bahrain—India Exhibition and Conference'; *India Speaks*, No. 52, November 2013.
50. 'Remittances to India on the Rise', *Trade Arabia*, 2 June 2013, available at: http://www.tradearabia.com/news/BANK_237035.html/.
51. CIA, *The World Factbook*, available at: https://www.cia.gov/library/publications/the-world-factbook/geos/ba.html/.
52. 'India—Bahrain Bilateral Relations', Embassy of India.
53. 'Bahrain Economic Quarterly—December 2013'; 'India—Bahrain Economic Relations'.
54. 'King Hamad's Visit to Boost Bahrain-China Relations', *Gulf News*, 13 September 2013, available at: http://gulfnews.com/news/gulf/bahrain/king-hamad-s-visit-to-boost-bahrain-china-relations-1.1230640/.
55. 'Bahrain, China Trade "May Hit $1.9bn"', *Trade Arabia*, 20 October 2013, available at: http://www.tradearabia.com/news/BANK_244708.html/.
56. 'Indian Missions Abroad', Ministry of External Affairs; 'King Hamad's Visit to Boost Bahrain—China Relations', *Gulf News*.
57. 'Pakistan Attaches Great Importance to its Relations With Bahrain: President', *The Nation (Pakistan)*, 12 September 2013, available at: http://www.nation.com.pk/islamabad/12-Sep-2013/pakistan-attaches-great-importance-to-its-relations-with-bahrain-president/.
58. 'PM For Enhanced Cooperation with Bahrain', *Prime Minister's Office*, Islamic Republic of Pakistan, Islamabad, 4 December 2013, available at: http://www.pmo.gov.pk/press_release_detailes.php?pr_id=259/.

59. Demographics of Bahrain, available at: https://www.princeton.edu/~achaney/tmve/wiki100k/docs/Demographics_of_Bahrain.html/.
60. 'Al Khalifah Seeking Legitimacy from Pakistani Citizens', *Islam Times (Pakistan)*, 13 April 2011, available at: http://www.islamtimes.org/vdcev78p.jh8neik1bj.html/.
61. 'Bahrain, Pakistan Trade Set to Double', *Trade Arabia*, 4 November 2012, available at: http://www.tradearabia.com/news/BANK_224940.html/.
62. Sehar Kamran, 'Pak-Gulf Defense Security and Cooperation', *Center for Pakistan and Gulf Studies*, January 2013, available at: http://cpakgulf.org/documents/Pak-Gulf-Security-Ties-final.pdf/.
63. 'Pakistani Troops Aid Bahrain's Crackdown', *Al Jazeera*, 30 July 2011, available at: http://www.aljazeera.com/indepth/features/2011/07/2011725145048574888.html/.
64. Elliot Abrams, 'A Glint of Hope in Bahrain', *Pressure Points*, Council on Foreign Relations, 12 March 2013, available at: http://blogs.cfr.org/abrams/2013/03/12/a-glint-of-hope-in-bahrain/.
65. Ibid.
66. 'Saudi Arabia–Bahrain', *Railpage*, 16 February 2012, available at: http://www.railpage.com.au/f-p1868769.htm/.

3

Iran

Alvite Singh Ningthoujam

Key Information

Area: 1,648,195 sq km; **Population:** 80,840,713 (2014 est.); **Native:** 61 per cent; **Expats:** 49 per cent; **Youth:** 18.7 per cent; **Population growth rate:** 1.22 per cent; **Life expectancy at birth:** 70.89 years; **Major population groups:** Persian 61 per cent, Azeri 16 per cent, Kurd 10 per cent, Lur 6 per cent, Baloch 2 per cent, Arab 2 per cent, Turkmen and Turkic tribes 2 per cent, others 1 per cent; **Religious groups:** Shia 90–95 per cent, Sunni 5–10 per cent, Zoroastrians, Jews and Christians 0.3 per cent, others 0.3 per cent (2011); **GDP:** US$987.1 billion; **Per capita income:** US$12,800; **Foreign trade:** US$125.64 billion; **Oil reserves:** 151.2 billion bbl (2013); **Gas reserves:** 33.07 billion m³; **Ruling party:** Combatant Clergy Association; **Supreme Leader (Wilayat-e-Faqih):** Ali Khamenei (since 4 June 1989); **President:** Hassan Rouhani (since 15 June 2013); **National Day:** 1 April; **Defence budget:** 4.95 per cent of GDP; **HDI rank:** 76; **Literacy rate:** 85 per cent; **UN education index:** 0.707; **Gender inequality index:** 0.496; **Labour force:** 27.72 million; **Unemployment rate:** 16 per cent; **External debt:** US$15.64 billion (December 2013); **Sovereign wealth fund:** US$58.6 billion; **Infant mortality rate:** 39 deaths out of 1,000; **Last national census:** 2011; **Parliament:** 290-member Majlis; **Last parliament election:** 2 March 2012; **Number of Indians:** NA; **Last Indian prime minister to visit:** Manmohan Singh, August 2012.

Sources: CIA, The World Factbook, https://www.cia.gov/library/publications/the-world-factbook/; UN Human Development Report, Statistics, http://hdr.undp.org/en/statistics/; United States Commission on Religious Freedom, US Department of State; Annual Report 2013; Briefs on Foreign Relations, Ministry of External Affairs, Government of India and Centre for Arms Control and Proliferation (Washington, D.C.).
Note: All figures for 2013.

Iran attracted immense global attention during 2013 mainly because of the presidential election and the interim nuclear deal. Hassan Rouhani, a moderate cleric, was elected president and he tried to break international isolation through an interim deal with the P5+1. It helped Iran's domestic situation as Western economic sanctions were eased off, while it also de-escalated the rhetoric of military confrontation. However, on the top of developments over Syria, the deal created some furore in the region. The US postures with Iran caused heartache for Saudi Arabia while Israel too rejected such measures as futile. While Indo-Iranian relations continued to remain on the same page as in previous years, India's response to the interim deal was measured and cautious to balance ties with three regional rivals.

DOMESTIC DEVELOPMENTS

In 2013, one of the most anticipated and a closely watched political event was the June Iranian presidential elections. Since the beginning of the year, Supreme Leader Ayatollah Ali Khamenei talked of an intense competition amongst various political parties, and he even warned of intervention by internal and external enemies of Iran.[1] In late-January, there were instances of violence in some cities, including clashes and arrest of journalists, and they were believed to be election related. As a result, the leader emphasized on free-and-fair elections, and not to repeat 'errors' of the controversial 2009 election when Mahmoud Ahmadinejad was reelected.[2] Ahmadinejad was believed to have good rapport with Khamenei but things turned sour when the former named some of his loyalists for top posts. Moreover, the tension increased in February when Iranian Parliamentary speaker Ali Larijani's brother Fazel allegedly sought a bribe in exchange for political favours from one of Ahmadinejad's closest allies, Saeed Mortazavi, the former Tehran prosecutor.[3] The issue further escalated when the Supreme Leader Khamenei warned that any top official from the three branches of the state who entered into any public bickering, particularly in the lead-up to a presidential election in June, would be guilty of treason. Ahmadinejad, who wanted to protect the 'legacy and his welfare' did not pay heed to such warnings.[4] In May, he was charged with violating rules by accompanying his chief adviser Esfandiar Rahim Mashaei to the election registry office.[5] The outgoing president's opponents had accused him of using public funds to promote Mashaei.

The seed for this bitterness was planted by the increasing confrontation between Ahmadinejad and the ruling clerics. Some of the important candidates in the June elections were independent Mohsen Rezaei, reformist Hassan Rouhani and Mostafa Kavakebian, and principlist Kamran Baqeri Lankarani, Alireza Zakani, Mohammad Reza Bahonar and Ali Akbar Velayati.[6] Election agendas of these candidates included elimination of unemployment and inflation; more youths in the cabinet and enhancement of academics; increase in domestic productions; improvement of agricultural sectors; economic reforms; extirpate corruption; ensuring justice and spread the word of Islam; end of the US-led sanctions, etc. A few of them even emphasized the need to improve Iran's ties with the West, especially the US. When elections were announced, 680 candidates,[7] including 30 women,[8] aspired to contest but the Guardian Council approved only eight men. In an apparent move to consolidate the Supreme Leader's grip over power, candidacies of former president Hashemi Rafsanjani and Ahmadinejad's adviser Esfandiar Rahim Mashaei were rejected.[9] Many Iranians found this incompatible with Khamenei's call for free and fair elections. Ahmadinejad sought to challenge this restriction. Furthermore, candidacies of about 30 women were also banned by the Guardian Council. Its members were of the view that allowing women to contest the highest elected office would be against the country's constitution. According to one of its members Ayatollah Mohammad Yazdi, 'not only does the law bar a female from the presidency, it prohibits a woman from appearing on the ballot.'[10]

The presidential elections were held on 14 June where 72 per cent of the 50 million eligible Iranians cast their votes. Belying pre-election forecast, reformist leader and former nuclear negotiator Hassan Rouhani[11] secured just over 50 per cent of the votes and emerged winner (Table 3.1 and Figure 3.1).[12]

Despite the restriction on women to contest the presidential elections, 2013 saw some positive developments, especially following the election of Rouhani. The most notable was the appointment of Marzieh Afkham as the spokesperson of the Iranian Foreign Ministry.[13] This was the first time the Islamic republic had named a woman to the position. While

Table 3.1
Iranian Presidential Elections, June 2013

Name of the candidate	Name of the party	Votes secured	Percentage
Hassan Rouhani	Moderation and Development Party	18,613,329	50.88
Mohammad Bagher Ghalibaf	Society of Engineers	6,077,292	16.46
Saeed Jalili	Revolutionary Stability	4,168,946	11.31
Mohsen Rezaei	Development and Justice Party	3,884,412	10.55
Ali Akbar Velayati	Islamic Coalition	2,268,753	6.16
Mohammad Gharazi	Independent	446,015	1.22
Valid votes		35,458,747	96.58
Blank or invalid votes		1,245,409	3.42
Total votes cast		36,704,156	100
Registered voters turn out		50,483,192	72.70

Source: Adapted from Ministry of Interior, Islamic Republic of Iran, available at: http://www.moi.ir/Portal/Home/ShowPage.aspx?Object=News&CategoryID=cc1 955c9-7610-428d-b15c-fafc947cc884&WebPartID=47942904-35b9-4ecc-bfc4-4d6d3bee26d8&ID=ab52b9a8-e2a6-41e4-bbcc-15665125a6b2/.

a section of ulema was reportedly opposed to her appointment, the new moderate president apparently asked his officials to name women to high-ranking posts. Another case was the election of first Baluchi woman, Samiyeh Balochzehi, as the mayor of Kalat, a southern Iranian city. It is one of the most underprivileged and conservative provinces in Iran. This had been considered as a significant step that could inspire Baluchi women to work for more rights and break boundaries that have been created by both the state and society.[14] These developments had indicated gradual changes, both in political and social spheres.

During 2013, the Iranian economy remained severely hit due to the Western sanctions over its nuclear programme. This was exasperated by other domestic issues which contributed to economic hardships. As early as in January, Iran faced severe problems with its pharmaceutical

Figure 3.1
Iranian Presidential Elections, June 2013

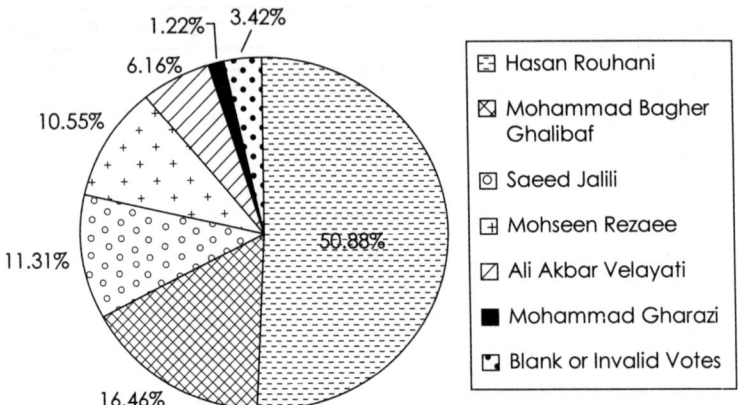

Source: Adapted from Ministry of Interior, Islamic Republic of Iran, available at: http://www.moi.ir/Portal/Home/ShowPage.aspx?Object=News&CategoryID=cc1 955c9-7610-428d-b15c-fafc947cc884&WebPartID=47942904-35b9-4ecc-bfc4-4d6d3bee26d8&ID=ab52b9a8-e2a6-41e4-bbcc-15665125a6b2/.

supplies, leading to a flourishing black market sector.[15] Apparently, rising poverty[16] was attributed to the soaring medical expenses.[17] While the medicine and humanitarian supplies are not covered by economic embargoes on Iran, it had indirect impact on them as international banking networks were hit. Vital Iranian automobile industry was also affected as the currency, Rial, was targeted by the sanctions.

The deteriorating Iranian economy was evident from rising inflation that was estimated to be about 40 per cent during most of 2013.[18] As a result, millions of Iranians suffered from sanctions and poor fiscal management and faced severe problems, such as rising food prices. Furthermore, oil exports and banking system were badly affected. Youth unemployment in 2013 was estimated at 35 to 40 per cent.[19] With regard to the budget deficit, spokesperson of the Iranian parliament's Energy Committee Hossein Amiri-Khamkani said that the administration would face US$40.4 billion deficit during the year 2013, but there were others who predicted US$28.25 billion deficit.[20] Alongside this, Iran's gross domestic product (GDP) in 2013 shrank by 5 to 6 per cent.[21]

On the energy front, Iranian crude shipments dropped to 700,000 barrels per day (bpd); average monthly revenue from oil sales during the first half of 2013 was estimated to be about US$3.4 billion, while it was US$8 billion in 2011 and US$6.3 billion in 2012.[22] However, with the interim nuclear deal, Iran's crude exports are likely to increase. It should be noted that oil exports make up to 80 per cent of Iran's total export earnings and 50 to 60 per cent of government revenue.[23] Economic recovery became the most daunting challenge facing Rouhani. In December, the president presented a US$315 billion annual budget to the parliament towards tackling high inflation and unemployment in 2014. The government's budget is expected at around US$75 billion.[24] The leader vowed to increase Iran's oil exports at an average of 1.1 million bpd at a cost of US$100 per barrel.[25] More rational and moderate policies are key to improving the economic climate in the country.

Iranian foreign policy had seen significant changes during 2013, particularly following Rouhani's election. Rebuilding cordial ties with its immediate neighbours, especially with Gulf Cooperation Council (GCC) countries and Central Asia, became Rouhani's top foreign policy agenda.[26] The most important development, however, was thaw in Iran–US relations. While the much anticipated 'historic-handshake' between Rouhani and Obama did not happen on the sideline of the UN General Assembly meeting in New York, a 15-minute telephone call by President Obama to Rouhani on 27 September seemed to have paved the way for a possible resolution of the nuclear crisis between the two countries.[27] This was the first direct talk between American and Iranian leaders since the Islamic revolution of 1979.

As a follow-up to the above event, in November, Iran had struck an interim nuclear agreement with the US and five other world powers.[28] With Iran's consent to curb its nuclear enrichment programme, the Western powers had decided to ease some on their sanctions on Tehran.[29] Besides an increase in Iranian crude export, the Geneva deal also signalled the start of a game-changing rapprochement between Iran and the West. However, while many Iranians celebrated this thaw,[30] some hardliners, including officials from Iran's Revolutionary Guard forces, criticized Rouhani for succumbing to the West.[31]

The Geneva deal, however, did elicit reservations and criticisms from some of the key allies of the US, especially Israel[32] and Saudi Arabia.[33] The Iran–US thaw became an irritant factor in Washington's relations with these two countries leading to speculations of understanding between the Jewish state and the Custodian of the Two Holy Places.[34]

In the defence sector, Iran made some progresses in its military modernization programmes, especially in submarines, advanced torpedoes, surveillance, combat unmanned aerial vehicles (UAVs), fighter jets and various kinds of missiles.[35] Defence Minister Hossein Dehqan stressed on the importance of defence cooperation with other countries, wherein Tehran could export some of its defence products. In November, Iran unveiled its domestically developed UAV, *Fotros*, which can be used for reconnaissance and combat operations.[36] With a range of 2,000 km, this UAV can cover much of the Middle East, including Israel and is manufactured by Iran Aircraft Manufacturing Industries Company. Earlier, an army commander announced the production of a new indigenous UAV, *Ra'ad 85*, which is capable of attacking air and ground targets.[37] Similar progress was made for missile and missile defence systems, such as *Talash*, capable of destroying modern fighter jets and drones.[38] Iranian Air Force ended the year by successfully test firing its long-range (of 200 km) *Qader* cruise missile in December.[39] Iran continued to emphasize that its military might is based entirely on deterrence and does not pose a threat to other countries.

BILATERAL RELATIONS

There were considerable political, economic and cultural engagements between India and Iran during 2013. The US–Iran thaw following the Geneva deal was seen as a positive development that would immensely benefit the bilateral relations and minimize, if not remove, some of the hurdles facing India.

Political Relations

The year 2013 started with the visit of Iran's Supreme National Security Council Secretary and Chief Nuclear Negotiator Saeed Jalili in January.[40] The visit was important as Iran reaffirmed its ties with India, especially at a time when the US-led sanctions reduced crude imports from Iran. Jalili met Indian National Security Advisor (NSA) Shivshankar Menon, Finance Minister P. Chidambaram and External Affairs Minister Salman Khurshid. Iranian leader had come to India to convince the latter to continue buying its oil amid the US sanctions. Moreover, both sides discussed means of enhancing cooperation in Afghanistan following the impending withdrawal of the US troops in December 2014.[41]

At the same time, Jalili 'ruled out any direct role for India in facilitating the start of the dialogue on the nuclear issue but stressed that both countries faced "common threats in the region"—listing terrorism and piracy as some of them.'[42] Importance was attached to the visit as he was considered a potential successor to President Ahmadinejad.[43] In the same month, Gholamreza Ansari presented his credentials to President Pranab Mukherjee as the new Iranian ambassador to India.[44] During their meeting, both the leaders discussed the historical ties and traditions that bind the Indo-Iranian relations, and pledged to take it further.[45]

The Iranian Majlis speaker Ali Larijani paid a five-day visit to India in February during which he held meetings with the Indian President, Prime Minister, External Affairs Minister, NSA and his Indian counterpart Lok Sabha Speaker Meira Kumar.[46] Giving importance to enhanced political relations, leaders from both the countries discussed ways to improve regional security, especially in Afghanistan.[47] For the first time in 2013, the Iranian speaker discussed the deteriorating political and security situation in Syria and both sides urged the need for internal dialogue among the conflicting parties to find a resolution.[48] The nuclear talks between Iran and P5+1, then underway in Kazakhstan,[49] and energy security figured in these talks.[50]

During 2013, most of India's exchanges with Iran heavily concentrated on improving energy ties, investments, development of Chabahar port and the situation in Afghanistan. These issues figured prominently when the Iranian ambassador to India met Rajnath Singh, president of the Bharatiya Janata Party (BJP)[51] and Secretary General of Communist Party of India (Marxist) (CPI-M) Prakash Karat in April.[52] Iran's willingness to reach out to different political parties exhibited its interest to seek a wider domestic audience in India. Amidst these engagements, the Indian Prime Minister sent a message of condolence for the loss of lives and destruction in the April earthquake in Iran and offered assistance.[53]

In May, External Affairs Minister Salman Khurshid visited Iran for the 17th meeting of the India–Iran Joint Commission.[54] During this visit, he met top Iranian leaders, including Advisor to the Supreme Leader Ali Akbar Velayati and Speaker of the Iranian Majlis Ali Larijani, and called on President Ahmadinejad. The meeting covered a wide range of issues, including Indian participation in Chabahar port, Iran–Pakistan–India (IPI) gas pipeline and economic and security development of Afghanistan.[55]

Chabahar has become important to India as it sees the port as a strategic conduit for smooth and uninterrupted passage of goods to Afghanistan, bypassing Pakistan.[56] The Syrian crisis was also discussed and both sides denounced violence and reiterated their support for a political settlement through dialogues.[57] India and Iran welcomed the Geneva communiqué, particularly the Six-Point Plan proposed by the UN-Arab League Special Envoy Kofi Annan.[58]

The highlight of the 17th commission meeting was the three memorandums of understanding (MoUs) signed by India and Iran.[59] They are as follows:

- MoU between Institute of Standards and Industrial Research of Islamic Republic of Iran (ISIRI) and Bureau of Indian Standards (BIS).
- MoU between the Foreign Service Institute and School of International Relations of the Iranian Foreign Ministry.
- MoU between the two governments on cooperation in the field of water resources management.

On the Iranian nuclear controversy, Salman Khurshid reiterated Tehran's 'indispensable right to use nuclear energy for peaceful purposes'.[60] In the words of one analyst,

> The recent visit by the external affairs minister can be viewed as continuation of new diplomatic push to strengthen bilateral cooperation with Iran 'despite the difficulties of economic sanctions imposed by the US and EU. However, the real test for both the countries is to maintain and sustain the current momentum....[61]

In continuation to its political outreach, New Delhi welcomed the election of Rouhani. Prime Minister Manmohan Singh was quick to congratulate Rouhani and expressed his desire to strengthen the relationship further by 'harnessing its enormous potential in the coming years'.[62] This change in the Iranian political leadership has been expected to usher in a 'new hope' in the Indo-Iranian ties as Rouhani is 'likely to bring to the presidency not only wisdom, maturity and pragmatism but also a matchless wealth of expertise derived from having served on one or another of Iran's leading institutions'.[63] Around this time, Foreign Secretary Ranjan Mathai announced India's support for Iran's presidency of the Conference on Disarmament, the UN's panel on nuclear disarmament.[64]

It should be noted that India had engaged with Rouhani during his earlier tenure as the National Security Council, including a meeting between him and India's National Security Adviser Brajesh Mishra in 2002.[65] In August 2013, the Vice-President of India M. Hamid Ansari represented India at the inauguration ceremony of the new Iranian President.[66] On the sideline of the event, Ansari met with several top Iranian leaders, including Ali Larijani and Iranian Deputy Minister of Foreign Affairs Abbas Araghci.[67]

The Geneva interim nuclear deal concluded in late November opened a new opportunity for both countries. Welcoming the deal, Ministry of External Affairs (MEA) observed:

> As the agreement between Iran and the P5 plus 1 has been agreed to just a few hours ago we are in the process of obtaining details from our key interlocutors, however, based on initial information available at this stage I can say that India welcomes the prospect of resolving questions related to Iran's nuclear programme, through dialogue and diplomacy. We also welcome the earlier agreement reached on November 11 between Iran and the IAEA, which is the only competent technical agency to verify the exclusively peaceful nature of Iran's nuclear activities, on practical measures for enhanced IAEA verification activity at Iranian nuclear sites.[68]

India's support for dialogue and diplomatic approach to resolve the Iranian nuclear crisis became apparent and evoked favourable response from strategic analysts, academicians, politicians and economists. There were also voices of caution.[69] In the aftermath of the deal, there was a suggestion that India was likely to start paying for Iranian crude oil in Euros[70] but this did not materialize in 2013.

Iranian Deputy Foreign Minister Ebrahim Rahimpour visited New Delhi and met Foreign Secretary Sujatha Singh on 25 November.[71] The talk which was a part of the high-level Foreign Office consultations enticed a wide attention as it happened right after the Geneva interim nuclear deal. During his meetings in India, both agreed to 'keep Saudi Arabia engaged in order to remove its misgivings about Tehran's interim understanding with the six global powers reached in Vienna'.[72]

Economic Relations

For many years, economic relations have remained as the mainstay of the bilateral ties and often superseded political relations. However, a downfall could be seen with regard to India's imports from Iran during 2012–13 which stood at US$11.59 billion, or 15.92 per cent less than in 2011–12 which was US$13.79 billion (Table 3.2 and Figure 3.2). Moreover, both Iranian share in total oil imports and share of oil in total imports from Iran have seen decline during the past three years (Table 3.3 and Figure 3.3). While the value for Indian export to Iran for the same period stood at US$3.35 billion, a growth of 38.97 per cent from US$2.41 billion during 2011–12 (Table 3.2). This fluctuation in the volume of trade was attributed to the US-led sanctions imposed on Iran.

In 2013, India and Iran had tried to revive their economic relations and sped up reciprocal visits and consultations to explore trade opportunities. As early as in January, the issue of unresolved payment crisis captured headlines. With dipping exports to Iran, India has been trying

Table 3.2
India–Iran Bilateral Trade (in US$ Million)

	2009–10	2010–11	2011–12	2012–13
India's exports to Iran	1,853.17	2,492.90	2,411.33	3,351.07
India's imports from Iran	11,540.85	10,928.21	13,790.16	11,594.46
Total bilateral trade	13,394.01	13,421.12	16,201.48	14,945.53
Share of Iran in India's total trade	2.87	2.16	2.04	1.89

Source: Adapted from Directorate General of Foreign Trade, New Delhi, available at: www.dgft.gov.in/.

Figure 3.2
India–Iran Bilateral Trade

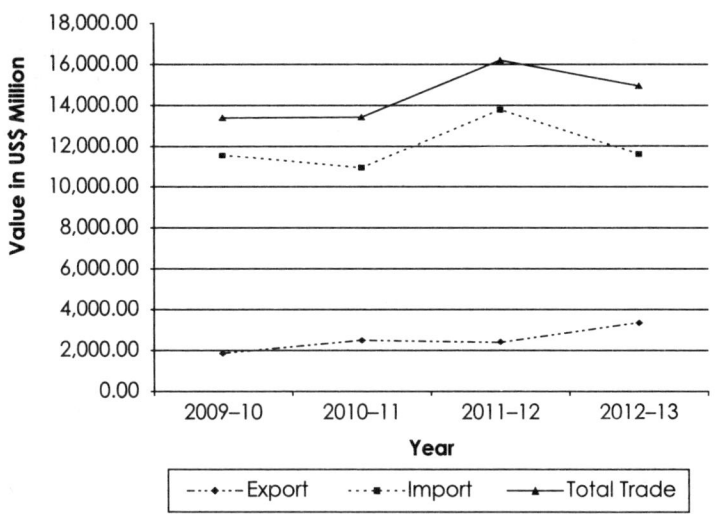

Source: Adapted from Directorate General of Foreign Trade, New Delhi, available at: www.dgft.gov.in/.

Table 3.3
Share of Oil in India's Imports from Iran (in US$ Million)

Year	Oil imports from Iran	Total oil imports	Iranian share in total oil imports	Imports from Iran	Per cent of oil in imports from Iran
2009–10	10,362.04	96,321.16	10.76	11,540.85	89.79
2010–11	9,377.88	115,929.02	8.09	10,928.21	85.81
2011–12	11,764.01	172,753.97	6.81	13,790.16	85.31
2012–13	9,716.39	181,344.67	5.36	11,594.46	83.80

Source: Adapted from Directorate General of Foreign Trade, New Delhi, available at: www.dgft.gov.in/.

to identify products that carry export potential and 'expedite contracts to set off a larger portion of the country's oil import bill'.[73] Towards this end both decided to set up a working group of experts on specific products to fast-track contracts. Some of the items identified by India included gems and jewellery, engineering goods and pharmaceuticals products.

Figure 3.3

Share of Oil in India's Total Imports from Iran

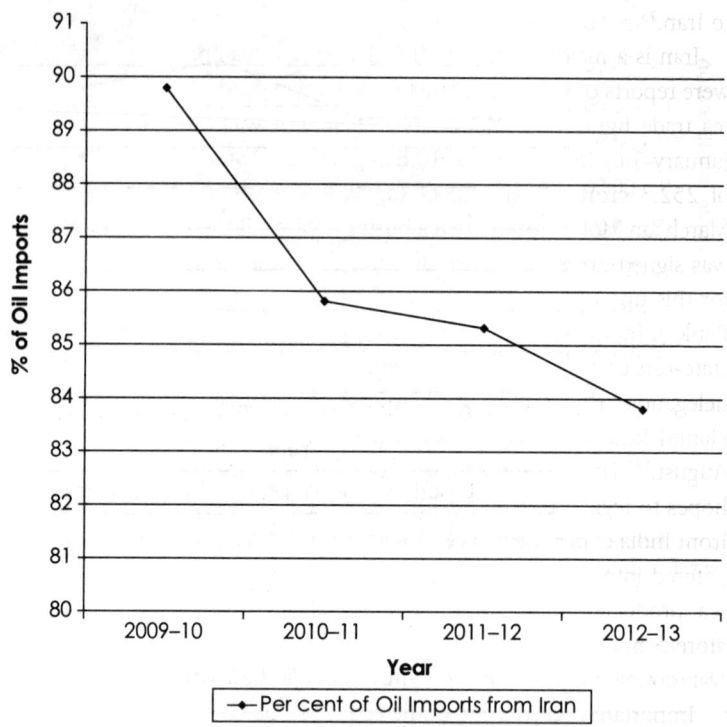

Source: Adapted from Directorate General of Foreign Trade, New Delhi, available at: www.dgft.gov.in/.

In January, there were reports of an agreement by Indian major pharmaceutical companies, such as Ranbaxy, Cipla, Glenmark and Ind-Swift Laboratories, to supply life-saving drugs to Iran.[74] Iran has been facing shortage of medicines due to the international sanctions. India wanted to provide assistance in this field and payment for such transactions would be made in Indian currency. Most of the demands from Iran were for bulk drugs, active pharmaceutical ingredients (APIs) and generic formulations that would be useful in the treatment of lung and breast cancers, brain tumours, heart ailments and other key diseases. To facilitate more trade in this area, Pharmaceutical Export Promotion Council of India (Pharmexcil), the apex body which is responsible for promotion of India's pharmaceutical exports, pledged to continue supplying drugs to Iran.[75] Iran is a major consumer of Indian-origin tea and in February, there were reports of India bartering tea for Iranian crude oil.[76] While the exact tea trade figure for 2013 is not available, it was estimated that during January–July India exported 10.8 million kg of tea with an estimated value of 252.3 crore Indian rupees (approximately US$41.88 million).[77] In March, an MoU to promote tea business worth 30 million kg in two years was signed during a visit by an Indian tea delegation to Iran. Optimism for this upsurge emerged due to the permission granted by the Reserve Bank of India (RBI) to Central Bank of Iran to open rupee accounts with state-run UCO Bank. Tea trade got a major boost when a nine-member delegation headed by the chairperson of Iran Tea Association (ITA), Hamid Reza Movassaghi, paid a five-day visit to Kolkata and Assam in August.[78] The visiting officials toured the tea gardens and expressed hopes to regain a substantial trade in this field by doubling the imports from India exports during 2014–15. Soon thereafter an Iranian importer entered into an agreement to buy at least 10 million tonne of orthodox tea produced in Golukpur Tea estate of North Tripura.[79] With the aforementioned frameworks to enhance tea trade, Indian tea exports to Iran doubled to 16.47 million during late 2013.[80]

Important components of the economic ties are soymeal, wheat, basmati rice, sugar, urea, etc. During early-March, it was reported that Iran would purchase higher supplies of Indian soymeal worth 0.8 million tonne by the end of the month, and 0.75 million tonnes during the leaner season of April–September.[81] An interesting fact is that by purchasing 870,776 tonnes by 31 March, Iran has become the largest importer of Indian soymeal beans surpassing Japan.[82] This was the second time Iran emerged as the top buyer of this grain from India consuming nearly one-third of the latter's total supplies.[83] India signed deals for 600,000 tonnes of soymeal to be exported during October and December 2013.[84]

On a similar note, rice continued to remain an important item in India–Iran trade. The price of Indian basmati rice was all-time high due to strong demands from Iran. The rupee-payment mechanism which had been in place since June 2012, to some extent, eased the bilateral trade. Iran purchased around 130,000 tonnes of Indian basmati rice till mid-2013, and the overall export for the financial year could grow by 6.5 per cent, soaring up to around 3.2 million tonnes.[85] This was a significant volume considering the difficulties faced by both the countries while navigating economic sanctions. By May, India began exporting a blend of basmati and non-basmati rice to Iran and, 'the non-basmati variety, which Iran is buying from India, costs around US$750 per tonne, while the basmati variety costs around US$1,600 per tonne'.[86]

There were speculations that India's near-monopoly in rice exports to Iran might be hit by the Geneva nuclear deal in November. This was primarily because of the possible resurgence of rice exports from Thailand and Pakistan due to easing sanctions on Iran. It was reported that India's share could be about 80 per cent of Iran's import of rice, which would be about 1.4–1.5 million tonne in 2013–14.[87]

The need for a robust trade in non-oil items was often endorsed. In late April, a 23-member business delegation from Federation of Andhra Pradesh Chamber of Commerce and Industry (FAPCCI) and the Chamber of Commerce for Iran Trade Promotion (CCITP) went to Iran to explore opportunities in bilateral trade.[88] The delegation signed three MoUs with chambers of commerce of Tehran, Shiraz and Bushehr and it was hoped that bilateral trade could reach US$25 billion within the next four years.[89]

Along with the above three items, the import of urea from Iran also surfaced in 2013 as India announced that it would continue importing urea from Iran. Till 15 February, India imported 1.6 million tonnes of Iranian urea.[90] India has started to think of setting up a urea factory in Chabahar,[91] and the issue figured during Khurshid's talks in May. This had come about when India was exploring opportunities in the Chabahar region and in the proposed Chabahar–Faraj–Bam railway.[92] An Indian delegation from the Fertiliser Ministry, Rashtriya Chemicals and Fertilisers (RCF), Gujarat Narmada Valley Fertilisers and Chemicals (GNFC) and Gujarat State Fertilisers and Chemicals Limited (GSFCL) visited Iran in December to discuss gas supply and prices for the proposed urea plant.[93]

During 2013, there were other important steps taken by both the countries to strengthen the overall economic ties. As an effort to boost trade, India proposed a preferential tariff arrangement to Iran.[94] A delegation led by Commerce Secretary S. R. Rao visited Tehran in April to sort out issues related to payment mechanisms and to push further trade agreements. Further, the Indo–Iranian Joint Commission meeting held the following month had investments in infrastructural developments and oil explorations on the agenda. For its part, Iran offered India a production-sharing agreement on exploration of a major oil block in its territory.[95] Notwithstanding economic sanctions against Iran, New Delhi had decided to scale up its commercial ties with the former. After EAM's visit to Iran, there was a report that India might ask the cash surplus Kandla and Jawaharlal Nehru ports to develop and operate cargo terminals at Chabahar port, to facilitate more trade. [96]

Furthermore, in May, in a move to ease payment for Iranian oil in rupee, India had agreed to outsource automobiles and pharmaceuticals products.[97] Iran was interested in importing Indian-made engineering materials, steel, auto parts, etc. Trade in these commodities was beneficial to India as it was a boon for the Indian automobile sectors. In the same month, both negotiated a swap deal for crude oil and gas condensates for India's textile machinery and raw materials.[98] If both manage to reach an agreement on textile trade, the value of Iranian imports from India would be approximately US$400 million.

In a move to bolster economic ties, Iran expressed its desire to open branches of four of its banks in India. Owing to the cumbersome procedures and regulations of the Reserve Bank of India (RBI), the initiative has been delayed. Opening of branches of Iranian banks could facilitate more trade. In the words of Masood E. Khaleghi, Iran's Consulate General in Mumbai:

> The high tariff structure maintained by India restricts further growth, which needs to be rationalised as preferential tariff system between India and Iran shall boost trade ties between the nations.[99]

The issue of opening of Iranian bank figured during December talks between Iran's industry minister Mohammad Reza Nematzadeh and his Indian counterpart Anand Sharma on the sidelines of the World Trade Organization (WTO) summit in Bali.[100] Meanwhile, the opening of Letters of Credit (LC) from Iran under the rupee payment mechanism became impressive, touching about US$400 million on a monthly basis.[101] Towards the end of 2013, when the news of the nuclear deal was announced, New Delhi hoped to revitalize its trade with Tehran. This development was welcomed by several Indian exporters and the Engineering Export Promotion Council (EEPC).[102]

A couple of trade-related visits in November and December ended the year on a positive note. In November, an Iranian delegation led by Yahya Ale-es Hagh, the president of Tehran Chamber of Commerce, Industries, Mines and Agriculture, visited India and invited industrialists from sectors, such as agriculture, mining, petrochemicals, educational services, infotech and infotech-enabled services, pharmacy, infrastructure, railway, telecom, energy, engineering, steel and dry fruits.[103] During this visit, FAPCCI signed another MoU with the Iran Chamber of Commerce, Industries and Mines and Commercial Organization of Khorasan province to promote trade and investment. In December, Federation of Indian Chambers of Commerce and Industry (FICCI) organized an exhibition in Tehran showcasing a variety of Indian products.[104]

From the above developments, it is quite evident how intensively both countries engaged to enhance economic ties. To give further impetus to it, an Indian panel headed by the Commerce Secretary was formed in December to chalk out strategy to boost trade.[105]

Energy Relations

In India–Iran relations, energy has always been the most important factor and it often overshadowed other aspects. However, since late 2000s, this issue came under wider scrutiny due to paymentimbroglio brought by the US-led sanctions on Iran. In 2013, New Delhi and Tehran tried unrelentingly to overcome the limitations in their energy ties. During 2012–13, India imported US$9.7 billion worth of Iranian crude oil (Table 3.4). In 2013, it imported 195,600 bpd of oil and condensate, which was a decline of 38 per cent compared with 315,200 bpd in 2012.[106] Energy relations between India and Iran in 2013 were fluctuating.

When both the countries were gearing up to ease energy ties, the sanction had an early impact on India–Iran ties. In January, the US-based California Public Employees' Retirement System (CalPERS), one of the world's largest pension funds, raised serious concerns over investments in shares of a few Indian oil companies, such as Oil India

Table 3.4
India's Energy Imports from Iran (in US$ Million)

	2009–10	2010–11	2011–12	2012–13
Energy imports from Iran	10,362.04	9,377.88	11,764.01	9,716.39
Total energy imports	96,321.12	115,929.02	172,753.92	181,344.67
Total energy imports from the Persian Gulf	55,904.14	66,688.4	105,056.26	105,859.15
Share in total energy imports (in per cent)	10.76	8.09	6.81	5.36
Share in energy imports from Persian Gulf (in per cent)	18.53	14.00	11.09	9.18

Source: Adapted from Directorate General of Foreign Trade, New Delhi, available at: www.dgft.gov.in/.

and Petronet LNG, because of their trade links with Iran.[107] CalPERS even blocked future investments in many state-run energy suppliers as it was reportedly monitoring Oil and Natural Gas Corp (ONGC) for possible Iranian ties.

In January, an Indian insurance scheme reportedly allowed Iran's state-run National Iranian Tanker Company (NITC) to bolster oil exports by chartering a vessel insured by India's state-run firms, industry and shipping.[108] This was used to transport oil cargo from Mangalore Refinery and Petrochemicals Limited (MRPL). NITC struggled many times to keep the oil flowing as it lacks small vessels that could be docked at the Mangalore port. Soon after this, there were reports of India cutting Iranian oil imports, including by MRPL and plans to reduce oil imports from Iran by 17 per cent[109] before the financial year ended. For MRPL, it was difficult to hire contract tankers. It planned to import only 3.8 million metric tonnes, or about 74,000 barrels a day during 2012–13, as against its previous target of 5.0 million tonnes.[110]

Payment-related issues and problems of shipping had major impacts on India–Iran energy ties. In February, the state-owned Hindustan Petroleum Corporation Limited (HPCL) announced its plan to halt Iranian oil imports on the ground that it could not renew insurance for its refineries to process the crude.[111] HPCL's move came at a time when India talked of reducing deliveries from Iran.

Since April 2012, India was paying in Euros to clear 45 per cent of its purchases of Iranian oil through Ankara-based Turkiye Halk Bankasi, while the balance were paid in rupees.[112] Iran was forced to keep its oil revenues in local Indian bank accounts and could use the money in purchasing commodities, such as food, medicine and other medical equipment. As a result, from mid-February, India started paying in rupees that was only partly convertible. Responding to such pressures, during February visit, Larijani called on India to prevent 'powerful countries from taking control of energy chokepoints'.[113]

In March, oil imports faced fresh hurdles when India's Mercator Lines halted offering a ship for transporting Iranian oil to India due to pressures from the US.[114] In the absence of such small vessels, National Iranian Oil Corp (NIOC) had to use only partially loaded suezmax ships to deliver crude to the MRPL plant. Such problems hindered the growth of energy trade between the two countries and became a major setback for the plants as well for the Iranian economy. On a similar note, during the same month, Chennai Petroleum Corporation Limited (CPCL) was hit as European companies were reluctant to provide technology licensing for six-million tonne units.[115] Along with it, MRPL, HPCL and ONGC also struggled for obtaining reinsurance due to the US sanctions, thereby forcing Indian refineries to look for other options including Kuwait and Saudi Arabia. CPCL faced similar problems in 2012 as well. With no viable solution in sight, in March MRPL's Managing Director P. P. Upadhya said that India would have to halt importing Iranian oil as there would not be any insurance cover due to the sanctions. In between, Iran replaced an Indian consortium led by ONGC by its Iranian Offshore Oil Company (IOOC) for the development of an offshore hydrocarbon block in the Persian Gulf.[116]

By the end of March, a 2,000-crore Indian rupees Energy Insurance Pool (EIP) fund was created to back Indian firms. The state-run Oriental Insurance Company and New India Assurance Company were picked as initial contributors as they underwrote risks of state-run MRPL and private Essar Oil Limited.[117] According to an agreement, Indian government would also provide sovereign guarantee for losses up to 10,000 crore Indian rupees. This initiative came as a big relief to firms, such as MRPL, whose insurance cover was running out. Among the other measures taken to streamline energy trade included India's approval for two Iranian ship underwriters who were not part of a global body and 'whose liability cover against risks, including oil spills and collisions for foreign ships calling at India's ports, will be accepted by the port authorities'.[118] Even though the Prime Minister emphasized on the 'strategic partnership' with Iran, by mid-2013 India drastically cut down its oil imports from Iran.[119]

For its part, Iran pushed harder for enhancing energy ties with India. In May, Minister Ali Akbar Salehi, during his meeting with his Indian counterpart, offered a new production-sharing regime for oil exploration by Indian companies. According to his plan, 'a production sharing contract will give the foreign country ownership of the oil explored and produced as also the freedom to ship it wherever they want'.[120] To enhance energy ties, Iranian Oil Minister Rostam Qasemi paid a three-day visit a few days later.[121] Iran even offered a gas pipeline through sea by avoiding Pakistan.[122] In June, India felt some relief when the US granted exemption to nine countries from sanctions for importing oil from Iran.[123] It was done because countries including India significantly reduced its dependence on Iran in the recent months.

With the 180-day waiver granted by the US, India's MRPL was prepared to resume oil imports from Iran in July and secured local reinsurance for claims of up to US$83 million. A refinery that witnessed a significant jump was Essar Oil Limited, which purchased 138,900 bpd of Iranian crude oil in June alone.[124] Simultaneously, the rupee-payment mechanism (through UCO Bank) that was in place also favoured the Indo-Iranian energy trade, and benefitted the state-owned Indian Oil Corporation (IOC).[125] Furthermore, to keep the oil flowing into India, Tehran offered to underwrite insurance worth US$1 billion per incident for its vessels. India, too, had sought sovereign guarantees for the Kish and Moallem protection and indemnity (P&I) clubs that insure Iranian vessels against personal injury and environment clean up claims.[126]

Despite this incident, India was keen to import more crude oil from Iran to offset earlier disruptions and Economic Affairs Secretary Arvind Mayaram indicated India's desire to import up to 11 million tonnes of oil from Iran in 2013–14.[127] A similar opinion was raised by the oil minister who speculated that imports from Iran could save up to US$8.5 billion in foreign exchange when the rupee was weakening against the dollar.[128] There were plans to include the private refiners, such as Essar, to enjoy the benefit of insurance cover for Iranian crude. Indian planners decided on creating 2,000-crore Indian rupees fund through contributions from public sector insurers and Oil Industry Development Board (OIDB). In this 1,000 crore Indian rupees would be contributed by the insurers while the OIDB would bring in the rest.[129]

By late 2013, the rupee-payment crisis again surfaced. Iran began to show reluctance to accept rupee payment beyond the current 45 per cent of the total amount because of its fear that its imports from India would not be sufficient enough to utilize the rupee balance.[130] In late September, Iran turned down India's request for this payment mode for oil imports, and started new rounds of negotiations. The options of paying Iran in Japanese yen, Russian Rouble or Chinese Yuan cropped up.[131] Meanwhile, Indian Department of Economic Affairs (DEA) unsuccessfully tried to convince Iran to sign an MoU for 100 per cent rupee payment. There were suggestions that the Rouhani government had withdrawn offers made under Ahmadinejad to attract Indian firms to help develop Iranian oilfields, such as Farsi block.[132] This was a major setback to India, particularly after expecting robust energy trade under the new Iranian government. To overcome the recurring difficulties, Iran offered to use Oman as a conduit to collect crude oil payments due from India.[133] This came to light when Muscat approached New Delhi for revising the mechanism which could facilitate transfer of oil payments by India but 2013 did not see any breakthrough on this front.

In December, some efforts were made to end the year on a positive note. To bolster ties, an Iranian delegation led by Gholamali Kamyab, deputy governor at Iranian Central Bank, visited India and met officials from the finance ministry, and Reserve Bank of India discussed issues related to shipping insurance, as well as ways to increase oil imports from Iran and exports from India.[134] Another effort to bridge energy cooperation was the negotiations between National Iranian Gas Exports Company (NIGEC) and Indian companies to deliver natural gas to India through a deepwater pipeline crossing the Sea of Oman.[135]

Cultural Relations

One arena that was not undermined by payment-related row and other differences was the cultural ties. Constant efforts were taken by both the countries to enhance relations, especially in the field of education, film, art and literature, etc. Cinema plays an important role in bridging the cooperation between the two. The year opened with Iran's participation at the Jaipur International Film Festival in January. Movies such as *A Look towards the Sky* directed by Hadi Mohaqqeq and *Suddenly, Zinat* by Navid Nikkhah Azad won Special Jury Mention in the festival.[136] In March, Iran participated at the Ninth IAWRT Asian Women's Film Festival held in New Delhi.[137] Likewise, many other Iranian film directors also participated in various Indian film festivals held in 2013. Iranian film-maker Alireza Shahrokhi participated as a jury member at the Ladakh International Film Festival (LIFF) in September 2013.[138] As it was in 2012, Iranian films competed in International Film Festival of Kerala (IFFK) and Chennai International Film Festival (CIFF), both held in December and received accolades.[139]

In February, an all-girl Iranian band Ghazal performed in New Delhi,[140] and this was the time when they expressed solidarity with a similar Kashmiri-women band which faced a fatwa from a senior clergy. In April, Hossein Cheraghi, the director of a popular Iranian paper puppet theatre, *The Puppet Theatre Group*, visited India to participate in a puppet festival.[141] A special issue volume containing valuable articles by Indo-Iranian scholars was released in New Delhi in November.[142] The Iranian consulate in Hyderabad released a collection of Persian poems by Maharaja Kishen Pershad Shaad of former Hyderabad State in March.[143]

In a move to uplift cultural cooperation, Indian Cultural Centre was inaugurated in Tehran during the visit of Salman Khurshid in May. The centre was a response to 'great contributions Iran has made to the growth of the Indian culture'.[144] A little earlier, Iran's Cultural Fairs Institute and India's National Book Trust (NBT) signed an agreement to expand their cooperation on international book fairs and marketing.[145]

On the social front, the problem related with Sikh-marriage registration under Iranian laws was discussed during Salman Khurshid's visit to Tehran. This was done in the interest of the 3,000-odd Indian-origin citizens in Iran; out of which one-third of them belong to the

Sikh community.[146] Iran has been considered to be sacred by the Sikhs due to the belief that Guru Nanak crossed through Afghanistan, Iran and Iraq on his way to Mecca. Moreover, to strengthen movements of people, more flights have been introduced between Hyderabad (in India) and Mashhad (in Iran).[147] Possibility for a visa-on-arrival facility is believed to be under consideration.

Defence Relations

Military relations between India and Iran have become a passé since mid-2000s. Several factors have been attributed for this dormancy. In the past, India assisted in refitting and maintaining Iranian armoured tanks and other military vehicles, and conducted a few joint naval exercises.[148] There were even discussions of Indian arms sales to Iran in early 2000s. Relations in this field were given further boost with the signing of a strategic partnership accord in January 2003, during then Iranian President Mohammad Khatami's visit to New Delhi. Cooperation in this field remained non-existent for the last one decade.

India's increasing focus on Iran has brought the possibility of a resumption of military ties. In July, Iranian ambassador to India expressed his desire to enhance defence ties with India. Reciprocating this sentiment, Defence Minister A. K. Antony welcomed the idea of more bilateral defence exchanges with Iran.[149] Acknowledging the achievements made by defence industries of both the countries, the Iranian envoy emphasized on his country's readiness to exchange experience with India. Further, in December, Iranian warships, *Alborz*, *Bandar Abbas*, and Russian-origin Kilo-class submarine, *Younes*, paid a goodwill visit to Mumbai.[150] Naval officials from both the countries called for a close naval cooperation and the need for outlining a 'framework for joint cooperation and provision of security for merchant vessels in India's western waters all the way to the Persian Gulf' was suggested.[151]

External Players

The US: Like previous years, the role of the US in Indo-Iranians was very visible during 2013. The reduction in India's import of crude from Iran was primarily due to the US-led sanctions. During his visit to India in January, Iran's Chief nuclear negotiator Saeed Jalili expressed concerns over the influence of the US on India's ties with Iran. It is essential to recognize that, on one hand, New Delhi is facing pressure from Iran to continue oil imports but, on the other, India is facing immense pressure from the US to move in the opposite direction and cut back imports from the Islamic Republic. In the words of Harsh V. Pant,

> While it is not in New Delhi's interest to jeopardize ties with Washington, India should not be expected to drastically curb its relations with Iran in response to pressures emanating from the US. To understand India's interest in Iran, one must first consider the country's dire need for energy security and the apparent issues with alternative options.[152]

For the US, the year opened with concerns over India's hesitation in implementing US-led sanctions against Iran.[153] Despite payment problems, India continued its oil imports from Iran. However, New Delhi was very concerned when another round of sanction was imposed in February. India could no longer use Turkish Halk Bank to pay for the Iranian oil.[154] In March, US charged Iran of carrying out certain unspecified clandestine activities in a few countries, including India.[155] While India refrained from issuing any formal reply, the pressures were palpable.

To bolster energy relations with India, several US lawmakers favoured exports of American natural gas to India. The Indo-Iranian energy relations figured prominently in the debate in the US Congress. This was primarily to curtail New Delhi's approach to Tehran for its energy needs. Indian ambassador to the US Nirupama Rao admitted, 'Export of US natural gas to India would provide a steady, reliable supply of clean energy that would help reduce India's crude oil imports from the Middle East and provide reliable energy to India.'[156] Though, no breakthrough was reported on this front, gas supply by the US would pose a stiff competition to Iran.

For its part, Iran also expressed its concerns over the transfer of nuclear material and technology by the US to India, and the decision of the Nuclear Suppliers Group to exempt New Delhi despite being a non-signatory to the Nuclear Non-Proliferation Treaty.[157] Without naming India, in May, Iranian representative to International Atomic Energy Agency (IAEA) Ali Asghar Soltanieh strongly condemned such non-compliant attitude of the US and EU and said,

> I have to warn that the extension of full nuclear cooperation to non-parties, exemption from strict export regulations of nuclear material and technology, such as NSG, which is an admiration for non-adherence to the NPT,

is a crystal clear non-compliance of the non-proliferation provisions of the Treaty by western countries, specifically the US and the EU.[158]

Amidst these tensions, the only solace for India was the US decision in November to grant a six-month waiver on Iran sanctions. This, however, came only after India drastically reduced imports from Iran. Things began to improve in late 2013; there were signals of a possible resolution to longstanding nuclear controversy. This had come to the great relief of India whose energy ties with Iran has been affected by the US sanctions. The landmark Geneva deal evoked mixed reactions within India. Most hinted at the resurgence of overall India–Iran bilateral relations.[159] Some were of the view that the Indo-Iranian relationship would continue to be engulfed by various challenges, notwithstanding what happens on the US–Iran front.[160] In the words of one,

> With Israel and Saudi Arabia not happy with the latest nuclear deal between Iran and leading world powers, India may not be able to derive any appreciable advantages in its overall relations with Iran. On the contrary, India needs to be extremely cautious while handling the challenges posed by the emerging Iran–US engagement.[161]

The above scholar is also of the view that without proper mechanisms to resolve the issues pertaining to payment of oil, banking insurance, shipping, etc., India–Iran ties would continue to be plagued by problems. From the above developments, it is visible that the US has remained as the most important external factor in Indo-Iranian ties.

China: Sino-Iranian relations during 2013 did not pose a major challenge to India's engagement with Iran. However, both the countries made constant efforts to enhance their bilateral relations. While Iran has remained China's top crude oil supplier,[162] the latter's main export items to Tehran are linked to construction, transportation and manufacturing sectors. China invested heavily in Tehran's subway systems, dams, fishery and cement factories. The bilateral trade between China and Iran in 2013 was estimated to be around US$27.5 billion, and is expected to shoot up to US$38 billion by early 2014.[163] This is an evidence of robust economic relations between the two countries. China also faced problems in its energy trade with Iran due to the US sanctions but felt a relief when the US extended six-month waivers in November, and more Iranian oil is expected to flow into China in 2014.

For India, China's involvement in the pipeline project between Iran and Pakistan in 2013 became a concern. There were suggestions that China offered US$1 billion in assistance for building gas pipeline.[164] Upon completion of this project, Pakistan could import 750 million cubic feet per day (mmcfd) of gas from Iran, extendable to one billion cubic feet. Another important concern was Beijing's interest to finance the Chabahar port project.[165] The move would significantly strengthen China's position in the Middle East and would undermine India's long involvement in the construction and maintenance of the port. Partly to counter Chinese presence in Iran, India had agreed to upgrade the Chabahar port, providing financial assistance.[166]

Pakistan: Iran and Pakistan continued to share cordial relations during the year 2013. Most of their engagements were focused on improving their bilateral ties but major emphasis was given to trade and gas pipeline project. While their total trade volume was estimated to be about US$1.5 billion in 2013, they have agreed to increase it to US$10 billion annually.[167] During 2013, leaders from both the countries acknowledged the need to enhance their trade transactions by speeding up their projects. To facilitate this, a Pakistani official encouraged the establishment of a joint banking system and urged both sides to turn to their national hard currencies instead of the American dollar in reciprocal trade exchanges.[168] Further, both the countries expressed their desires to enhance relations in the field of science and technology, and also the investment opportunities by the Pakistani business community in the agricultural, tourism and metal industry of Iran.

A major concern for India was the initiatives taken by Iran and Pakistan to strengthen their cooperation through gas pipeline. In early January, Iran pitched for the extension of this pipeline to India via Pakistan but New Delhi turned down this offer because of security concerns.[169] On 11 March, despite difficulties due to the US sanctions, President Ahmadinejad inaugurated construction work of a long-delayed US$7.5 billion gas pipeline.[170] By early 2014 Iran has constructed 900 km of the pipeline on its soil. This has remained a concerning development for India whose energy projects with Iran are in a limbo, mainly due to the sanctions and other security issues.

Simultaneously, there were reports of India's eagerness to join the Iran–Pakistan (IP) pipeline project. In March, Indian Oil Minister Moily described the IP pipeline project to be beneficial to New Delhi but emphasized the need to sort out certain 'sensitive issues'.[171] India started to reconsider its stand owing to the rising demands for energy but no visible progress was made during 2013 on this front. In fact, in late 2013, Iran and Pakistan had their own shares of problems regarding gas purchase agreement and pricing, and the cancellation of US$500 million loan by Iran undermined Pakistan's dream to complete the project.[172] Iran's crumbling economy due to the sanctions led to this development.

Israel: The unresolved issue of the alleged Iranian terror attack on an Israeli diplomat in New Delhi in February 2012 continued. To speed up the probe, New Delhi had sent Letter Rogatory as a reminder to five countries, including Iran, seeking urgent cooperation. This was done after the case hit a dead-end due to Iranian non-cooperation in executing arrest warrants against four of its nationals.[173] The terror attack figured prominently during the eighth meeting of India–Israel Joint Working Group (JWG) on counter-terrorism held on 20 February in New Delhi.[174] The non-resolution of the terror attack tests India's ability to balance its ties with Israel and Iran.

In June, Israel's President Shimon Peres urged India not to remain 'neutral' to Iran's 'aggressive attempt' to become a regional hegemon by possessing nuclear capabilities.[175] The President also reminded India's own concerns with nuclear capacities in its region. The Iranian nuclear programme is one issue in which India and Israel have different views.[176]

Challenges and Problems

Apart from the aforementioned energy-related issues, there were other problems that caused major concerns to both India and Iran. As in the past, certain activities of Iranian students in India captured media attention in 2013. However, they were fewer than in the previous year. In October, the Pune police arrested an Iranian student, who, even after being deported from the city in 2009, returned via Nepal and was found living in the city again.[177] This case drew added attention because of reports of movements of terror suspects in and out of India via Nepal border. In November, Iranian student Sahel Rabiani was deported on charge of violating visa rules.[178]

The issue of treatment of Bahais in Iran tangled India–Iran relations.[179] In the past, there were instances of such mistreatment of this community in Iran, especially its students. Several Indian leaders and human rights activists appealed to both Iranian and Indian leaders to protect the rights of this community.[180] Another Iranian demand bothered India. For the first time, in December, it wanted an Indian delegation to get tests for HIV, Hepatitis C and Tuberculosis before issuing visas, which New Delhi considered 'discriminatory and politically incorrect'.[181]

When both were trying to resolve problems related to oil payment and banking insurance difficulties, on 13 August, Iranian Revolutionary Guard Corps (IRGC) detained an Indian oil-carrying ship *MT Desh Shanti* and created furore in Delhi.[182] The vessel was detained on the pretext that it was causing environmental concerns by polluting the Iranian water, a claim that was refuted by New Delhi.[183] This was seen as a retaliatory move against the detention of an Iranian cargo vessel, *Diyanat*, by Indian authorities in early 2012.[184] Finally, after intense negotiations, in September, Iran ordered the release of the Indian tanker only after submitting a letter of undertaking by the ship's owner to compensate for damages if the claim of pollution was proved.[185] Meanwhile, in November, Iran had agreed to release 10 Indian sailors who were imprisoned on the ground of violating international maritime boundary.[186]

CONCLUSION

When compared to recent year, 2013 was a less successful year for India and Iran, particularly due to the difficulties in maintaining their energy cooperation. Trade ties remained low as compared to the previous year since the banking systems were hit due to the sanctions. At the same time, both countries sought to expand their overall bilateral ties, and this was evidenced by the constant and reciprocal high-level visits. Such moves open a wide avenue for cooperation, and a desire to resume security-related cooperation was acknowledged by both the countries. India and Iran should promote further cooperation in the fields of socio-cultural, academic, and science and technology. Such initiatives could lead to a fair understanding of each other's country. In this regard, the initiative to begin visa-on-arrival facility for the Iranians visiting India should facilitate more people-to-people contacts. Lastly, New Delhi should try to capitalize on the thawing of relations between Iran and the US, and try to streamline those issues, mainly energy-related, which have significantly undermined their bilateral ties in recent years. At the same time, it is essential to recognize that as long as India continues to walk under the shadow of the US–Iran tension, difficulties in the India–Iran bilateral relations are inevitable.

NOTES

1. 'Iran Presidential Election 2013: Khamenei Will Have Tight Grip on Candidate Field after Ahmadinejad', *The Huffington Post*, 7 March 2013, available at: http://www.huffingtonpost.com/2013/03/07/iran-presidential-election-2013-khamenei_n_2826304.html/.
2. 'Iranian Presidential Hopefuls Detail Agendas', *Press TV (Iran)*, 30 April 2013, available at: http://www.presstv.com/detail/2013/04/30/301147/iran-presidential-hopefuls-set-agendas/.
3. 'Ahmadinejad vs. Ayatollah Khamenei: Iran's President, Supreme Leader Clash over Political Authority', *Reuters*, 8 February 2013, available at: http://www.huffingtonpost.com/2013/02/08/ahmadinejad-vs-ayatollah-khamenei_n_2647337.html/.
4. Ibid.
5. 'Iran's President Faces Sanctions over Breaking Election Rules', *The Guardian (London)*, 12 May 2013, available at: http://www.theguardian.com/world/2013/may/12/iran-president-charges-breaking-election-rules/.
6. 'Iranian Presidential Hopefuls Detail Agendas', *Press TV*, 30 April 2013, available at: http://www.presstv.com/detail/2013/04/30/301147/iran-presidential-hopefuls-set-agendas/
7. Tara Kangarlou, 'Who's Running in Iran's Presidential Election?' *CNN*, 13 June 2013, available at: http://edition.cnn.com/2013/06/04/world/meast/iran-election-candidates-profile/.
8. 'Iran Election: Cleric Rules Out Women Candidates', *BBC*, 16 May 2013, available at: http://www.bbc.com/news/world-middle-east-22560976/.
9. Colin Freeman, 'Iran Bans Hashemi Rafsanjani from Running in Presidential Election', *The Telegraph (London)*, 21 May 2013, available at: http://www.telegraph.co.uk/news/worldnews/middleeast/iran/10072084/Iran-bans-Hashemi-Rafsanjani-from-running-in-presidential-election.html/.
10. Lisa Daftari, 'Religious Leaders Ban 30 Women from Running for Iran's Presidency', *Fox News*, 17 May 2013, available at: http://www.foxnews.com/world/2013/05/17/religious-leaders-ban-30-women-from-running-for-iran-presidency/.

11. For a brief biography of Hassan Rouhani, see, 'Rohani Becomes Iran's New President', *Press TV*, 15 July 2013, available at: http://www.presstv.com/detail/2013/06/15/309169/rohani-becomes-irans-new-president/.

12. 'President-elect Rohani Urges West to Respect Iran's Rights', *Press TV*, 16 June 2013, available at: http://www.presstv.com/detail/2013/06/16/309324/west-must-respect-iran-rights-rohani/.

13. 'Iran Foreign Ministry Appoints First-Ever Spokeswoman', *Al Arabiya*, 29 August 2013, available at: http://english.alarabiya.net/en/News/middle-east/2013/08/29/Iran-foreign-ministry-appoints-first-ever-spokeswoman.html/.

14. 'Baluchi Sunni Woman Elected Mayor is First for Iran', *Al-Monitor*, 5 December 2013, available at: http://www.al-monitor.com/pulse/originals/2013/12/sunni-woman-first-iran-mayor.html#/.

15. 'Iran Medical Crisis Deepens as Sanctions Hit Economy', *The Huffington Post*, 8 January 2013, available at: http://www.huffingtonpost.com/2013/01/08/iran-medical-crisis_n_2432629.html/.

16. 'Iran: Rising Poverty, Declining Labour Rights', *International Federation for Human Rights* (FIDH), 10 June 2013, available at: http://www.fidh.org/en/asia/iran/iran-rising-poverty-declining-labour-rights-13403/.

17. Arash Karami, 'Medical Expenses Force 7.5% of Sick Iranians into Poverty Annually', *Al-Monitor*, 6 December 2013, available at: http://iranpulse.al-monitor.com/index.php/2013/12/3414/medical-expenses-force-7-5-of-iranians-into-poverty-annually/. In 2013, 7.5 per cent of sick Iranians were dropping below the poverty line/.

18. For a report on the inflation, see Arash Karami, 'With Record Inflation, Iran Plans to Reduce Subsidies by 30%', *Al-Monitor*, 7 October 2013, available at: http://iranpulse.al-monitor.com/index.php/2013/10/2962/with-record-inflation-iran-plans-to-reduce-subsidies-by-30/.

19. 'Iranian Youth Struggle with Unemployment', *Al Jazeera*, 13 June 2013, available at: http://www.aljazeera.com/video/middleeast/2013/06/20136136295061524.html/. Also see, Vali R. Nasr, 'Iran's Economic Crossroads', *The New York Times*, 4 December 2013, available at: http://www.nytimes.com/2013/12/05/opinion/nasr-irans-economic-crossroads.html?_r=0/.

20. 'Iranian MP: Administration to Face $40.4 Billion Budget Deficit', *Trend (Azerbaijan)*, 17 September 2013, available at: http://en.trend.az/regions/iran/2190961.html/.

21. Nasr, 'Iran's Economic Crossroads'.

22. Timothy Gardner, 'Iran's Oil Revenues Drop 58 Percent since 2011 as Sanctions Bite: U.S.', *Reuters*, 30 August 2013, available at: http://www.reuters.com/article/2013/08/30/us-usa-iran-sanctions-idUSBRE97T0S220130830/.

23. Dalga Khatinoglu, 'Iran's Oil Revenues Reached $34 Bln in 9 Months', *Trend*, 9 January 2014, available at: http://en.trend.az/regions/iran/2228363.html/.

24. 'Rouhani Submits Budget Draft for Next Year to Majlis', *Press TV*, 8 December 2013, available at: http://www.presstv.com/detail/2013/12/08/338841/rouhani-submits-budget-draft-to-majlis/.

25. Najmeh Bozorgmehr, 'Iran President Vows to Tackle Inflation and Un-
    employment', *The Financial Times*, 8 December 2013, available at: http://
    www.ft.com/intl/cms/s/0/43af605c-6024-11e3-916e-00144feabdc0.
    html#axzz2sTJsz8Or; and Marcus George and Isabel Coles, 'Iran President
    Rouhani Targets Stagflation in First Budget', *Reuters*, 8 December 2013,
    available at: http://www.reuters.com/article/2013/12/08/us-iran-budget-
    idUSBRE9B703120131208/.
26. Abbas Maleki, 'Rouhani Stresses Regionalism in Iranian Foreign Policy',
    Al-Monitor, 13 July 2013, available at: http://www.al-monitor.com/pulse/
    originals/2013/07/rouhani-stresses-regionalism-in-iranian-foreign-policy.
    html#/.
27. Dan Roberts and Julian Borger, 'Obama Holds Historic Phone Call with
    Rouhani and Hints at End to Sanctions', *The Guardian*, 28 September 2013,
    available at: http://www.theguardian.com/world/2013/sep/27/obama-phone-
    call-iranian-president-rouhani/.
28. Five other countries were France, Germany, Britain, China and Russia.
29. For some of the agreements between Iran and the West, see Julian Borger
    and Saeed Kamali Dehghan, 'Iran Seals Nuclear Deal with West in Return
    for Sanctions Relief', *The Guardian*, 24 November 2013, available at: http://
    www.theguardian.com/world/2013/nov/24/iran-nuclear-deal-west-sanc-
    tions-relief/.
30. Aryn Baker, 'Iranians Celebrate Nuclear Deal', *Time*, 24 November 2013,
    available at: http://world.time.com/2013/11/24/iranians-celebrate-nuclear-
    deal/.
31. 'Iranian General Criticises Rouhani Government', *Al Jazeera*, 11 December
    2013, available at: http://www.aljazeera.com/news/middleeast/2013/12/
    iranian-general-criticises-rouhani-government-20131211159757812.
    html/. Also see, Azadeh Moaveni, 'Not Everyone's Happy: Hardliners in
    Iran Criticize Geneva Nuclear Deal', *Time*, 25 November 2013, available
    at: http://world.time.com/2013/11/25/not-everyones-happy-hardliners-in-
    iran-criticize-geneva-nuclear-deal/.
32. Jodi Rudoren, 'Israeli Leaders Denounce Geneva Accord', *The New
    York Times*, 24 November 2013, available at: http://www.nytimes.
    com/2013/11/25/world/middleeast/israeli-leaders-decry-iran-accord.html/.
33. Atul Aneja, 'Geneva Nuclear Success Impacts Saudi–Iran Ties', *The
    Hindu*, 26 November 2013, available at: http://www.thehindu.com/news/
    international/world/geneva-nuclear-success-impacts-saudiiran-ties/arti-
    cle5394317.ece/.
34. Daniel Dolan, 'Why Saudi Arabia and Israel Have Teamed up against Iran',
    The US Navy Institute (USNI) News, 13 January 2014, available at: http://
    news.usni.org/2014/01/13/opinion-saudi-arabia-israel-teamed-iran/.
35. Zachary Keck, 'Iran to Unveil New Submarine, UAVs, Fighter Jets and Missiles',
    The Diplomat, 24 August 2013, available at: http://thediplomat.com/2013/08/
    iran-to-unveil-new-submarine-uavs-fighter-jets-and-missiles/.

36. 'Iran Unveils Biggest Indigenous Drone', *Press TV*, 18 November 2013, available at: http://www.presstv.com/detail/2013/11/18/335294/iran-un-veils-biggest-indigenous-drone/.

37. 'Iran Builds New Indigenous UAV Dubbed Ra'ad 85', *Press TV*, 28 September 2013, available at: http://www.presstv.com/detail/2013/09/28/326567/iran-builds-new-indigenous-uav/.

38. 'Iran Announces New Air Defence Missile System amid Nuclear Talks', *The Jerusalem Post*, 9 November 2013, available at: http://www.jpost.com/Iranian-Threat/News/Amid-nuclear-negotiations-in-Geneva-Iran-announces-new-air-defense-missile-331052/.

39. 'Iran Boasts Successful Test of 200 KM Range Missile', *Arutz Sheva (Israel)*, 21 December 2013, available at: http://www.israelnationalnews.com/News/News.aspx/175384#.UvhTePmSwWI/.

40. *Annual Report 2012–13*, Ministry of External Affairs, New Delhi, p. 41, available at: http://www.mea.gov.in/Uploads/PublicationDocs/21385_Annual_Report_2012-2013_English.pdf/. For a relevant report, see Saurabh Chaturvedi, 'Under Fire, Iran Bolsters India Ties', *LiveMint*, 4 January 2013, available at: http://blogs.wsj.com/indiarealtime/2013/01/04/under-fire-iran-bolsters-india-ties/.

41. 'Tehran Looks to Hold Fresh Round of Talks this Month', *LiveMint*, 4 January 2013, available at: http://www.livemint.com/Politics/NXFiH0CeJ6GAdMa-Go0a3xJ/Iran-looks-to-deepen-security-ties-with-India.html/.

42. Ibid.

43. Harsh V. Pant, 'In Mutual Interest: India and Iran', *The Telegraph (Kolkata)*, 12 January 2013, available at: http://www.telegraphindia.com/1130112/jsp/opinion/story_16429609.jsp#.UuNpzBC6bIW/.

44. 'Indian President Receives Credentials of Iran's New Ambassador', *Tehran Times*, 22 January 2013, available at: http://www.tehrantimes.com/politics/105087-indian-president-receives-credentials-of-irans-new-ambassador/.

45. 'Iran and India Have a Special Relationship, Indian President Says', *Press TV*, 23 January 2013, available at: http://www.presstv.ir/detail/2013/01/23/285038/iran-india-have-a-special-relationship/.

46. 'Iran, India Set to Forge Closer Parliamentary Relations: Larijani', *Press TV*, 24 February 2013, http://www.presstv.com/detail/2013/02/24/290627/iran-india-to-boost-parliamentary-ties/.

47. 'Iran, India, Russia Must Join Hands to Counter Terrorism: Larijani', *Press TV*, 28 February 2013, available at: http://www.presstv.com/detail/2013/02/28/291202/iran-russia-india-must-unite-forces/.

48. 'India and Iran Are Friendly Countries: Larijani', *Tehran Times*, 1 March 2013, available at: http://tehrantimes.com/politics/106061-iran-and-india-are-friendly-countries-larijani-/.

49. For an analysis, see Meir Javedanfar, 'Iran Celebrates Limited Victory After Latest P5+1 Talks', *Al-Monitor*, 27 February 2013, available at:

http://www.al-monitor.com/pulse/originals/2013/02/p51-talks-iran-winner-analysis-almaty-kazakhstan.html#/.

50. Ibid.; 'Iranian Speaker in India to Explore Communication Links', *The Hindu*, 26 February 2013, available at: http://www.thehindu.com/news/national/iranian-speaker-in-india-to-explore-communication-links/article4452840.ece/.

51. 'Iranian Envoy Meets BJP Chief', *The Indian Express*, 10 April 2013, available at: http://archive.indianexpress.com/news/iranian-envoy-meets-bjp-chief/1100086/.

52. 'Iranian Envoy Calls on CPM Secretary General in New Delhi', *Islamic Republic News Agency (IRNA)*, 12 April 2013, available at: http://www.irna.ir/en/News/80610919/Politic/Iranian_envoy_calls_on_CPM_secretary_general_in_New_Delhi/.

53. 'PM Condoles the Loss of Lives in Iran Earthquake', *Press Release*, Prime Minister of India, New Delhi, 17 April 2013, available at: http://pmindia.nic.in/press-details.php?nodeid=1607/.

54. 'Visit of External Affairs Minister to Iran for the 17th India–Iran Joint Commission Meeting', *Press Release*, Ministry of External Affairs, New Delhi, 2 May 2013, available at: http://www.mea.gov.in/press-releases.htm?dtl/21643/Visit+of+External+Affairs+Minister+to+Iran+for+the+17th+IndiaIran+Joint+Commission+meeting/. This meeting was scheduled for 19 November 2012 in Tehran but was postponed as it coincided with the Parliament session in India.

55. 'Khurshid Visiting Iran from Friday', *The New Indian Express*, 3 May 2013, available at: http://www.newindianexpress.com/nation/Khurshid-visiting-Iran-from-Friday/2013/05/03/article1573060.ece/.

56. 'Salman Khurshid to Leave for Iran: India Looks for Access to Chabahar PORT', *The Economic Times*, 3 May 2013, available at: http://articles.economictimes.indiatimes.com/2013-05-03/news/39009655_1_gwadar-port-chabahar-port-indian-goods/.

57. Meena Singh Roy, 'India and Iran Relations: Sustaining the Momentum', *IDSA Issue Brief*, 20 May 2013, available at: http://idsa.in/issuebrief/India-IranRelations_msroy_200513/.

58. Ever since the Syrian crisis began in the early 2011, there has been no viable solution to bring an understanding between the ruling Syrian government and the protesters. With such stalemate, the former United Nations and Arab League envoy to Syria, Kofi Annan, submitted what has been called as 'Six-Point Peace Plan' to the UN Security Council on 16 March 2012. For the relevant resolution and the Six-Point Plan on Syria, see 'Security Council Unanimously Adopts Resolution 2042 (2012)', *Department of Public Information*, United Nations Security Council, New York, 14 April 2012, available at: http://www.un.org/News/Press/docs/2012/sc10609.doc.htm/.

59. 'Joint Press Statement on 17th India–Iran Joint Commission Meeting', *Press Release*, Ministry of External Affairs, New Delhi, 4 May 2013, available at:

http://www.mea.gov.in/press-releases.htm?dtl/21652/Joint+Press+Stateme
nt+on+17th+IndiaIran+Joint+Commission+Meeting/.

60. 'India Reiterates Iran's Right to Access N. Technology', *Fars News Agency*,
    5 May 2013, available at: http://english2.farsnews.com/newstext.php?nn=
    9107167276/.

61. Roy, 'India and Iran Relations'.

62. 'PM Congratulates President-Elect Rouhani of Iran', *Press Release*, Prime
    Minister of India, New Delhi, 19 June 2013, available at: http://pmindia.
    nic.in/press-details.php?nodeid=1641/.

63. Satish Chandra, 'New Hope for Indo-Iran Ties', *The New Indian Express*, 20
    June 2013, available at: http://www.newindianexpress.com/opinion/New-
    hope-for-Indo-Iran-ties/2013/06/20/article1642887.ece/.

64. 'India Supports Iran's Presidency of Conference on Disarmament', *The Times
    of India*, 19 June 2013, available at: http://articles.timesofindia.indiatimes.
    com/2013-06-19/india/40068688_1_nuclear-programme-ranjan-mathai-
    former-nuclear-negotiator/.

65. Shubhajit Roy, 'India a Foreign Policy Priority, Says Rouhani', *The Indian
    Express*, 11 July 2013, available at: http://indianexpress.com/article/news-
    archive/web/india-a-foreign-policy-priority-says-rouhani/.

66. 'Visit of Vice President of India to Iran', *Press Release*, Ministry of External
    Affairs, New Delhi, 2 August 2013, available at: https://www.mea.gov.in/
    press-releases.htm?dtl/21991/Visit+of+Vice+President+of+India+to+Iran/.

67. 'Indian Vice President to Attend Rohani Swearing-In Ceremony', *Press
    TV*, 2 August 2013, available at: http://www.presstv.com/detail/2013/
    08/02/316895/india-vp-to-attend-rohani-inauguration/.

68. 'Official Spokesperson's Response to the P5 Plus 1 Agreement With Iran
    on the Iran Nuclear Issue', *Press Release*, Ministry of External Affairs, New
    Delhi, 24 November 2013, available at: http://www.mea.gov.in/media-
    briefings.htm?dtl/22522/Official+Spokespersons+response+to+the+P5+plu
    s+1+agreement+with+Iran+on+the+Iran+Nuclear+Issue/.

69. 'Iran Accord Will be Advantageous to India, Help Region', *Business Stan-
    dard*, 27 November 2013, available at: http://www.business-standard.
    com/article/international/iran-accord-will-be-advantageous-to-india-help-
    region-113112700207_1.html/. For further analysis, see Sunil Dasgupta,
    'India Readjusts Ties with Iran', *Asia Times*, 12 December 2013, available at:
    http://www.atimes.com/atimes/South_Asia/SOU-01-121213.html/.

70. 'Post-deal with World Powers, Iran Briefs India on Moving Ahead', *Deccan
    Chronicle*, 25 November 2013, available at: http://www.deccanchronicle.
    com/131125/news-current-affairs/article/post-deal-world-powers-iran-
    briefs-india-moving-ahead/.

71. 'Foreign Secretary's Meeting with Deputy Foreign Minister of Iran', *Press
    Release*, Ministry of External Affairs, New Delhi, 25 November 2013, avail-
    able at: https://www.mea.gov.in/press-releases.htm?dtl/22525/Foreign+Sec
    retarys+Meeting+with+Deputy+Foreign+Minister+of+Iran/.

72. Sandeep Dikshit, 'India, Iran Agree to Keep Wary Saudi Arabia Engaged', *The Hindu*, 26 November 2013, available at: http://www.thehindu.com/todays-paper/tp-national/india-iran-agree-to-keep-wary-saudi-arabia-engaged/article5391819.ece/.

73. 'Exports to Iran Back on Track, up 6.7% in April–Nov', *Business Line*, 8 January 2013, available at: http://www.thehindubusinessline.com/economy/exports-to-iran-back-on-track-up-67-in-aprilnov/article4287488.ece/.

74. 'India to Supply Life-saving Medicines to Iran', *Rediff.com*, 8 January 2013, available at: http://www.rediff.com/business/slide-show/slide-show-1-india-to-supply-life-saving-medicines-to-iran/20130108.htm/.

75. 'India Woos Iran with its Affordable Generic Drugs', *The Economic Times*, 31 January 2013, available at: http://articles.economictimes.indiatimes.com/2013-01-31/news/36659039_1_pharmexcil-pharmaceuticals-export-promotion-council-pharma-exports; and 'India, Iran Finalise Rupee as Trade Currency', *Financial Express*, 10 December 2013, available at: http://pharma.financialexpress.com/latest-updates/1480-india-iran-finalise-rupee-as-trade-currency/.

76. 'India May Barter Tea for Crude Oil from Iran', *Business Line*, 1 February 2013, available at: http://www.thehindubusinessline.com/industry-and-economy/agri-biz/india-may-barter-tea-for-crude-oil-from-iran/article4369474.ece?ref=wl_industry-and-economy/.

77. Indrani Dutta, 'Iranian Market Keeps Indian Tea Exporters Guessing', *The Hindu*, 10 December 2013, available at: http://www.thehindu.com/business/iranian-market-keeps-indian-tea-exporters-guessing/article5440886.ece/.

78. 'Iranian Tea Delegation on Visit to Kolkata', *Business Standard*, 6 August 2013, available at: http://www.business-standard.com/article/companies/iranian-tea-delegation-on-visit-to-kolkata-113080601449_1.html/.

79. 'Iranian Trader to Import Orthodox Tea from India', *The Times of India*, 1 September 2013, available at: http://articles.timesofindia.indiatimes.com/2013-09-01/guwahati/41662416_1_tea-production-orthodox-tea-ctc-tea/.

80. Shaoli Chakrabarty, 'Tea Exports to Iran Double', *The Telegraph*, 25 December 2013, available at: http://www.telegraphindia.com/1131226/jsp/business/story_17721058.jsp#.UuKoaxC6bIU/.

81. 'Benefits of Higher Soya Export to Iran', *Business Line*, 6 March 2013, available at: http://www.thehindubusinessline.com/opinion/benefits-of-higher-soya-export-to-iran/article4482182.ece/.

82. Swansy Alfonso, 'Iran Pays High Premium for Staples from India', *LiveMint*, 17 May 2013, available at: http://www.livemint.com/Politics/5tjPmcmPoqnc9Kf3k2jb0I/Iran-pays-high-premium-for-staples-from-India.html/.

83. 'Iran Set to be Top Importer of Soymeal from India Again—Trade', *Reuters*, 6 August 2013, available at: http://in.reuters.com/article/2013/08/06/india-oilmeal-exports-idINL4N0G629320130806/.

84. 'India Agrees 600,000 T Soymeal Export Deals for Oct–Dec', *Business Recorder*, 21 September 2013, available at: http://www.brecorder.com/markets/commodities/asia/136988-india-agrees-600000-t-soymeal-export-deals-for-oct-dec.html/.

85. 'Iran Demand Boosts India Basmati Rice Price', *The Wall Street Journal*, 9 April 2013, available at: http://online.wsj.com/news/articles/SB10001424127887323550604578412201442386828?mg=reno64-wsj&url=http%2F%2Fonline.wsj.com%2Farticle%2FSB10001424127887323550604578412201442386828.html/.

86. 'India Begins Exporting Basmati & Non-Basmati Blend to Iran', *The Economic Times*, 16 May 2013, available at: http://articles.economictimes.indiatimes.com/2013-05-16/news/39310641_1_india-rice-exporters-association-basmati-vijay-setia/. The blended rice is a mixture of aromatic non-basmati rice and pusa-1121 basmati variety.

87. For an analysis, see Tejinder Narang, 'Basmati to Stay on Iran's Plate', *Business Line*, 19 December 2013, available at: http://www.thehindubusinessline.com/opinion/basmati-to-stay-on-irans-plate/article5479163.ece/.

88. 'Iran for More Trade with India in Non-oil Sectors', *Deccan Herald*, 11 May 2013, available at: http://www.deccanherald.com/content/331760/iran-more-trade-india-non.html/.

89. 'India, Iran Trade Poised to Cross $25 B in 4 Years', *Business Line*, 11 May 2013, available at: http://www.thehindubusinessline.com/economy/india-iran-trade-poised-to-cross-25-b-in-4-years/article4706199.ece/.

90. 'Urea Imports from Iran Not Banned: Government', *The Economic Times*, 22 February 2013, available at: http://articles.economictimes.indiatimes.com/2013-02-22/news/37242115_1_urea-imports-urea-requirement-mt/.

91. 'India to Set up Urea Factory in Iran', *Press TV*, 30 April 2013, available at: http://www.presstv.ir/detail/2013/04/30/301032/india-to-set-up-urea-factory-in-iran/.

92. Atul Aneja, 'India Considering More Investments in Iran', *The Hindu*, 4 May 2013, available at: http://www.thehindu.com/news/international/world/india-considering-more-investments-in-iran/article4684077.ece/.

93. 'Indian Delegation May Visit Iran for Discussions on Urea Plant', *The Times of India*, 25 November 2013, available at: http://articles.timesofindia.indiatimes.com/2013-11-25/india/44449068_1_urea-plant-chabahar-chahbahar/.

94. 'India May Propose Preferential Trade Deal with Iran', *The Economic Times*, 23 April 2013, available at: http://articles.economictimes.indiatimes.com/2013-04-23/news/38763300_1_rupee-payment-mechanism-iranian-importers-iranian-crude/.

95. 'India Set to Scale up Ties with Iran: Joint Exploration on Cards', *The Economic Times*, 6 May 2013, available at: http://articles.economictimes.indiatimes.com/2013-05-06/news/39065037_1_chabhar-sanctions-issue-khurshid/.

96. 'Kandla, JN Ports May be Asked to Operate Iranian Cargo Terminals', *Business Line*, 7 May 2013, available at: http://www.thehindubusinessline. com/industry-and-economy/logistics/kandla-jn-ports-may-be-asked-to-operate-iranian-cargo-terminals/article4695503.ece/.

97. 'Iran to Source Vehicles, Medicines from India', *The Economic Times*, 17 May 2013, available at: http://articles.economictimes.indiatimes.com/2013-05-17/news/39336799_1_iran-auto-exports-pharma-exports/.

98. 'Iran, India Reach Basic Barter Trade Agreement', *Press TV*, 22 May 2013, available at: http://presstv.com/detail/2013/05/22/304924/iran-india-in-talks-on-barter-trade-deal/.

99. 'Four Iranian Banks Plan to Open Branches in India', *The Economic Times*, 31 May 2013, available at: http://articles.economictimes.indiatimes. com/2013-05-31/news/39655949_1_aiai-india-and-iran-trade-promo-tion/. It should be noted that the Indian Ministry of Home Affairs, in 2012, declined the security clearance for three Iranian banks (Parsian Bank, Bank Pasargad and Eghtesad-e-Novin Bank) which intended to open branches in India. While these banks could have eased trade relations between India and Iran, there was also fear of using them for money laundering and terror financing.

100. 'Iran Asks India to Open Banking Channels', *The Times of India*, 5 December 2013, available at: http://timesofindia.indiatimes.com/business/india-business/Iran-asks-India-to-open-banking-channels/articleshow/26876937.cms/.

101. 'India Allows Re-Export of Imported Products to Iran', *Business Line*, 11 June 2013, available at: http://www.thehindubusinessline.com/economy/india-allows-reexport-of-imported-products-to-iran/article4803858.ece/.

102. 'As Iran, US Settle Nuclear Talks, India Focuses on Boosting Trade', *Business Standard*, 15 November 2013, available at: http://www.business-standard. com/article/economy-policy/as-iran-us-settle-nuclear-talks-india-focuses-on-boosting-trade-113112500427_1.html/.

103. 'Iran Keen to Tap Investment From India, Says FAPCCI', *The Economic Times*, 26 November 2013, available at: http://economictimes.indiatimes. com/news/economy/foreign-trade/iran-keen-to-tap-investment-from-in-dia-says-fapcci/articleshow/26426225.cms/.

104. 'Exhibition & Buyer Seller Meet (BSM)', *Press Release*, FICCI-B2B, 15–19 December 2013, available at: http://www.ficci-b2b.com/business-meet-ings/outbound-meeting/product-showcase-exhibition-buyer-seller-meet-in-iran/18/index.htm/. For a similar report, see 'Iran, India Should Gain Better Understanding of Each Other's Economy: Indian Official', *Tehran Times*, 15 December 2013, available at: http://www.tehrantimes.com/politics/112827-iran-india-should-gain-better-understanding-of-each-others-economy-indian-official/.

105. 'Panel Meets Today to Review India–Iran Trade', *Business Standard*, 17 December 2013, available at: http://www.business-standard.com/

article/economy-policy/panel-meets-today-to-review-india-iran-trade-113121600876_1.html/.

106. Nidhi Verma, 'India Imported Nearly 40% Less Iranian Oil in 2013', Live-Mint, 30 January 2014, available at: http://www.livemint.com/Money/Nt2jqQzWW675fMllJxdhWK/India-imported-nearly-40-less-Iranian-oil-in-2013.html/.

107. 'CalPERS Dumps Indian Oil Stocks on Iran Concerns', Business Standard, 7 January 2013, available at: http://www.business-standard.com/article/markets/calpers-dumps-indian-oil-stocks-on-iran-concerns-113010700098_1.html/.

108. 'Iran Charters Oil Ship with Indian Insurance: Sources', NDTV, 15 January 2013, available at: http://www.ndtv.com/article/india/iran-charters-oil-ship-with-indian-insurance-sources-317831/. The vessel was Omvati Prem, owned by Mumbai-based Indian shipper Mercator Limited. Many a times, NITC had to change the names of its tankers as it keeps adopting new tactics to keep Iran's oil exports flowing in response to sanctions.

109. 'India to Reduce Iran Oil Imports', Gulf News, 16 January 2013, available at: http://gulfnews.com/business/markets/india-to-reduce-iran-oil-imports-1.1133178/.

110. 'Mangalore Refinery Cuts Crude Imports from Iran', The Wall Street Journal, 31 January 2013, available at: http://online.wsj.com/news/articles/SB10001424127887323701904578275771019052916?mg=reno64-wsj&url=http%3A%2F%2Fonline.wsj.com%2Farticle%2FSB10001424127887323701904578275771019052916.html/.

111. 'UPDATE 1-India's HPCL May Have to Halt Iran Oil Imports from June', Reuters, 12 February 2013, available at: http://uk.reuters.com/article/2013/02/12/india-iran-hpcl-idUKL4N0BC42M20130212/.

112. Nidhi Verma, 'Indian Pays for Iran Oil in Rupees, Turkey Route Halted: Sources', Reuters, 18 February 2013, available at: http://www.reuters.com/article/2013/02/18/us-india-iran-imports-idUSBRE91H0AN20130218/.

113. 'Iran, India Should Cooperate to Head off Energy Monopoly: Larijani', Press TV, 25 February 2013, available at: http://www.presstv.com/detail/2013/02/25/290759/iran-india-can-avert-energy-monopoly/.

114. 'India's Mercator Says Will Not Use Ship for Iran Oil Imports', Reuters, 1 March 2013, available at: http://www.reuters.com/article/2013/03/01/india-iran-mercator-idUSL4N0BR72L20130301/.

115. 'Iran Crisis May Hit Expansion Plans of Indian Refiners', Business Standard, 4 March 2013, available at: http://www.business-standard.com/article/companies/iran-crisis-may-hit-expansion-plans-of-indian-refiners-113030400013_1.html/.

116. 'Iran Replaces Indian Company with IOOC in Offshore Field', Press TV, 20 March 2013, available at: http://www.presstv.ir/detail/2013/03/20/294556/iran-awards-field-to-domestic-company/. In 2002, NIOC signed

a five-billion-dollar deal with an Indian consortium led by ONGC, for the development of Farsi Block, which comprises Binaloud Oil Field and Farzad B Gas Field.

117. 'India to Create Rs 2,000 Cr Energy Pool to Reinsure Iran Crude Imports', *The Financial Express*, 30 March 2013, available at: http://www.financialexpress.com/news/india-to-create-rs-2000-cr-energy-pool-to-reinsure-iran-crude-imports/1095247/.

118. 'India Approves Two Iranian Ship Underwriters', *LiveMint*, 8 April 2013, available at: http://www.livemint.com/Politics/Zj4wSehxxwyTc5i29I3tYM/India-approves-2-Iranian-ship-underwriters.html/. These underwriters were Kish P&I Club, founded by a group of Iranian ship owners on Kish Island located in the Persian Gulf, and Tehran-based Moallem Insurance Co.

119. 'India's Iran Oil Imports Plunge 26.5 Pct in Fy13—Trade', *Reuters*, 24 April 2013, available at: http://www.reuters.com/article/2013/04/24/india-iran-oil-idUSL3N0D935X20130424/.

120. 'Iran Offers New Oil Contracts to Lure India', *Business Line*, 4 May 2013, available at: http://www.thehindubusinessline.com/economy/iran-offers-new-oil-contracts-to-lure-india/article4683765.ece/.

121. 'Iran, India Set to Expand Energy Relations: Iran Oil Minister', *Press TV*, 26 May 2013, available at: http://www.presstv.com/detail/2013/05/26/305553/iran-india-set-to-boost-energy-ties/.

122. 'Iran Offers Sweeteners to Push More Oil', *The Times of India*, 28 May 2013, available at: http://articles.timesofindia.indiatimes.com/2013-05-28/india/39579205_1_iran-pakistan-india-eu-sanctions-farzad-b-gas-field/.

123. 'U.S. Exempts India, 8 Others from Sanctions for Iranian Oil', *The Hindu*, 6 June 2013, available at: http://www.thehindu.com/news/international/world/us-exempts-india-8-others-from-sanctions-for-iranian-oil/article4786925.ece/. Eight other countries were China, Malaysia, Republic of Korea, Singapore, South Africa, Sri Lanka, Turkey and Taiwan.

124. Ibid.; 'India's Iranian Oil Imports More Than Halve in June—Trade', *Reuters*, 23 July 2013, available at: http://www.reuters.com/article/2013/07/23/india-iran-oil-idUSL4N0FO33E20130723/.

125. 'Iran Oil Payments Bring Relief for Rupee', *The Indian Express*, 22 July 2013, available at: http://archive.indianexpress.com/news/iran-oil-payments-bring-relief-for-re/1144782/. Till mid-2013, Indian Oil Corporation imported Iranian crude oil worth US$7 billion.

126. 'Iran Offers India $1 Billion Sovereign Guarantee for Oil Shipments', *LiveMint*, 23 July 2013, available at: http://beta.livemint.com/Politics/DNooI-wBhN3TERj9U00eCeJ/Iran-offers-India-1-billion-sovereign-guarantee-for-oil-shi.html?ref=also_read/.

127. 'India Plans Crude Import from Iran to Offset Supply Problems', *Hindustan Times*, 29 August 2013, available at: http://www.hindustantimes.com/business-news/india-plans-crude-import-from-iran-to-offset-supply-problems/article1-1114753.aspx/.

128. 'India to Save $8.5 Billion in Oil Imports from Iran: Veerappa Moily to PM', *The Economic Times*, 1 September 2013, available at: http://articles. economictimes.indiatimes.com/2013-09-01/news/41663227_1_crude-oil-imports-halkbank-indian-oil-corp/.

129. 'Oil Imports From Iran: Insurance Cover Likely for Private Refiners Too', *Business Line*, 29 September 2013, available at: http://www.thehindubusi-nessline.com/industry-and-economy/oil-imports-from-iran-insurance-cover-likely-for-private-refiners-too/article5182692.ece/.

130. Ibid.

131. 'India Starts New Line of Negotiations with Iran', *Business Standard*, 1 October 2013, available at: http://www.business-standard.com/article/economy-policy/india-pushing-iran-to-accept-rs-for-oil-imports-113100100005_1. html/.

132. 'Rohani May Be Playing Nice with US, but Not with India', *Iran Times*, 4 October 2013, available at: http://iran-times.com/rohani-may-be-playing-nice-with-us-but-not-with-india/.

133. Amitav Ranjan, 'Oman to the Rescue, Asks India to Route Iran Oil Payments through Muscat', *The Indian Express*, 14 October 2013, available at: http://archive.indianexpress.com/news/oman-to-the-rescue-asks-india-to-route-iran-oil-payments-through-muscat/1182523/.

134. Manoj Kumar and Nidhi Verma, 'Iran, India Meet to Discuss Oil Exports, Payments', *Reuters*, 10 December 2013, available at: http://in.reuters.com/article/2013/12/10/india-iran-oil-idINDEE9B906S20131210/.

135. 'Iran to Deliver Gas to India via Oman', *Times of Oman*, 16 December 2013, available at: http://www.timesofoman.com/News/Article-27052. aspx/.

136. 'Two Iranian Films Win at Jaipur International Film Festival', *Press TV*, 5 February 2013, available at: http://www.presstv.com/detail/2013/02/05/287359/indian-filmfest-hails-iranian-films/.

137. 'Iran "Facing Mirrors" to Open Indian Women Film Festival', *Press TV*, 2 March 2013, available at: http://www.presstv.ir/detail/2013/03/02/291507/iranian-film-to-open-indian-filmfest/.

138. 'Leh Warms up to 2nd International Film Festival', *DNA India*, 12 September 2013, available at: http://www.dnaindia.com/entertainment/report-leh-warms-up-to-2nd-international-film-festival-1887682/.

139. '"Parviz" Nabs Top Award at Kerala Film Festival', *Press TV*, 15 December 2013, available at: http://www.presstv.com/detail/2013/12/15/340146/iran-film-shines-in-indian-filmfest/.

140. 'Sufi Music Is an Expression of Peace', *The Hindu*, 7 February 2013, available at: http://www.thehindu.com/todays-paper/tp-national/tp-newdelhi/sufi-music-is-an-expression-of-peace/article4387978.ece/.

141. '5,000-year History Binds Iranian, Indian Puppets', *Deccan Herald*, 9 April 2013, available at: http://www.deccanherald.com/content/324900/5000-year-history-binds-iranian.html/.

142. 'Rah-e-Islam on "Imam Hussain and Revolution" Released', *News, Islamic Culture and Relations Organisation, Cultural Centre of the Islamic Republic of Iran*, New Delhi, 25 November 2013, available at: http://fa.newdelhi.icro.ir/index.aspx?siteid=159&pageid=11649&newsview=605824/.

143. 'Persian Poetry Penned by Former Ruler of Hyderabad Released', *The Times of India*, 13 March 2013, available at: http://articles.timesofindia.indiatimes.com/2013-03-13/hyderabad/37681731_1_persian-poetry-prime-minister-iran/.

144. 'Indian Cultural Centre Inaugurated in Tehran', *Press TV*, 6 May 2013, available at: http://www.presstv.com/detail/2013/05/06/302067/india-launches-cultural-center-in-iran/.

145. 'Iran, India Ink Cooperation Agreement on Book Fairs', *Press TV*, 12 February 2013, available at: http://www.presstv.ir/detail/2013/02/12/288586/iran-india-to-collaborate-on-book-fairs/.

146. 'India Raises the Issue of Sikh Marriage Registration with Iran', *Hindustan Times*, 4 May 2013, available at: http://www.hindustantimes.com/world-news/india-raises-the-issue-of-sikh-marriage-registration-with-iran/article1-1054902.aspx/.

147. 'Flight between Hyderabad, Iran's Mashhad City from June 30', *The Times of India*, 11 May 2013, available at: http://articles.timesofindia.indiatimes.com/2013-05-11/india/39185823_1_hassan-nourian-direct-flight-south-india/.

148. For a brief analysis of India–Iran military ties, see Monika Chansoria, 'India–Iran Defence Cooperation', *Indian Defence Review*, Vol. 5, No. 1, January–March 2012, available at: http://www.indiandefencereview.com/interviews/india-iran-defence-cooperation/.

149. 'Iran Seeks Enhanced Defence Ties with India', *The Times of India*, July 22, 2013, available at: http://articles.timesofindia.indiatimes.com/2013-07-22/india/40726537_1_defence-ties-defence-equipment-defence-minister/.

150. 'Iranian Warships on Three-Day Goodwill Visit to Mumbai', *The Times of India*, 5 December 2013, available at: http://articles.timesofindia.indiatimes.com/2013-12-05/india/44806541_1_iranian-warships-indian-ocean-goodwill-visit/.

151. 'Iran, India Stress Expansion of Naval Cooperation', *Press TV*, December 9, 2013, available at: http://www.presstv.ir/detail/2013/12/06/338496/iran-india-stress-naval-cooperation/.

152. Harsh V. Pant and Julie M. Super (2013), 'Balancing Rivals: India's Tightrope between Iran and the United States', *Asian Policy*, Vol. 15, January, pp. 69–88.

153. 'India Hesitant to Implement US, EU sanctions on Iran: Report', *The Times of India*, 19 January 2013, available at: http://articles.timesofindia.indiatimes.com/2013-01-19/india/36431347_1_eu-sanctions-deputy-oil-minister-european-union-sanctions/.

154. Indrani Bagchi and Sanjay Dutta, 'New US Sanctions Create Panic, India's Oil Imports from Iran Could be Hit Hard from Feb 6', *The Times of India*, 25 February 2013, available at: http://timesofindia.indiatimes.com/business/india-business/New-US-sanctions-create-panic-Indias-oil-imports-from-Iran-could-be-hit-hard-from-Feb-6/articleshow/18186715.cms/.

155. 'Iran Using India for Clandestine Activities: US', *Hindustan Times*, 6 March 2013, available at: http://www.hindustantimes.com/world-news/iran-using-india-for-clandestine-activities-us/article1-1021882.aspx/.

156. 'Fearing Iran Entry, US Congressmen Favour Export of Natural Gas to India', *The Indian Express*, 27 April 2013, available at: http://archive.indianexpress.com/news/fearing-iran-entry-us-congressmen-favour-export-of-natural-gas-to-india/1108443/.

157. Shubhajit Roy, 'India Upset over Iran's Poser on US Nuclear Transfer', *The Indian Express*, 28 May 2013, available at: http://archive.indianexpress.com/news/india-upset-over-irans-poser-on-us-nuclear-transfer/1121478/0/.

158. Ibid.

159. 'Iran Accord Will Be Advantageous to India, Help Region', *Business Standard*, 27 November 2013, available at: http://www.business-standard.com/article/international/iran-accord-will-be-advantageous-to-india-help-region-113112700207_1.html/.

160. Harsh V. Pant, 'Iran–India Relations Will Remain Constrained in the Near Future', *The National (Abu Dhabi)*, available at: 13 October 2013, http://www.thenational.ae/thenationalconversation/iran-india-relations-will-remain-constrained-in-the-near-future/.

161. For a detailed analysis, see P. R. Kumaraswamy, 'India and Iran-Nuke Deal', *Geopolitics*, January 2014, Vol. 4, No. 8, pp. 72–74.

162. 'Iran's Frozen Assets in China: $22bn, or $47bn?' *Trend*, 30 October 2013, available at: http://en.trend.az/regions/iran/2206261.html/. According to this report, China imported 16.01 million tonnes of Iranian oil during first nine months of 2013. The amount equalled 428,160 bpd.

163. 'Iran–China Annual Trade to Hit US$38b', *Business Times*, 13 December 2013, available at: http://www.btimes.com.my/Current_News/BTIMES/articles/20131213154208/Article/index_html/.

164. Zafar Bhutta, 'Anonymous Donor: "Friendly" Country Offers $1b For Iran–Pakistan Pipeline', *The Express Tribune*, 28 November 2013, available at: http://tribune.com.pk/story/638053/anonymous-donor-friendly-country-offers-1b-for-iran-pakistan-pipeline-business/.

165. Zachary Keck, 'China Makes Play for Iran's Chabahar Port', *The Diplomat*, 1 July 2013, available at: http://thediplomat.com/2013/07/china-makes-play-for-irans-chabahar-port/. For a similar report, see Zachary Keck, 'India–China Rivalry Threatens US Sanctions on Iran', *The Diplomat*, 15 August 2013, available at: http://thediplomat.com/2013/08/india-china-rivalry-threatens-us-sanctions-on-iran/.

166. 'In a $100 Million Move to Counter China, India to Upgrade Iran's Chabahar Port', *NDTV*, 4 May 2013, available at: http://www.ndtv.com/article/india/in-a-100-million-move-to-counter-china-india-to-upgrade-iran-s-chabahar-port-362599/.

167. 'Iran, Pakistan to Boost Bilateral Trade', *UPI.Com*, 13 September 2013, available at: http://www.upi.com/Top_News/World-News/2011/09/13/Iran-Pakistan-to-boost-bilateral-trade/UPI-38831315892170/.

168. 'Pakistan, Iran Bent on Boosting Trade Volume', *Press TV*, 20 January 2013, available at: http://presstv.com/detail/2013/01/20/284605/iran-pakistan-to-boost-trade-volume/.

169. Sachin Parashar, 'Iran Pitches Extending Pipeline to India via Pakistan', *The Times of India*, 5 January 2013, available at: http://articles.timesofindia.indiatimes.com/2013-01-05/india/36161052_1_jalili-iran-pitches-india-and-pakistan/.

170. 'Iran, Pakistan Inaugurate IP Gas Pipeline', *Press TV*, 11 March 2013, available at: http://www.presstv.com/detail/2013/03/11/292995/iran-pakistan-inaugurate-ip-gas-pipeline/. The 2,000-km pipeline would enable the export of 21.5 million cubic metres of Iranian natural gas to Pakistan on a daily basis.

171. 'IP Gas Pipeline Project Beneficial to India: Indian Minister', *Press TV*, 28 March 2013, available at: http://www.presstv.com/detail/2013/03/28/295542/ip-gas-pipe-line-beneficial-to-india/.

172. 'Iran Cancels Pakistan Gas Pipeline Loan', *Dawn.Com (Pakistan)*, available at: http://www.dawn.com/news/1073896/iran-cancels-pakistan-gas-pipeline-loan/. For a detailed report, see 'Pakistan Loses Ground to India in Iran Ties', *Press TV*, 25 December 2013, available at: http://www.presstv.ir/detail/2013/12/25/341795/pakistan-loses-ground-to-india-in-iran-ties/.

173. 'Israeli Attack Case: India Seeks Iran's Help Again', *Outlook India*, 19 February 2013, available at: http://news.outlookindia.com/items.aspx?artid=790285/. Other four countries were Israel, Malaysia, Thailand and Georgia.

174. 'Israel Prods India on Iran', *The Telegraph*, 21 February 2013, available at: http://www.telegraphindia.com/1130222/jsp/nation/story_16591943.jsp#.UtJUpfQW0WJ/. Also see, 'India–Israel Joint Working Group on Counter Terrorism, New Delhi, 20 February 2013', *Press Release*, Ministry of External Affairs, New Delhi, 20 February 2013, available at: http://www.mea.gov.in/press-releases.htm?dtl/21204/IndiaIsrael+Joint+Working+Group+on+Counter+Terrorism/.

175. 'India Cannot Stay Neutral towards Iran: Shimon Peres', *The Economic Times*, 23 June 2013, available at: http://articles.economictimes.indiatimes.com/2013-06-23/news/40147126_1_president-mahmoud-ahmedinejad-shah-mohammad-reza-pahlavi-iran-and-israel/.

176. P. R. Kumaraswamy, 'Israel Confronts Iran: Rationales, Responses and Fall-outs', *IDSA Monograph Series*, No. 8, November 2012; also by the same author, 'India's Iran Defiance', *IDSA Comment*, 19 March 2012, available at: http://www.idsa.in/idsacomments/IndiasIranDefiance_prkumaraswa-my_190312/.

177. 'Deported Iranian Student Returns via Nepal, Arrested', *The Indian Express*, 31 October 2013, available at: http://archive.indianexpress.com/news/deported-iranian-student-returns-via-nepal-arrested/1189467/.

178. 'Vizag: Iranian Student Deported for Visa Rules Violations', *Business Standard*, 16 November 2013, available at: http://www.business-standard.com/article/pti-stories/vizag-iranian-student-deported-for-visa-rules-viola-tions-113111601253_1.html/.

179. For a relevant report on restrictions and abuses, see 'Iran', *International Religious Freedom Report for 2012*, US Department of State, available at: http://www.state.gov/j/drl/rls/irf/religiousfreedom/index.htm#wrapper/. 'The Bahais number approximately 300,000 and are heavily concentrated in Tehran and Semnan.'

180. 'Baha'is to Seek India's Help against Harassment in Iran', *The Indian Express*, 7 April 2007, available at: http://archive.indianexpress.com/news/baha-is-to-seek-india-s-help-against-harassment-in-iran/27716/; 'India's Former Deputy Prime Minister L. K. Advani and other Prominent Indians Appeal to Iran for Justice', *News*, Baha'i Faith, 17 December 2010, avail-able at: http://www.bahai.in/news/national-news-of-the-bahais-of-india/indias-former-deputy-prime-minister-lk-advani-and-other-prominent-indians-appeal-to-iran-for-justice.html/; and 'Baha'is Want India to Push Iran to Treat Minorities Better', *The Times of India*, 11 November 2013, available at: http://articles.timesofindia.indiatimes.com/2013-11-11/india/43929185_1_baha-is-national-spiritual-assembly-hassan-rouhani/.

181. 'New Delhi Miffed as Iran Asks India Inc Visitors for HIV, Hepatitis, TB tests', *The Indian Express*, 10 December 2013, available at: http://archive.in-dianexpress.com/news/iran-to-india-inc-visitors-hiv-test-please/1205746/.

182. 'Iran Seizes Indian Ship Carrying Oil from Iraq', *The Times of India*, 15 August 2013, available at: http://articles.timesofindia.indiatimes.com/2013-08-15/india/41412731_1_hormuz-indian-ocean-irgc/.

183. 'Iran's Interception of Indian Oil Tanker Not Political: Tehran', *Press TV*, 16 August 2013, available at: http://www.presstv.com/de-tail/2013/08/16/318994/no-political-side-to-india-ship-detention/. 'Tank-er was detained because it discharged its oily ballast water 30 miles away from Iran's Lavan Island in the Persian Gulf which caused a 10-mile-long oil slick on the sea.'

184. 'Now, Iran Summons Indian Envoy in Diplomatic Tit-for-Tat', *The Times of India*, 29 August 2013, available at: http://articles.timesofindia.indiatimes.com/2013-08-29/india/41579470_1_indian-ship-iranian-ship-irgc/.

185. 'Iran Releases Indian Crude Oil Tanker', *Business Line*, 7 September 2013, available at: http://www.thehindubusinessline.com/industry-and-economy/logistics/iran-releases-indian-crude-oil-tanker/article5103690.ece/.
186. 'Ten Indian Sailors Released from Iran Jail Reach Gujarat', *NDTV*, 2 November 2013, available at: http://www.ndtv.com/article/india/ten-indian-sailors-released-from-iran-jail-reach-gujarat-440853/.

4

Iraq

Anjani Kumar Singh

Key Information

Area: 438,317 sq km; **Population:** 32,585,692 (2014 est.); **Native:** NA; **Expats:** NA; **Youth:** 19.6 per cent; **Population growth rate:** 2.23 per cent; **Life expectancy at birth:** 71.42 years; **Major population groups:** Arab 75–80 per cent, Kurdish 15–20 per cent, Turkoman, Assyrian or others 5 per cent; **Religious groups:** Shia 60–65 per cent, Sunni 32–37 per cent, Christian and others 3 per cent; **GDP:** US$248 billion; **Per capita income:** US$7,100; **Foreign trade:** US$158.6 billion; **Oil reserves:** 143.1 billion bbl (2013); **Gas reserves:** 3.171 trillion m³; **Ruling party:** Da'wa Party; **Ruler:** President Jalal Talabani (since 6 April 2005); **National Day:** 14 July; **Defence budget:** 8.6 per cent of GDP; **HDI rank:** 131; **Literacy rate:** 78.2 per cent; **UN education index:** 0.498; **Gender inequality index:** 0.557; **Labour force:** 8.9 million; **Unemployment rate:** 16 per cent; **External debt:** US$59.49 billion (December 2013); **Sovereign wealth fund:** US$18 billion; **Infant mortality rate:** 37.53 deaths out of 1,000; **Last national census:** 1987; **Parliament:** 325-member Council of Representatives; **Last parliament election:** 7 March 2010; **Number of Indians:** NA; **Last Indian prime minister to visit:** Indira Gandhi, January 1975.

Sources: CIA, The World Factbook, available at: https://www.cia.gov/library/publications/the-world-factbook/; UN Human Development Report, Statistics, available at: http://hdr.undp.org/en/statistics/; United States Commission on Religious Freedom, US Department of State; Annual Report 2013; Briefs on Foreign Relations, Ministry of External Affairs, Government of India and Centre for Arms Control and Proliferation (Washington, D.C.).
Note: All figures for 2013.

The trauma of war and conflict remained a visible legacy in Iraq during 2013. The polity, society and economy have been coping with the consequences of the US-led invasion of 2003. After the withdrawal of American combat forces in December 2011, Iraq has been grappling with internal security and stability even as its petroleum production and exports have gone up. Iraq's location in a volatile region and its internal fault lines based on religious and ethnic identities are major challenges to its stability. Significantly, Iraq's resources are not evenly divided across sectarian–demographic lines. Most known hydrocarbon resources are concentrated in the Shia areas of the south and the ethnic Kurdish region in the north, with few resources in control of the Sunni minority in central Iraq.[1] Any further consolidation of bilateral relations would have to factor in the external and internal environments of Iraq.

DOMESTIC DEVELOPMENTS

Domestically the biggest challenge facing the country has been the societal cleavages engendered by the conflict since 2003 and its resultant political manifestations. According to the United Nations (UN), 2013 was the deadliest in terms of civilian casualty since 2008 and by all indications, the situation seemed to be worsening.[2] The resurgence of al-Qaeda led by the Islamic State of Iraq and the Levant (ISIL) is a major concern for stability in Iraq.

On the political front, the Shia–Sunni and the Arab–Kurd divide are far from bridged and this brings into question the prospects of short-to-medium-term stability in Iraq. The leadership of Nouri al-Maliki has appeared to be stable but many see in it the signs of authoritarianism.[3] This certainly leaves the quest for unity a moot question. According to a Congressional Research Service (CRS) Report, the absence of President Jalal Talabani due to health reasons in 2013 opened up a political crisis resulting in the flaring up of sectarian rift.[4] However, according to Freedom House Iraq's political rights rating improved in 2013 from six to five due to an increase in political activity by opposition parties during provincial elections held in April and June.[5] The autonomous northern Kurdish region is a parallel power centre and the concentration of significant resources in the region has resulted in a constant tussle with the central authority in Baghdad.

The Kurdish Regional Government (KRG) headed by Masoud Barzani is an important player in Iraqi politics and, thus, has a crucial role in political stability. In the preceding years, there was a tussle between Baghdad and Irbil which made national reconciliation difficult. Among the few positive developments, for the first time in two years, Prime Minister Maliki visited Irbil on 10 June and Barzani paid a return visit to Baghdad on 7 July, since his last visit in late 2010. The two sides subsequently established seven joint committees to try and resolve contentious issues, such as federalism, security cooperation, revenue sharing and balancing powers between the central and regional governments.[6]

The impact of conflict on the recovery of economy cannot be denied. Despite improvement in its per capita income and gross domestic product (GDP) owing to expanding petroleum trade,[7] a large section of Iraqi population lives below poverty line and does not have access to decent living conditions. The economy suffers from its excessive dependence on the oil sector for revenue generation. The irony is that despite being the largest sector of the economy, the petroleum segment is a meagre employment generator. This makes the diversification of economy an imperative for the Iraqi government. The political instability and sectarian violence[8] meant a skewed regional distribution of development. At the level of governance, corruption remains a big problem to be tackled; Iraq ranked 171 in the 2013 Corruption Perception Index of the Transparency International.[9]

Regionally both Saudi Arabia and Iran seek to influence the developments inside Iraq. Under Prime Minister Nouri al-Maliki, Iraq was inclined towards Iran much to the chagrin of Saudi Arabia.[10] The significant progress in the Iranian impasse with the Western countries would have its impact on Iraq too. The Iraq–Iran factor is being watched with interest in the world oil markets for its impact upon the Organization of Petroleum Exporting Countries (OPEC) and on the international petroleum trade.[11] Even after its withdrawal, the US remains a constant presence in Iraqi politics. The security situation and regional scenario have made Iraq an important customer of arms and the US has been actively pushing arms sales to Iraq in the name of security cooperation and, thus, a significant sum of revenue is spent in the security sector.[12] Among other actors in its neighbourhood, the situation in Syria remains a threat for Iraq. The ongoing crisis in Syria has resulted in the influx of large number of refugees. According to the

UN, the total number of registered refugees from Syria in Iraq stood at 216,271 as of 22 January 2014.[13]

BILATERAL RELATIONS

Even a decade after the US-led invasion, Iraq resembles an unstable powder keg rather than a self-reliant state. The emergence of ISIL indicates the fragility of the domestic political situation. The equitable distribution of resources and participative framework of growth and development are the goals that Iraq is in need of. While the geographical location of Iraq is unchangeable, its polity and society remain in a flux. Under the circumstances, to view Iraq only through the prism of crude resources is one folly that India would be well advised to avoid. The bilateral relations need to transcend governments and connect with the people and the country as a whole.

Political Relations

If bilateral visits are taken as the markers of health of relations, then the year 2013 augured well. To begin with the India's External Affairs Minister Salman Khurshid paid a two-day visit to Iraq in June.[14] It was the first such visit since the then Foreign Minister I. K. Gujral visited Iraq in 1990. It was also the first high-level visit from India to Iraq since 2003. Veerappa Moily, Minister for Petroleum and Natural Gas, led a 25-member delegation for the Joint Commission Meeting that was held in July in Baghdad; this was the first Joint Commission meeting since 2007.[15]

The most important visit of the year was by the Prime Minister of Iraq Nouri al-Maliki in August. It was the first head of the government-level visit since Prime Minister Indira Gandhi visited Iraq in 1975.[16] Four memorandums of understanding (MoUs) were signed during the visit of Iraqi Prime Minister:[17]

- MoU in the field of energy between the two oil ministries
- MoU regarding periodic Foreign Office Consultations
- MoU between the Foreign Service Institutes of the two foreign ministries

- MoU between the Ministries of Water Resources on bilateral cooperation in water resources development and management

Moreover, Iraqi Deputy Prime Minister for Energy Hussain Ibrahim Saleh al-Shahristani visited India to deliver the IISS-Oberoi lecture in Mumbai on 14 August. In the month of December, the Iraqi National Security Advisor Falih al-Fayyadh visited India and held meetings with Indian officials. The issue of bilateral relations and the means to further them were discussed in a meeting between the Indian Ambassador Suresh K. Reddy and the deputy Prime Minister of Iraq Salih al-Mutleg in Baghdad held in July.[18]

During these high-level visits and meetings, India and Iraq shared views on issues such as Afghanistan and Syria where both the countries hold similar positions. Both are in agreement with the need of reforming the UN to make the world body inclusive and reflective of changing global scenario. Iraq reiterated its support to India's candidature for a permanent membership in the United Nations Security Council (UNSC).

Security Cooperation

Bilateral security cooperation including the possibility of India training the Iraqi armed force personnel was discussed during External Affairs Minister Salman Khurshid's visit to Iraq in June.[19] The issue of bilateral security cooperation was discussed on 19 December in a meeting between the National Security Adviser of Iraq Falih al-Fayyadh and Indian Minister for Home Affairs Sushil Kumar Shinde.[20] In his deliberations with the Indian strategic community, al-Fayyadh identified two ways of cooperation in counter-terrorism operations between India and Iraq; one, direct cooperation involving transparency in exchange of information, experience sharing and capacity building/investments in Iraq to enhance anti-terrorism infrastructure, and, two, indirect cooperation which might include adopting common anti-terrorism policy and voicing concerns at an international platform.[21] He further added that there was a need to encourage diplomatic visits and exchange. A bilateral agreement was also signed between Institute for Defence Studies and Analyses (Delhi) and Al-Nahrain Center for Strategic Studies (Baghdad).[22] In an important move India eased restriction on the export of arms and related material to Iraq in February 2014.[23]

Economic Relations

Economic relations between the states have become key drivers of inter-national politics. India and Iraq are not an exception and both are trying to constructively engage in the economic arena. With a bilateral trade in excess of US$21 billion in 2012–13, Iraq and India poised to take their engagement to higher levels.[24] Interestingly, in terms of numbers the bi-lateral trade exceeded that of India's trade with countries such as Japan, Russia and South Korea.[25] Economic relations between India and Iraq are largely dominated by the petroleum trade; however, the potential of non-oil economic ties is significant. Iraqi need for investments in the re-construction efforts following debilitating wars for much of the last three decades can provide an opportunity for India to diversify its economic relations with Baghdad.

India and Iraq shared an important economic relationship since the days of India's independence in 1947. Interestingly, the Indian rupee was used as currency in Iraq from 1917 until Iraq's independence from Britain in 1932, when it was replaced by the Iraqi dinar.[26] In the initial days, the agreement granting most favoured nation status to each other in 1962 made Iraq an important market for Indian tea, jute textiles and spices.[27] The relations received a renewed impetus in the 1970s under the Ba'ath party rule. An important feature of this phase was the Rupee–Rouble trade agreement that involved Soviet Union and enabled India to import Iraqi oil and pay in Indian currency.[28]

As indicated by the Minister of Commerce and Industries Anand Sharma on 23 August both countries are exploring the possibility of bilateral trade in domestic currencies.[29] The issue is important for India as trade in local currencies would partially help India in dealing with the exchange rate volatility and declining value of rupee. To facilitate the participation of Indian industries, for its part, Iraq 'is also working on making the tendering process for sourcing equipments amenable for Indian companies; goods of Indian origin were not allowed to participate in tenders floated by Iraqi companies'.[30] The Indo-Iraqi trade continued to increase in 2013. As shown in Table 4.1 and Figure 4.1 the trade with Iraq as a component of India's total foreign trade increased from 1.56 per cent in 2010–11 to 2.59 per cent in 2012–13. Bouyed by increased demand for oil, the trade links are poised to continue their upward trend in the coming year. Tea, foodgrains, meat and poultry products,

Table 4.1
India–Iraq Bilateral Trade (in US$ Million)

	2009–10	*2010–11*	*2011–12*	*2012–13*
India's exports to Iraq	477.13	678.14	763.97	1,278.13
India's imports from Iraq	7,026.93	9,008.30	18,918.47	19,247.31
Total bilateral trade	7,504.06	9,686.44	19,682.44	20,525.44
Share of Iraq in India's total trade	1.61	1.56	2.47	2.59

Source: Adapted from Directorate General of Foreign Trade, available at: www.dgft.gov.in/.

Figure 4.1
India–Iraq Bilateral Trade

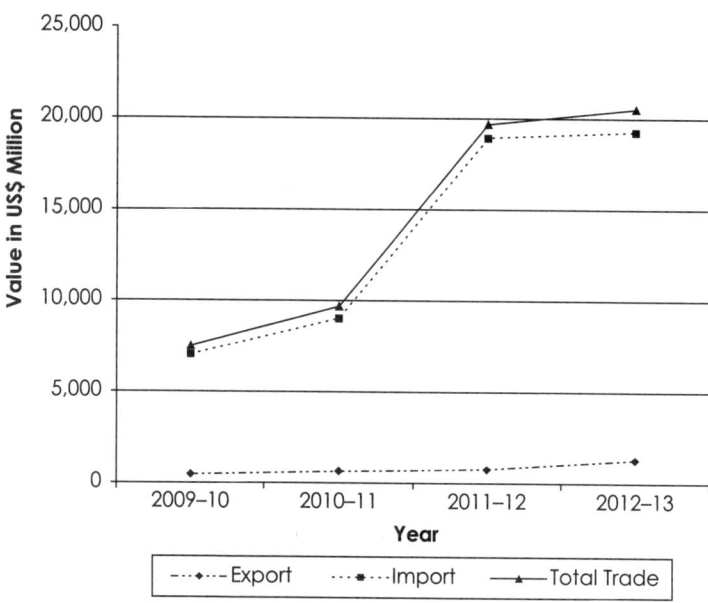

Source: Adapted from Directorate General of Foreign Trade, New Delhi, available at: www.dgft.gov.in/.

pharmaceutical and medical equipments are some of the products that can provide India a foothold in the Iraqi market. Similarly, trade in services especially information and communication technology is also an untapped area in the economic ties between India and Iraq.

Energy

Energy trade comprises the bulk of trade between India and Iraq. The importance of energy trade between the two countries is complementary; India needs a secure and stable supply of petroleum and Iraq needs a market to sell its chief produce. Iraq became second largest supplier of petroleum crude to India after Saudi Arabia in the year 2013. According to the US Energy Information Administration, Iraq revised its estimate of proven oil reserves from 115 billion barrels in 2011 to 141 billion barrels as of 1 January 2013.[31] The Iraqi oil production is estimated to grow to five million barrels a day by 2035; much of it would be going to the Asian market. As a consequence, Iraq is planning to increase its output based on demands from India and China.[32]

However, India should not be expecting any special treatment in pricing. Iraqi Deputy Prime Minister in charge for Energy Shahristani categorically ruled out any special price to India because the Iraqi laws do not allow for such concessions.[33] Thus, Iraq offers an option for diversification of supplies but any quest for the special concessional terms such as those prevalent in the 1970s and 1980s has to take a backseat for now.

In 2013, India focused its efforts on converting the traditional buyer–seller energy relations with Iraq into a long-term strategic partnership. The need for collaborative arrangements in a wide array of activities such as exploration, fertilizer plants and joint ventures was regularly highlighted by the Indian side. Expressing the same spirit Prime Minister Manmohan Singh said, 'We agreed our energy trading relationship should be turned into a strategic partnership, including joint ventures in oil exploration, petrochemical complexes and fertilizer plants. The Memorandum of Understanding on Cooperation in energy will provide a very strong framework to diversify cooperation....'[34]

During the visit of the Iraqi Prime Minister, the ONGC Videsh Limited (OVL) and Petroleum Contracts and Licensing Directorate (PCLD) of Iraq initiated long pending negotiations for Block-8 contract.[35] Iraq also offered three new oil blocks—namely Kifil, West Kifil, and Merjan—in the undeveloped Middle Furat Oil Field on a nomination basis to Indian public sector oil companies. India has agreed to study and submit a proposal to PCLD for discussions and negotiations. Earlier, during the 17th Joint Commission meeting held in Dubai on 7 July,

Iraq expressed its interest in investing in the upcoming 15 mmt oil refinery at Paradip in India. The Iraqi response to India's request for abolition of Letters of Credit (LC) and to increase in interest-free credit period from 30 days to 60 days was positive.[36] In a sign of growing engagement of Indian companies in building Iraq's energy infrastructure, BGR Energy Systems signed a contract worth US$246 million for engineering, procurement and construction (EPC) of 4×125 MW gas-based power project at Nasiriya with the Iraqi Ministry of Electricity. The contract entails the scope of engineering, procurement and construction services of balance of plant (BOP), civil works and erection, testing and commissioning of gas turbine-generator sets supplied by General Electric, as well as, operation and maintenance of power project for six months.[37] As shown in Table 4.2 and Figure 4.2 the petroleum and oil imports comprised more than 99 per cent of the total imports from Iraq keeping in with the trends of preceding years. Moreover, Iraq's share in India's oil imports and imports from Persian Gulf region has consistently increased (Table 4.3).

Sociocultural Ties

The sociocultural and historical aspects of India–Iraq ties were high-lighted by the Deputy Prime Minister of Iraq in the IISS-Oberoi lecture of 2013 at Mumbai with these words:

Table 4.2
Share of Oil in India's Imports from Iraq (in US$ Million)

Year	Oil imports from Iraq	Total oil Imports	Iraqi share in oil total imports	Imports from Iraq	Per cent of oil in imports from Iraq
2009–10	6,981.32	96,321.12	7.25	7,026.93	99.35
2010–11	8,954.66	115,929.02	7.72	9,008.30	98.80
2011–12	18,826.19	172,753.92	10.90	18,918.47	99.51
2012–13	19,166.06	181,344.67	10.57	19,247.31	99.58

Source: Adapted from Directorate General of Foreign Trade, New Delhi, available at: www.dgft.gov.in/.

Figure 4.2

Share of Oil in India's Total Imports from Iraq

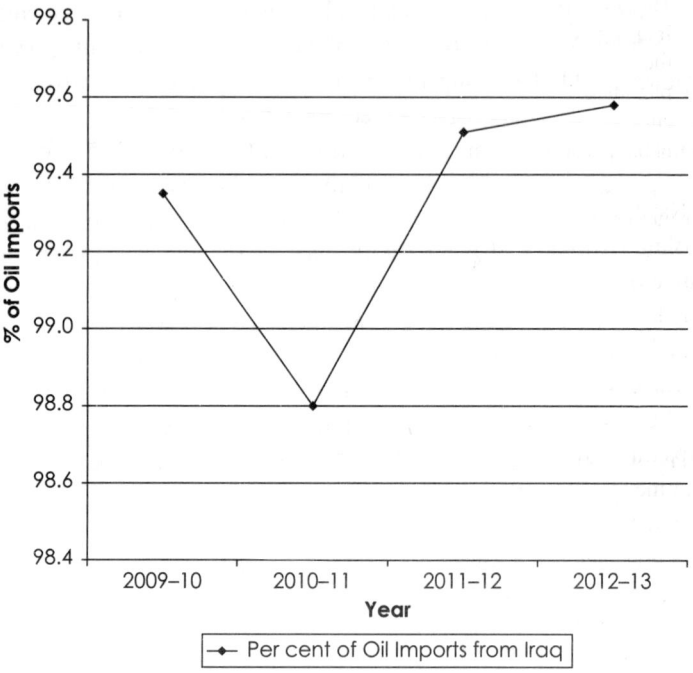

Source: Adapted from Directorate General of Foreign Trade, New Delhi, available at: www.dgft.gov.in/.

Table 4.3

India's Energy Imports from Iraq (in US$ Million)

	2009–10	2010–11	2011–12	2012–13
India's energy imports from Iraq	6,981.32	8,954.66	18,826.19	19,166.06
India's total energy imports	96,321.12	115,929.02	172,753.92	181,344.67
India's total energy imports from persian gulf	55,906.14	66,688.4	105,056.26	105,859.15
Share of Iraq in total energy imports (in per cent)	7.25	7.72	10.90	10.57
Share of Iraq in imports from Persian Gulf (in per cent)	12.49	13.43	17.92	18.11

Source: Adapted from Directorate General of Foreign Trade, New Delhi, available at: www.dgft.gov.in/.

... our connections predate the British occupation, and there were very strong centuries-old religious and economic ties between our two nations. The gold that covers the domes and minarets of the shrines of the Imams in Iraq were donated by Indian Rajas. Our trading and merchant families sent their sons to settle in India, as well as many Indian families that came on pilgrimage chose to settle in Iraq. They brought with them Indian culture and cuisine. In the Basra area in the south of Iraq, people still use many varieties of biryani and other spicy dishes, which other Iraqis find difficult to handle.[38]

Najaf and Karbala are the holy sites for a large population of Shia Muslims in India and pilgrimage to these sites has been an important source of exchange of people and cultures. The visit and stay of Guru Nanak Dev to Baghdad in 1511 and his relation with Sheikh Bahlul are etched in the common cultural heritage of India and Iraq.[39]

The government estimates that there are somewhere between 10,000 to 12,000 Indians working in Iraq. At present, India offers 150 scholarships through Indian Technical and Economic Cooperation (ITEC) Programme to Iraqi students in technical courses. There are 50 scholarships offered by Indian Council of Cultural Relations (ICCR) in postgraduate studies and an estimated 10,000 Iraqi students are pursuing various postgraduate courses all over India.[40] Almost 200 to 250 medical visas are issued by Indian embassy in Baghdad on a daily basis for Iraqis.[41] People-to-people contacts through cultural exchanges, educational engagements and medical tourism are an important part of deepening Indo-Iraqi ties; more importantly, this is an area which provides avenues for engendering goodwill without being a drag on economic resources.

External Powers

The US: The US is responsible in more than one way for the state of affairs in Iraq. Needless to say both countries have a complex but close relationship. After the withdrawal of the US combat troops in 2011, the Strategic Framework Agreement (SFA) guides the overall relationship between the two states.[42] Under the provisions of SFA, the fourth meeting of Higher Coordination Committee under the leadership of Iraq's Prime Minister Nouri al-Maliki and the US Vice President Joseph Biden took place in Washington in November 2013.[43] Since the end of the US-led war to liberate Kuwait in early 1991, the US has played a role in promoting Iraq's Kurdish autonomy.[44]

The US policy in Iraq is focused around five points, as enunciated by US Deputy Assistant Secretary Brett McGurk on 13 November:[45]

1. Maintaining a unified and federal Iraq
2. Supporting increases in production and export of oil resources
3. Promoting Iraq's strategic independence and regional integration
4. Countering the re-emergence of al Qaida in Iraq (AQI)
5. Supporting Iraq's democratic institutions and trajectory

The US would play an active role in Iraq for the foreseeable future and any actor interested in Iraq would have to be aware that the US identifies the Iraqi hydrocarbon sector as vital to its interests in the region.

China: If Iraq has become one of the largest oil producers in recent years, China has become its largest buyer.[46] In 2008 after waiting on the sidelines for situation to improve, China signed the first major oil deal Iraq made with a foreign country since 2003 to provide technical advisers, oil workers and equipment to help develop the al-Ahdab oil field in Wasit province southeast of Baghdad.[47] China has been aggressively bidding for petroleum resources abroad as a part of its diversification strategy. As a consequence, while its oil imports from traditional suppliers, such as Saudi Arabia and Russia, declined, imports from Iraq grew by roughly 50 per cent in 2013, making Iraq the fifth largest supplier to China.[48]

In the year 2012, Iraq became the fourth largest Arab trade partner of China. The bilateral trade volume reached US$17.569 billion, with a year-on-year growth of 23.13 per cent. China imported 15.68 million tonnes of crude oil from Iraq, with a year-on-year growth of 13.87 per cent.[49] With upstream projects and service agreements to develop oil fields, such as al-Ahdab, Halfaya and Rumaila, China has been consolidating its engagement with Iraq. The role of China is a matter of envy to many as Robert Kaplan noted in 2011 that the US 'liberated Iraq so that Chinese firms can extract its oil'.[50] China, on the other hand, considers its engagement with Iraq a 'natural result of China's economic rise'.[51] India faces competition from large Chinese firms in the petrochemical as well as reconstruction sectors in Iraq.

Pakistan: Pakistan and Iraq share a commonality in terms of being influenced by the US policies as well as grappling with internal instability. In the pre-2003 days, Pakistan and Iraq did not enjoy the best of relations. However, ever since 2003 Pakistan has tried to upgrade its relations with Baghdad. In the year 2013, Pakistan and Iraq agreed in principal to upgrade their defence cooperation. According to its Ambassador in Baghdad Shah M. Jamal, Pakistan intends to sign agreements with Iraq ensuring defence cooperation including the training of Iraq's Armed Forces personnel by Pakistan.[52] The need for enhanced trade and economic relations was stressed by Pakistan's Prime Minister Nawaz Sharif in his meeting with the visiting Speaker of Iraqi Assembly Osama Abdul Aziz al-Nujaifi in Islamabad on 7 December.[53] Iraq–Pakistan trade relations mainly involve export of crude oil, crude materials, excluding fuels, food and live animals by Iraq, and food, medicine and manufactured goods from Pakistan.[54] India faces competition from Pakistan in terms of export of foodgrains to Iraq. Acting on its intentions of forwarding ties with Iraq, Pakistan signed deals to supply basic trainer aircraft to the Iraqi Air Force and help train its personnel.[55]

Challenges and Prospects

During his visit, Iraqi Prime Minister indicated India's importance when he said: 'We rely heavily on India for the reconstruction and development of Iraq which has been devastated by war and adventure.'[56] The reconstruction in Iraq provides both an opportunity and challenge. While, on the one hand, the 2003 war has left signs of destruction all around, it meant a weakening of institutional capabilities of Iraq and, hence, fast tracking of bilateral relations would have to accommodate the process of reconstruction. On the other hand, however, the reconstruction process provides India an opportunity to partner Iraq in its efforts and provide a much needed broader and deeper basis to the engagement going beyond energy trade. India has been active in reconstruction efforts in Afghanistan and the same should be attempted in Iraq. Building schools, power plants and transmission lines, providing health care and augmenting Iraq's petroleum industry are some of the areas which go beyond the buyer–seller relationship and have the potential to generate societal goodwill which would help in going a long way in a sustainable bilateral engagement. The economic ties between India and Iraq are heavily skewed towards petroleum; this is one area where India needs to augment its potential towards diversified engagement. The regional politics and circumstances have given rise to many questions regarding India's position vis-à-vis Saudi Arabia, Iraq and Iran.

The internal conflict within Iraq is beyond India's control. India has done well to keep out of the internal wrangling of various factions. However, India can certainly engage various communities and groups to exchange views within the purview of diplomatic means and help Iraq built capabilities towards social cohesion through experience sharing and training programmes. Given the Indian expertise in IT sector, the lack of cooperation is a lacunae that needs to be addressed and the first step towards that can be the creation of a dedicated webpage of Indian Embassy in Baghdad. India has dedicated embassy websites in countries such as Iran, Saudi Arabia and United Arab Emirates (UAE).

CONCLUSION

India and Iraq moved towards strengthening their engagement in the year 2013 as was evident through diplomatic activities and high-level exchange. Trade between the two countries has grown significantly since 2003 and all indicators point towards an upward movement. Iraq is going to be an important player in the world energy market and India is poised to be one of the largest expanding markets, thus there is a complementarity in this field. The relationship with Iraq is valuable in itself and when seen in the context of the Persian Gulf it is going to remain a key actor provided it does not fall prey to the various fault lines within. Thus, it is in India's interest to partake in the reconstruction of Iraq which not only provides an economic opportunity for India Inc., but also offers a platform for a long-term and sustainable relationship. That India is neither a superpower towering above nor a profit-seeking behemoth, are factors that can be sources of strength. The need is for the Indian policymakers and diplomats to set their priorities in order and for the Indian business to be ready for the opportunities that lay ahead. *Phronesis* may be the key word here.

NOTES

1. 'Analysis Briefs: Iraq', *US Energy Information Administration (EIA)*, 2 April 2013, available at: http://www.eia.gov/countries/analysisbriefs/Iraq/iraq.pdf/.

2. 'UN Casualty Figures for December, 2013 Deadliest since 2008 in Iraq', United Nations Iraq, 2 January 2014, available at: http://www.uniraq.org/index.php?option=com_k2&view=item&id=1499:un-casualty-figures-for-december-2013-deadliest-since-2008-in-iraq&Itemid=633&lang=en/.

3. Hassan Barari, 'Al-Maliki's Policies Pose Bigger Threat than Al-Qaeda', *Arab News*, 5 November 2013, available at: http://www.arabnews.com/news/472541/.

4. Kenneth Katzman, 'Iraq: Politics, Governance, and Human Rights', *Congressional Research Service*, 5 February 2014, available at: https://www.fas.org/sgp/crs/mideast/RS21968.pdf/.

5. 'Freedom in the World 2014', *Freedom House*, available at: http://www.freedomhouse.org/sites/default/files/Freedom%20in%20the%20World%202014%20Booklet.pdf/.

6. 'Testimony of Deputy Assistant Secretary Brett McGurk House Foreign Affairs Subcommittee on the Middle East and North Africa Hearing: Iraq', *House Committee on Foreign Affairs United States, Washington DC*, 13 November 2013, available at: http://docs.house.gov/meetings/FA/FA13/20131113/101473/HHRG-113-FA13-Wstate-McGurkB-20131113.pdf/.

7. Since 2005, the GDP has steadily increased. The GDP growth of Iraq in 2006 was just 1.6 per cent which increased to 8.4 per cent in 2012. This has been attributed to the growing petroleum export and in 2013 Iraq was the sixth largest petroleum exporter in the world, *The World Bank*, available at: http://data.worldbank.org/indicator/NY.GDP.MKTP.KD.ZG/countries/IQ?display=graph/; and 'Iraq Returns as World's Fastest-Growing Oil Exporter', *Reuters*, 5 March 2014, available at: http://www.reuters.com/article/2014/03/05/iraq-oil-idUSL6N0M22P120140305/.

8. Due to the sectarian violence, the number of Iraqi refugees and internally displaced people is estimated to be around one million. Since 2010, around 500,000 Iraqi refugees from Syria have returned to Iraq. According to Iraq Body Count, a monitoring group, approximately 13,046 deaths have been reported in Iraq due to sectarian conflict in 2013, *Iraq Body Count*, available at: https://www.iraqbodycount.org/database/.

9. 'Corruption by Country/Territory: Iraq', *Transparency International*, 2013, available at: http://www.transparency.org/country#IRQ/.

10. Salah Nasrawi, 'Iraq and Saudi Arabia: Between a Rock And a Hard Place', *Al Jazeera*, 29 November 2013, available at: http://www.aljazeera.com/indepth/opinion/2013/11/iraq-saudi-arabia-between-rock-hard-place-20131128638344586.html/.

11. 'OPEC: Iran–Iraq Alliance Weakens Saudis', *UPI*, 4 January 2013, available at: http://www.upi.com/Business_News/Energy-Resources/2013/01/04/OPEC-Iran-Iraq-alliance-weakens-Saudis/UPI-68701357323613/.

12. 'Pentagon Proposes $2.7B in Iraq Arms Sales', *Defense News*, 6 August 2013, available at: http://www.defensenews.com/article/20130806/DEFREG02/308060014/Pentagon-Proposes-2-7B-Iraq-Arms-Sales/.

13. 'Syrian Situation in IRAQ Inter-agency Update No. 57, 31 December 2013', *United Nations*, 24 January 2014, available at: http://www.uniraq.org/index.php?option=com_k2&view=item&task=download&id=244_de06dea1f70 0553fedc5ccb5f0a1206d&Itemid=626&lang=en/.

14. 'Visit of External Affairs Minister to Iraq (June 19–20, 2013)', *Outgoing Visit*, Ministry of External Affairs, New Delhi, 16 June 2013, available at: http://www.mea.gov.in/outoging-visit-detail.htm?21824/Visit+of+External+Affairs+Minister+to+Iraq+June+1920+2013/.

15. 'India–Iraq Relations', Ministry of External Affairs, New Delhi, 2013, available at: http://www.mea.gov.in/Portal/ForeignRelation/India-Iraq_Relations.pdf/.

16. 'State Visit of Prime Minister of Iraq Mr. Nouri al-Maliki to India (August 22–25, 2013)', *Incoming Visit*, Ministry of External Affairs, New Delhi, 21 August 2013, available at: http://www.mea.gov.in/incoming-visit-detail.htm?22088/State+visit+of+Prime+Minister+of+Iraq+Mr+Nouri+alMaliki+to+India+2225+August+2013/.

17. 'List of Documents Signed during the State Visit of Mr Nouri al-Mailiki, Prime Minister of Republic of Iraq to India (August 22–25, 2013)', *Bilateral/Multilateral Documents*, Ministry of External Affairs, New Delhi, 23 August 2013, available at: http://www.mea.gov.in/bilateral-documents.htm?dtl/22114/List+of+Documents+signed+during+the+State+Visit+of+Mr+Nouri+alMailiki+Prime+Minister+of+Republic+of+Iraq+to+India+Augu st+2225+2013/.

18. Ahmed Hussein, 'Mutleg, Indian Ambassador to Iraq Discuss Bilateral Relations', *Iraqi News*, 3 July 2013, available at: http://www.iraqinews.com/baghdad-politics/mutleg-indian-ambassador-to-iraq-discuss-bilateral-relations/#axzz2tDgNOJub/.

19. Shubhajit Roy, 'Security Top on Agenda of Khurshid's Iraq Visit', *The Indian Express*, 19 June 2013, available at: http://indianexpress.com/article/news-archive/web/security-top-on-agenda-of-khurshids-iraq-visit-2/.

20. 'Bilateral Security Cooperation between India and Iraq', *Press Release*, Press Information Bureau, New Delhi, 19 December 2013, available at: http://pib.nic.in/newsite/PrintRelease.aspx?relid=102024/.

21. 'Talk by Mr. Falih Al-Fayyadh, National Security Adviser, Republic of Iraq', *Events*, Institute for Defence Studies and Analyses (IDSA), New Delhi, 20 December 2013, available at: http://idsa.in/event/FalihAlFayyadhNSARepublicofIraq/.

22. 'India and Iraq Must Cooperate to Counter Terrorism: National Security Advisor of Iraq', *Press Release*, Institute for Defence Studies and Analyses

(IDSA), New Delhi, 20 December 2013, available at: http://www.idsa.in/pressrelease/IndiaandIraqMustCooperatetoCounterTerrorism/.

23. 'Export of Arms and Related Materials to Government of Iraq', Directorate General of Foreign Trade India, 12 February 2014, available at: http://dgft.gov.in/exim/2000/NOT/NOT13/not6813.htm/.

24. 'State Visit of Prime Minister of Iraq, Mr. Nouri al-Maliki to India (22–25 August, 2013)', *Incoming Visit*, Ministry of External Affairs, 21 August 2013, available at: http://www.mea.gov.in/incoming-visit-detail.htm?22088/State +visit+of+Prime+Minister+of+Iraq+Mr+Nouri+alMaliki+to+India+2225+A ugust+2013/.

25. Rajeev Sharma, 'India's Red Carpet for Iraqi PM Nouri Al-Maliki is Good Diplomacy', *First Post*, 24 August 2013, available at: http://www.firstpost.com/world/indias-red-carpet-for-iraqi-pm-nouri-al-maliki-is-good-diplomacy-1057991.html/.

26. Hussain Ibrahim Saleh al-Shahristani, 'Recent Trends in the Global Energy, Oil & Gas Economy', *Events*, IISS-Oberoi Lecture, Mumbai, 14 August 2013, available at: http://www.iiss.org/en/events/events/archive/2013-5126/august-1e98/recent-trends-in-global-energy-1218/.

27. Prithvi Ram Mudiam, *India and the Middle East* (London: British Academy Press, 1994), p. 62.

28. See Lok Shabha Questions, Part II Proceedings other than Questions and Answers (XIV Lok Sabha), 'Discussion under Rule 193: Situation in Iraq', 6 July 2004, available at: http://164.100.47.132/LssNew/psearch/result-14Participitants.aspx?dbsl=187/.

29. Sujay Mehdudia, 'India, Iraq Exploring Payment in Domestic Currency: Anand Sharma', *The Hindu*, 23 August 2013, available at: http://www.the-hindu.com/business/Industry/india-iraq-exploring-payment-in-domestic-currency-anand-sharma/article5052675.ece/.

30. 'Iraqi PM Addresses Captains of Indian and Iraqi Industry', *Press Release*, Federation of Indian Chambers of Commerce and Industry (FICCI), 23 August 2013, New Delhi, available at: http://www.ficci.com/PressRelease/1318/PressRelease.pdf/.

31. 'Analysis Briefs: Iraq'.

32. Khalid Al-Ansary and Kadhim Ajrash, 'Iraq to Boost Oil Output This Year as Asian Demand Strengthens', *Bloomberg News*, 23 October 2013, available at: http://www.bloomberg.com/news/2013-10-23/iraq-to-boost-oil-output-this-year-as-asian-demand-strengthens.html/.

33. 'Iraq Will Not Sell Crude to India at a Special Price: Shahristani', *The Financial Express*, 16 August 2013, available at: http://www.financialexpress.com/news/-iraq-will-not-sell-crude-to-india-at-a-special-price-shahristani/1155860/.

34. 'India Proposes 10-Yr Oil Deal with Iraq', *The Indian Express*, 24 August 2013, available at: http://archive.indianexpress.com/news/india-proposes-10yr-oil-deal-with-iraq/1159331/.

35. 'Joint Statement during the State Visit of H.E. Mr. Nouri Al-Maliki, Prime Minister of Iraq to India (August 22–25, 2013)', *Speeches & Statements*,

Ministry of External Affairs, New Delhi, 23 August 2013, available at: http://www.mea.gov.in/Speeches-Statements.htm?dtl/22115/Joint+Stateme nt+during+the+State+Visit+of+HE+Mr+Nouri+Al+Maliki+Prime+Minister+ of+Iraq+to+India++August+2225+2013/.

36. Nidhi Verma, 'Iraq Offers Longer Credit to Indian Oil Buyers', *Reuters*, New Delhi, 11 November 2013, available at: http://uk.reuters.com/article/2013/11/11/india-iraq-oil-idUKL4N0IW3XD20131111/.

37. 'BGR Energy Bags $246-M Contract from Iraq Govt', *The Financial Express*, 16 October 2013, available at: http://www.financialexpress.com/news/bgr-energy-bags-246m-contract-from-iraq-govt/1183004/.

38. Hussain Ibrahim Saleh al-Shahristani, 'Recent Trends in the Global Energy, Oil & Gas Economy', *Events*, IISS-Oberoi Lecture, 14 August 2013, available at: http://www.iiss.org/en/events/events/archive/2013-5126/august-1e98/recent-trends-in-global-energy-1218/.

39. 'India–Iraq Relations', Ministry of External Affairs, New Delhi, 2013, available at: http://www.mea.gov.in/Portal/ForeignRelation/India-Iraq_Relations.pdf/.

40. Ibid.

41. 'Transcript of Media Briefing by Official Spokesperson', *Media Briefings*, Ministry of External Affairs, New Delhi, 21 August 2013, available at: http://www.mea.gov.in/media-briefings.htm?dtl/22090/Transcript+of+Media+Bri efing+by+Official+Spokesperson+August+21+2013/.

42. 'The Strategic Framework Agreement (SFA) and U.S.–Iraqi Bilateral Relations', Embassy of the United States, Iraq, Baghdad, available at: http://iraq.usembassy.gov/american-iraqi.html/.

43. 'Joint Statement by the United States of America and the Republic of Iraq', *Press Release*, Prime Minister's Office Iraq', 2 November 2013, available at: http://pmo.iq/pme/press/2013/11en/02112013_1en.htm/.

44. Katzman, 'Iraq'.

45. 'Testimony of Deputy Assistant Secretary Brett McGurk House Foreign Affairs Subcommittee on the Middle East and North Africa Hearing'.

46. Tim Arango and Clifford Krauss, 'China Is Reaping Biggest Benefits of Iraq Oil Boom', *The New York Times*, 2 June 2013, available at: http://www.nytimes.com/2013/06/03/world/middleeast/china-reaps-biggest-benefits-of-iraq-oil-boom.html?pagewanted=all&_r=0/.

47. Erica Goode and Riyadh Mohammed, 'Iraq Signs Oil Deal with China Worth up to $3 Billion', *The New York Times*, 28 August 2008, available at: http://www.nytimes.com/2008/08/29/world/middleeast/29iraq.html/.

48. Wayne Ma and Brian Spegele, 'New Suppliers Boost China Oil Imports', *The Wall Street Journal*, 21 January 2014, available at: http://online.wsj.com/news/articles/SB10001424052702303802904579334411874909686/.

49. 'Bilateral Relations between China and Iraq', Embassy of the People's Republic of China in the Republic of Iraq, Baghdad, 11 April 2013, available at: http://iq.chineseembassy.org/eng/zygx/zygxgk/.

50. Robert Kaplan, 'The Middle East Crisis Has Just Begun', *The Wall Street Journal*, 26 March 2011, available at: http://online.wsj.com/news/articles/SB 10001424052748704050204576218842399053176/.
51. Wang Zhaokun, 'Beijing Not Post-War "Victor" in Iraq', *Global Times*, 21 March 2013, available at: http://www.globaltimes.cn/content/769526.shtml#.Uv9puTssWvc/.
52. 'Pakistan, Iraq to Sign Defence Cooperation Pact', *The Nation (Pakistan)*, 25 March 2013, available at: http://www.nation.com.pk/national/25-Mar-2013/pakistan-iraq-to-sign-defence-cooperation-pact/.
53. 'Pakistan, Iraq Should Boost Bilateral Trade: PM', *The Nation*, 7 December 2013, available at: http://www.nation.com.pk/islamabad/07-Dec-2013/pakistan-iraq-should-boost-bilateral-trade-pm/.
54. 'Iraq', The Federation of Pakistan Chambers of Commerce & Industry, available at: http://www.fpcci.com.pk/products/subcat_pdf_82.pdf/.
55. Usman Ansari, 'Pakistan Sells Trainer Aircraft to Iraq, Seeks Further Contracts', *Defense News*, 11 February 2014, available at: http://www.defensenews.com/article/20140211/DEFREG04/302110026/Pakistan-Sells-Trainer-Aircraft-Iraq-Seeks-Further-Contracts/.
56. Mehdudia, 'India, Iraq Exploring Payment in Domestic Currency'.

5

Kuwait

Paulami Sanyal

Key Information

Area: 17,818 sq km; **Population:** 2,742,711 (2014 est.); **Native:** NA; **Expats:** NA; **Youth:** 15.3 per cent; **Population growth rate:** 1.7 per cent; **Life expectancy at birth:** 77.64 years; **Major population groups:** Kuwaiti 45 per cent, other Arab 35 per cent, South Asian 9 per cent, Iranian 4 per cent, others 7 per cent; **Religious groups:** Sunni 59.5 per cent, Shia 25.5 per cent, others 15 per cent; **GDP:** US$165.8 billion; **Per capita income:** US$42,100; **Foreign trade:** US$136.42 billion; **Oil reserves:** 101.5 billion bbl (2013); **Gas reserves:** 11.73 billion m³; **Ruling family:** al-Sabah; **Ruler:** Emir Sabah al-Ahmad Jabir al-Sabah (since 29 January 2006); **Crown Prince:** Prince Nawaf al-Ahmad al-Jaber al-Sabah (since 7 February 2006); **National Day:** 25 February; **Defence budget:** 5.3 per cent of GDP; **HDI rank:** 54; **Literacy rate:** 93.3 per cent; **UN education index:** 0.620; **Gender inequality index:** 0.274; **Labour force:** 2.38 million; **Unemployment rate:** 3.4 per cent; **External debt:** US$34.41 billion (December 2013); **Sovereign wealth fund:** US$410 billion; **Infant mortality rate:** 7.51 deaths out of 1,000; **Last national census:** 2011; **Parliament:** 65-member partially elected National Assembly; **Last parliament election:** 27 July 2013; **Number of Indians:** over 500,000; **Last Indian prime minister to visit:** Indira Gandhi, May 1981.

Sources: CIA, *The World Factbook*, available at: https://www.cia.gov/library/publications/the-world-factbook/; *UN Human Development Report*, Statistics, available at: http://hdr.undp.org/en/statistics/; United States Commission on Religious Freedom, US Department of State; *Annual Report 2013; Briefs on Foreign Relations*, Ministry of External Affairs, Government of India and Centre for Arms Control and Proliferation (Washington, D.C.).
Note: All figures for 2013.

Kuwait has witnessed internal political disturbances in the wake of Arab Spring. Fresh elections for the National Assembly were held in July 2013 but problems continued as Jaber al-Mubarak al-Sabah returned as Prime Minister. Despite disturbances, Kuwaiti economy has continued to remain steady riding on energy exports and strong showing by the service sector. India–Kuwait relations witnessed fresh momentum during the year with the visit of the Kuwaiti Prime Minister in November, the first visit by a Kuwaiti head of the government in 10 years. Bilateral trade continued in the same wane while efforts at taking the economic engagements to a step further can lead to rise in trade in the coming years.

DOMESTIC DEVELOPMENTS

The small emirate of Kuwait used to be one coastal desert village, inhabited by fishermen, merchants and pearl divers who arrived mainly from interiors of Arabian Peninsula in the eighteenth century. Today, it is a city-state with 104 billion barrels of proven reserve oil, which is 8 per cent of world's total oil reserve and has natural gas reserves of 1.586 trillion cubic metres. Petroleum accounts for half of the gross domestic product (GDP), 95 per cent of export revenues and 80 per cent of government income.[1] Kuwait's climate is not suitable for agriculture thus making it dependant on the imports from other countries for its food requirements. To meet its water needs, Kuwait depends on desalination or import.[2]

The Emir is the head of the state, with the power to appoint Prime Minister who then chooses the cabinet. Emir also serves as Commander-in-Chief of the Armed Forces, appoints judges and has the power to suspend the National Assembly for limited periods of time. Prime Minister has always been a member of al-Sabah family and till 2003 he used to be the Crown Prince. Usually the Kuwaiti cabinet has three out of four deputy prime ministers from the family. The present Prime Minister is Jaber al-Mubarak al-Sabah who was reappointed after the July election.

Kuwait's National Assembly has 50 seats and was established under Kuwait's 1962 constitution having more legislative authority than other Arab countries in its neighbourhood. It can introduce, consider legislation and vote on legislations introduced by the government. It cannot confirm cabinet nominees, but it can, by simple majority, express 'no confidence' and remove individual ministers. The opposition comprising most of Liberals, Sunni Islamists, youths and intellectuals has been demanding more powers for the National Assembly and less power for the cabinet, which is largely an extension of al-Sabah family.[3]

Since 1990s the voting rights in Kuwait was extended gradually and in 2005 women were given the right to vote and contest elections to the National Assembly. Political parties are banned but different groups can compete in elections as 'currents', 'trends' or 'political societies'.[4] Many of them form *diwaniyas* which are primarily informal social gatherings held at night by elites belonging to different political ideologies and backgrounds. The Arab Spring had an impact in Kuwait and led to unrest and dissolution of the Assembly. Elections were held on 27 July that returned supporters of the royal family in majority. Two women were elected which was one less than in 2012.[5] There were about 300 candidates in the fray of which eight were female. Some opposition groups including those associated with Muslim Brotherhood boycotted the election (Table 5.1 and Figure 5.1).[6] Of about 439,911 registered voters, 228,314 used their franchise accounting for 52 per cent.[7] Even though opposition forces are working outside the system, there have been no major public demonstrations. Opposition demands are confined to demands for constitutional monarchy, where the elected parliament would select the cabinet.[8]

Table 5.1
Kuwaiti Parliamentary Elections, July 2013

Date of election	Result of election	Number of registered candidates	Percentage of registered women candidates	Number of seats	Distribution of seats according to sex
27 July 2013	Sunni Islamists 3, Liberals 9, Popular Action Bloc 0; Shiite 8; Sunni Independents 30	329 (321 men, 8 women)	2.4	50	Men: 48 Women: 2

Source: Kenneth Katzman, 'Kuwait: Security, Reform, and US Policies', *Congressional Research Service*, 30 January 2014, available at: http://www.fas.org/sgp/crs/mideast/RS21513.pdf/.

Figure 5.1
Kuwaiti Parliamentary Elections, July 2013

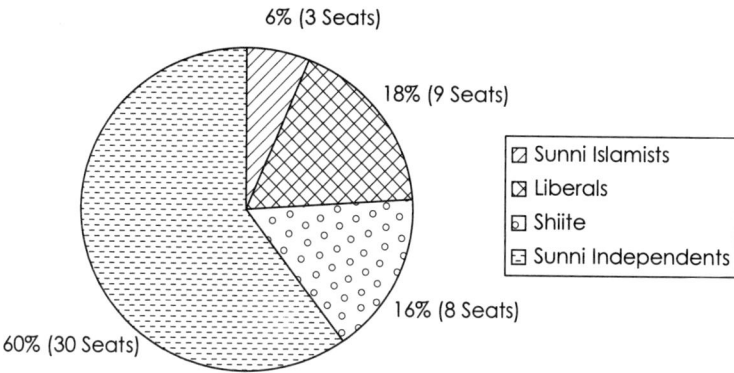

Source: Adapted from Kenneth Katzman, 'Kuwait: Security, Reform, and US Policies', *Congressional Research Service,* 30 January 2014, available at: http://www.fas.org/sgp/crs/mideast/RS21513.pdf/.

Kuwait is the second smallest land area within Organization of Petroleum Exporting Countries (OPEC) yet producing the third largest volume of oil and its economy is heavily dependent on hydrocarbon production.[9]

However, presently it is attempting to diversify its economy and is expected to sign contracts of more than US$117 billion in different sectors during 2012–16 which would include oil and gas sector, both upstream and downstream, construction including new cities, hospitals and housing units, infrastructure, including roads, airport, port, metro and railway projects, power and transmission, petrochemicals, gas processing, pipeline, etc.[10] Moreover, in 2013 the Ministry of Finance signed a contract with Hongkong and Shanghai Banking Corporation (HSBC) for the first solar power plant of 280 MW which would be able to generate 15 per cent of renewable energy by 2030.[11]

Energy policy in this country is decided by the Supreme Petroleum Council, overseen by the Ministry of Petroleum, and executed by the Kuwait Petroleum Corporation and its subsidiaries. Kuwait has an active sovereign-wealth fund, the Kuwait Investment Authority, which oversees all state expenditures and international investments. Kuwait bans foreign ownership of its resources but the government has taken certain measures (for example, Project Kuwait) to increase foreign participation in the oil and gas sectors.[12] According to *Oil and Gas Journal*, as of January 2013, Kuwait's territorial boundaries have an estimated 102 billion barrels of proven oil reserves and 63 trillion cubic feet of proven natural gas reserves. Estimated natural gas reserves have remained static since 2006. Kuwait's intent to diversify its economy has spurred an extensive drive in natural gas exploration. Additional reserves of oil are held in the Partitioned Neutral Zone (PNZ), which it shares with Saudi Arabia.[13]

Regarding minorities, troubles related to Biduns did not cease in spite of the new law passed by parliament in March to naturalize 4,000 of them by 2013.[14] Although it addressed the problem of statelessness, the Bidun activists have a different account of this law. According to them, this measure has not benefitted their community, 'but is being used to grant citizenship to children born to Kuwaiti mothers and foreign fathers'.[15] The government, however, claims that Biduns have benefitted from the law.

Although women have been granted some political rights, their social position continues to be a cause for concern. Kuwait has no laws prohibiting domestic violence, sexual harassment or marital rape. There are several non-governmental organizations working for women rights as many women face domestic abuse.[16] Human trafficking has continued despite the authorities taking some measures to deal with the problem. The 2013 US State Department annual report on trafficking classified Kuwait as Tier Three, which stands for the most problematic countries, for the seventh year in a row. The report cited that Kuwait has been a failure when it comes to reporting arrests, prosecutions, convictions or sentences of traffickers for either forced labour or sex trafficking, and that Kuwait has very weak victim protection measures.[17]

Moreover, freedom of speech has remained under stress particularly because of the Article 25 of the 1970 penal code 'which prescribes a sentence of up to five years in prison for anyone who publicly "objects to the rights and authorities of the emir or faults him"'.[18] The authorities brought at least 29 cases against those who criticized government on Twitter, Facebook or any other social media during 2013. Article 25 does not detail what constituted offending the Emir. There are eight examples that Human Rights Watch reported as political statements that do not amount to incitement of violence but still they were found guilty under the Article. In mid-April, former parliamentarian Musallam al-Barrak was sentenced to five years in prison for insulting the Emir. However, his sentence was overturned in May. In November, a court sentenced a Kuwaiti man to five years in prison for a Twitter comment about Sunni and Shia theology. In December, the Constitutional Court rejected a challenge to Article 25 of the penal code.[19]

According to the Kuwaiti constitution, Islam is the official religion and Sharia is the primary source of legislation. Majority of Kuwaiti Muslims are Sunnis.[20] Most of the remaining ones are Shia along with a small number of Christian and Bahai citizens. The Christian churches which are recognized by Kuwaiti government are Roman Catholic Church, Coptic Orthodox Church, National Evangelical (Protestant) Church, Armenian Orthodox Church, Greek Orthodox Church (referred to in Arabic as the Roman Orthodox Church), Greek Catholic (Melkite) Church and the Anglican Church. There are also some unrecognized Christian groups and an estimated 100,000 Buddhists and 10,000 Sikhs, the majority of whom are non-citizens.[21] The preamble of the constitution states that the country and its rulers are established in the name of Allah and that faith is important in promotion of Arab nationalism and world peace. Part 1 Article 2 of the constitution depicts Islam as the state religion and Article 12 says that state has the responsibility to safeguard Arab and Islamic heritage. Freedom of religion is identified only when it conforms to established customs, provided that it does not conflict with public policy or morals. Religious groups need official recognition and should be registered with the Ministry of Awqaf and Islamic Affairs. However, there is no official list of recognized religious institutions.[22]

BILATERAL RELATIONS

Bilateral relations have come a long way from the rupture faced when India was found wanting in condemning the Iraqi occupation of Kuwait during 1990–91.[23] A new era started with the June 2006 visit of Kuwaiti Emir Sabah al-Ahmad al-Jaber al-Sabah. The ties have grown since, with both recognizing other's importance in the regional dynamics, but are driven mainly by trade and commerce.

Political Relations

In 2013, political relations came to the fore with the 7 to 10 November visit of Kuwaiti Prime Minister Jaber al-Mubarak al-Hamad al-Sabah.[24] He was accompanied with a high-level delegation consisting of

Deputy Prime Minister and Minister of Foreign Affairs Sabah al-Khalid al-Hamad al-Sabah, Minister of Oil Mustafa Jassem al-Shamali, Minister of Commerce and Industry Anas Khalid al-Saleh and senior officials and business leaders. Apart from having bilateral discussions and consultations with Prime Minister Manmohan Singh, he also called on President Pranab Mukherjee, Vice President Hamid Ansari and held meetings with UPA chairperson Sonia Gandhi and Indian officials. Jaber al-Sabah attended a business luncheon meeting organized by the three business forums, namely Federation of Indian Chambers of Commerce and Industry (FICCI), Confederation of Indian Industry (CII) and Associated Chambers of Commerce and Industry of India (ASSOCHAM).[25]

A number of bilateral agreements were signed during his visit, including one on facilitating the transfer of sentenced person to serve their remaining sentences of imprisonment or any other form of punishment in their own country.[26] A Memorandum of Understanding (MoU) between Foreign Service Institute (FSI) of Ministry of External Affairs of India and Kuwait Diplomatic Institute (KDI) was signed to promote cooperation regarding exchange of information on structure and content of training programmes, exchange of trainees, students, faculty members, experts and researchers. Moreover, an MoU in the field of sports and an educational exchange programme was also signed.

Moreover, during the visit, India and Kuwait agreed to broaden the areas of bilateral engagement and to develop existing spheres of mutual interest including energy, power, petrochemicals, investments, infrastructure development, project exports, environment and remediation of contaminated soil, education, culture, health, human resource and information technology. The two sides discussed regional and international issues, especially the security situation in Middle East and South Asia, and agreed for a regular exchange of views on various regional and international issues.[27] The two also exchanged views on the role of institutions in strengthening democracy. Both the Prime Ministers expressed their satisfaction with the first dialogue between the National Security Council Secretariat of India and the National Security Bureau of Kuwait in October. It was agreed that the security dialogue would take place annually between the two countries. The two Prime Ministers condemned terrorism in all shapes and forms.[28]

From the perspective of the Gulf region, it was agreed to further strengthen the relationship between India and Gulf Cooperation Council (GCC) countries by finalizing an early date for India–GCC Free Trade Agreement. The two countries shared their concern about the situation in Syria and called for an effort by the UN–Arab League special envoy to Syria Lakhdar Brahimi to facilitate appropriate atmosphere for the Geneva-II Conference. Regarding the Afghanistan issue, both supported the Afghan-led reconciliation process and committed to help Afghanistan achieve its objective of peace, stability, independence and development at an early date.

Earlier, Minister of Amiri Diwan Affairs Nasser al-Sabah al-Ahmad al-Jaber al-Sabah visited India during 10–13 March at the invitation of External Affairs Minister Salman Khurshid. He was accompanied by senior officials from different institutions including Kuwaiti hydrocarbon sector and Kuwait Investment Authority. During this visit, he called on the Prime Minister and the Vice President and met Ministers of Finance, Petroleum and Natural Gas, Commerce, Industry and Textiles and Deputy Chairman of Planning Commission. During these meetings, discussions about bilateral cooperation on energy, trade and investment were emphasized.[29]

From the Indian side, Minister of State for External Affairs E. Ahamed visited Kuwait in January to take part in the International Humanitarian Pledging Conference on Syria.[30] Another important high-level visit was by Montek Singh Ahluwalia, Deputy Chairman of the Planning Commission in July.

Economic Relations

Trade balance has conventionally remained in favour of Kuwait owning mainly to oil imports. Importantly, exports from India to Kuwait have further witnessed decline during the past three years. India has been among the top 10 trade partners for Kuwait.[31] Bilateral trade during 2012–13 accounted for US$17.65 billion, a share of 2.23 per cent in India's total trade (Table 5.2 and Figure 5.2). India's exports to Kuwait stood at US$1.06 billion during 2012–13, a 10 per cent decline from the previous year, whereas imports from Kuwait stood at US$16.58 billion, recording a meagre growth of 1 per cent (Table 5.2). Major items exported from India cover a broad range including food items, textiles, garments, electrical and engineering equipment, metal products, pressure vessel

Table 5.2
India–Kuwait Bilateral Trade (in US$ Million)

	2009–10	2010–11	2011–12	2012–13
India's exports to Kuwait	782.45	1,856.01	1,181.41	1,061.08
India's imports from Kuwait	8,249.49	10,313.64	16,439.64	16,588.13
Total bilateral trade	9,031.95	12,169.65	17,621.05	17,649.21
Share of Kuwait in India's total trade	1.93	1.96	2.22	2.23

Source: Adapted from Directorate General of Foreign Trade, available at: www.dgft.gov.in/.

Figure 5.2
India–Kuwait Bilateral Trade

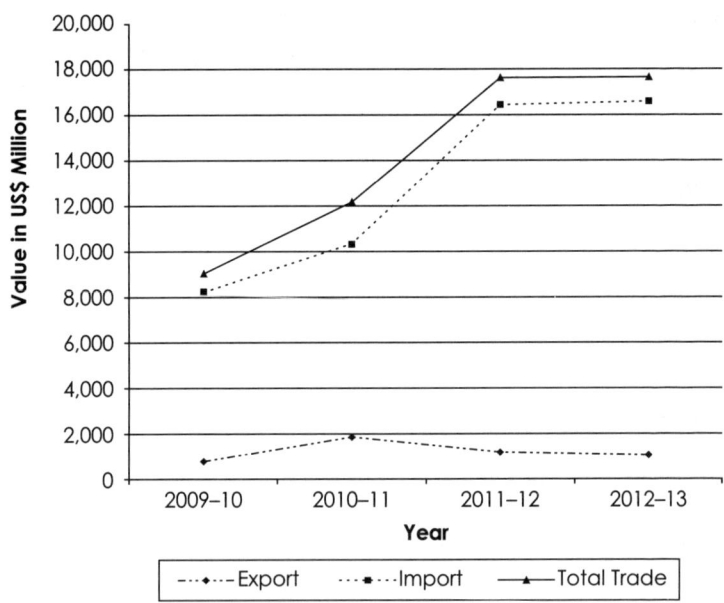

Source: Adapted from Directorate General of Foreign Trade, New Delhi, available at: www.dgft.gov.in/.

reactors, industrial valves, boilers, machinery and mechanical appliances, articles of iron or steel, etc., on the other hand, oil accounted for nearly 95 per cent of imports from Kuwait with a bill of US$15.73 billion (Table 5.3 and Figure 5.3).

Table 5.3

Share of Oil in India's Imports from Kuwait (in US$ Million)

Year	Oil imports from Kuwait	Total oil imports	Kuwaiti share in total oil imports	Imports from Kuwait	Per cent of oil in imports from Kuwait
2009–10	7,909.80	96,321.16	8.21	8,249.49	95.88
2010–11	9,729.09	115,929.02	8.39	10,313.64	94.33
2011–12	15,718.33	172,753.92	9.10	16,439.64	95.61
2012–13	15,737.46	181,344.67	8.68	16,588.13	94.87

Source: Adapted from Directorate General of Foreign Trade, available at: www.dgft.gov.in/.

Figure 5.3

Share of Oil in India's Imports from Kuwait

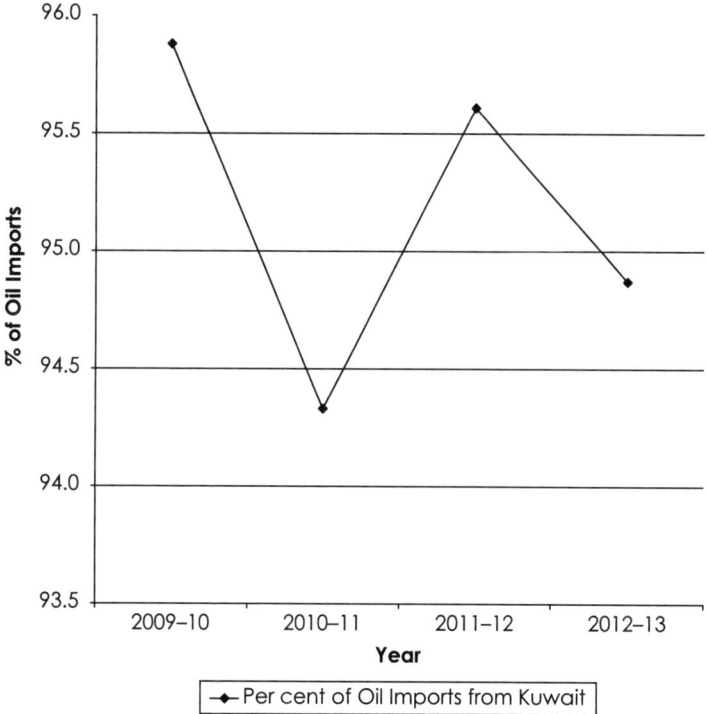

Source: Adapted from Directorate General of Foreign Trade, New Delhi, available at: www.dgft.gov.in/.

There have been several high-level delegates' meetings on economic issues between the two countries throughout 2013. The most important of them was the visit of Kuwaiti Prime Minister, which focused on economic cooperation, investment and diversification of non-oil trade sector. The two countries decided that they would encourage regular participation in each other's trade fairs and exhibitions and facilitate other trade promotional measures. Jaber al-Sabah said that Kuwait recognized the potential in the Indian economy and discussed ways to increase Kuwaiti investments. Both the parties urged for the exchange of information on available investment opportunities and discussed to establish a joint mechanism to develop investments between the two countries. They identified the need for meetings between Kuwait Investment Authority (KIA) and Indian public and private sector companies.[32] While discussing Kuwaiti investment it should be noted that mostly Kuwaiti investment to India has been directed through international investment companies or through Mauritius, Singapore or other countries providing tax breaks. So far, Kuwaiti investments in India are about US$3 billion of which US$2.4 billion is by KIA, made in the last few years. An investment delegation led by Ravi Mathur, Secretary (Disinvestment), visited Kuwait on 13 November and held discussions with senior officials of KIA led by its Managing Director Bader al-Sa'ad. KIA is considering more investments into India, besides the recent equity investment worth US$5.37 million in the Power Grid Corporation of India Limited. Other significant Kuwaiti investments in India include those by Alghanim Group of Kuwait, the KAPICO Group, Agility Logistics, Hasibat Holding Co., KGA Group, KCIC, KIPCO, Global Investment House and Kuwait Finance House.[33]

During the meeting between the two Prime Ministers, the Kuwaiti side also welcomed India's disinvestment of its public sector undertakings and appreciated the efforts taken towards economic reforms, increased de-regulation and the creation of an environment agreeable for foreign direct investments. The Kuwaiti side agreed to consider the Indian suggestion to open an office of KIA in India. During a meeting organized jointly by the FICCI, CII and ASSOCHAM India sought Kuwait's help towards an early conclusion of a Free Trade Agreement with GCC.[34]

It was also decided in the meeting between the two Prime Ministers to enhance cooperation between the financial institutions of the two countries, such as Securities and Exchange Board of India, Capital Markets Authority of Kuwait and the respective Central Banks. Moreover, they agreed to encourage cooperation in the steel sector, including through joint venture for setting up a steel plant in Kuwait. Both sides appraised each other of their plans for the respective development of infrastructure.[35] A delegation of the KIA would visit India to explore opportunities for investing in the country as part of the US$350-billion fund which is growing by US$25 billion annually. India expressed interest in a US$100 billion Kuwaiti infrastructure renewal programme.[36]

During 1–3 July, Deputy Chairman of India's Planning Commission Montek Singh Ahluwalia visited Kuwait to promote economic relations between the two countries particularly in the field of investment. During his stay, he held discussions with different Kuwaiti ministers and members of Indian Business Council in Kuwait.[37] In October, a 15-member delegation of FICCI visited Kuwait and held discussions with Kuwaiti Business community.[38]

Energy

Kuwait is the fourth largest supplier of crude oil to India and energy relations between the two countries clearly take key position when it comes to bilateral relations. Kuwait has consistently supplied approximately 8 per cent of India's energy imports in recent years (Table 5.4). During 2012–13, India imported US$105 billion worth of petroleum from Persian Gulf countries and Kuwait had a share of 14.87 per cent (Table 5.4).

During the Fifth Asian Ministerial Energy Roundtable in Seoul on 12 September, Minister of Oil of Kuwait Mustafa Jassem al-Shamali

Table 5.4

India's Energy Imports from Kuwait (in US$ Million)

	2009–10	*2010–11*	*2011–12*	*2012–13*
Energy imports from Kuwait	7,909.80	9,729.09	15,718.33	15,737.46
Total energy imports	96,321.12	115,929.02	172,753.92	181,344.67
Total imports from Persian Gulf	55,904.14	66,688.4	105,056.26	105,859.15
Share in total energy imports	8.21	8.39	9.10	8.68
Share in energy imports from Persian Gulf	14.15	14.59	14.96	14.87

Source: Adapted from Directorate General of Foreign Trade, available at: www.dgft.gov.in/.

met his Indian counterpart M. Veerappa Moily and the two discussed several energy-related issues, such as enhancing cooperation, training and human resources development, cooperation in research and development, joint ventures in petrochemical complexes and cooperation in joint exploration in India and other countries. The two leaders also emphasized the need for partnership in strategic reserves storage facility available in India.[39] The Indian side gave details about developing capabilities of Indian companies in building large refinery and upstream projects. It was agreed that an Indian business delegation with companies having expertise in oil sector projects would visit Kuwait to discuss business opportunities. The technical manpower requirement project in Kuwaiti oil sector was discussed and it was decided that India would try to provide capacity-building and personal training programmes to assist Kuwait.[40]

To meet its increasing energy demand, India proposed a long-term agreement of at least 10 years, better terms, including abolition of Letter of Credit (LC) and increase in interest free credit period up to 60 days. The Kuwaiti side agreed to consider the demands favourably. During the Kuwaiti Prime Minister's visit in November both sides expressed happiness on the development of trade between the two countries in the energy sector.[41]

Defence Relations

Defence cooperation between India and Kuwait comprises high-level military visits, training and port calls by naval ships. To further strengthen bilateral ties and interaction between the two countries, two Indian Naval ships INS Mysore and INS Tarkash paid a goodwill visit to Kuwait during 10–13 September. India and Kuwait are also members of Indian Ocean Naval Symposium (IONS), which is a voluntary and cooperative initiative among 35 countries of the Indian Ocean Region and has served as an ideal forum for sharing information and cooperation on maritime issues.[42]

Cultural Relations

Regular cultural exchanges take place between India and Kuwait. For example, in February, an Indian classical music concert featuring Maestros Kala Ramnath (Violin), Rupak Kulkarni (Flute) and Yogesh Samsi

(Tabla) was organized by the Indian embassy in Kuwait. In May, an exhibition of photographs of *Islamic Monuments of India* by Benoy K. Behl was held and another on *The Travelling Lens* by Shreekant Somany was held in November.[43] Indian embassy in Kuwait, in association with Indian Tourism Ministry, organized *Incredible India* show in June highlighting India's tourism potential and attractions.[44] An MoU in science and technological cooperation was signed between Council of Scientific and Industrial Research and Kuwait Institute for Scientific Research (KISR) in November.[45] Developments of the scientific capability of the two countries were included in the discussions during Kuwait Prime Minister's visit in November. Both wanted the concerned agencies to work in finalizing a cooperation programme in the field of science and technology as well as in agriculture, biotechnology, environment, information and communications technology, and non-conventional energy technologies.[46]

In the field of health, India supplies Kuwait with top specialists along with paramedical staff of high reputation. An MoU has been signed in April 2012 for cooperation in medical and health sector.[47] Both sides wanted Joint Working Group on medical cooperation to train the Kuwaiti doctors in India and choose the right recruiting companies by the Kuwaiti side.[48] In the field of sports and youth affairs, an MoU was signed on bilateral cooperation during the visit of the Kuwaiti Prime Minister.[49] In terms of higher education, an Educational Exchange Programme was signed in November, aimed at strengthening bilateral cooperation. These exchanges should not to be limited to students and researchers but include academicians and specialists from various fields. Moreover, special focus should be given to conducting research seminars in the fields of science and education, exchange of books, publications, audio-visual materials, microfilm and archival resources and other information to assist researchers in their fields of operations.

Migrant Workers

Among the total Kuwaiti population of 2.7 million, migrant workers make up approximately 1.2 million, including more than 600,000 domestic workers.[50] The Indian expatriate community is the largest group, numbering approximately 700,000 according to the Kuwaiti Minister of Interior.[51] The Indian community is regarded as the community of first preferences in Kuwait. A large proportion of them are engaged in unskilled and semi-skilled works. There are also professionals such as engineers, doctors, chartered accountants, scientists, software experts, management consultants, architects and skilled workers, such as technicians and nurses. The number of the highly qualified Indian experts in hi-tech areas, especially in the software and financial sector, is on an increase. The total remittance from Kuwait to India is estimated to be more than US$3 billion annually. The Indian community consists of approximately 300 associations representing different types of regional, professional and cultural interests. Among them, 128 associations are registered with the Indian Embassy.[52] There are 19 Indian schools affiliated to the Central Board of Secondary Education (CBSE) where around 46,000 Indian students are enrolled.[53]

In March, the Kuwaiti government declared its intention to reduce the total number of migrant workers down to one million by annually reducing 100,000 for the next 10 years. To meet that goal, the following month, Kuwait started a policy of deporting migrants who had committed a major traffic violation. By September, according to local human rights organizations, the Ministry of Interior had deported 1,258 expatriates for this reason. In August, the health ministry announced that it would deport any expatriates who suffer from confirmed cases of infectious diseases. In early 2014, Human Rights Watch reported that there have been no deportations under this clause but other categories of deportations were taking place without any judicial review.[54]

Kuwait has also adopted indirect methods to force the departure of migrants. For example, in March, Kuwait adopted a regulation that required expatriates who apply for a driving licence to be 18 or over, pass a driving test, be a legal resident for at least two years, have a university degree, and earn at least KWD400 or US$1,400 per month. There are reports in the local media that in August Kuwaiti authorities evicted expatriate tenants from Kuwaiti citizen's homes. The reason for this action, according to local NGOs, was that those residential buildings rented to expatriates have to be classified as 'investment accommodations'.[55]

Domestic workers in Kuwait suffer most from such laws and their implementations. According to Human Rights Watch, labour issues are on the rise due to *kafala* (sponsorship) system which ties a migrant worker's legal residence to a sponsoring employer. Migrant workers who have worked for their sponsor for less than three years can only transfer with their sponsor's consent (migrant domestic workers always require consent). If a worker leaves their sponsoring employer, including when fleeing due to abuse, the employer must register the worker as absconding and this could lead to detention and deportation.[56] Under these provisions, almost 3,000 Indian workers and at least 11,800 workers in total have been deported from Kuwait during 2013.

The ongoing campaign has affected the Indians particularly as they are the largest community of expatriates in Kuwait and the Indian embassy puts the estimated number of illegal workers at 20,000.[57] The ambassador assured that the Indian citizens were not specifically targeted and asked Kuwaiti authorities to deal with the Indian expatriates with more dignity.[58] However, according to Undersecretary of Ministry of Social Affairs and Labour Jamal al-Dosari, the Kuwait authorities are going to replace the existing sponsorship system with a new project Public Authority for Manpower (PAM). The logistical details of this new project are still being worked out.[59]

External Players

The US: Kuwait always has played a very important role in US interventions in the Persian Gulf since 1980s. Kuwait has the US presence within its territory since the Iran–Iraq war. To meet the regional hostilities Kuwait has always taken help from Washington. Presently, Kuwait is suspicious of the Iranian intentions in spite of maintaining an apparently normal economic and political relation with Iran. However, regarding Iran's increasing power in the region, Kuwait is not taking any direct measures lest they provoke Iran to take military actions. Such regional issues were discussed when Kuwaiti Emir Sabah al-Ahmad al-Jaber al-Sabah met President Barack Obama in Washington on 13 September. The US never took interest in the changing political scenario of Kuwait. This has been reflected in the official statement at the end of the meeting between President Obama and Kuwaiti Emir which did not indicate that any discussion on the political situation of Kuwait took place.[60] During this meeting, the two discussed about Kuwaiti detainees in Guantanamo, securing a fair prosecution, current political changes in Middle East and their repercussions at different levels, particularly the case of Palestine and the situation in Syria.[61]

In the post-Iraq phase, the US has 13,500 troops in Kuwait who are expected to remain there for an indefinite period. Some of these US forces present in Kuwait are combat forces and not exactly support groups, so it can be deduced that the US would be anticipating attack from Iraq or Iran and has taken this path as a preventive measure.[62] Kuwaiti defence has always been supported by the West in general and the US in particular. Its defence requirement will continue to be met by the US.[63] At present, Kuwait plans to procure missile defence equipments towards enhancing gulf security. The Defence Security Cooperation Agency notified a potential sale to Kuwait of one C-17 cargo aircraft and associated equipment which costs US$371 million and technical support to its US-made F-18s which would cost approximately US$150 million.[64]

China: China is emerging as a rapidly growing economy and in the words of Kuwaiti Deputy Prime Minister and Foreign Minister Muhammad Sabah al-Salim al-Sabah, 'it is the "economic dragon" which is likely to be the cornerstone of the global economic growth in the twenty-first century'.[65] Kuwait was the first country among the GCC to establish diplomatic relations with China in 1971. It has consistently adhered to China's policy of 'one China' and never supported the claims of Taiwan. Kuwait is China's eighth largest crude oil supplier and supplies about 4.6 per cent of Chinese oil imports. However, the Kuwait Petroleum Commission seeks to increase its export to China to 500,000 barrels per day by 2015. Kuwait was the first Arab country to invest in China and the first Gulf state to offer soft loans to China.

China's economy has been growing at a very steady rate and to keep pace with this developing economy China's demand for the energy is increasing every day. Gulf countries who are dependent on oil and with huge sovereign wealth fund, such as Kuwait, have been leaning more towards East than West due to the protectionist policies of the US. China being one of the most important economies of Asia, the major share of this sovereign wealth fund is moving out to China.[66] This development of relationship is visible from the increasing trade between China and Kuwait which rose to US$2 billion (12.55 billion Yuan), an increase of 11 per cent from 2012. During the China–Arab states Expo in September,[67] in which Kuwait was the 'Guest of Honour',[68] Kuwait held a China–Kuwait Cooperation Forum of about 200 representatives who discussed cooperation in the field of bilateral trade and investment relations between both the nations.[69]

Pakistan: Relationship between Kuwait and Pakistan had started even before the discovery of oil, and after the oil boom, like other countries of South Asia, Pakistan sent a large number of migrant workers to Kuwait. In spite of facing some troubles in their relations regarding Kuwait's awarding visas to Pakistani nationals during 2011,[70] they are presently enjoying cordiality in terms of diplomatic relations. Both the countries celebrated their 50 years' anniversary of diplomatic relationship on 8 October 2013.[71]

The relationship is focused mainly on trade as Pakistan is one of the biggest buyers of Kuwaiti diesel.[72] During 2013, the first round of Bilateral Political Consultations was held between the two countries. During this event, held on 7 October, both sides agreed on joint cooperation in the field of mutual interests, including promotion of investments, regular holding of Joint Ministerial Commission Meeting and completion of development projects under Kuwait Fund. Emphasis was put on high-level exchanges including parliamentary delegations and private sector visits.[73] Pakistan is also keen on increasing its exports to Kuwait and Lahore Chambers of Commerce and Industry is focussed on Halal food products, textile sector and rice exports to Kuwait.[74]

The political relation received a boost when Prime Minister of Kuwait Jaber al-Mubarak al-Sabah, the first in seven years, visited Pakistan during 10–12 November.[75] During this visit, both sides signed agreements and MoUs in the areas of investment, extradition and labour and visa waivers at the diplomatic and official level.[76] The two sides emphasized on Kuwaiti investments in different sectors of Pakistan. Pakistan's President Mamnoon Hussain invited Kuwaiti investors to access the huge potential of Pakistan in diverse fields including trade and investment, defence, energy, oil and gas.[77]

Challenges and Opportunities

The relationship between Kuwait and India is not free of challenges and problems. The otherwise cordial relationship has been facing problems regarding the migration. The Indian community forms the largest expatriate group in the country. Troubles surrounding the expatriate community can strain the relationship between the two. The most vulnerable section of Indian community are the domestic workers who are not provided security under the Kuwaiti labour laws and often face troubles related to the adverse working conditions, non-payment of salaries, confiscation of their passports, etc. Indians in Kuwait also face problems related to renewal of passports which are kept pending. There were cases where companies failed to provide return airfares to workers on completion of their contracts. Many times, these Indian workers go to Kuwait illegally and sometimes they lack the attestation from the Indian embassy in Kuwait.

Sometimes, the Indian expatriates face problems related to school textbooks published by National Council of Educational Research and Training (NCERT). The NCERT does not have any sole distributer in Kuwait but one company, Sakina International Trading Company, brought out a court injunction preventing other companies or agencies from importing books into Kuwait for the Indian schools.

Another major point of concern is the aggressive policies of Kuwaitization or an attempt to increase the number of Kuwaitis in manual work. This would hamper the future migrants in certain fields of work. However, it is found that most of the Indians are blue-collar workers and Kuwaitization process is taking place in the white-collar sector.[78] Another trouble that the expatriates are confronted with is the suppression of freedom of religion. Freedom of religion is not available to certain sects which are not recognized. For example, Sikhs are not allowed to worship in private homes. They face difficulties in finding landlords who would provide them spaces of worship or finding crematorium.[79] Buddhists and Hindus are not recognized and, hence, can only pray in private homes.[80]

Kuwait is a country of importance for India. The current India–Kuwait bilateral trade is more than India's trade with countries such as Russia and the UK.[81] There has been significant development between the two countries too, as a state visit, which took place during 2013. This high-level political engagement stands for the fact that both the countries are rendering equally substantial amount of attention towards each other. As a result of this development in political relation, the two countries have engaged in several dialogues on trade and investment issues.

There have been troubles in the bilateral trade sector due to the poor quality of products from India's manufacturing sectors and lack of proper advertisements from the Indian side. However, during different meetings and dialogues with Kuwait, India emphasized on its infrastructural development of the productions. From this, a development in the quality of products can be expected. This year the focus of economic discussions was more on increasing cooperation in investment. A joint body was proposed to be formed for directing investment cooperation between the two countries which is a significant improvement because, till now, Kuwaiti investment to India was made indirectly via other countries.

In the bilateral trade, India's negative trade balance with Kuwait is one permanent problem. However, both the countries have discussed about diversifying non-oil trade sector during the state visit on 2013. Domestically, Kuwait is attempting to deviate from its oil dependence and is trying to work on various other projects. Moreover, India asked Kuwait's help in the conclusion of Free Trade Agreement with GCC and if attained, this would help to develop the trade between India and GCC countries.

CONCLUSION

There has been substantial development of relationship between the two countries in 2013. The visit of Kuwaiti premier came at the right time. Trade and business continued to flourish, while efforts at improving relations in other areas, such as two-way flow of investments and defence and security, have become a priority. However, such efforts will come to fruition only if India takes some necessary measures, shows eagerness in developing bilateral relations and follows up on agreements and MoUs. Mere signing of agreements and dialogues will not lead the relations anywhere and it is up to India to make these dialogues mutually beneficial.

NOTES

1. Khizar Niazi, 'Kuwait Looks towards the East: Relations with China', *Policy Brief* (Washington, D.C.), No. 26, 1 September 2009, available at: http://www.mei.edu/content/kuwait-looks-towards-east-relations-china-0/.
2. 'Brief on India–Kuwait Trade and Economic Relation', Embassy of India, Kuwait, available at: http://indembkwt.org/pendind/indokuwaiteconomic.php/.
3. Kenneth Katzman, 'Kuwait: Security, Reform, and US Policies', *Congressional Research Service*, 30 January 2014, available at: http://www.fas.org/sgp/crs/mideast/RS21513.pdf/.
4. Ibid.
5. Human Rights Watch, *World Report 2014: Kuwait*, available at: http://www.hrw.org/world-report/2014/country-chapters/kuwait/.
6. Katzman, 'Kuwait'.
7. 'State of Kuwait', *Election Guide: Democracy Assistance and Electoral News*, 27 July 2013, available at: http://www.electionguide.org/elections/id/1668/.
8. Katzman, 'Kuwait'.
9. 'Kuwait', *US Energy Information Administration (EIA)*, 8 July 2013, available at: http://www.eia.gov/countries/cab.cfm?fips=KU/.
10. 'Brief on India–Kuwait Trade and Economic Relation'.
11. 'Kuwait to Build the First Solar Power Plant', *Kuwait Times*, 30 September 2013, available at: http://news.kuwaittimes.net/kuwait-build-first-solar-power-plant/.
12. 'Kuwait', *EIA*.
13. Ibid.
14. For background of Bidun problem see, Mona Kareem, 'Is Kuwait Serious about Bedoon Naturalization', *Al-Monitor*, 27 March 2013, available at: http://www.al-monitor.com/pulse/originals/2013/03/kuwait-bedoon-naturalization.html#/.
15. *World Report 2014: Kuwait*.
16. Katzman, 'Kuwait'.
17. *World Report 2014: Kuwait*.
18. Ibid.
19. Katzman, 'Kuwait'.
20. Official Religion of Kuwait, *Kuwait Government Online*, available at: http://www.e.gov.kw/sites/kgoenglish/portal/Pages/Visitors/AboutKuwait/CultureAndHeritage_ReligiousPractices.aspx/.
21. 'Kuwait', *International Religious Freedom Report for 2012*, US Department of State, available at: http://www.state.gov/j/drl/rls/irf/2012/nea/208398.htm/.
22. 'Religious Freedom in Kuwait', *Institute on Religion and Public Policy Report*, available at: http://lib.ohchr.org/HRBodies/UPR/Documents/Session8/KW/IRPP_UPR_KUW_S08_2010_InstituteonReligionandPublicPolicy.pdf/.
23. P. R. Kumaraswamy, 'Re-energizing the Gulf Bilateral', *The Indian Express*, 13 June 2006, available at: http://www.indianexpress.com/news/reenergising-the-gulf-bilaterals/6327/.

24. Rajeev Sharma, 'Decoding the Relevance of Kuwaiti PM's Visit to India', *FirstPost*, 10 November 2013, available at: http://www.firstpost.com/world/decoding-the-relevance-of-kuwaiti-pms-visit-to-india-1220773.html/.

25. 'Joint Statement during the State Visit of HH Seikh Jaber Al-Mubakrak Al-Hamad Al-Sabah, Prime Minister of Kuwait to India (November 7–10, 2013)', *Bilateral/Multilateral Documents*, Ministry of External Affairs, New Delhi, 9 November 2013, available at: http://www.mea.gov.in/bilateral-documents.htm?dtl/22464/; 'Kuwait's PM Seikh Jaber to Pay Four-Day Visit to India from November 7', *The Economic Times*, 31 October 2013, available at: http://articles.economictimes.indiatimes.com/2013-10-31/news/43561308_1_kuwaiti-minister-energy-security-trade-and-investment/.

26. 'Documents Signed during the State Visit of HH Seikh Jaber Al-Mubarak Al-Hamad Al-Sabah, Prime Minister of Kuwait to India (November 7–10, 2013)', *Bilateral/Multilateral Documents*, Ministry of External Affairs, New Delhi, 8 November 2013, available at: http://mea.gov.in/bilateral-documents.htm?dtl/22456/.

27. 'Joint Statement during the State Visit of HH Seikh Jaber Al-Mubakrak Al-Hamad Al-Sabah,.

28. Ibid.

29. 'Visit of HE Sheikh Nasser Sabah Al Ahmed Al Jaber Al Sabah, Minister of Al-Diwan Al-Amiri Affairs of the State of Kuwait to India', *Press Release*, Ministry of External Affairs, New Delhi, 13 March 2013, available at: http://mea.gov.in/press-releases.htm?dtl/21373/Visit+of+HE+Sheikh+Nasser+Sabah+Al+Ahmed+Al+Jaber+Al+Sabah+Minster+of+AlDiwan+AlAmi"ri+Affairs+of+the+State+of+Kuwait+to+India/.

30. 'India Seeks Stronger Ties with Kuwait, Peace in Syria', *Business Standard*, 31 January 2013, available at: http://www.business-standard.com/article/pti-stories/india-seeks-stronger-ties-with-kuwait-peace-in-syria-113013100450_1.html.

31. 'Kuwait', Ministry of External Affairs, New Delhi, 15 January 2014, available at: http://www.mea.gov.in/Portal/ForeignRelation/Kuwait_January_2014.pdf/.

32. 'Joint Statement during the State Visit of HH Seikh Jaber Al-Mubakrak Al-Hamad Al-Sabah.

33. 'Kuwait', Ministry of External Affairs.

34. 'India Seeks Kuwait's Support for GCC Free Trade Agreement', *Business Standard*, 8 November 2013, available at: http://www.business-standard.com/article/news-ians/india-seeks-kuwait-s-support-for-gcc-free-trade-agreement-113110800972_1.html.

35. 'Joint Statement during the State Visit of HH Seikh Jaber Al-Mubakrak Al-Hamad Al-Sabah.

36. 'India, Kuwait to Take Relationship beyond Buyer–Seller Partnership', *The Hindu*, 9 November 2013, available at: http://www.thehindu.com/news/national/india-kuwait-to-take-relationship-beyond-buyerseller-partnership/article5330790.ece/.

37. 'Visit of Dr. Montek Singh Ahluwalia to Kuwait', *Press Release*, Embassy of India, Kuwait, 7 July 2013, available at: http://www.indembkwt.org/DispNews.aspx?ID=259/.

38. 'FICCI Delegation Explore Business Opportunities in Kuwait', *The Economic Times*, 31 October 2013, available at: http://articles.economictimes.india-times.com/2013-10-31/news/43561453_1_business-delegation-ficci-kcci/.

39. 'Kuwait and India Discuss Joint Petroleum Projects', *Arab Times*, 13 September 2013, available at: http://www.arabtimesonline.com/NewsDetails/tabid/96/smid/414/ArticleID/199749/reftab/96/t/Kuwait—India-discuss-joint-petroleum-projects/Default.aspx/.

40. Ibid.

41. 'Joint Statement during the State Visit of HH Seikh Jaber Al-Mubakrak Al-Hamad Al-Sabah.

42. 'Indian Naval Ships Visit to Kuwait', *Press Release*, Embassy of India, Kuwait, 9 September 2013, available at: http://www.indembkwt.org/DispNews.aspx?ID=267/.

43. 'Kuwait', Ministry of External Affairs.

44. 'Indian Tourism Promotion Event Held in Kuwait', *Business Standard*, 13 June 2013, available at: http://www.business-standard.com/article/pti-stories/india-tourism-promotion-event-held-in-kuwait-113061300480_1.html/.

45. 'Kuwait', Ministry of External Affairs.

46. 'Joint Statement during the State Visit of HH Seikh Jaber Al-Mubakrak Al-Hamad Al-Sabah.

47. 'India Kuwait Relations', *Indo-Kuwait Friendship Society*, available at: http://www.indo-kuwaitfriendshipsociety.com/india_kuwait_relations.html/.

48. 'Joint Statement during the State Visit of HH Seikh Jaber Al-Mubakrak Al-Hamad Al-Sabah.

49. 'Documents Signed during the State Visit of HH Seikh Jaber Al-Mubarak Al-Hamad Al-Sabah.

50. *World Report 2014: Kuwait*.

51. Cited by Indo-Kuwait Friendship Society, available at: http://www.indo-kuwaitfriendshipsociety.com/india_kuwait_relations.html/.

52. 'India Kuwait Relations', *Indo-Kuwait Friendship Society*.

53. Ibid.

54. *World Report 2014: Kuwait*.

55. Ibid.

56. Ibid.

57. 'Indian Official Voices Concern over Kuwait Deportations', *arabianbusiness.com*, 11 June 2013, available at: http://www.arabianbusiness.com/indian-official-voices-concern-over-kuwait-deportations-504737.html/.

58. Ibid.

59. 'Kuwait to Scrap Sponsorship System for Foreign Workers', *The Hindu*, 24 September 2013, available at: http://www.thehindu.com/todays-paper/

tp-national/kuwait-to-scrap-sponsorship-system-for-foreign-workers/article5162492.ece/.
60. Katzman, 'Kuwait'.
61. 'Amir Briefs Cabinet on Visit to US-Praise for "Positive" Political Relationship', *Kuwait Times*, available at: http://news.kuwaittimes.net/amir-briefs-cabinet-visit-us-praise-positive-political-relationship/.
62. Katzman, 'Kuwait'.
63. Niazi, 'Kuwait Looks towards the East'.
64. Katzman, 'Kuwait'.
65. Niazi, 'Kuwait Looks towards the East'.
66. Ibid.
67. 'China, Kuwait Looking for Expanding Cooperation', *Xinhuanet.com*, 18 November 2013, available at: http://news.xinhuanet.com/english/china/2013-11/18/c_132897082.htm/.
68. Nasser Al-Otaibi, 'China–Kuwait Economic Cooperation Forum Kicks off NW China', *Kuwait News Agency*, 16 September 2013, available at: http://www.kuna.net.kw/ArticleDetails.aspx?id=2333929&language=en/.
69. 'China, Kuwait Looking For Expanding Cooperation', *Xinhuanet.com*.
70. Andy Sambidge, 'Kuwait Mulls Lifting Ban on Pakistani Visas', *arabianbusiness.com*, 12 January 2013, available at: http://www.arabianbusiness.com/kuwait-mulls-lifting-ban-on-pakistani-visas-485352.html/.
71. 'Pakistan Kuwait Hold 1st Round of Political Consultations', *Kuwait News Agency*, 9 October 2013, available at: http://www.kuna.net.kw/ArticleDetails.aspx?id=2338118&language=en/.
72. 'Pakistan Has "Close and Cordial Relations" with Kuwait, Says Ambassador', *Kuwait News Agency*, 9 November 2013, available at: http://www.kuna.net.kw/ArticleDetails.aspx?id=2343182&language=en/.
73. 'Pakistan, Kuwait to Boost Cooperation in Different Fields', *The Nation (Pakistan)*, 9 October 2013, available at: http://www.nation.com.pk/business/09-Oct-2013/pakistan-kuwait-to-boost-cooperation-in-different-fields/.
74. 'Kuwait Is Potential State for Pakistan Exports', *Dawn.com (Pakistan)*, 28 March 2013, available at: http://www.dawn.com/news/798572/kuwait-is-potential-state-for-pakistan-exports/.
75. Masroor Ahmed Khan, 'PM Kuwait Visits Pakistan', *The News Tribe*, 11 November 2013, available at: http://www.thenewstribe.com/2013/11/11/pm-kuwait-visits-pakistan/.
76. Shoaib A. Raja, 'Pakistan, Kuwait Inks Four Agreements to Boost Ties', *The News International (Pakistan)*, 12 November 2013, available at: http://www.thenews.com.pk/Todays-News-13-26604-Pakistan-Kuwait-ink-four-agreements-to-boost-ties/.
77. 'President Urges for Concerted Steps to Promote Pakistan–Kuwait Ties', *Associated Press of Pakistan*, 10 November 2013, available at: http://www.app.com.pk/en_/index.php?option=com_content&task=view&id=248767/.

78. 'Kuwait', The Ministry of Overseas Indian Affairs, New Delhi, 2 August 1990, available at: http://moia.gov.in/pdf/kuwait.pdf/.
79. Religious Freedom in Kuwait, *Institute on Religion and Public Policy Report*.
80. Ibid.
81. Sharma, 'Decoding the Relevance of Kuwaiti PM's Visit to India'.

6

Oman

Marimuthu Ulaganathan

Key Information

Area: 309,500 sq km; **Population:** 3,219,775 (2014 est.); **Native:** less than 70 per cent; **Expats:** more than 30 per cent; **Youth:** 19.9 per cent; **Population growth rate:** 2.06 per cent; **Life expectancy at birth:** 74.97 years; **Major population groups:** Arabs, Baluchi, South Asian and African (distribution not available); **Religious groups:** Ibadhi Muslims 75 per cent, others 25 per cent; **GDP:** US$94.86 billion; **Per capita income:** US$29,800; **Foreign trade:** US$86.97 billion; **Oil reserves:** 4.902 billion bbl (2013); **Gas reserves:** 849.5 billion m³; **Ruling family:** al-Said; **Ruler:** Sultan Qaboos bin Said al-Said (since 23 July 1970); **Crown Prince:** not nominated, **National Day:** 18 November; **Defence budget:** 11.4 per cent of GDP; **HDI rank:** 84; **Literacy rate:** 81.4 per cent; **UN education index:** 0.576; **Gender inequality index:** 0.340; **Labour force:** 968,800; **Unemployment rate:** 15 per cent; **External debt:** US$10.84 billion (December 2013); **Sovereign wealth fund:** US$14.2 billion; **Infant mortality rate:** 14 deaths out of 1,000; **Last national census:** 2010; **Parliament:** 71-member nominated Upper House, 84-member elected Majlis al-Shura; **Last parliament election:** 15 October 2011; **Number of Indians:** 500,000; **Last Indian prime minister to visit:** Manmohan Singh, November 2008.

Sources: CIA, *The World Factbook*, available at: https://www.cia.gov/library/publications/the-world-factbook/; *UN Human Development Report*, Statistics, available at: http://hdr.undp.org/en/statistics/; United States Commission on Religious Freedom, US Department of State; *Annual Report 2013; Briefs on Foreign Relations*, Ministry of External Affairs, Government of India and Centre for Arms Control and Proliferation (Washington, D.C.).
Note: All figures for 2013.

Oman, an important country in the Gulf, has diligently protected its independent foreign policy that was again displayed during 2013 when it refused the Saudi proposal for a Gulf union. Unlike other Gulf Cooperation Council (GCC) constituents, it has pursued relations with Iran and is reported to have facilitated Iranian talks with Western powers over its nuclear programme. On the domestic front, Sultan Qaboos has remained in control despite sporadic disturbances that have continued since the outbreak of Arab Spring in 2011. In order to deal with the situation, the ruler has tried to find solutions for the economic hardships through diversification efforts as hydrocarbon reserves continue to diminish. As far as India–Oman relations are concerned, 2013 proved to be a good year for bilateral trade but India seems to have failed in making up for the problem that led to cancellation of Sultan Qaboos's visit as chief guest for 2013 Republic Day parade.

DOMESTIC DEVELOPMENTS

Oman's strategic location in the trade route between East and West has helped it maintain its maritime power since the sixth century when Arab traders made a base in Muscat. Although it remained in touch with outside world due to maritime trade, Oman has preserved a strong sense of tradition and culture. The present ruling al-Said dynasty was founded in 1774, and during the colonial period it was briefly governed as a British protectorate. The current ruler Sultan Qaboos bin Said succeeded his father in 1970 and began building the sultanate with the help of oil-wealth. Skilfully using limited oil resources Sultan showed himself as a benevolent ruler domestically and a skilful diplomat externally.[1]

The dominant political culture is to respect the tribal patrimonial leadership and there is a general acceptance of the Sultan's rule. Even the demonstrations during January–May 2011 over political, economic and social issues in major cities such as in Sohar, Muscat and Salalah asserted their loyalty to the Sultan and were directed against the high officials. In 2012, the Sultanate held its first ever municipal elections that witnessed over 1,600 candidates for the 192 available seats. Forty-eight women were also in the fray, of which four were elected.[2]

However, Oman's problems continued in 2013; in February around 50 activists including journalist and bloggers went on a hunger strike to get attention of their incarceration and to persuade the Omani Supreme Court to hear their appeal.[3] They were arrested on the charges of defaming the Sultan and violating Oman's cyber laws. Subsequently, in an effort towards reconciliation, the Sultan pardoned 35 of them and they were released on 21 March.[4] The act was seen as a positive step towards gradual political change as outlined in the Basic Law of 1996. The demonstrators of Sohar protest who went on hunger strike were also pardoned by Sultan Qaboos in July and were reinstated in their previous jobs, whether in public or private sectors.[5] Sporadic labour unrest was noticed during 2013. Small strikes were held by oil sector workers and employees in Muscat's new international airport. Strikingly, both Omani nationals and expatriates participated in these strikes.[6] In response, the government decided to limit the number of foreign workers and announced a sharp rise in wages for Omani citizens.

In an important development in April, a member of Shura council tabled a motion to amend the state laws to give nationality rights to children born to non-Omani father but Omani mother. Presently, Omani nationality can only pass through Omani father. The 84-member Shura council is yet to adopt the bill[7] but a discussion over recognizing their citizenship rights is indeed an indication of changing attitude towards women. The UN Human Development Report 2013 ranked Oman at 59 out of 148 countries in the gender inequality index. Female participation in the workforce has improved over the years and 28.3 per cent of women were in the workforce as of 2013.[8] Although it is remarkably low in comparison to male proportion that stands at 81.6 per cent, it is better than neighbouring monarchies. The proportion of women in the parliament has gradually improved and currently stands at 9.6 per cent.[9] Moreover, health and sanitation facilities for women have improved over time; for example, maternal mortality rate has declined to 32.

Oman presently gives high priority to education and the need to diversify its economy to employ educated Omani youths. In 1986, the country's first university, Sultan Qaboos University was opened. It has continued to expand, recently added a law college, and remains the country's only major public university. Recently, the Omani government constructed about 25 public post-secondary education institutions, technical colleges, teacher training colleges, and health institutes. To encourage Omani students to pursue higher studies in the US, Europe, Australia, Japan and Singapore, the Sultanate announced a new programme to provide 1,000 scholarships over the next five years.[10]

While maintaining political control at home, the ruling dispensation has continued to follow an independent foreign policy. The matter over the proposed Gulf union came to a head when Oman turned down the suggestion, which made other Gulf states, especially Saudi Arabia and Qatar, furious. During a meeting of the GCC in Kuwait on 7 December, Omani Foreign Minister Yusuf bin Alawi bin Abdullah said that: 'We will not prevent the Union but, we will not be part of the new body.'[11] Importantly, Oman has maintained good relations with Iran, and hence it does not want to upset the larger neighbour at the cost of joining an uncertain union. In August Sultan Qaboos undertook a much awaited visit to Iran. He is the only Arab leader to maintain good understanding and personal relations with the Iranian regime. The visit focused on economic and diplomatic issues. Oman has reportedly facilitated the negotiations between the West and Iran over its nuclear programme through a secret channel that culminated in the Geneva nuclear deal concluded in November.[12] In the past, Oman has often acted as an intermediary between Western countries and Iran, especially in resolving the issue of kidnapped US citizens.[13]

Oman is middle-level oil power as compared to other oil-rich countries of the Middle East. The oil revenue is the mainstay of income and a major part of GDP. Oman's oil reserves have been depleting fast compared to other GCC states and hence, the government has been seeking economic diversification by encouraging agriculture, tourism, and gas sector and other non-oil industries. Oman vigorously promotes the private sector to play a role in the country's growth.[14] It is increasingly becoming difficult for the government to provide jobs to its citizens and privatization is seen as an alternative. Oman wants to transform itself as a trading hub, asserting that ships that offload at its Salalah port pay lower insurance rates than other Gulf cities like Dubai, and Abu Dhabi and Bahrain.[15]

In 2013 the budget rose to US$33.5 billion and the major portion of spending went to education, health, housing and social welfare.[16] Due to 2011 protests, the GCC pledged to provide US$1 billion annual aid from 2013 for the next 10 years to promote infrastructure development such as Oman–GCC railway project.[17] In 2013, Oman declared that in promoting small and medium enterprises (SMEs), Omani nationals' entry would be promoted and that not more than 33 per cent expatriates would be allowed to work in such enterprises. The government also increased Omani nationals' salary by 62 per cent from July due to workers protests. The government has asked private sector to cut down on unnecessary expatriate work force.[18]

The Fifth Five-year Plan had aimed for a national expenditure in research and development in the public and private sectors to 1 per cent of GDP for 2011–15. But this goal appears extremely difficult after the Arab Spring and the resultant spending priorities.[19] According to *Vision 2020*, the government would boost measures of diversification into service, industrial and financial sectors. Advancing new industries and increasing downstream oil operations such as petrochemicals have been a cornerstone of Oman's aim to cut excessive dependence upon hydrocarbon exports. It is also expected to generate new jobs.[20] The government earmarked investments of up to US$15 billion in new petrochemical and infrastructure projects at the Salalah port over the next 10 years. Oman expects to boost growth and employment through the 1,000 km long, US$13 billion railway network across the country. It is also investing heavily in the airport and port operations in the southern city of Salalah near the border with Yemen. These projects are part of a plan to provide the private sector a larger role in the economic diversification and minimise dependence on oil production that accounts for 77 per cent of government incomes and half of the economic output.

New railway system in the Sultanate of Oman along with other GCC states is under way. Rail network inside Oman will extend approximately over 2,244 km over nine divisions between Oman and United Arab Emirates (UAE) border in the north to Yemen in the south. The specialization of track system is non-electrified and is a continuous welded rail system. The track will be used for both freight and passenger travel throughout the Sultanate.[21] Moreover, as part of economic diversification the government plans to expand its mining industry including copper, chromites, limestone and non-metallic items, marble, etc. The new Omani mining law came into force in 2013 and many domestic and international companies are keen to invest in this sector.[22] In Al-Wustah region, a new dry dock has been built at a cost of US$1.5 billion, and this dock is considered to be the second biggest after Dubai.[23] This can challenge Dubai's dominance in being trading and transporting hub in the region as a large number of ships plying from Asia to Europe hug Oman's coast en route to the Suez Canal.

Despite efforts to diversify its economy, oil exports produce about 60 per cent of government incomes. According to SHELL and Royal Dutch Omani oil reserves stand at 5.5 billion barrels and are depleting and would last only for the next 15 years.[24] Oman now considers exploring natural gas fields in the interior desert region. Principal area of extraction is called as Khazzan and is likely to be as deep as 4,500 meters.[25] In addition, Oman has tried to maximize the utilization of its hydrocarbon reserves. The recently introduced, Enhanced Oil Recovery (ECR) techniques have been instrumental in increasing the oil production after 2008. Oman is considered a pioneer in this technique which ensures steady rise of oil output and helps insulate the effects of decline in the global oil prices.[26] Oman's total oil supply in 2012 was 924,000 barrels and in 2013 oil production rose slightly to 957,000 barrels per day. The value of oil trade in 2013 was US$23.5 billion which is around 80 per cent of its GDP.[27] Oman is the fifth largest dry natural gas producer in the Middle East and 26th worldwide. The Sultanate has been using majority of its natural gas for producing electricity at home but it also exports some. Oman's natural gas export value stood at US$3.9 billion in 2013.

BILATERAL RELATIONS

India's relations with Oman can be traced back to the time of Indus Valley Civilization.[28] The ties continued to flourish during the British period and grew further after Sultan Qaboos came to power in 1970.[29] India and Oman have similar views on a number of international issues. Oman has been supportive of India's stance on the Kashmir issue, arguing in favour of resolving the conflict through bilateral negotiations. Cooperation at multilateral forums such as the Indian Ocean Rim Association for Regional Cooperation (IOR-ARC) has further boosted bilateral relations.

Political and Defence Relations

India and Oman have signed many agreements including those for combating crime, cooperation in agriculture and civil aviation sectors, and cooperation between the State Audit Institution of Oman and the Comptroller and Auditor General of India. Moreover, it has agreements on Avoidance of Double Taxation, Bilateral Investment Promotion and Protection, Treaty of Extradition, memorandum of understanding (MoU) on Manpower, MoU on Joint Investment Fund and MoU on Cultural Cooperation.[30] The 2008 visit of Prime Minister Manmohan Singh gave a boost to bilateral ties between India and Oman. However, India awaits the visit of Sultan Qaboos Bin Said al-Said to receive the Jawaharlal Nehru Award for International Understanding awarded to him for his contribution to peace in the region.

Despite some issues, political relations have remained smooth. The ninth and 10th India–Oman Strategic Consultative Group (IOSCG) Meetings were held at Muscat and New Delhi in 2012 and 2013, respectively. This secretary-level meet which began in 2003 provides a forum for open and frank exchange of views on bilateral, regional and international issues.[31] India sent many public and private missions to Oman during 2013. These began with a visit by the Minister of State for External Affairs E. Ahamed in March. This was followed by visits by Minister of State for Consumer Affairs, Food and Public Distribution, K. V. Thomas in September. In October, Deputy National Security Adviser Nehchal Sandhu visited Oman and held meetings with his counterpart the Secretary General of the National Security Council of Oman as well as with Omani Minister of Royal Office, Minister Responsible for Foreign Affairs, Inspector-General of Police & Customs; and the Chief of Staff of the Armed Forces.[32]

Moreover, business and political visits from Oman continued. A delegation led by the head of the Public Authority for Investment Promotion of Export Development (PAIPED) Salem Nasser al-Ismaily visited India in December. An eleven-member Shura Council delegation headed by Abdulla Salim Nasser al-Kakhani visited India on 27–28 February 2014 and interacted with the members of Lok Shaba and Rajya Sabha. Apart from these two big delegations, many business groups visited India throughout the year. India has yet to sort out the issue that led to the cancellation of Qaboos's visit for Republic Day in 2013. It is important that an affable solution is found to facilitate his visit at the earliest, given India's interest in the country and the region.

Defence has been an important area of cooperation between India and Oman. Chief of the Naval Staff Admiral Devendra Kumar Joshi visited Oman in April and held discussions with senior Defence Officials and toured many units of the Royal Navy of Oman. He also delivered a speech at the Command and Staff College, Bait Al Falaj.[33] The Biennial Indian Navy-Royal of Oman exercise has been conducted since 1993 under the title of *Naseem Al Bahr*. The ninth edition of training held on 25 September 2013 in the Northern Arabian Sea celebrated 20 years of joint exercise between the two navies. The exercise was aimed at deriving mutual benefit from the experiences of both the navies and the scope and content of exercise have also increased progressively. The focus of the exercise in 2013 was on surface warfare, anti-air warfare, air operation, advanced helo operations and maritime interdiction operations. From the Indian side *INS Mysore* (guided missile destroyer), *INS Tarkash* and *INS Tabar* (stealth frigates) and *Aditya* (fleet tanker) took part under the Command of the Flag Officer Commanding Western Fleet, Rear Admiral Anil Kumar Chawla.[34] The Royal Omani Navy was represented by Royal Navy of Oman Vessels (RNOV) missile and gun vessels, *Al Muazzar*, *Al Mussandam*, *Al Naja* and a Landing ship RNOV *Temsah*, along with Royal Air Force of Oman aircraft F-16, Hawks and Jaguars, amongst others.[35]

From strategic point of view Oman can be a great interlocutor to Indian defence in maritime trade and naval forces. Due to India's dependence on imported oil from the Gulf region, it is imperative to maintain a strong naval presence in the region to save Indian merchant vessels from sea-piracy, and Oman port can be a middle point to monitor transportation in the Arabian Sea.

Economic Relations

A number of institutional mechanisms like Joint Commission Meeting (JCM) and Joint Business Council (JBC) have been set up to oversee economic cooperation between India and Oman. During the past four years, India–Oman bilateral trade has hovered around US$4.5 billion (see Table 6.1 and Figure 6.1). Exports to Oman have witnessed a sustained growth and in 2012–13 trade balance tilted in India's favour with a 96.61 per cent growth. However, imports from Oman saw a sudden

Table 6.1

India–Oman Bilateral Trade (in US$ Million)

	2009–10	2010–11	2011–12	2012–13
India's exports to Oman	1,032.93	1,086.48	1,322.13	2,599.49
India's imports from Oman	3,499.89	4,002.07	3,345.94	2,009.72
Total bilateral trade	4,532.82	5,088.55	4,668.08	4,609.21
Share of Oman in total trade	0.97	0.82	0.59	0.58

Source: Adapted from Directorate General of Foreign Trade, New Delhi, available at: www.dgft.gov.in/.

Figure 6.1

India–Oman Bilateral Trade

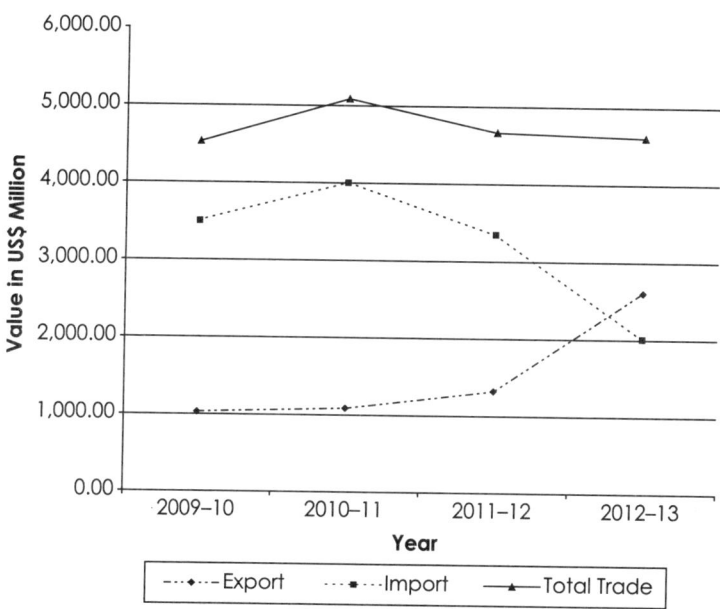

Source: Adapted from Directorate General of Foreign Trade, New Delhi, available at: www.dgft.gov.in/.

decline of 40 per cent during 2012–13 owing mainly to decline in oil imports (see Table 6.2 and Figure 6.2). Overall trade also witnessed a decline of US$600 million and Oman's share in India's total trade stood at 0.58 per cent during 2012–13 (see Table 6.1 and Figure 6.1).

Table 6.2
Share of Oil in India's Imports from Oman (in US$ Million)

Year	Oil imports from Oman	Total oil imports	Omani share in total oil imports	Imports from Oman	Per cent of oil in imports from Oman
2009–10	2,904.41	96,321.12	3.02	3,499.89	82.99
2010–11	3,293.14	115,929.02	2.84	4,002.07	82.29
2011–12	2,083.84	172,753.92	1.21	3,345.94	62.28
2012–13	507.88	181,344.67	0.28	2,009.72	25.27

Source: Adapted from Directorate General of Foreign Trade, New Delhi, available at: www.dgft.gov.in/.

Figure 6.2
Share of Oil in India's Imports from Oman

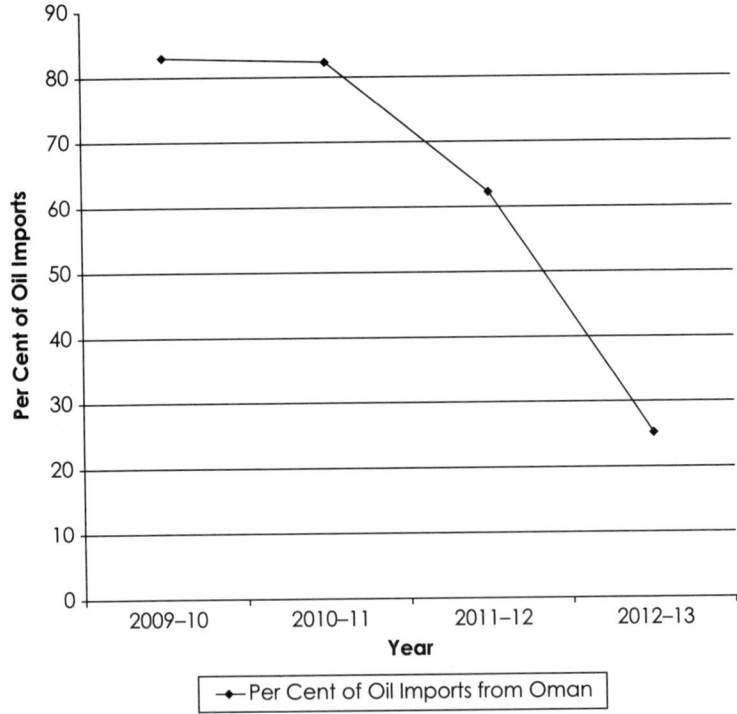

Source: Adapted from Directorate General of Foreign Trade, New Delhi, available at: www.dgft.gov.in/.

A number of Indian companies have established businesses in Oman through joint ventures. The total number of joint ventures in Oman is 1,517 with an overall value of US$7.5 billion including US$4.5 billion Indian investment.[36] The first India–Oman joint venture is the US$969 million, Oman India Fertilizer Company (OMIFCO); India's largest joint venture abroad began in August 2002 at Sur and was inaugurated on 28 January 2006.[37] Other joint ventures include Bharat Oman Refineries Limited (BORL) that has set up a 6 million metric tonnes per annum (MMTPA) low-cost refinery at Bina in Sagar district of Madhya Pradesh at the cost of US$2.4 billion and was formally launched in May 2011.[38]

Jindal Steel and Power Ltd. (JSPL) was the first Indian private company to enter Oman when it acquired the Oman-based Shadeed Iron and Steel Co. for US$464 million in May 2010 and has been operating a 1.5 million tonnes per annum (MTPA) gas-based hot briquetted iron plant at Sohar Industrial port area of Oman since October. Another Indian multi-national Company Larsen & Toubro (L&T) has established four mega joint ventures: L&T Oman, L&T Electromac, L&T Modular Fabrication Yard and L&T Heavy Engineering in Oman. The L&T has a strong presence in Oman's heavy industries sector and contributes significantly to the Omani economy. It recently won the US$3.55 million bid for completion of Phase-4 of the proposed Batinah Expressway project. It also got a contract for procurement and construction worth about US$235 million from Petroleum Development Oman (PDO). L&T also bagged an Engineering, Procurement and Construction (EPC) contract worth US$72 million from Oman Electricity Transmission Co. (OETC) for the construction of two 132/33 KV grid stations in Amerat and Mabella, along with the installation of 132 KV overhead lines and cables in Muscat.[39]

Indian business presence has increased tremendously in recent years. A number of small and big Indian companies have started businesses in Oman. Indian financial institutions such as Bank of Baroda (since 1975), State Bank of India (since 2004), New India Assurance Company, Life Insurance Corporation, ICICI Bank and HDFC Bank have a strong presence in Oman. In April, a leading Indian travel company, a division of Akbar Group, opened its fourth branch at a prominent business location in Muscat.[40] Likewise, the contract for 43-kilometre Batinah Expressway was won by India's Simplex Infrastructure with capital expenditure of US$291 million. Oman's first ferrochrome production has started at the Sohar Free Zone. This project is a 50:50 joint venture between Muscat Overseas Group and India's Indsil Group. The joint company has already invested US$35 million in the first phase of development to spur production at 6,000 tonnes per month as of mid-2013. Moreover, India–Oman Joint Investment Fund (IOJIF) has acquired a 4.7 per cent stake in India's agri–commodity exchange, the National Commodity and Derivatives Exchange (NCDEX), by brokerage firm Jaypee Capital Services Ltd. After this acquisition, IOJIF owns 2.38 million of NCDEX's 50.68 million shares.[41] Indian Telecom Company bagged US$5.5 million worth projects from Omantel.[42]

Indian ventures have actively participated and organized business and trade expo in Muscat leading to promotion of India–Oman trade. From 31 January to 1 February HDFC organized the Indian Property Show 2013 in partnership with Oman International Trade and Exhibition (OITE).[43] In June another property Expo was organized by The Times of India and Arabian Gate Expo and had participation from Malaysia, Kuwait, UAE, Bahrain as well as India.[44] A number of Indian companies from construction and infrastructure sector participated in Infra Oman exhibition at Oman International Exhibition Centre held in September-October.

Government agencies have also pursued bilateral engagements giving impetus to trade and business ties. The IOJIF was signed in New Delhi in July 2010 and started its operations from February 2011 with a corpus of US$100 million. In 2013 it was decided that fund would be raised to US$1.5 billion. In March, Indian Embassy arranged a seminar, under the title of 'India Business Seminar', to promote bilateral commercial relations and showcase attractive investment sectors.[45] On 24 June, India sent a two-member delegation from Ministry of Finance for talks on the revision of the Double Taxation Avoidance Agreement with their Omani counterpart.[46]

Similarly, many Omani delegations visited India during 2013 indicating towards growing interests in bilateral trade. In May, chairman of the Public Authority for Investment Promotion and Export Development (PAIPED) led an Omani business group and met with the top business leaders in India for drawing further investments in Oman. Another Omani delegation from Sohar Free Zone came to India to meet potential

investors for a US$250 million project. A three member business delega-
tion from Omani Ministry of Commerce and Industry visited India in
September, to explore the business opportunities available for dry dates
in Indian market.[47] Another Omani official delegation visited in October
to certify the poultry production units in India and inspected those poultry for export to Oman.

On the invitation of Omani Chamber of Commerce and Industry
(OCCI), Confederation of Indian Industries (Southern Region) visited
Oman to participate in the Med-Health and Wellness Exhibition
2013 and to explore business opportunities and investment options.
A 22-member delegation visited Oman from 23 to 25 September.[48]
Air travel between India and Oman increased in 2013; IndiGo started
daily flight from Muscat to Mumbai and Spice-jet started operating the
Muscat–Ahmadabad route.[49]

Energy Relations

India–Oman trade and commerce in energy is limited; energy imports
from Oman during 2012–13 witnessed a sharp decline of 76 per cent
(Table 6.3). Oman's share in India's total energy imports declined to
0.28 per cent, while its share among Persian Gulf countries stood at 0.48
per cent. Notwithstanding the decline in oil imports, trade and commerce in petrochemical sector has witnessed growth in recent years and
Oman's bid to diversify its economy provides an opportunity for Indian
oil and petrochemical companies to invest in the Omani market.

Cultural Relations

Cultural relations revolve around the Indian community that constitute
the largest expatriate community in Oman. Indian music and films are
popular among expatriates as well as among native population. Many
Indians occupy key positions in the government and private sectors. A
large number of Indian doctors, approximately 2,000, are working in
Oman. About 30 are working in Sultan Qaboos University as faculty.
Moreover, there are a large number of Indians working as engineers,
charted accountants, nurses, managers and in other white-collared positions.[50] There are 19 Indian schools across Oman that mainly cater to

Table 6.3
India's Energy Imports from Oman (in US$ Million)

	2009–10	2010–11	2011–12	2012–13
India's energy imports from Oman	2,904.41	3,293.14	2,083.84	507.88
India's total energy imports	96,321.12	115,929.02	172,753.92	181,344.67
Total energy imports from the Persian Gulf	55,904.14	66,688.40	105,056.26	105,859.15
Share in total energy imports (in per cent)	3.02	2.84	1.21	0.28
Share in energy imports from Persian Gulf (in per cent)	5.20	4.94	1.98	0.48

Source: Adapted from Directorate General of Foreign Trade, New Delhi, available at: www.dgft.gov.in/.

the educational needs of more than 40,000 Indian children and follow CBSE curriculum. In 2013, Bhartiya Vidya Bhavan International School was inaugurated by Ambassador J. S. Mukul in Muscat.

India also provides scholarship to Omani students for higher studies, who mainly come to pursue science and technology education. Presently, the number of scholarships offered to Omani student has gone from 50 to 125.[51] Moreover, the Indian embassy in Muscat organizes cultural events to promote awareness about Indian culture and heritage and to attract tourists and students. In February, Indian Embassy organized *Indian Technical and Economic Cooperation Day*, with an impressive turnout of about 250 alumni from Oman. In the same month, young *Bharat Natyam* dancers from Sridevi Nrithyalaya, Chennai, visited Oman and participated in the *Muscat International Folklore Festival*. On 31 December, India sent a two-member committee from Ministry of Culture and the officiating Director-General of the National Archives of India. This committee discussed with the National Records and Archives Authority of Oman to enhance the mutual assistance in the field of archives.

External Powers

The US: Oman is strategically located in the Strait of Hormuz and the Indian Ocean and plays a role in maritime security and fighting piracy. Oman has strong relations with the US, based on Gulf security-oriented alliance. Protests in Oman during 2011–12 and the official response did not change the attitude of the Obama administration towards Oman. Every year Oman sends about 500 students to study in the US through its Middle East Peace Initiative Scholarship programme.[52] The Omani police gets assistance and training from the US security force to enhance security capabilities at the maritime and land borders. To prevent illegal entry from Yemen, the US has been providing weapons since 2008. In May, Oman announced its plans to procure US-made Thermal High Altitude Area Defence (THAAD), a sophisticated missile defence system at the cost of US$2.1 billion. Secretary of State John Kerry visited Oman to help finalize the deal.[53] In the same visit, Kerry reportedly held a meeting with Sultan Qaboos requesting Omani help in securing the freedom of ex-Marine Amir Hekmati, a dual citizen jailed in Iran in August 2011, and retired FBI agent Robert Levinson, who went missing in Iran in 2006.[54] An Iranian national Mojtaba Atarodi, Assistant Professor of electrical engineering at Sharif University of Technology, who had been detained in California on 7 December 2011 for allegedly buying high-tech US laboratory equipments, was finally released on 27 April, reportedly on humanitarian grounds.[55]

The Geneva nuclear deal was largely possible due to Qaboos's ability to negotiate with Iranian leadership. Earlier he had secured the freedom of US hikers in late 2010 and 2011. Secret informal discussions between middle-level US and Iranian officials began at the start of 2013.[56] Reports indicated that US officials, including Deputy Secretary of State William Burns, have been visiting Oman since early 2013 well before the moderate Hassan Rouhani was elected Iranian president in June, to explore the possibility of renewed relations and a nuclear settlement.[57] These talks which gained momentum after Rouhani took office in August coupled with Sultan Qaboos's visit to Iran, helped pave the way for US–Iran diplomatic overtures in September. On 24 November, an interim nuclear deal was signed between Iran and the P5+1.[58]

China: In January, Chinese Vice Foreign Minister Zhai Jun and Secretary General of Omani Foreign Ministry Sayyid Badr bin Hamad bin Hamoud al-Busaidi held the seventh round of strategic consultations in Muscat. The two countries exchanged views on bilateral relations and international and regional problems of common concern. The Chinese deputy foreign minister said that 'the relationship between China and Oman has maintained the momentum of rapid development in recent years with deepening mutual political trust, fruitful pragmatic cooperation, and close cultural and educational exchanges.'[59] China is ready to further friendly relations with Oman and continue to expand areas of cooperation in order to promote the bilateral relationship to a new level.

An OCCI delegation visited China and attended the China Arab States Economic and Trade Forum in Yinchuan city in September. From China three leading companies Ningxia Qinlong Pipes Industry Co Ltd, SANY Heavy Industry and Bright Oceans Corporation are looking at Oman as a prospective venture place for pipe manufacturing, construction of machinery production, energy and mining.[60] This delegation was accompanied by Omani–Chinese Friendship Society in China.[61] The OCCI delegation deemed that modern technologies can be used to develop and upgrade the quality of production and services in Oman's private sector, particularly small and medium-sized enterprises that enjoy more attention and progress in the Sultanate.

Oman has issued a commemorative stamp celebrating Oman–China relations prized at 200 baiza, which are now available at all post offices in Oman.[62] The commemorative stamp showcases Qasrul al Alam, the ceremonial palace of His Majesty Sultan Qaboos bin Said and Tiananmen Square, the large city square in the centre of Beijing. Oman plans to further boost external investments with the help of China by another 17 per cent by the end of 2014.

Pakistan: Pakistan and Oman share historical relations and use the Arabian Sea for their maritime trade. The ethnic Baloch community in Oman migrated from Sindh and Gwader provinces of Pakistan. The Gwader province was earlier under the control of Oman and was handed over to Pakistan in 1958. In 2010, Pakistani Prime Minister Syed Yousef Raza Gilani visited Oman, and signed an agreement on enhancing the defence cooperation amongst the armed forces, defence procurement, joint exercises, training and exchange of defence delegations.[63] Pakistan and Oman have strong relations in the field of education. During 2013, a 41-member delegation headed by Khaliq-ur-Rehman, Vice Chancellor, Government College University, Lahore, visited Sultan Qaboos University.[64]

The two have robust trade and commerce ties. The two-way trade totalled US$485 million in 2011–12. Investments from both countries have increased in various sectors such as construction, telecommunications and banking. According to Nawabzada Aminullah Khan Raisani, Pakistani Ambassador to Oman, bilateral trade and economic relations were 'marching forward satisfactorily' and are expected to boost further.[65] Moreover, the Pakistan and Oman Joint Business Council is expected to provide a thrust to the bilateral trade relations and focus on ways to improve trade ties while searching for newer avenues to encourage investments.[66] Trade in commodities such as oil products, leather products and petrochemical products is vibrant.

There is a strong Pakistani expatriate community estimated to be 235,000 in Oman that has played an important role in strengthening bilateral ties. A number of festivals and events are organized by Pakistani embassy and private organizations to improve trade and commerce and promote cultural ties. For example, a Pakistan Mango Festival was held in Muscat from 8 to 14 July.[67]

United Kingdom: Oman and UK have been maintaining a seminal relationship throughout the century. The closeness of the relationship was highlighted by the visit of Queen Elizabeth to Muscat on 27 November 2010 for the 14th anniversary of Sultan Qaboos's rule and the visit of Prince of Wales and Duchess of Cornwall in March 2013 as guests of the Sultan.[68] Oman and UK's relationship is diversified but the UK enjoys close and fruitful engagement in trade, investment, defence, security, health, parliamentary, diplomatic, education and cultural fields.[69] The fifth UK–Oman Joint Working Group took place in London on 8 October.[70] The Oman–UK trade is in favour of the latter. In December 2012, Oman ordered for 12 Typhoon fighter jets and eight Hawk military aircrafts, for US$4.18 billion. In June 2012, the international housing bank HSBC merged with Oman International Bank to create the second largest bank in the Sultanate. This investment has created a large number of jobs for Omanis, including jobs at the most senior levels.[71]

According to an agreement reached on 17 December, British Petroleum (BP) would drill around 300 wells to flush gas trapped deep under the Omani desert over the next 15 years and Oman is relying on Khazzan project estimated at US$16 billion to keep its economy growing. The Khazzan tight gas project, which aims to extract around 1 billion cubic feet (bcf) of gas per day from sandstones at depths of up to 4,500 m in central Oman, is a showcase for BP's tight gas extraction technology.[72] Some of the Omani and the British educational institutions cooperate closely. Many leading British financial service companies and law firms have branches in Muscat. British engineering, architectural and construction companies are also active in Oman.[73]

CONCLUSION

Since the beginning of this century, Oman has undergone some degree of economic reform but limited political reform. India and Oman relationship has remained smooth in 2013. Oman is trying to diversify its economy through non-oil sectors due to its depleting oil resources. This needs expertise and skilled labour which India can pool. Currently, Indian expatriate community is acting as a bridge between the two nations through their professional and cultural contribution. In future, both countries can deepen support for each other in the international institutions. India wants a safe maritime trade in Arabian Sea and wants to act as a responsible actor in the region to suppress maritime piracy. Finally, India and Oman need to work to establish security through cooperation rather than conflict on land or in sea.

NOTES

1. Joseph A. Kéchichian, *Oman and the World: The Emergence of Independent Foreign Policy* (Santa Monica: Rand Corporation, 1995).
2. 'Four Women Win Elections, Make History', *Times of Oman*, 23 December 2012, available at: http://www.timesofoman.com/News/Article-4507.aspx/.

3. Sunil K. Vaidya, 'Hunger Strike by Oman Activists Continue', *Gulf News*, 21 February 2013, available at: http://gulfnews.com/news/gulf/oman/hunger-strike-by-oman-activists-continues-1.1149236/.

4. Amnesty International, 'Sultan of Oman Pardons Activists', 22 March 2013, available at: http://www.amnestyusa.org/news/news-item/sultan-of-oman-pardons-activists/.

5. Human Rights Watch, 'Oman: Drop Charges Against Activist-Blogger Accused of Undermining "Prestige of the State"', 24 July 2013, available at: http://www.hrw.org/news/2013/07/24/oman-drop-charges-against-activist/.

6. Amnesty International, *Annual Report: Oman 2013*, 3 February 2014, available at: http://www.amnestyusa.org/research/reports/annual-report-oman-2013/.

7. Sunil K. Vaidya, 'Allow Women to Pass on Nationality Says Oman MP', *Gulf News*, 3 February 2014, available at: http://gulfnews.com/news/gulf/oman/allow-women-to-pass-on-nationality-says-oman-mp-1.1168526/.

8. United Nations, *Human Development Report 2013—The Rise of the South: Human Progress in a Diverse World—Oman*, available at: http://hdr.undp.org/sites/default/files/Country-Profiles/OMN.pdf/.

9. Ibid.

10. Ryan Harrison, 'Special Country Report: Oman 2013', *Gulf Business*, 3 March 2013, available at: http://gulfbusiness.com/2013/03/the-life-of-oman/#.Uw9gfKKyDIX/.

11. 'Gulf Union Meet on GCC Agenda', *Times of Oman*, 8 December 2013, available at: http://www.timesofoman.com/News/Article-26729.aspx/.

12. Geoff Dyer and Hugh Carnegy, 'Iran Deal Has its Roots in Secret Talks with the US', *Financial Times*, 25 November 2013, available at: http://www.ft.com/cms/s/0/4fc9e936-55fa-11e3-96f5-00144feabdc0.html#axzz2wyNNdbI9/.

13. 'Oman's Sultan Qaboos in Tehran for Energy Talks', *Al Arabiya*, 25 August 2013, available at: http://english.alarabiya.net/en/business/energy/2013/08/25/Oman-s-Sultan-Qaboos-in-Tehran-for-energy-talks-html/.

14. Bertelsmann Stiftung, *Oman, Country Report 2014*, available at: http://www.bti-project.org/reports/country-reports/mena/omn/index.nc?tx_itaoreport_pi1[action]=show/.

15. Kenneth Katzman, 'Oman: Reform, Security, and U.S. Policy', *Congressional Research Service*, 27 September 2013, available at: http://www.fas.org/sgp/crs/mideast/RS21534.pdf/.

16. 'Oman 2013 Budget Spending up 30%', *Arabian Business,* 2 January 2013, available at: http://www.arabianbusiness.com/oman-2013-budget-spending-up-30—484264.html/.

17. Bertelsmann Stiftung, *Oman, Country Report 2014*.

18. Katzman, 'Oman'.

19. Ibid.

20. Harrison, 'Special Country Report'.

21. 'Oman to Launch $15bn Rail Construction in Q4 2014', *Al Arabiya*, 30 December 2013, available at: http://english.alarabiya.net/en/business/aviation-and-transport/2013/10/30/Oman-to-launch-15bn-rail-construction-in-Q4-2014.html/.

22. 'The Special Report: Oman 2014—Industry and Mining', *Oxford Business Group*, available at: http://www.oxfordbusinessgroup.com/news/subterranean-windfall-new-mineral-discoveries-hold-potential-growth/.

23. 'Oman's New Port—Sleepy No More—A Grand Plan for a Fishing Village May, with Luck, Transform the Country', *The Economist*, 6 April 2013, available at: http://www.economist.com/news/middle-east-and-africa/21575819-grand-plan-fishing-village-may-luck-transform-country-sleepy-no?zid=308&ah=e21d923f9b263c5548d5615da3d30f4d/.

24. Jeff Gerth and Stephen Labaton, 'Oman's Oil Yield Long in Decline, Shell Data Show', *The New York Times*, 8 April 2004, available at: http://www.nytimes.com/2004/04/08/business/08OIL.html/.

25. 'BP and Oman Agree to Jointly Develop a Gas Field with Bigger Goals in Mind', *The New York Times*, 16 December 2013, available at: http://www.nytimes.com/2013/12/17/business/international/bp-and-oman-agree-to-develop-gas-field.html?ref=oman&_r=0#h/.

26. 'Country: Oman 2013', *US Energy Information Administration (EIA)*, 10 October 2013, available at: http://www.eia.gov/countries/cab.cfm?fips=mu/.

27. Ali Abdulla Al Riyami, 'Oman Oil and Gas Industry', Ministry of Oil and Gas, Sultanate of Oman.

28. For a background discussion, see Anisur Rehman, 'The Socio-Cultural Dimensions of Indo-Omani Relations', *International Politics*, 2009, Vol. 2, No. 3, p. 99.

29. Kéchichian, *Oman and the World*.

30. 'India–Oman Relations', *Press Release*, Ministry of External Affairs, New Delhi, January 2014, available at: http://www.mea.gov.in/Portal/ForeignRelation/Oman_January_2014.pdf/.

31. 'India–Oman Bilateral Ties Well-Established', *MuscatDaily.Com*, 15 August 2013, available at: http://www.muscatdaily.com/Archive/Business/India-Oman-bilateral-ties-well-established-2hf6/.

32. 'India–Oman Relations'.

33. 'Indian Naval Chief Visits RNO Units, Meet Officials', *Times of Oman*, 18 April 2013, available at: http://www.timesofoman.com/News/Article-13530.aspx/.

34. 'Naseem Al Bahr', a Naval Exercise between Indian & Oman Navy Held', *Press Release*, Indian Navy, available at: http://www.indiannavy.nic.in/press-release/naseem-al-bahr-naval-exercise-between-indian-oman-navy-held/.

35. 'India and Oman Navies Conduct Naseem Al Bahr 2013 Biennial Navel Exercise', *Naval Technology.com*, 25 September 2013, available at: http://www.naval-technology.com/news/newsindia-oman-navies-bienniel-naval-exercise/.

36. 'Indian–Oman Bilateral Ties Well-Established'.

37. 'India–Oman Relations'.
38. Ibid.
39. 'L&T Oman Secures US$72mn EPC Contract from OETC', *Technical Review-Middle East*, available at: http://technicalreviewmiddleeast.com/power-a-water/transmission/l-t-oman-secures-us-72-million-epc-contract-from-oetc, accessed on 29 January 2014/.
40. 'Akbar Travels India Opens Branch in Barka', *Times of Oman*, 7 April 2013, available at: http://www.timesofoman.com/News/Article-12742.aspx/.
41. 'Indo-Oman Fund Acquires 4.7% in Indian Exchange', *MuscatDaily.com*, 11 November 2013, available at: http://www.muscatdaily.com/Archive/Business/Oman-India-fund-acquires-4.7-in-Indian-exchange-2pqk/.
42. 'India–Oman Relations', *Press Release*, Ministry of External Affairs.
43. 'HDFC Presents Indian Homes Fair', *MuscatDaily.com*, 30 January 2013, available at: http://www.muscatdaily.com/Archive/Oman/HDFC-presents-India-Homes-Fair-20bo/.
44. 'Times Property Exhibition to Attract Builders from India on Feb 21', *MuscatDaily.com*, 20 January 2014, available at: http://www.muscatdaily.com/Archive/Oman/Times-property-exhibition-to-attract-builders-from-India-on-February-21-2y88/.
45. 'India offers Enormous Investment Opportunities for Omani Businessmen', *Times of Oman*, 27 March 2013, available at: http://www.timesofoman.com/News/Article-11857.aspx/.
46. 'India-Oman Relations'.
47. Ibid.; 'Oman keen on Marketing its Dates in India', *Business Line*, 30 September 2013, available at: http://www.thehindubusinessline.com/news/states/oman-keen-on-marketing-its-dates-in-india/article5186440.ece/.
48. 'India–Oman Relations'; 'CII Train Young Omani Entrepreneurs', *Business Line*, 13 September 2013, available at: http://www.thehindubusinessline.com/economy/cii-to-train-young-omani-entrepreneurs/article5123192.ece/.
49. 'India–Oman Relations'.
50. Ibid.
51. 'Sultanate Get More Itec Scholarships', *MuscatDaily.com*, 19 February 2013, available at: http://www.muscatdaily.com/Archive/Business/Sultanate-to-get-more-ITEC-scholarships-21wq
52. 'Opportunities in Oman's Higher Education Sector', US Department of State, available at: http://m.state.gov/md205822.htm/.
53. 'Sultanate of Oman to Buy the Air Defence System THAAD from United States', *Army Recognition*, 27 May 2013, available at: http://www.armyrecognition.com/may_2013_news_defence_army_military_industry_uk/sultanate_of_oman_to_buy_the_air_defense_missile_system_thaad_from_united_states_2705134.html/; Katzman, 'Oman'.
54. Shashank Bengali, 'U.S.–Iran Thaw Began with Months of Secret Meetings', *Los Angeles Times*, 24 November 2013, available at: http://www.latimes.com/world/la-fg-1125-iran-tic-toc-20131125,0,2689052.story#axzz2uJwSDpdn/.

55. 'US Frees Iranian Scientist after More Than Year in Custody, Oman Says', *NBC NEWS*, 26 April 2013, available at: http://worldnews.nbcnews.com/_news/2013/04/26/17924156-us-frees-iranian-scientist-after-more-than-year-in-custody-oman-says?lite/.

56. 'Secret US–Iran Talks Cleared Way for Historic Nuclear Deal', *The Telegraph (London)*, 24 November 2013, available at: http://www.telegraph.co.uk/news/worldnews/middleeast/iran/10471030/Secret-US-Iran-talks-cleared-way-for-historic-nuclear-deal.html/.

57. Ibid.

58. Paul Richter, 'Oman Sultan's Visit to reportedly a Mediation Bid between Iran and U.S.', *Los Angeles Times*, 30 August 2013, available at: http://www.latimes.com/world/worldnow/la-fg-wn-us-iran-oman-nuclear-standoff-20130830,0,6785814.story#axzz2uJwSDpdn/.

59. 'China and Oman Hold the 7th Round of Strategic Consultations between the Two Foreign Ministers', *China News*, Embassy of the People's Republic of China in the Sultanate of Oman, Muscat, 31 January 2013, available at: http://lv.china-embassy.org/eng/zgyw/t1010788.htm/.

60. 'Oman Attracts Chinese Attention', *Oman Daily Observer*, 6 November 2013, available at: http://main.omanobserver.om/?p=27855/.

61. 'Omani Trade Delegation Visits China–Arab States Expo 2013', *Muscat-Daily.com*, 16 September 2013, available at: http://www.timesofoman.com/News/Article-22696.aspx/.

62. 'Oman Post Issues Stamp to Mark 35 Years of Relations with China', *Muscat-Daily.com*, 27 May 2013, available at: http://www.muscatdaily.com/Archive/Oman/Oman-Post-issues-stamp-to-mark-35-years-of-relations-with-China-2ah7/.

63. 'Pakistan Eyes Maritime Trade with Oman', *Dawn.com*, 27 December 2010, available at: http://www.dawn.com/news/594057/pakistan-eyes-maritime-trade-with-oman/.

64. 'Visit of Top Position holder of Pakistani Students to Oman', *Press Release*, Embassy of Pakistan, Sultanate of Oman, Muscat, 29 June 2013, available at: http://www.mofa.gov.pk/oman/pr-details.php?prID=1523/.

65. 'Oman, Pakistan Trade Ties Booming, Says H E Raisani', *MuscatDaily.com*, 27 March 2013, available at: http://www.muscatdaily.com/layout/set/print/Archive/Oman/Oman-Pakistan-trade-ties-booming-says-H-E-Raisani-24yr/.

66. 'Oman–Pakistan Joint Business Council Soon', *Oman Daily Observer*, 11 July 2013, available at: http://main.omanobserver.om/?p=1191/.

67. Ibid.

68. 'Queen Flies to Oman as State Visit Continues', *BBC News*, 25 November 2010, available at: http://www.bbc.co.uk/news/uk-11843072/.

69. British Embassy Muscat 'British Ambassador's Interview with German News Agency', 11 June 2013, available at: https://www.gov.uk/government/

world-location-news/british-ambassadors-interview-with-germen-news-agency/.

70. 'Oman-UK Joint Working Group Discusses SME Development', *Muscat-Daily.com*, 10 October 2013, available at: http://www.muscatdaily.com/Archive/Oman/Oman-UK-Joint-Working-Group-discusses-SME-development-2mfe/.

71. 'British Ambassador's interview with German News Agency'.

72. 'BP Signs $16bn Deal to Develop Large Gas Project in Oman', *Al Arabiya*, 17 December 2013, available at: http://english.alarabiya.net/en/business/energy/2013/12/17/BP-signs-16bn-gas-deal-in-Oman.html/; and Stanley Reed, 'BP and Oman Agree to Jointly Develop a Gas Field with Bigger Goals in Mind', *The New York Times*, 16 December 2013, available at: http://www.nytimes.com/2013/12/17/business/international/bp-and-oman-agree-to-develop-gas-field.html?ref=oman&_r=0#h/.

73. 'Oman', *Middle East Association, UK*, available at: http://the-mea.co.uk/countries/oman/.

7

Qatar

Manjari Singh

Key Information

Area: 11,586 sq km; **Population:** 2,123,160 (2014); **Native:** NA; **Expats:** NA; **Youth:** 13.4 per cent; **Population growth rate:** 3.58 per cent; **Life expectancy at birth:** 78.38 years; **Major population groups:** Arab 40 per cent, Indian 18 per cent, Pakistani 18 per cent, Iranian 10 per cent, others 14 per cent; **Religious groups:** 77.5 per cent, Christian 8.5 per cent, others 14 per cent (2004); **GDP:** US$198.7 billion; **Per capita income:** US$102,100; **Foreign trade:** US$52.28 billion; **Oil reserves:** 15.57 million bbl (2013); **Gas reserves:** 25.2 trillion m³; **Ruling family:** al-Thani; **Ruler:** Sheikh Tamim bin Hamad bin Khalifa al-Thani (since 25 June 2013); **Crown Prince:** not nominated; **National Day:** 18 December; **Defence budget:** 10 per cent of GDP; **HDI rank:** 36; **Literacy rate:** 96.3 per cent; **UN education index:** 0.629; **Gender inequality index:** 0.546; **Labour force:** 1.424 million; **Unemployment rate:** 0.3 per cent; **External debt:** US$149.4 billion (December 2013); **Sovereign wealth fund:** US$170 billion; **Infant mortality rate:** 6.42 deaths out of 1000; **Last national census:** 2010; **Parliament:** 45-member partially elected Majlis al-Shura; **Last parliament election:** June 2013; **Number of Indians:** close to 500,000; **Last Indian prime minister to visit:** Manmohan Singh, November 2008.

Sources: CIA, *The World Factbook*, https://www.cia.gov/library/publications/the-world-factbook/; *UN Human Development Report*, Statistics, available at: http://hdr.undp.org/en/statistics/; United States Commission on Religious Freedom, US Department of State; *Annual Report 2013; Briefs on Foreign Relations*, Ministry of External Affairs, Government of India and Centre for Arms Control and Proliferation (Washington D.C.).
Note: All figures for 2013.

Emboldened by its oil and gas resources and the accompanying financial clout, the small state of Qatar has emerged as a major force not only in the international energy market but also as an important player in the Middle Eastern diplomacy. With active role in a number of crises facing the region, Qatar has been seeking to increase its influence and profile internationally. While the rate of success has been limited, some of the crucial issues in the region would not have been resolved without a helping hand from Doha. The willingness of the Emir to voluntarily abdicate in favour of his son has set a precedent for other monarchs in the region. The contours and progress of the Indo–Qatari relations have to be located within this wider but complex context.

DOMESTIC DEVELOPMENTS

The Qatar Peninsula is on the north-easterly coast of the much larger Arabian Peninsula and borders Saudi Arabia to the south while the rest of its territory is surrounded by the Persian Gulf. Qatar is an absolute monarchy that has been ruled by the al-Thani family since the mid-nineteenth century. Before the discovery of oil in 1939, Qatar was noted mainly for pearling and sea trade. It remained a British protectorate until it gained independence on 3 September 1971. On 27 June 1995, Hamad bin Khalifa al-Thani deposed his father Khalifa bin Hamad al-Thani in a peaceful coup and became the Emir. In a surprise move on 25 June 2013, Hamad stepped down in favour of his son Tamim, who was the Crown Prince since 5 August 2003.[1]

The decision-making power, including on foreign policy, is confined to the ruling family, especially the current Emir and his team. According to a research conducted by the Centre for Strategic and International Studies (CSIS), the new Emir Tamim's beliefs regarding his country's role in Middle East will 'largely determine Qatar's actions'.[2] Importantly, 'Like his father, Tamim is thought to be a supporter of the Muslim Brotherhood while simultaneously maintaining warm and strong relations with the West.'[3]

Sheikh Tamim unveiled his new cabinet a day after taking over from his father. Abdullah bin Nasser bin Khalifa al-Thani replaced Hamad bin Jassim al-Thani as the prime minister, while Energy and Industry Minister Mohammed Saleh al-Sada has kept his post. Khalid al-Attiyah was named the Foreign Minister and Ali Sherif al-Emadi became the Finance Minister.[4] The Emir also named Hessa al-Jaber as Minister of Communication and Information Technology, making her the third woman minister in the country's history. Naming a woman to a ministerial position is not unprecedented, but remains an uncommon occurrence. The first woman to serve in Qatar's cabinet was Ahmed al-Mahmoud, who was named the Education Minister in 2003, while Ghalia bint Mohammed al-Thani had served as the Minister of Public Health.[5]

In one of his first foreign policy statements, the 33-year-old Emir said that his country 'rejects divisions in Arab societies on sectarian lines'.[6] According to him, the Qataris seek to preserve relations with all governments and countries and respect all sincere, active and effective political directions in the region. He also added that the country still faced a number of challenges which needs to be tackled.[7]

In recent years, Qatar's relations with its immediate neighbours were not always good. The monarchy has territorial problems with Bahrain and Saudi Arabia. Long-running tensions with Bahrain over the Hawar islands were resolved in 2001 through the verdict of the International Court of Justice. The border conflicts with Saudi Arabia during 1992–94 were resolved through the signing of border demarcation agreement in 2001.[8]

Under the new Emir, Qatar has sought to increase cooperation with Saudi Arabia and the US while reducing tensions with the Islamic Republic of Iran. According to reports, Tamim has garnered a consensus within the royal family to reduce Qatar's high-profile diplomacy and focus on national and regional issues. The Emir argued that as a tiny country Qatar was making too many enemies and needed to take a step back.[9] As a result, Qatar decided to reduce its profile in the Sunni revolt in Syria as well as in Egypt. Doha is also trying to reach out to Saudi Arabia, which became the main supporter of the Syrian rebels. Qatar's new policy led to the immediate removal of Prime Minister Hamad Bin Jassim, who for 20 years was regarded as the most powerful politician in the emirate. Under Hamad Bin Jassim, Qatar sought to mediate in the Afghanistan crisis and allowed the Taliban movement to open an office in Doha. This move was partly aimed to facilitate talks between the US and Afghan movement in light of the impending American withdrawal by December 2014. But one of the first steps taken by Tamim was to reverse that decision and order the closure of the Taliban office in Doha.[10] Interestingly, as crown prince, Tamim had been looking after the internal security for the past five years.

Many observers believe that the regime change in Qatar could ease tensions with countries such as Egypt, Iran and the US.[11] In recent times, Egypt and Iran were angered by Qatar's financing of Islamist militias while Washington was unhappy with Qatar's aid to Syrian groups associated with al-Qaeda. Turkey, however, appeared troubled by the departure of Hamad Bin Jassim. Under the outgoing Prime Minister, Ankara and Doha coordinated to help Sunni rebels in Syria and the Hamas regime in the Gaza Strip. 'Qatar's active foreign policy has come to an end,' lamented Sinan Ulgen, chairman of the Istanbul-based Centre for Economic and Foreign Policy Studies. He went on to add: 'With the new ruler, it is not possible to see Qatar playing an active role in regional issues, including Syria—a situation which would have a negative impact on Turkey's foreign policy.'[12]

On the energy front, Qatar has the world's third largest natural gas reserves and the oil reserves are in excess of 25 billion barrels. The skilful use of the energy assets has enabled Qatar to emerge as the world's richest country in per capita terms. With the highest human development in the Arab World, it is ranked 37th at the global level. Furthermore, it is recognized as a high-income economy by the World Bank and the 19th most peaceful country in the world.[13] Taking into account that all its neighbours have oil or gas deposits, Qatar has found itself in a situation where it could not enjoy much weight in the regional politics solely on the basis of rich resources. Even more, sometimes Qatar's economic activities were restricted due to the absence of cooperation with other Persian Gulf monarchies.

Therefore, willing to be more independent in the region, especially from the dominating role played by Saudi Arabia, Qatar decided to seek relations beyond the Persian Gulf. As a major oil and gas exporter Qatar was an interesting candidate for partnership for many nations in the West and in Asia.[14] In the words of an Israeli analyst Yoel Guzansky: 'Qatar's readiness to use its immense economic power for political purposes, coupled with the weakness of several regional actors in the wake of the "Arab Spring," has put the emirate's foreign policy in the spotlight,' but it is 'likely to change'.[15]

In December 2013, *Forbes* observed that Qatar has prospered in the last several years with a continued high real GDP growth. Throughout the financial crisis that plagued the global economy, Qatari authorities sought to protect the local banking sector with direct investments. The GDP grew sharply from 2010 onwards because of the increasing oil prices and expanding gas sector. The Qatari economic policy has been focused on developing non-associated natural gas reserves and increasing private and foreign investments in non-energy sectors. At the same time, oil and gas still account for more than 50 per cent of GDP, roughly 85 per cent of export earnings and 70 per cent of government revenues. Oil and gas have made Qatar the world's highest per capita income nation with lowest unemployment rate. The proven oil reserves, which are in excess of 25 billion barrels, should enable Qatar to continue with the current level of output for the next 57 years.[16]

Qatar's proven natural gas reserves exceed 25 trillion cubic metres and this is more than 13 per cent of the world's total. Qatar's successful 2022 World Cup bid is likely to accelerate large-scale infrastructural projects such as Qatar's metro system, light rail system and the Qatar–Bahrain causeway. The Hamad International Airport was projected to open by the end of 2013 but was postponed to April 2014 due to cost overruns.[17] It is expected to have an annual passenger capacity of 24 million. On 11 August 2013, *Forbes* again placed Qatar as the world's top-saving countries for 2013. Qatar's gross national savings, a measure that accounts for both private and public savings, stand at an astronomical 59 per cent of its GDP.[18]

Inspite of the impressive performance of its economy, Qatar faces some severe problems. It relies heavily on foreign labour for its economic growth, to the extent that migrant workers comprise 94 per cent of the workforce. According to the International Trade Union Confederation (ITUC), the visa sponsorship system, currently in vogue in Qatar, leads to forced labour by making it difficult for a migrant worker to leave an abusive employer or travel overseas without permission.[19] According to Human Rights Watch statistics, Qatar has a population of about two million, of whom only 10 per cent are Qatari nationals. The number of economically active foreign nationals increased by 122,000, almost 10 per cent, during a 12-month period from April 2012, and is expected to rise further in response to a burgeoning construction sector.[20]

During 2013, the human rights climate in Qatar remained problematic, particularly for the large and growing migrant worker population. Migrants continued to experience serious violations of rights, including forced labour and arbitrary restrictions on the right to leave Qatar, which exposed them to exploitation and abuse by their employers. Qatar's already poor record on freedom of expression declined further with the announcement of a draft cyber-crime law in May.[21] International criticisms over abuse of migrant workers intensified during 2013; Human Rights Watch said in January that without major reforms, the tens of thousands of migrant workers who are building the infrastructure for the 2022 FIFA World Cup would face exploitation and misery. Appalling living and working conditions and high death rates of migrant workers have dogged preparations for the mega sport event. But despite mounting international criticism, Qatari authorities have not given any indication that they are prepared to carry out reforms.[22]

Migrant workers are also subjected to a labour system that facilitates trafficking and forced labour. In contravention of Qatari laws, workers often pay exorbitant recruitment fees and employers confiscate their passports upon their arrival in the country. The *kafala* (sponsorship) system ties a migrant worker's legal status to a sponsoring employer, thereby requiring workers to get an exit visa from that sponsor before leaving Qatar. Workers often live in cramped, unsanitary conditions, and many complain of excessive working hours and unpaid wages. British newspaper *The Guardian* reported that between 4 June and 8 August, 44 Nepalese workers died in Qatar, many from cardiac arrest and work-related accidents.[23]

The Qatari Constitution stipulates Islam as the state religion, and national law incorporates both secular legal traditions and Sharia (Islamic law). In practice, the government generally respects religious freedom, with some restrictions.[24] There are both Sunni and Shia Muslims though they reside in different regions. According to the Qatar Statistic Authority, Sunni Muslims constitute the majority of citizens; Shia Muslims number between 5 per cent and 15 per cent.[25] The government does not release figures regarding religious affiliations. However, the *Religious Freedom Report* annually published by the US State Department provides some estimates regarding the religion composition of the expatriate community. Most non-citizens are Sunni or Shia Muslims or Hindus,

Christians, or Buddhists. There are about 200,000 Roman Catholics, 20,000–25,000 Anglicans and about 3,000 Egyptian Coptic Christians. There are no estimates regarding the small Greek and other Eastern Orthodox population. The Hindu community is almost exclusively from India and Nepal and is estimated at more than 450,000, while Buddhists are from South, Southeast and East Asia and are estimated at 100,000. There are an estimated 100 Bahais of Iranian origin, some of whom are nationals of the country.[26]

The Constitution and Qatari laws provide for freedom of association, public assembly, and worship, within limits of public order and morality concerns. The law prohibits proselytization by non-Muslims and places restrictions on public worship. Converting to another religion from Islam is considered an apostasy and technically a capital offense; however, since the country gained independence in 1971, there has been no recorded punishment for such an act.[27] Christian group worship is permitted among the six registered Christian denominations at a government-provided area in Mesaymir. Unregistered churches and congregations are required to worship under the patronage of one of the six legally recognized Christian denominations. Hindus, Buddhists, Bahais and other religious groups do not have authorized facilities in which to practice their religions. The government generally considers members of these religious groups as transient members of the community not requiring permanent religious facilities or clergy, though worship by these groups in private homes and workplace are allowed.

BILATERAL RELATIONS

Qatar and India have good relations revolving around trade, investment and defence cooperation. India's bilateral trade with Qatar increased from US$1.2 billion in 2005 to US$14 billion in 2012, and efforts are being made to further target Qatar's fast growing markets. Additionally, with 500,000 Indians living and working in Qatar (meaning Indian inhabitants are twice the number of Qatari nationals), remittances going back to India are substantial.[28] The Qatar Investment Authority (QIA) has plans to invest US$10 billion in India over several years starting in 2012 and India has been working to enable such investments.[29] While

Qatar does have military ties with Pakistan, it seems to be balancing this besides ties with India. In 2008, India and Qatar signed a defence agreement that was said to be 'just short of stationing troops' and laid out a structure for joint maritime security.[30]

Political Relations

President of India Pranab Mukherjee sent a message of warm greetings and congratulations to Tamim bin Hamad al-Thani on his assumption of office as the Emir of Qatar. A message of congratulations and warm greetings was also sent by Prime Minister Manmohan Singh who also extended a message of warm greetings to the new Qatari Prime Minister Abdullah bin Nasser bin Khalifa al-Thani.[31] The political relationship between the two countries is close and multi-dimensional. The large Indian community acts as a catalyst for enhancing ties across a spectrum of relations. There is a growing synergy in hydrocarbon and other sectors. In recent years, a number of steps have been taken to further strengthen and expand bilateral relations. These include exchange of high-level visits, consultations in different areas, cooperation in multilateral institutions, in recent years.[32]

Finance Minister P. Chidambaram paid an official visit to Doha during 18–19 May and held extensive discussions with his counterpart Yousef Hussein Kamal towards enhancing bilateral economic relations, especially Foreign Direct Investment in India. He also met the Emir and reviewed the entire gamut of bilateral relations.[33] Qatar is among the few countries in the region with which India has a structure for joint maritime security and training. By signing a defence pact with Oman in 2008, India has signalled its readiness to play a larger-than-before role in the region providing maritime security in the Indian Ocean and Gulf of Aden. The pact allows India to take care of the defence requirements of Qatar, including intelligence sharing and manpower training.[34] Further, on 12 September, the Indian Ambassador to Qatar Sanjiv Arora said that India is keen to further strengthen its existing military ties with Gulf Cooperation Council (GCC) countries and argued that India looks 'forward to further strengthen its existing co-operation in the area of defence with GCC nations and the ongoing goodwill visits by four naval ships of its Western Fleet to the region, is in the framework of the country's excellent long-standing relations with the respective states'.[35]

INS Tabar was the third of the three Talwar class frigates of the Indian navy, which made a port call at Doha during a four-day visit in September. Another ship *INS Aditya* also visited Doha and the other two vessels of the foursome, *INS Mysore* and *INS Tarkashare*, visited Kuwait. The four joined in the UAE on 15 September. Among the things on the agenda was the renewal of the defence ties with Qatar at a two-day meeting of the Joint Committee of the Defence Co-operation (JCDC) in Doha in September. This was the third meeting of the joint commission after the earlier meetings in Doha in 2008 and in New Delhi in 2011.[36]

Moreover, during his tenure, Emir Hamad visited India on three different occasions and Queen Sheikha Mozah bint Nasser al-Missned who accompanied him during these visits also made a separate visit to India in February 2006. From the Indian side, the last state visit to Qatar took place in 2008, when Prime Minister Manmohan Singh visited that country.

Economic Relations

India's bilateral trade with Qatar increased from US$13.72 billion in 2011–12 to US$16.38 billion in 2012–13, a 19.35 per cent increase (Table 7.1 and Figure 7.1). Indian exports witnessed a decline of 14.95 per cent from US$807.95 million in 2011–12 to US$687.18 million in 2012–13 (Table 7.1 and Figure 7.1). Qatar's exports to India amounted to US$15.69 billion in 2012–13, a 21.5 per cent growth from the previous year, owing mainly to increased volume of oil imports by India amounting to US$14.57 billion (Table 7.2 and Figure 7.2).

Table 7.1
India–Qatar Bilateral Trade (in US$ Million)

	2009–10	2010–11	2011–12	2012–13
India's exports to Qatar	536.97	375.39	807.95	687.18
India's imports from Qatar	4,648.52	6,819.87	12,916.35	15,693.08
Total bilateral trade	5,185.49	7,195.27	13,724.30	16,380.26
Share of Qatar in total trade	1.11	1.16	1.73	2.07

Source: Adapted from Directorate General of Foreign Trade, New Delhi, available at: www.dgft.gov.in/.

Figure 7.1
India–Qatar Bilateral Trade

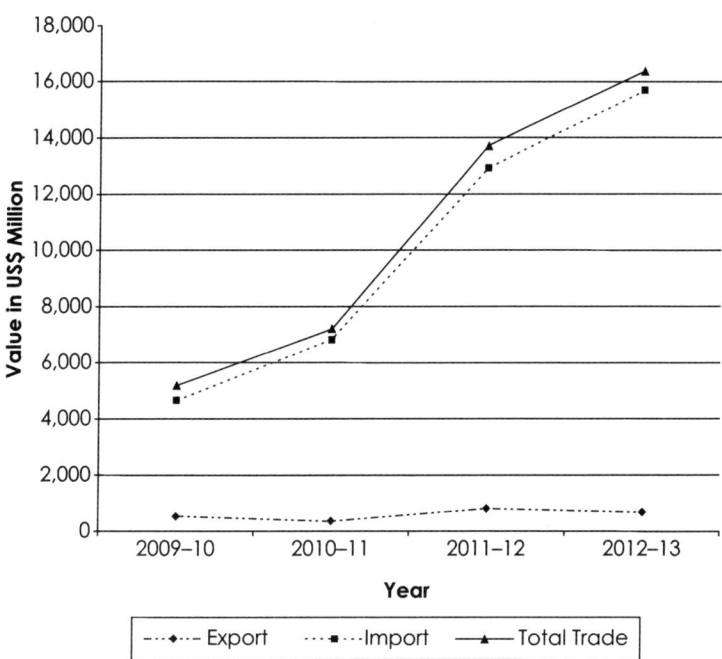

Source: Adapted from Directorate General of Foreign Trade, New Delhi, available at: www.dgft.gov.in/.

Table 7.2
Share of Oil in India's Imports from Qatar (in US$ Million)

Year	Oil imports from Qatar	Total oil imports	Qatar's share in total oil imports	Imports from Qatar	Per cent of oil in imports from Qatar
2009–10	4,101.68	96,321.16	4.26	4,648.52	88.24
2010–11	6,060.95	115,929.02	5.23	6,819.87	88.87
2011–12	11,697.83	172,753.92	6.77	12,916.35	90.57
2012–13	14,578.34	181,344.67	8.04	16,380.26	89.00

Source: Adapted from Directorate General of Foreign Trade, New Delhi, available at: www.dgft.gov.in/.

176   MANJARI SINGH

Figure 7.2
Share of Oil in India's Total Imports from Qatar

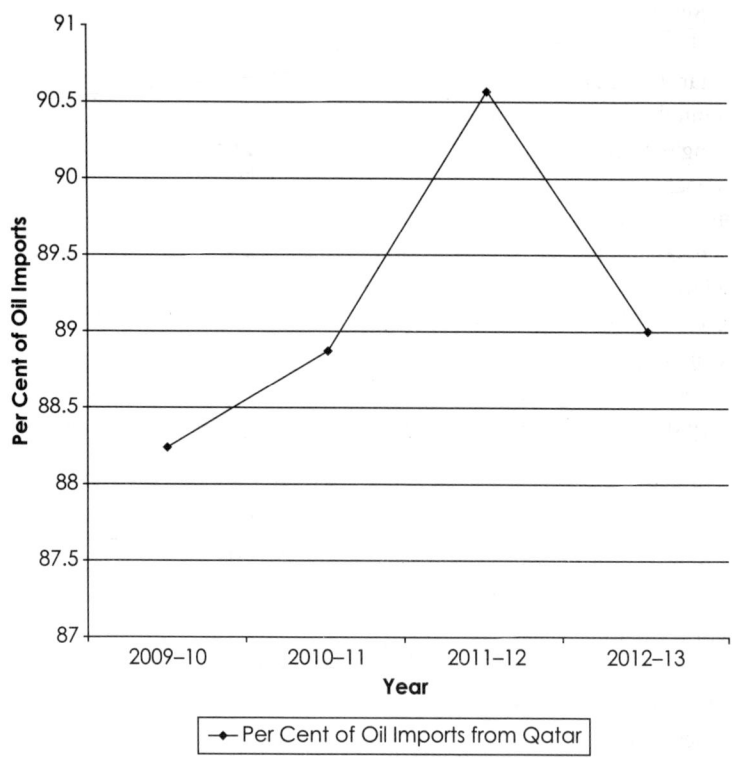

Source: Adapted from Directorate General of Foreign Trade, New Delhi, available at: www.dgft.gov.in/.

Major items of Indian exports are machinery and equipments, transport equipment, textiles, food products, ores and minerals, etc.[37] India is the fourth largest export market for Qatar after Japan, South Korea and Singapore. In terms of imports into Qatar, India ranks 10th. A large number of Indian companies, such as Larsen and Turbo, Punj Lloyd, Voltas, Dodsal, Simplex, Shapoorji Pallomji, TCS, Tech Mahindra, Satyam Mahindra, Wipro, NIIT, HCL, etc., have set up their offices in Qatar and have secured major contracts or businesses. A number of premier Indian banks, such as State Bank of India, Canara Bank, Syndicate Bank, Bank of India, ICICI Bank, are operating in Qatar, either under the Qatar Financial Centre or under private exchanges. These banks are, however, not authorized to do retail banking.

Recent investments between the two countries include a US$100 million joint venture to be set up in Mesaieed Industrial area between Qatar Industrial Manufacturing Company (QIMC) and KLJ Organic Limited. This would enable manufacturing of Chlorinated Paraffin Wax along with caustic soda, hydrochloric acid, calcium chloride and sodium hypochlorite as by-products and co-products. It would also enable the purchase of majority stakes of the Indian basmati rice seller, Bush Foods Overseas, by Hassad Food of Qatar with an investment of over US$100 million and a deal with Qatar Foundation Endowment to buy 5 per cent stakes in Bharti Airtel with an investment of US$1.26 billion. These are positive developments between the two countries but Qatar's investment has been more in other countries.

In the last few months of 2013, there have been several trade missions from India to Qatar. These include a 20-member Federation of Indian Chambers of Commerce and Industry (FICCI) delegation (in September 2012) and a 12-member Chemical and Allied Export Promotion Council of India (CAPEXIL) delegation (in February 2013). Besides these, Indian companies participated in the Doha Trade Exhibition (in January), and World Chambers Congress hosted by Qatar Chamber of Commerce and Industry (in April). For the first time, the Associated Chambers of Commerce and Industry in India (ASSOCHAM), along with 30 Indian companies, participated in the 'Qatar Project' exhibition in May that focused on the infrastructural sector. Other important visits included a FICCI delegation in October and Small and Medium Enterprises (SMEs) Chamber delegation in September–October.[38]

Seeking to enhance bilateral trade and cooperation, Finance Minister P. Chidambaram held discussions with Qatar's Minister of Economy and Finance Yousuf Hussain Kamal and interacted with business leaders during his visit to Doha on 18 May. Among others, he also met the CEO of QIA and CEO of Qatari Business Association. He attended an Investors Meeting which included the CEOs of leading Qatar companies and banks, and CEOs of Pension Funds and top investors.[39] Though the economic relations are good and trade ties positive, there are still problems and challenges. As in previous years, India has a negative trade balance with Qatar which has been a concern for India.

Energy Relations

The hydrocarbon sector, both upstream and downstream, has been identified as a potential area for the further enhancement and expansion of bilateral cooperation. India is a major buyer of ethylene, propylene, ammonia, urea and polyethylene from Qatar. Even though 90 per cent of India's imports from Qatar comprises hydrocarbons (Table 7.2), India has not been a major customer for Qatari crude oil and natural gas.[40] During 2012–13, Qatar's share in India's total energy imports was 8.04 per cent and its share among imports from Persian Gulf countries was 13.78 per cent (Table 7.3).

Liquefied Natural Gas (LNG) imports constitute a priority area for India. Qatar has made major investments in the exploitation of its LNG reserves and is the world's largest LNG supplier.[41] Geographical proximity and long-term energy requirements make India a prime market for the Qatari LNG exports. In pursuance of these complementarities, the two sides had signed a memorandum of understanding (MoU) in January 1998 for cooperation in the gas, oil and industrial sector. The MoU envisages a number of steps to exploit the potentials in these areas, with the purchase of LNG from Qatar as its primary component.

Table 7.3
India's Energy Imports from Qatar (in US$ Million)

	2009–10	2010–11	2011–12	2012–13
India's energy imports from Qatar	4,101.68	6,060.95	11,697.83	14,578.34
India's total energy imports	96,321.16	115,929.06	172,753.97	181,344.67
Total energy imports from the Persian Gulf	55,904.14	66,688.40	103,915.24	105,809.19
Share in total energy imports (in per cent)	4.26	5.23	6.77	8.04
Share in energy imports from Persian Gulf (in per cent)	7.33	9.09	11.26	13.78

Source: Adapted from Directorate General of Foreign Trade, New Delhi, available at: www.dgft.gov.in/.

Subsequently, an agreement for the supply of 7.5 million metric tonnes of LNG per year, for 25 years, to India was signed in June 1999 in London. Under this agreement, 5 million tonnes of gas per year was to be supplied for 25 years beginning from January 2004 and further 2.5 million tonnes for another 25 years beginning from 2009. In addition, 1.25 million tonnes was supplied as special cargos between July 2007 and September 2008. During the visit of the Indian Prime Minister in November 2008, India sought additional supplies of LNG. Qatar currently has put an embargo on fresh commitments till it concludes its detailed assessment of LNG reserves which is expected to last at least till 2013–14.[42] Qatar has agreed to provide some additional spot cargos. The possibility of diverting some supplies committed to other destinations is being explored.[43]

Cultural Relations

Cultural ties between India and Qatar are strong. The first Agreement that was signed, following establishment of diplomatic relations between the two countries in 1973, was on Cultural and Technical Cooperation (1980). This was replaced with an agreement in the field of cultural cooperation during the visit of the Emir Hamad to India in April 2012.[44] It stresses on the vital role of cultural cooperation in strengthening the bilateral relations and promoting and encouraging exchange of cultural activities between the two countries. The presence of the large Indian population contributes significantly in promoting Indian art, culture and tradition in this country. Reflecting its diversity, the Indian community has about 100 associations and most of them are affiliated to the Indian Culture Centre (ICC),[45] an umbrella association that works under the aegis of the Embassy, with the Indian Ambassador as its patron. There are two other umbrella associations that function under the aegis of the Embassy, which addresses the humanitarian, sociocultural and economic and commercial needs of the Indian community. These are Indian Community Benevolent Forum (ICBF) and Indian Business and Professional Network (IBPN).

Indian cinema is popular in Qatar. There are a number of theatres that play Indian movies throughout the year. The fourth edition of Doha Tribeca Film Festival held in Doha, late last year, opened with Mira Nair's *The Reluctant Fundamentalist*. The Indian community is the single largest expatriate group in Qatar and acts as a catalyst for enhancing bilateral ties. The exact number of Indian nationals in Qatar is not documented, but by the end of 2012, it was estimated to be close to 500,000, which is approximately 26 per cent of Qatar's total population of 1.9 million. Indians are highly respected in Qatar for their sincerity, hard work, technical expertise and law-abiding nature and are employed in different capacities, in almost every local establishment, governmental or private.[46]

While a majority of the Indian community continues to be engaged in unskilled and semi-skilled work and belonging therefore to the low- or lower-middle income groups, in recent years, an increasing number of Indian nationals have been engaged in professional jobs as doctors, engineers, chartered accountants, bankers, etc. The number of Indians who have established themselves as entrepreneurs is small, but they are affluent. Separate figures for male and female Indian employees are not available.

Indian professionals and businessmen constitute a small but important component of the Indian community in Qatar. IBPN, Institution of Engineers (India), Indian Medical Association and the Institute of Chartered Accountants maintain active chapters in Qatar with an expanding membership and on-going activities. In addition, there are a number of specialists working in other fields like management, education, pharmacies, software, etc. As Qatar's economic development accelerates, the numbers of Indians and their involvement at all levels in Qatar is expected to grow despite a reduction in the number of visas issued for labourers, etc.[47]

However, there have been incidents of violation of Indian workers' rights in Qatar. On 26 September, *The Guardian* reported that Qatar's construction frenzy ahead of the 2022 World Cup has already cost the lives of at least 4,000 migrant workers.[48] The International Trade Union Confederation (ITUC) had been scrutinizing builders' deaths in the emirate for the past two years and concluded that at least half a million extra workers from countries including Nepal, India and Sri Lanka are expected to flood in to complete the construction of stadiums, hotels and infrastructure in time for the World Cup kickoff. It warned that the annual death toll among those working on building sites could rise to 600 a year—almost a dozen a week—unless Doha makes urgent reforms.[49]

While it admits that the cause of death is not clear in many cases—with autopsies often not being conducted and the routine attribution to heart failure—the ITUC believes that harsh and dangerous working conditions and cramped and squalid living quarters are to be blamed. Some workers complained of forced labour under 50 degree Celsius heat, accused employers of retaining salaries for several months and confiscating passports, hence making it impossible for them to leave. Some even complained of being denied free drinking water. The investigation found that sickness is endemic among workers living in overcrowded and unsanitary conditions and hunger has also been reported.[50] In a statement issued in February 2014, the Indian ambassador said that 82 Indian workers died in the first five months of 2013 and 1,460 complained to the Embassy about labour conditions and consular problems. More than 700 Indian workers died in Qatar between 2010 and 2012.[51]

External Players

The US: In view of the level of coordination and cooperation with the US that exists since diplomatic relations were established in 1972, and the concentration of US military power on the tiny peninsula, it is natural for Qatar to move in parallel with the US strategic and regional plans. According to the US State Department, 'bilateral relations are strong,' while both countries coordinate diplomatically and cooperate on regional security and have a defence pact. 'Qatar hosts US Central Command (CENTCOM) Forward Headquarters', and supports NATO and US regional military operations.[52] Qatar is also an active participant in the US-led efforts to set up an integrated missile defence network in the Gulf region. Moreover, Qatar hosts the US Combined Air Operations Centre and three American military bases, namely Al-Udeid Air Base, Assaliyah Army Base and Doha International Air Base, which are manned by approximately 5,000 US forces.[53]

At the same time, in recent months Qatar has emerged as the major sponsor of various Islamist political movements. It now appears that the Qatari regime has become one of the principal benefactors of the Muslim Brotherhood, although, it was reportedly, disbanded in Qatar in 1999. Qatar is seen by the US as a crucial player in the region. The *Al Jazeera* network and Qatar's close ties with the Hamas leader Khaled

Meshaal have always presented a headache for the US, whose policy towards Hamas was largely governed by its need to align closely with Israeli thinking on the subject. Famously, the former senator and now Secretary of State John Kerry had claimed in 2009 that 'Qatar ... can't continue to be an American ally on Monday that sends money to Hamas on Tuesday.'[54] Despite this, Qatar continues to send money, and the Americans remain their allies. On 29 April, there was a meeting between Vice President Joe Biden and US Secretary of State John Kerry, and the delegation of the Arab League represented by the then Prime Minister of Qatar, Sheikh Hamad bin Jassim al-Thani. This meeting was devoted to the Israeli–Palestinian peace process in which Qatar is supposed to be playing a crucial role.[55]

Strategically, the Al-Udeid military base (the headquarters of US CENTCOM) and the increasing importance of Qatar as a regional actor and financial investor have made the relationship between the US and Qatar closer in recent years. Thus, their differences concerning Israel, the occasionally troublesome *Al Jazeera* network, and Qatar's hosting and funding of hard-line Islamists have been papered over in favour of larger strategic visions that ensure the interests of both parties.[56]

China: The strengthening of relations with Qatar is evident in China's desire to be a major player in the Middle East. It is also a sign that China is willing to be, and is being embraced as, an alternative to traditional influences, such as the US.[57] The latest step taken in China–Qatari relations came in the form of the opening of *Dragon Mart*, a Chinese superstore selling Chinese-made products, in Doha, in February. The mart, which is expected to emerge as a gateway for supplying Chinese products in the booming Qatar, would offer Chinese traders and manufacturers a unique platform to cater to the needs of this sizeable market. The launching of *Dragon Mart* came shortly after it was revealed that the bilateral trade between the two nations totalled US$8.45 billion in 2012, a 45 per cent increase from the year before.[58]

While exports from Qatar totalled US$7.2 billion, exports from China totalled just over US$1.2 billion. The booming bilateral trade in 2012 coincided with the visits of the Chinese Premier Wen Jiabao to Qatar during 18–19 January 2012 and Qatar's Prime Minister Hamad to China in April 2008. Such high level visits are indicative of the mutual desire for strong political and economic relations, which include increased Chinese involvement in the wealthy Middle Eastern nation. Besides geopolitical influence, China's growing interest in Qatar mainly lies in its continuing demand for energy resources. China has allowed greater access to Qatar in investing in China as part of the strengthening bilateral relations. This is important for Qatar as it seeks to diversify its predominantly energy-dominated economy.

Qatar has partnership with China in various Solar Projects, the leader in solar photovoltaic (PV) panel manufacturing. It is the presence of these Chinese firms that has driven down the price of PV panels by 75 per cent in the last five years, pushing rival US firms into bankruptcy. 'China has quadrupled its solar capacity target to 50GW by 2020, and is addressing the oversupply of panels through accelerated domestic installations, which may help it weather the storm of import duties coming from the US,' said Tom Whitehouse, chairman of the London Environmental Investment Forum.[59]

In line with the decisions of the G-77 to reduce greenhouse gas emissions, Qatar has set a target of 20 per cent. Hence, it was a good move for Doha to join hands with China in launching its first solar power project in early 2013. Currently, Qatar Solar Technologies (QSTec) is collaborating with Germany's Solar World but as a senior analyst with a Doha investment fund observed, China is likely to play a larger role in future.[60] On 21 September, Abdullah bin Hamad al-Attiyah, the Deputy Prime Minister and Minister of Energy and Industry, met Chinese ambassador Yue Xiaoyong. Their talks covered bilateral relations between the two countries, especially in oil and gas sectors. The Qatari leader showed optimism on energy cooperation and both sides expressed willingness to further develop potential in that field.[61]

Pakistan: Pakistan and Qatar have been expressing the desire to enhance their relations, both politically and economically. This was reflected when, Ali Bin Abdullah al-Thani, a senior member of the Qatari royal family and the Chairperson of the Pak-Qatar Takaful Group (a cooperative financial company) called on the Pakistani Prime Minister Raja Parwez Ashraf on 1 March and discussed their bilateral interests. Qatar has constructed a model village in Rahim Yar Khan District of Pakistan, comprising of 200 houses of two rooms each, two schools, playground, mosques and a shopping area. The village was constructed to rehabilitate the several people displaced during floods. It plans to construct several such villages in Pakistan.[62]

On 29 March, Emir Tamim, then the heir apparent honoured Pakistan's Ambassador to Qatar, with a medal as a farewell.[63] In August, Speaker of the National Assembly of Pakistan Sardar Ayaz Sadiq urged the investors of Qatar to take advantage of upcoming business opportunities in Pakistan and invest in various sectors especially the energy and manufacturing sectors.[64] On 26 September, there was a meeting between Prime Minister Nawaz Sharif and the Emir of Qatar on the sidelines of the UN General Assembly. The two agreed to transform the bilateral relations into 'mutually beneficial economic partnership.' The discussion focused in particular on cooperation in the energy and power sectors, including LNG.[65] Following these events, in December Prime Minister Nawaz Sharif invited Qatar's petroleum and gas companies to invest in Pakistan's oil and gas exploration and production sector.[66]

Problems, Challenges and Opportunities

An important dimension of the Indo–Qatari relations is the presence of a large Indian community in Qatar. A majority of the Indian population in Qatar are engaged in unskilled and semi-skilled work and professionals constitute a small component of the Indian community in Qatar.[67] Even though the remittance to India is very high, the condition of migrant workers is not very good. There are several instances where the Indian expatriates are abused by their employers. Another major threat and problem for the Indians are the recruitment agencies. There are many cases of fraud and extortion by such recruitment agencies.[68] Many of the housemaids are exploited through the present system of recruitment of domestic workers.[69]

There are cases of non-observance of terms of contracts by employers, which cause distress to many Indian workers. Many Indians are vulnerable to neglect, diseases, accidents, and unemployment. Many of the expatriates want their children to get an education in India and there is a growing demand for quota or such facilities in this direction.[70]

According to the labour agreement which was signed in 1985, the sponsors in Qatar are required to execute an employment contract indicating, inter-alia, salient features such as wages and other benefits. The contract is first required to be attested by the Department of Labour and the Ministry of Foreign Affairs in Qatar and is then presented to the Indian Embassy for further attestation. On the basis of such attested contract the sponsor can either arrange recruitment of manpower through the Government of India or its agent or an agent registered with the Government of India or one directly from the market. In case of a dispute between the employee and the sponsor or in the event of breach of employment contract, the Department of Labour, Government of the State of Qatar intervenes and adjudicates, failing which the case is referred to the Labour Court for a decision. This is a tiring and cumbersome process.

However, the Indo–Qatar Labour agreement of 1985 does not cover drivers, cooks, houseboys and housemaids, who make-up a large portion of Indian workers. An additional labour protocol was signed on 20 November 2007 in New Delhi between Indian Minister for Overseas Indian Affairs Vayalar Ravi and Qatar's Minister of Labour and Social Affairs (MOLSA), Sultan bin Hassan al-Dhabit al-Doussari. The agreement extended the provisions of the original 1985 Labour Agreement to cover domestic workers. However, it did not cover on work conditions. This is the biggest problem and a threat to the welfare of Indian workers in Qatar who work for minimal pay.[71] Moreover, in 2013 there were no high level visits between the two countries and the only exception was the visit by Finance Minister P. Chidambaram in May.

CONCLUSION

The relationship between India and Qatar looks very promising. However, 2013 witnessed less political contacts than the previous year. A lot has been promised on the business front and the two countries are working on various projects together. Not only energy and trade relations seem to get better but various Indian aviation projects and companies have their stakes in Qatar. A number of Indian banks and financial institutions have come up in Qatar. One can say that the relationship which was once based primarily on oil and gas is expanding to other realms as well. But the expatriate situation is under stress and the cultural relations can be better if the expatriate situation improves in Qatar. To further strengthen the ties, leaders of both the countries should meet on a regular basis to resolve the differences.

NOTES

1. 'Qatar's Emir Transfers Power to Son', *Al Jazeera*, 25 June 2013, available at: http://www.aljazeera.com/news/middleeast/2013/06/2013625516403468. html; and 'Qatar's New Emir: A Remarkable Emir Bows Out', *The Economist*, 29 June 2013, available at: http://www.economist.com/news/middle-east-and-africa/21580197-remarkable-emir-bows-out-hard-act-follow/.
2. Sadika Hameed et al., *Regional Dynamics and Strategic Concerns in South Asia: Gulf State's Role*, Centre for Strategic and International Studies, Washington, 2014, p. 5, available at: https://csis.org/files/publication/140124_Hameed_GulfStates_Web.pdf/; and Regan Doherty, 'Qatar Will Pursue Its "Independent Behaviour"—New Emir', *Reuters*, 26 June 2013, available at: http://uk.reuters.com/article/2013/06/26/uk-qatar-emir-idUK-BRE95O06220130626/.
3. Ibid.
4. 'Qatar's New Emir Sheikh Tamim Unveils New Cabinet', *BBC News*, 26 June 2013, available at: http://www.bbc.co.uk/news/world-middle-east-23071586/.
5. 'New Emir Appoints Female Cabinet Member in Qatar Government Shake-up', *Doha News*, 26 June 2013, available at: http://dohanews.co/new-emir-appoints-female-cabinet-member-in-qatar/.
6. 'Qatar's New Emir Sheikh Tamim Unveils New Cabinet'.
7. Ibid.
8. Mehran Kamrava, 'Royal Factionalism and Political Liberalization in Qatar', *The Middle East Journal* (2009), Vol. 63, No. 3, p. 411.
9. 'Qatar was "Making Too Many Enemies": New Emir, New Foreign Policy', *World Tribune*, 17 July 2013, available at: http://www.worldtribune.com/2013/07/17/qatar-was-making-too-many-enemies-new-emir-new-foreign-policy/.
10. Ibid.
11. Yoel Guzansky, 'Cutting Qatar Down to Size', *INSS Insight*, No. 476, 16 October 2013, available at: http://www.inss.org.il/index.aspx?id=4538&articleid=5827/.
12. Ibid.
13. 'The World's Richest Countries', *Forbes*, 22 February 2012, available at: http://www.forbes.com/sites/bethgreenfield/2012/02/22/the-worlds-rich-est-countries/; and 'International Human Development Indicators', *Human*

Development Report, 12 January 2013, available at: https://web.archive.org/web/20130112042847/http://hdr.undp.org/en/statistics/.

14. David G. Victor, Amy M. Jaffe, et al., *Natural Gas and Geopolitics from 1970–2040* (Cambridge: Cambridge University Press, 2006), p. 237.

15. Guzansky, 'Cutting Qatar Down to Size'.

16. 'Qatar', *Forbes*, December 2013, available at: http://www.forbes.com/places/qatar/.

17. 'Hamad International Airport Opening Postponed until 2014', *Doha News*, 5 September 2013, available at: http://dohanews.co/hamad-international-airport-opening-postponed-until/.

18. 'The World's Top-Saving Countries, 2013', *Forbes*, 11 August 2013, available at: http://www.forbes.com/sites/danalexander/2013/11/08/worlds-top-saving-countries-2013/.

19. International Trade Union Confederation (ITUC), 'International Unions Warn Qatar's Work Visa System Allows Employers to Use Forced Labour', 18 January 2013, available at: http://www.ituc-csi.org/international-unions-warn-qatar-s?lang=en/.

20. Human Rights Watch, *World Report 2014: Qatar*, available at: http://www.hrw.org/world-report/2014/country-chapters/qatar/.

21. 'Qatar Law Soon to Fight Cyber Crimes', *Gulf Times*, 30 May 2013, available at: http://www.gulf-times.com/qatar/178/details/354485/qatar-law-soon-to—fight-cyber—crimes/.

22. Human Rights Watch, 'Qatar: Serious Migrant Worker Abuses', 21 January 2014, available at: http://www.hrw.org/news/2014/01/21/qatar-serious-migrant-worker-abuses/.

23. *World Report 2014: Qatar*.

24. 'Qatar', *International Religious Freedom Report for 2012*, US Department of State, available at: http://www.state.gov/documents/organization/208620.pdf/.

25. Ibid.

26. 'Qatar', *Country Report on Human Rights Practices for 2011*, US Department of State, available at: http://www.state.gov/documents/organization/186656.pdf/.

27. Ibid.

28. 'Qatar, India Bilateral Trade Jumps to $14 Billion in 2012,' *Qatar Chamber*, 20 February 2013, available at: http://www.qatarchamber.com/qatar-india-bilateral-trade-jumps-to-14-billion-in-2012/.

29. SWF Institute, 'Qatar SWF Looks to India for Investments', 11 April 2012, available at: http://www.swfinstitute.org/swf-article/qatar-swf-looks-to-india-for-investments/.

30. 'India, Qatar Ink Key Defence Pact', *The Financial Express*, 11 November 2008, available at: http://www.financialexpress.com/news/india-qatar-ink-key-defence-pact/383907/.

31. 'India–Qatar Relations', Ministry of External Affairs, New Delhi, available at: http://www.mea.gov.in/Portal/ForeignRelation/Qatar_Dec_2013.pdf/.

32. 'India–Qatar Bilateral Relations', Embassy of India, Doha, Qatar, available at: http://www.indianembassyqatar.org/pages/bilateralrelations.php/.
33. 'FM to Meet Qatari Minister, Business Leaders Today', *Business Standard*, 18 May 2013, available at: http://www.business-standard.com/article/economy-policy/fm-to-meet-qatari-minister-business-leaders-to-day-113051800731_1.html/.
34. Hameed, *Regional Dynamics and Strategic Concerns in South Asia*.
35. 'India Keen to Strengthen Defence Ties with Gulf Countries', *Business Standard*, 12 September 2013, available at: http://www.business-standard.com/article/specials/india-keen-to-strengthen-defence-ties-with-gulf-countries-113091200370_1.html/.
36. Ibid.
37. 'India–Qatar Bilateral Relations', Embassy of India.
38. Ibid.; and 'India–Qatar Relations', Ministry of External Affairs.
39. 'FM to Meet Qatari Minister, Business Leaders Today', *Business Standard*, Dubai, 18 May 2013, available at: http://www.business-standard.com/article/economy-policy/fm-to-meet-qatari-minister-business-leaders-to-day-113051800731_1.html/; and 'Finance Minister Leaves Today for Five Day Foreign Visit to UK, France and Qatar: To Hold Discussions on Various Bilateral and Investment Related Issues', *Press Information Bureau*, New Delhi, 15 May 2013, available at: http://pib.nic.in/newsite/PrintRelease.aspx?relid=95989/.
40. Alessandro Bacci, 'Qatar and India: A Gas Relationship Due to Continue', DAO's Board of Directors, 23 March 2012, available at: http://www.daoonline.info/public/foto/BACCI%20-%20IKA%20-%20Qatar%20And%20IndiaMar%202012.pdf/.
41. 'Brookings Doha Energy Forum 2013 Policy Paper', *Brookings Doha Center – Brookings Energy Security Initiative Report*, No. 25, 1–2 April, available at: http://www.brookings.edu/~/media/research/files/reports/2013/08/06%20energy%20forum%20report/energy%20forum%20report_english.pdf.
42. 'India–Qatar Bilateral Economic Relations', Embassy of India, Doha, Qatar, available at: http://indianembassyqatar.org/pages/bilateraleconomic.php/.
43. Ibid; 'Brookings Doha Energy Forum 2013 Policy Paper'.
44. 'India–Qatar Bilateral Relations', Embassy of India.
45. For more, see India Cultural Centre (ICC), Embassy of India, Doha, Qatar, available at: http://iccqatar.com/.
46. 'India–Qatar Bilateral Relations', Embassy of India.
47. Ibid.
48. 'Qatar World Cup Construction Will Leave 4,000 Migrant Workers Dead', *The Guardian (London)*, 26 September 2013, available at: http://www.theguardian.com/global-development/2013/sep/26/qatar-world-cup-migrant-workers-dead/.
49. ITUC-Qatar, 'International Trade Union Confederation: Building Workers Power', available at: http://www.ituc-csi.org/qatar/.

50. Human Rights Watch, 'Human Rights in Qatar', available at: http://www. hrw.org/middle-eastn-africa/qatar/.
51. 'International Trade Union Confederation.
52. 'Qatar and U.S.: Collusion or Conflict of Interests', *pravadu.ru*, 24 January 2013, available at: http://english.pravda.ru/world/asia/24-01-2013/123571-qatar_usa-0/.
53. Ibid.
54. Cited in Christopher M. Blanchard, 'Qatar: Background and U.S. Relations', *Congressional Research Service*, 30 January 2014, available at: http://www. fas.org/sgp/crs/mideast/RL31718.pdf/.
55. 'Secretary Kerry's and Qatari Prime Minister Hamad's Remarks, April 2013', Council on Foreign Relations, 29 April 2013, available at: http://www. cfr.org/peacekeeping/secretary-kerrys-qatari-prime-minister-hamads-remarks-april-2013/p30590?cid=rss-palestine-secretary_kerry_s_and_qatari_p-042913/.
56. 'Qatar and the US Have a Working Relationship', *Open Democracy*, 30 April 2013, available at: http://www.opendemocracy.net/michael-stephens/qatar-and-us-have-working-relationship/; Lina Khatib, 'Qatar's Foreign Policy: The Limits of Pragmatism', *International Affairs*, 2013, Vol. 89, No. 2, pp. 417–31, available at: http://iis-db.stanford.edu/pubs/24060/INTA89_2_10_Khatib.pdf/; and Jean Shaoul, 'Qatar Plays Key Role in US Middle East/North Africa Plans', *World Socialist Web Site*, 9 February 2013, available at: http://www.wsws.org/en/articles/2013/02/09/qata-f09.html/.
57. Bruno de Paiva, 'Strengthening China–Qatar Relations Mutually Beneficial—Analysis', *Eurasia Review*, 16 March 2013, available at: http://www. eurasiareview.com/16032013-strengthening-china-qatar-relations-to-be-mutually-beneficial-analysis/.
58. 'Dragon Mart to Bring Chinese Flavour to Qatar', *The Peninsula (Doha)*, 27 February 2013, available at: http://thepeninsulaqatar.com/news/qatar/227105/dragon-mart-to-bring-chinese-flavour-to-qatar/.
59. Cited in Simon Watkins, 'China and Qatar: A New and Lucrative Fiscal Alliance', *The Edge*, 4 January 2013, available at: http://www.theedge.me/china-and-qatar-a-new-and-lucrative-fiscal-alliance/.
60. Ibid.
61. 'Qatari Deputy PM Meeting Chinese Ambassador', Embassy of People's Republic of China in the State of Qatar, Doha, 21 September 2013, available at: http://qa.china-embassy.org/eng/zkgx/t516408.htm/.
62. 'Diplomatic Pakistan Enjoys Brotherly Relations with Qatar, Prime Minister', *Pakistan Press International*, 1 March 2013, available at: http://ppinewsagency.com/101506/diplomatic-pakistan-enjoys-brotherly-relations-with-qatar-prime-minister/.
63. 'Heir Apparent Honours Pakistan's Ambassador', *Gulf Times*, 29 March 2013, available at: http://www.gulf-times.com/qatar/178/details/347216/heir-apparent-honours-pakistan%E2%80%99s-ambassador/.

64. 'Economic Relations: Pakistan Invites Qatar to Enhance Ties', *The Express Tribune (Islamabad)*, 1 August 2013, available at: http://tribune.com.pk/ story/584701/economic-relations-pakistan-invites-qatar-to-enhance-ties/.

65. 'Pakistan, Qatar to Boost Relations in Energy Sector', *Business Recorder*, 26 September 2013, available at: http://www.brecorder.com/top-news/108-pakistan-top-news/137709-pakistan-qatar-to-boost-relations-in-energy-sector.html/.

66. 'PM Invites Qatar's Energy Companies to Invest in Pakistan', *Aaj News*, Islamabad, 20 December 2013, available at: http://www.aaj.tv/2013/12/ pm-invites-qatar%E2%80%99s-energy-companies-to-invest-in-pakistan/; 'Pakistani PM Urges Qatari Firms to Invest in Pakistan', *Qatar Living.com*, 20 December 2013, available at: http://www.qatarliving.com/news/posts/ pakistani-pm-urges-qatari-firms-invest-pakistan/; and 'Deepening ties: PM Asks Qatar Companies to Invest in Pakistan', *The Express Tribune (Islamabad)*, 21 December 2013, available at: http://tribune.com.pk/story/648466/deep-ening-ties-pm-asks-qatar-companies-to-invest-in-pakistan/.

67. 'Qatar', Ministry of Overseas Indian Affairs, New Delhi, available at: http:// moia.gov.in/pdf/qatar.pdf/.

68. 'International Trade Union Confederation.

69. 'Qatar', MOIA.

70. Ibid.

71. Ibid.

8

Saudi Arabia

Md. Muddassir Quamar

Key Information

Area: 2,149,690 sq km; **Population:** 27,345,956 (2014 est.); **Native:** less than 70 per cent; **Expats:** more than 30 per cent; **Youth:** 19.3 per cent; **Population growth rate:** 1.49 per cent; **Life expectancy at birth:** 74.82 years; **Major population groups:** NA; **Religious groups:** Sunni 80–85 per cent, Shia 10–15 per cent; **GDP:** US$927.8 billion; **Per capita income:** US$31,300; **Foreign trade:** US$523.3 billion; **Oil reserves:** 264.6 million bbl (2013); **Gas reserves:** 8.018 trillion m³; **Ruling family:** al-Saud; **Ruler:** King Abdullah bin Abdulaziz al-Saud (since 1 August 2005); **Crown Prince:** Prince Salman bin Abdulaziz al-Saud (since 18 June 2012); **National Day:** 23 September; **Defence budget:** 10 per cent of GDP; **HDI rank:** 57; **Literacy rate:** 86.6 per cent; **UN education index:** 0.703; **Gender inequality index:** 0.682; **Labour force:** 8.412 million; **Unemployment rate:** 10.5 per cent; **External debt:** US$149.4 billion (December 2013); **Sovereign wealth fund:** US$681.2 billion; **Infant mortality rate:** 14.58 deaths out of 1,000; **Last national census:** 2010; **Parliament:** 150-member nominated Majlis al-Shura; **Last parliament appointment:** 2013; **Number of Indians:** 2.8 million; **Last Indian prime minister to visit:** Manmohan Singh, February–March 2010.

Sources: CIA, *The World Factbook,* available at: https://www.cia.gov/library/publications/the-world-factbook/; *UN Human Development Report,* Statistics, available at: http://hdr.undp.org/en/statistics/; United States Commission on Religious Freedom, US Department of State; *Annual Report 2013; Briefs on Foreign Relations,* Ministry of External Affairs, Government of India and Centre for Arms Control and Proliferation (Washington, D.C.).
Note: All figures for 2013.

Saudi Arabia's unique geostrategic and geo-economic positions make it an important country in the Middle East, especially in the Persian Gulf region. Domestic and regional developments in 2013 brought newer challenges for Saudi Arabia. *Nitaqat*, the new labour law, became one of the most talked about issues in Indian media due to its impact upon expatriate workers. Moreover, an interim deal between Iran and P5+1 in November over the decade-long nuclear controversy became an important concern for Saudi Arabia. Notwithstanding these issues, 2013 proved to be another good year for Indo-Saudi bilateral ties.

DOMESTIC DEVELOPMENTS

Saudi Arabia is going through a significant phase as far as its domestic situation is concerned. It has experienced slow but sustained sociopolitical transition due to reform initiatives taken by the monarchy in response to domestic demands and international pressures during the last two decades. Though it witnessed massive economic growth since the oil boom of 1970s, it was only in the aftermath of the 1990–91 Kuwaiti crises that one could notice increased political activity and demands for political opening.[1]

Some of the earlier decisions began bearing fruits in 2013 and strengthened the ongoing sociopolitical transformation. For example, in late 2012 the head of *Mutawwa* (Commission for the Promotion of Virtue and Prevention of Vice) was replaced and its powers were curtailed.[2] Women athletes were allowed to take part in the London Olympic Games.[3] In January, the king announced the 150 members of the sixth *Majlis al-Shura* including 30 women, with one of them being a Shia. This was in tune with the king's commitment in September 2011 to reserve 20 per cent of the seats for women and to allow participation and voting rights for women in municipal elections scheduled for early 2015. Saudi Arabia has faced international criticisms over the condition and status of women and their continued marginalization in public realm. However, the situation has slowly changed and is reflected in public debates during the year. An important propellant was the campaign for women's right to drive. The demand is not new but strongly resonated in the aftermath of the Arab Spring. Manal al-Sharif led the campaign in 2011 but it was curbed and she was arrested. A new campaign was started in late 2013 with the help of social media.

Though the women campaigns for driving rights have not succeeded, they have generated debates in local media about women's rights issues. Women belonging to different professions have voiced their opinion for their rights while some took up social media activism to raise their concerns. For example, Eman al-Nafjan, a female blogger based in Riyadh, launched the 26 October Women Driving Campaign through social media. She was joined by Loujain al-Hathloul, a Saudi currently studying in Canada, who volunteered to announce the beginning of the campaign through Keek.[4] However, as it gathered momentum, it evoked official crackdown leading to arrest of some of the participants including Tariq al-Mubarak, a schoolteacher, who had openly come out in support of the campaign.[5] Moreover, prominent women, such as Samar Fatany (journalist and writer), Amira Kashgary (professor), Surraya al-Obaid (member of Majlis al-Shura), Naila Attar (founder of Baladi initiative), Suhaila Zain al-Abideen (member of National Society for Human Rights) and Omaima al-Najjar (blogger and activist), have openly talked about women's rights and needs for reform.

A number of reform initiatives were seen during the year under review and can be termed as a limited response to rising voices in favour of granting women more rights. Apart from nomination of women in the Majlis al-Shura, women have now been allowed to practice law. Bayan Mahmoud al-Zahran was issued a licence to practice law in courts in November 2013, thereby becoming the first Saudi woman lawyer.[6] Efforts are continuing to improve female participation in education and economy. Nitaqat, launched to limit the number of expatriate workers, is expected to improve the employment opportunities for Saudis, both men and women, particularly in the private sector. The government plans to improve the network of school, colleges and vocational institutes to improve the education sector while seeking to diversify the economy to reduce youth unemployment. It has continued to provide scholarship for students who wish to study abroad through the King Abdullah Foreign Scholarship Programme.

While reform initiatives were started, some steps have been taken to curb dissent. Prosecution and conviction of some of the activists reflect the Saudi uneasiness over the Arab Spring. In March 2013, human rights activists Abdullah al-Hamid and Muhammad al-Qahtani were convicted on a number of charges including disruption of security and incitement by the Criminal Court in Riyadh.[7] The Saudi Civil and Political Rights Association (ACPRA) that was engaged in providing assistance to detainees held without charges or trial, founded by these two activists, was ordered to disband.[8] This was followed by the conviction of two Shia women rights activists—Wajeha al-Huweider and Fawzia al-Oyouni—on charges of 'undermining a marriage' by the District Court in Al-Khobar.[9] The conviction evoked criticisms from other activists, especially Manal al-Sharif who said in her blog that 'it was a sad day not only for the two activists but for all Saudi women'.[10] Many in the international media argued that the two have been targeted under a false case because of their human rights activities.[11] In September, the Appeal Court in Dammam confirmed their conviction.[12] Saudi Arabia has long faced criticisms over its human rights violations and, hence, these convictions are not very helpful.

Moreover, the institutionalized bias against the Shias continues. Although King Abdullah has taken some steps to mitigate the situation by allowing some religious freedom to the Shias, discriminatory practices have not ended. In the wake of Arab Spring some of the Shia-dominated areas, particularly in the Eastern Province, have witnessed disturbances but were brought under control.[13] In 2012, a number of Shia youth were held on charges of organizing demonstration and creating trouble. The situation, however, improved in 2013 but demands for release of those who are held for long without trial echoed throughout the year.[14]

In addition to these issues, succession remains an important political matter that resonated during 2013. On 14 February, Prince Khalid bin Bandar (b. 1951) was appointed Governor of Riyadh.[15] Interestingly, the same day Prince Muhammad bin Saad (b. 1944) was replaced with Prince Turki (b. 1971), son of King Abdullah, as Deputy Governor of Riyadh. In April, Prince Khalid bin Sultan (b. 1949) was removed as Deputy Minister of Defence and was replaced by Prince Fahd bin Abdullah bin Muhammad but he was removed within 20 weeks and Prince Salman bin Sultan (b. 1976) was appointed Deputy Minister of Defence in August. Meanwhile, in May Prince Mutaib (b. 1952), third son of King Abdullah, was elevated to the Council of Ministers as a new Ministry of National Guard that was created by abolishing the office of Commander of National Guard. In December, the Governor of Mecca Prince Khalid al-Faisal (b. 1940) was appointed Minister of Education, replacing the king's son-in-law Faisal bin Abdullah bin Mohammed al-Saud who held the position since 2009. Prince Mishaal bin Abdullah (b. 1970) was appointed the Governor of Mecca in December. These shuffling in government positions are important indicators of politics within the Royal family and may have come as a result of tensions over succession issue.

At the foreign policy front, two important developments took place towards the end of 2013. On 18 October, Saudi Arabia shocked the world by rejecting a non-permanent seat in the United Nations Security Council (UNSC) for which it was elected for the first time. The official Saudi statement said that it did not wish to accept the seat because the Security Council has 'failed in upholding its duties towards world peace', alleging that its 'double standards pushed the kingdom to take this stand'.[16] It was perhaps a reflection of Saudi unhappiness with the US policy towards Syria and Iran.[17] The issue attracted widespread discussions in the local media which was appreciative of the Saudi stand.[18] Moreover, Saudi apprehensions became true when in November, the P5+1 and Iran announced that they have agreed on an interim deal to resolve the long-standing Iranian nuclear crisis. Apart from the strong reaction from the Saudi government, the deal attracted criticism in the local Arabic media indicating deep-seated Saudi concern over Iranian ambitions in the region.[19]

Notwithstanding these developments, the Saudi economy continued to remain buoyant throughout 2013. The gross domestic product (GDP) recorded a mild growth to reach US$745 billion despite a decline in oil revenues by about 11 per cent.[20] Revenues from non-oil sector showed good signs with 14 per cent increase representing 10 per cent of total fiscal revenues. An important aspect of the economic performance was the 5.5 per cent growth in private sector (non-oil), represented mainly in construction, retail, transport, communication and manufacturing sector.[21] It was a result of a planned effort towards economic diversification to counter the effect of fluctuations in international oil market. Saudi Arabia is trying to diversify its economy particularly in the areas of power generation, telecommunication, natural gas exploration and petrochemical sector aimed at lowering dependence on oil revenues. Most of the non-oil sectors recorded good growth during 2013.

As per preliminary estimates, the government revenues are projected at US$301.6 billion for 2013 with expenditures projected to reach US$246.7 billion, leading to a US$54.9 billion surplus.[22] The budget for 2014 is estimated to be balanced with both revenues and expenditures projected at US$228 billion. Human resource development through education and training has been a priority area as far as fiscal budget is concerned during the past five years. The year 2013 witnessed an estimated 25 per cent budgetary expenditure on education sector, including foundation of new schools, colleges and vocational institutions.[23] Moreover, 16 per cent of the budget was spent on health and social affairs. Similarly, the 2014 budget focuses on education and health sectors with nearly 50 per cent planned allocation.[24] As a whole, the government plans to invest in areas that would enhance 'long-term strong and sustainable economic development and employment opportunities' for citizens.[25] It outlines education, health, services, infrastructure and science and technology as priority areas for government expenditure.

An important concern that Saudi Arabia is trying to address has been unemployment among youth. Unemployment rate was estimated to be 12 per cent in 2013 but was recorded to be higher among women at 34 per cent.[26] The rate, however, is higher among youth, both male and female, with estimates ranging up to 40 per cent in 2013. International Monetary Fund (IMF) argues that since Saudi economy has shown robust growth in the recent years and is expected to remain strong in 2013–14, it provides a good opportunity to tackle unemployment among youth.[27] The government has taken a number of measures to generate jobs and improve employment opportunities for Saudi nationals. *Nitaqat* is one of the steps in this direction that aims at limiting the number of expatriate workers in private sector. Moreover, it aims at enhancing the share of private sector in economy to reduce dependence on oil and improve employment opportunities. Simultaneously, plans have been laid down to enhance employability and skill development through education and training of youth to reduce unemployment. Furthermore, in 2011, the government had launched an unemployment allowance plan—*Hafiz*—that continued during 2013.

The domestic situation in Saudi Arabia remained calm and stable during 2013 unlike the previous year when some disturbances were reported. Overall, social, political and economic developments indicate a slow transformation which is steered by the monarchy and is endorsed by the populace.

BILATERAL RELATIONS

Despite millennia of commercial and civilizational linkages between the subcontinent and the peninsula, India's relations with Saudi Arabia remained confined to diplomatic ties after the British withdrawal. As the two charted different foreign policy courses, their paths seldom intersected until the 1990s. The period between 1947 and 1990 witnessed occasional high-level friendly visits but did not lead to close relations.[28] Trade remained limited and people-to-people contacts were primarily confined to Hajj pilgrimage. The situation changed to some extent in the aftermath of oil boom due to large inflow of Indian expatriate workers who earned goodwill for themselves and their country with their skills and hard work. The dynamics changed with the changing post-Cold War global order as both sides started to realign their international relations. Economy became the catalyst for a measured break from the past leading to enhanced relations and willingness for strategic cooperation due to concurring interests and concerns.

The 2006 visit of King Abdullah to India and Prime Minister Manmohan Singh's visit to Saudi Arabia in 2010 paved the way for expansion of bilateral relations in the last five years.[29] The year 2012 witnessed major breakthrough in the field of defence cooperation with the visit of Indian Defence Minister, joint meeting and extraditions of terror accused to India. Moreover, trade volume increased with Saudi Arabia agreeing to export more petroleum to compensate the loss due to sanctions on Iran. Efforts from private and government organizations on both sides continued to explore business and investment opportunities reaching fruition at times. A smooth Hajj with large Indian consignment and continuous outflow of Indian workers and professionals together with promising trade and business expansion marked the deepening of bilateral ties in 2012.

Political Relations

As a result of recognition of each other's importance and their domination to improve bilateral relations, India and Saudi Arabia recognized the need for high-level political exchanges. Apart from the visits of King Abdullah (2006) and Prime Minister Manmohan Singh (2010), the last five years have witnessed numerous bilateral visits.

From the Indian side, the visits included those by External Affairs Minister S. M. Krishna in March 2011 and Minister of Defence A. K. Antony in February 2012. Moreover, Minister of Overseas Indian Affairs Vayalar Ravi and Petroleum Minister S. Jaipal Reddy had visited Saudi Arabia in September 2010 and February 2011, respectively. Ministers of State for External Affairs E. Ahamed (April 2009 and 2011) and Shashi Tharoor (March 2010) visited the Kingdom. Chairperson of Hajj Committee of India Mohsina Kidwai (March 2011) and National Security Advisor Shivshankar Menon (December 2011) visited Saudi Arabia to discharge official duties. Furthermore, Deputy Chairman of Rajya Sabha K. Rahman Khan visited Saudi Arabia to attend the G-20 Parliament Speaker's Consultative Meeting in Riyadh during 25–26 February 2012 and held meetings with various Saudi leaders. Minister of Health and Family Welfare Ghulam Nabi Azad represented India at the funeral of Crown Prince Sultan in October 2011, while Minister of Law and Justice Salman Khurshid led a three-member delegation in June 2012 to offer condolences on the demise of Crown Prince Nayef.

Some of the important visits from the Saudi side included the visit of then Governor of Riyadh Prince Salman (Crown Prince since June 2012) in April 2010. Earlier, Intelligence Chief and now Second Deputy Prime Minister Prince Muqrin had come to India in January 2009. Abdulla Zainal Alireza, Minister of Commerce, had visited India in August 2009 and November 2010 to explore opportunities for enhancing bilateral trade and commerce. Other visits include Minister for Economy and Planning Khalid bin Muhammad al-Qusaibi's (February 2011); Prince Bandar bin Sultan, Secretary General of Saudi National Security Council (March 2011); Tawfiq Bin Fawzan al-Rabiah, Minister of Commerce and Industry (January 2012) and Deputy Minister of Petroleum and Mineral Resources Abdulaziz bin Salman al-Saud (February 2012).

The high point of political relations in 2013 was the visit of External Affairs Minister Salman Khurshid during 25–26 May.[30] This was his first visit to the region after taking charge of the ministry during which he met Crown Prince Salman, Second Deputy Prime Minister Prince Muqrin, Foreign Minister Prince Saud al-Faisal and Labour Minister Adel Fakeih.[31] He also delivered a personal letter from the Indian Prime Minister to King Abdullah and discussed various domestic, regional and international issues pertaining to Indo-Saudi relations. The principal focus of this visit, however, was the issue of *Nitaqat* and India thanked Saudi Arabia for allowing a grace period for Indian expatriate workers to correct their status or return without paying the penalty.[32] The issue of turmoil in Syria and concerns over Iranian nuclear programme also came in for discussion. Salman Khurshid, during the joint press conference with the Saudi Foreign Minister, expressed satisfaction at the progress of Indo-Saudi defence and security ties emphasizing that terror is a common enemy for both the countries and that the stability and security in the Gulf and South Asia are mutually interlinked.[33] Moreover, he highlighted the Indian willingness to enhance the already flourishing trade relations and invited more Saudi investments in India. He further argued that people-to-people contacts could enhance through educational cooperation and youth exchange programmes.

In addition, Minister of State for External Affairs E. Ahamed visited Saudi Arabia with members of Hajj delegation and met Bandar bin Mohammed al-Hajjar, Saudi Minister of Hajj, in Jeddah and signed the Hajj agreement for 2013.[34] Minister of Overseas Indian Affairs Vayalar Ravi visited Saudi Arabia on 27–30 April and was accompanied by E. Ahamed and T. K. A. Nair, Advisor to Prime Minister, and held meetings with Saudi leaders including Foreign Minister, Labour Minister and Deputy Interior Minister. Other visits included Attorney General G. E. Vahanvati's visit during 14–21 May when he met Interior Minister Prince Muhammad bin Nayef and Justice Minister Mohammed bin Abdulkareem al-Issa. On 3 July, Rajiv Mehrishi, Secretary in the Ministry of Overseas Indian Affairs (MOIA), visited the kingdom and held meetings with Saudi Vice Labour Minister Mufraj al-Haqbani and in August Ashok Kantha, Secretary (East), Ministry of External Affairs (MEA) visited Saudi Arabia to review the arrangements for Hajj.[35] Finance Minister P. Chidambaram visited Saudi Arabia to attend the India–Saudi Arabia Joint Commission Meeting held in Riyadh during 27–28 January 2014[36] while Crown Prince Salman was slated to visit India in February 2014.[37]

From the Saudi side, important political visits included Saudi Deputy Minister of Labour Ahmad Bin Fahad al-Fuhaid's to participate in a two-day meeting of Joint Working Group (JWG) on Labour issues between India and Saudi Arabia during 30–31 May. On the sidelines of the JWG meeting, he met Minister of Overseas Indian Affairs Vayalar Ravi.[38] In November, Saudi Deputy Minister for Law Fahad Abuhimed visited India for the Second Review Meeting of the ninth Joint Committee held in New Delhi. As a sign of deepening relations, a labour cooperation pact was signed between India and Saudi Arabia.[39]

Economic Relations

Trade and commerce are important areas of bilateral relations between India and Saudi Arabia. Two-way trade has constantly recorded growths during the past five years except for a minor decline during 2009–10. Saudi Arabia is the fourth largest trading partner of India and is second only to United Arab Emirates (UAE) in the Persian Gulf, which has emerged as the largest regional trading partner for India. The total trade between India and Saudi Arabia has recorded a growth of 16.75 per cent during 2012–13 in comparison to 2011–12 (Table 8.1 and Figure 8.1). Bilateral trade now comprises 5.53 per cent of India's total foreign trade. Trade balance remains skewed in favour of Saudi Arabia owing mainly to hydrocarbon imports that comprise nearly 90 per cent of India's total

Table 8.1
India–Saudi Arabia Bilateral Trade (in US$ Million)

	2009–10	2010–11	2011–12	2012–13
India's exports to Saudi Arabia	3,907.00	4,684.40	5,683.29	9,785.78
India's imports from Saudi Arabia	17,097.57	20,385.28	31,817.70	33,998.11
Total bilateral trade	21,004.57	25,069.68	37,500.99	43,783.89
Share of Saudi Arabia in India's total trade	4.50	4.04	4.72	5.53

Source: Adapted from Directorate General of Foreign Trade, New Delhi, available at: www.dgft.gov.in/.

Figure 8.1
India–Saudi Arabia Bilateral Trade

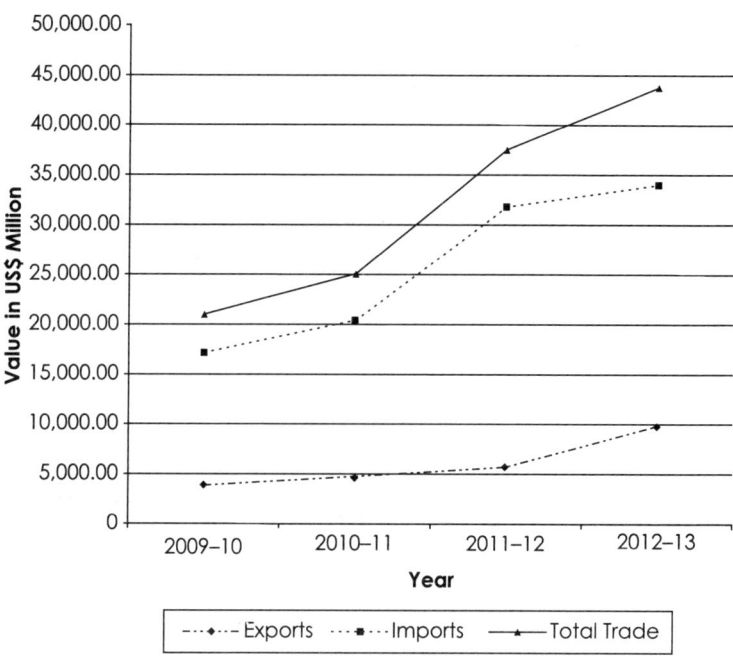

Source: Adapted from Directorate General of Foreign Trade, New Delhi, available at: www.dgft.gov.in/.

Table 8.2
Share of Oil in India's Imports from Saudi Arabia (in US$ Million)

Year	Oil imports from Saudi Arabia	Total oil imports	Saudi share in total oil imports	Imports from Saudi Arabia	Per cent of oil in imports from Saudi Arabia
2009–10	15,390.04	96,321.16	15.98	17,097.57	90.01
2010–11	17,932.31	115,929.06	15.47	20,385.28	87.97
2011–12	28,302.37	172,753.97	16.38	31,060.10	91.12
2012–13	29,896.53	181,344.63	16.49	33,998.11	87.94

Source: Adapted from Directorate General of Foreign Trade, New Delhi, available at: www.dgft.gov.in/.

Figure 8.2

Share of Oil in India's Imports from Saudi Arabia

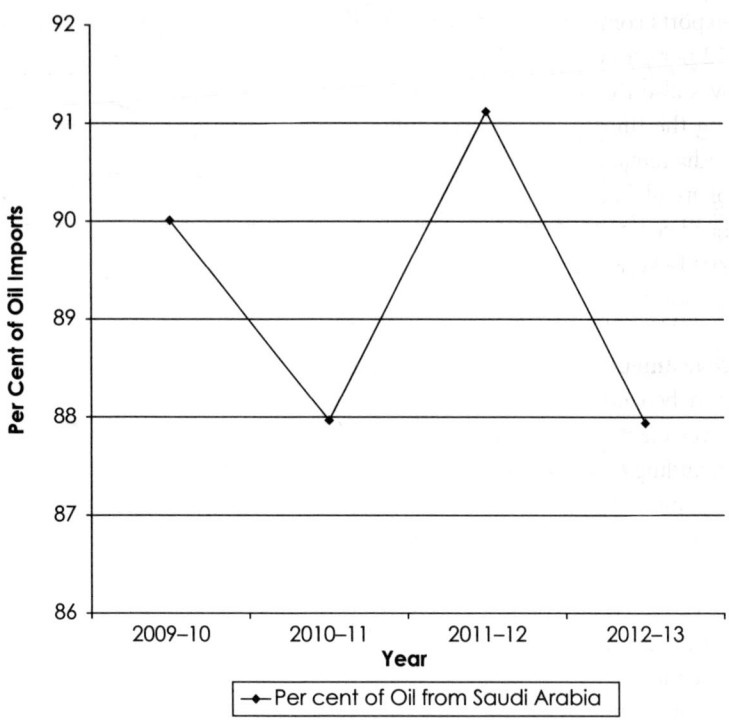

Source: Adapted from Directorate General of Foreign Trade, New Delhi, available at: www.dgft.gov.in/.

imports from Saudi Arabia (Table 8.2 and Figure 8.2). Saudi Arabia remains India's largest supplier of crude oil, accounting for almost one-fifth of its imports (Table 8.2).

In 2012–13, India's total imports from Saudi Arabia stood at US$33.99 billion, witnessing a growth of 6.85 per cent from the previous year (Table 8.1). There was not much difference in terms of commodities which comprised crude oil, chemicals and fertilizers, plastic and rubber products, paper and wood products, animal products, dry fruits and nuts, pearls, metals and metal articles, etc. Indian exports to Saudi Arabia grew to US$9.78 billion in 2012–13 (Table 8.1). Major exports comprised of petroleum products, animal and dairy products, machinery, cereals, fruits and vegetables, cotton and textile, animal fodder, and so on. During 2012–13, Saudi Arabia emerged as the seventh largest market for Indian exports comprising 3.25 per cent of total exports, which is a growth of 72 per cent compared to 2011–12. Moreover, in 2012–13, Saudi Arabia was also the source of 6.92 per cent of India's global imports, becoming the third largest supplier after China and UAE. For Saudi Arabia, India remains the fifth largest export market, accounting for 8.3 per cent of its global exports, but in terms of imports by Saudi Arabia, India has become the seventh largest source, which is an improvement from 2011–12 when it was ninth.[40] It now accounts for nearly 4 per cent of the former's total imports.[41]

Investments: In addition to imports and exports, economic relations have benefitted from two-way flow of investments. The prospects of Saudi investments in India have remained untapped due to various reasons, including a lack of confidence and less friendly investment environment. Not much headway was made in the US$750 million India–Saudi Joint Investment Fund that was announced during the ninth Joint Commission Meeting (JCM) held in New Delhi in January 2012. Meanwhile, during 2012–13, India received US$7.13 million worth of investments from Saudi companies recording a 10-fold growth in comparison to 2011–12 when it was US$0.7 million.[42]

Although the investments have witnessed growth, the cumulative long-term Saudi investments in India have remained constant at 0.02 per cent. In fact, Saudi Arabia fell back three steps to be 48th largest investor in Indian market in 2013.[43] According to figures released by the Department of Industrial Policy and Promotion between April 2000 and November 2013, Saudi companies have invested US$41.18 million in India.[44] These investments can be located in fields as varied as paper manufacturing, chemicals, computer software, granite processing, industrial products and machinery, cement, metallurgical industries, etc.[45] Moreover, among the Persian Gulf countries Saudi Arabia is the third largest source of foreign direct investment (FDI) into India after UAE and Oman.

Indian businesses have invested in Saudi Arabia to the tune of US$2.07 billion between 2000 and 2009.[46] Farah Naaz Gauri observes that Indian firms have shown remarkable interest in Saudi market after implementation of new Saudi laws and have established joint venture projects or wholly owned subsidiaries in the kingdom. According to the Indian Embassy in Saudi Arabia, the Saudi Arabian General Investment Authority (SAGIA) has issued 426 licences to Indian companies for joint ventures or fully owned subsidiaries till 2010, with expected investments worth of US$1.6 billion in Saudi Arabia.[47] According to latest figures available for 2012, nearly 350 Indian projects were functioning in the kingdom with US$1.6 billion in sectors such as construction, contracting, administrative consulting and IT.[48]

Low investment figures notwithstanding, both sides recognize the possibilities of enhancing two-way investments. During his visit to India in March 2013, Abdul Rahman al-Rabiah, Chairman of Saudi–India Joint Business Council (JBC) emphasized that 'Saudi Arabia is offering investment opportunities worth US$625 billion to Indian businessmen in vital sectors such as infrastructure, petrochemicals, electricity, IT, tourism, natural gas production, agriculture and education'.[49] Besides New Delhi, he visited Lucknow and Hyderabad to hold meetings with Indian businessmen and to invite them to invest in Saudi Arabia. Moreover, the Indian side is also keen on attracting Saudi investments in fields such as oil and gas, real estate and lucrative Indian financial market. During his visit to Saudi Arabia to participate in the 10th JCM in January 2014, Finance Minister P. Chidambaram

> discussed the importance of Saudi investment in India and presented specific projects in India including Delhi–Mumbai Industrial Corridor (DMIC); OpaL Petrochemical Complex, Gujarat; Petrochemical Complex at Mangalore, Karnataka; IOCL's LNG Project at Ennore, Tamil Nadu; Paradip Refinery/Petrochemical Project of IOCL at Paradip; and Kochi Petrochemical Project of BPCL.[50]

Owing to increased interests on both sides, some new projects have been muted and a few of them realized. For example, in December 2012, Tata Motors signed a letter of intent with Saudi Arabia to set up Land Rover plant in the country with an initial investment of US$1.2 billion.[51] Moreover, Saudi Basic Industries Corporation (SABIC), one of the world's biggest petrochemical companies, inaugurated a US$100 million state-of-the-art research and development (R&D) centre in Bangalore in December 2013.[52]

Energy Relations

The story of India's economic growth cannot be divorced from energy security concerns. India imports nearly 80 per cent of its energy requirements.[53] With an increase of 5.1 per cent in oil consumption, India has emerged as the third largest energy consumer in the world during 2012 after China and the US leaving behind Russia, Japan and Germany.[54] Saudi Arabia, on the other hand, is the largest producer and exporter of oil and has the largest known oil reserves in the world accounting for one-fifth of the proven oil reserves. It is the largest source of energy for India and supplies nearly one-fifth of India's energy requirements. Energy has been one of the driving forces behind India's relations with Saudi Arabia and it will continue to dominate the Indo-Saudi ties. As Table 8.3 shows, the Saudi share in total oil imports by India continues to range between 15 and 17 per cent during the past four years. Moreover, Saudi share in India's energy imports from the Persian Gulf countries hovers around 25 to 30 per cent during the past five years (Table 8.3 and Figure 8.3).

During 2012–13, a slight increase of US$1 billion was recorded in India's energy import bills from Saudi Arabia from the previous year. Energy relations remained limited to imports but India is seeking Saudi investments to develop in downstream petroleum industry and received a positive response. The two countries agreed to encourage cooperation

Table 8.3
India's Energy Imports from Saudi Arabia (in US$ Million)

	2009–10	2010–11	2011–12	2012–13
Energy imports from Saudi Arabia	15,390.04	17,932.31	28,302.37	29,896.53
Total energy imports	96,321.16	115,929.06	172,753.97	181,344.63
Total energy imports from Persian Gulf	55,904.14	66,688.40	95,915.24	105,809.19
Share in total energy imports	15.98	15.47	16.38	16.49
Share in energy imports from Persian Gulf	27.53	26.89	29.13	28.26

Source: Adapted from Directorate General of Foreign Trade, New Delhi, available at: www.dgft.gov.in/.

Figure 8.3

Share of Saudi Arabia in India's Oil Imports

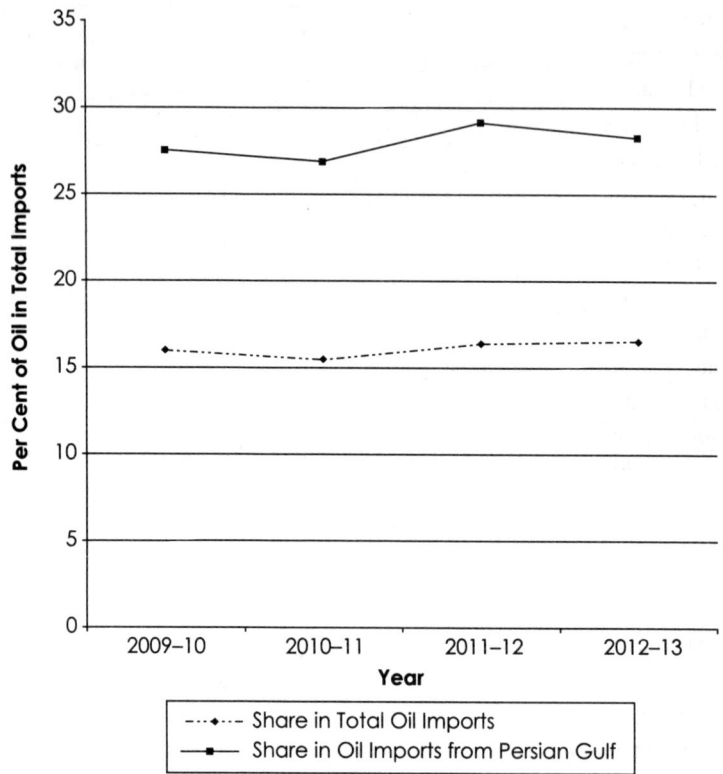

Source: Adapted from Directorate General of Foreign Trade, New Delhi, available at: www.dgft.gov.in/.

in the field of oil, gas and minerals through a Joint Technical Team during Finance Minister P. Chidambaram's visit to Saudi Arabia in January 2014.[55] These developments may lead to enhanced cooperation in the field of energy in the near future.

Defence Relations

Defence has been an important area of mutual concern for India and Saudi Arabia, which has led to cooperation for peace and security in the region. The previous year was an important milestone with the visit of Defence Minister A. K. Antony, and extradition of terror accused to India. Although defence and security remains a critical area of bilateral relations, 2013 did not witness any major development in this field. The two countries have continued to cooperate in anti-piracy operations in the Indian Ocean. Moreover, they had agreed to form a Joint Committee on Defence Cooperation in 2012 that held its first meeting in September 2012 in New Delhi. 'During the meeting both sides expressed their interest in further enhancing defence exchanges and interactions between their armed forces.'[56] However, things remained muted in 2013.

During his visit to Saudi Arabia in May, External Affairs Minister Salman Khurshid expressed satisfaction over the progress made in defence and security relations between the two countries.[57] He further said, 'The Security and stability in the Arabian Peninsula is closely linked to the security in South Asia', indicating the importance India attaches to Saudi Arabia with respect to domestic and regional security.[58] He told the Saudi English daily *Arab News*, 'India considers Saudi Arabia a centre of stability in the region,' and that 'Bilateral security cooperation between India and Saudi Arabia will contribute to regional stability and in addressing the common threat of terrorism in the region.'[59] This outlines Indian desire to cooperate with Persian Gulf countries to fight terror particularly cross-border terrorism.

With respect to security and defence, an important question that has reverberated in recent times is India's response to the security concerns of the Arab countries, particularly in the context of receding American strategic presence in the region. India till now has treaded a fine line without taking a clear stand. However, during the 2013 Manama Dialogue External Affairs Minister Salman Khurshid said that, 'India has the capabilities and the will to not only safeguard India's own coastline and island territories, but also contribute to keeping our region's SLOCs [sea lines of communication] open and flowing,' which is of vital importance for India's economy and security.[60] At the same time, he rejected speculations of India providing on-the-ground military assistance and security like the US.[61]

Cultural Relations

Cultural ties between India and Saudi Arabia have grown during recent years. India has a memorandum of understanding (MoU) on Cultural Cooperation with Saudi Arabia, an agreement in the field of youth and sports, and another MoU of Scientific and Educational Cooperation. Both the countries wish to increase cooperation in the field of education and research. It is in this regard that an MoU for joint research programmes was signed between the two countries. Moreover, an agreement was signed between King Abdulaziz Foundation for Research and Archives and India–Arab Cultural Centre at Jamia Millia Islamia, New Delhi, to translate important Arabic books on history and culture of the Kingdom into Indian languages.[62] However, nothing happened during 2013.

Tourism has emerged as an important area where both sides find possibilities of growth. Although both sides have expedited their efforts to attract tourists, things have not yet materialized into tangible results. India has tried to promote itself as a possible tourist destination for Saudis. The Indian embassy in Riyadh, in association with Ministry of Tourism, had organized road shows at various places in the Kingdom to encourage Indian tourism in Saudi Arabia. A proposal to sign an MoU to boost tourism was mooted by Indian side in 2012 but no progress has been made in this direction.[63] A number of events and visits had taken place during 2012 indicating enhanced interests in improving bilateral cultural relations. *Indian Cultural Week* was organized in Riyadh in November 2012[64] and a Saudi youth delegation had visited India in March 2012.[65] In May 2013, *Road Shows* were organized in the cities of Jeddah, Riyadh and Dammam to woo Saudi tourists to India.[66] A high-level delegation led by the Secretary Tourism, Government of India, Perwez Dewan, and consisting of State Tourism officers and private tour operators visited the Kingdom for the occasion.

Expatriates: Indians comprise the largest expatriate community in Saudi Arabia, accounting for nearly one-third of the total expatriate population.[67] Currently, the number of Indians engaged in various works in Saudi Arabia is estimated at 2.8 million. As much as 50 per cent comprise unskilled labours working in construction, oil industry and other unorganized sectors. Saudi Arabia continues to attract the largest number of Indian workers; during 2012 out of 747,041 workers that sought emigration clearance to go abroad for work, 357,503, that is, nearly 45 per cent went to Saudi Arabia.[68] India received US$70 billion in remittances from abroad during 2012, of which, nearly US$30 billion came from the Gulf Cooperation Council (GCC) countries.[69] Among the GCC, Saudi

Arabia is the largest source of remittances, amounting to US$3.5 billion annually, which is also the largest inward flow of foreign exchange from a single country.

An important area of problem with respect to Indian expatriates in the GCC countries, including in Saudi Arabia, has been exploitation of the workers as well as harsh living conditions. India has continuously raised the issue at bilateral forums and seeks bilateral agreements with destination countries to improve working conditions of Indian workers. India celebrates Pravasi Bhartiya Divas (PBD) to improve linkages with its diaspora every year. In 2013, an Indian businessman in Saudi Arabia Mohammed R. Karuvanthodi was awarded PBD award for business in 2013.[70] According to the Ministry of Overseas Indian Affairs, the exploitation of Indian workers in Gulf countries has come down during recent years due to steps taken by the government as well as efforts of Indian expatriate communities in the respective countries.[71]

Nitaqat: An important issue that emerged in 2013 was the Saudization programme launched in 2011, namely *Nitaqat.* It has been launched to improve job prospects for Saudi nationals in private sector. The issue reverberated in India due to its impact on the workers and their families. It was reported that Indian workers would be worst affected due to the policy because they constitute the largest number in small- and medium-sized enterprises that were worst hit by *Nitaqat.* Indian authorities took up the issue with Saudi Arabia and India–Saudi JWG was formed to work towards minimizing fallout of *Nitaqat.*[72] In April, King Abdullah 'announced a grace period allowing overstaying expatriates to correct status, get new jobs or leave the country without facing penal action till the end of the grace period', on 3 November.[73] Indian workers benefitted the most from the grace period and as much as 1.4 million Indians regularized their job status during the period.[74] However, nearly 75,000 Indian workers returned after they were issued emergency certificates by the Indian embassy in Riyadh.[75] A large chunk of these returnees belong to Kerala that has the largest number of expatriate workers in the Gulf. Though *Nitaqat* posed an important challenge for Indo-Saudi relations during 2013, it was handled carefully by the Indian authorities. The issue figured prominently during Salman Khurshid's visit to the kingdom in May.[76]

Hajj: India is home to a large population of Muslims who have travelled to the holy cities of Mecca and Medina to perform Hajj and Umrah (pilgrimage to Kaaba carried out not during Hajj) since the advent of Islam. India has continued to send one of the largest groups of pilgrims for Hajj in modern times. In 2010, a record number of 171,671 Indian pilgrims visited Saudi Arabia for Hajj, while in 2011 the number was 170,362. Despite a request by India for an increase in Hajj quota, the number for 2012 remained the same and a total of 169,971 Indian pilgrims visited Saudi Arabia to perform Hajj. Saudi Arabia had to cut down on the number of Hajj pilgrims for 2013 due to the ongoing expansion work in *Masjid al-Haram* in Mecca. Therefore, the number of Indian Hajj pilgrims came down to 135,938. However, more than 200,000 Indian pilgrims visited Saudi Arabia to perform Umrah during 2012–13.[77] Indian authorities have constantly worked towards providing a smooth Hajj for Indians through improved services, monitoring and consultation with Saudi authorities. In August, Secretary (East), MEA, Ashok Kantha visited Saudi Arabia to review arrangements for Hajj and expressed satisfaction over the preparations.

External Players

India's relations with Saudi Arabia are affected by important international and regional players such as the US, China, Pakistan, Iran and Israel, all of whom have stakes in the regional dynamics. The US dominance in Middle East is noticeably receding in recent times while China has been trying to enhance its presence, and both these developments pose strategic challenges for India. Pakistan has historically played the religious card to isolate India from Muslim states but the situation has started to change in recent times due to realignment in India's foreign policy and active diplomacy. However, Pakistan's 'brotherly' relations with Saudi Arabia remain a potent challenge for India. Additionally, Iran and Israel are two important regional players with whom India has good relations but both have an antagonistic relation with Saudi Arabia that can potentially affect the Indo-Saudi ties.

The US: The US is a *de facto* regional player because of its long presence and historical dominance in the Middle East and Persian Gulf. Saudi Arabia is a strategic ally of the US and the alliance goes back to the

1930s when oil exploration started in the kingdom. Moreover, towards the end of the Second World War, the US provided security to the Persian Gulf replacing Britain. Thus, the historical relations between the US and Saudi Arabia are forged in oil and security.[78] However, a number of developments in the recent times have indicated differences between the US and Saudi Arabia as well as changing regional dynamics and American policy in the region. This has become evident during the Arab Spring, particularly in the case of Egypt and Syria. In the case of Egypt, Saudi Arabia rushed to provide aid and support after the military dismissed Mohammed Morsi's government in July.[79] On the other hand, the US has taken a cautious approach, emphasizing on the need for restoration of peace and democracy.[80] In Syria's case, Saudi Arabia was pressing for external military intervention to remove Bashar al-Assad, particularly after the alleged use of chemical weapons by the regime in August.[81] However, the US chose to think otherwise and agreed to the Russian proposal whereby Syria consented to surrender its stockpile of chemical weapons.[82] This evidently angered the monarchy and Saudi Arabia refused to take the non-permanent seat in the UNSC, protesting against inaction on Syria.[83] Moreover, the interim nuclear deal between Iran and global powers has further exposed the fissure in US–Saudi relations.[84] Apart from the changing dynamics of US–Saudi relations, American interests and policy in the Persian Gulf have undergone substantial change. In fact, due to increasing domestic economic concerns and changing global and regional situation, the US influence in the region has started to recede, which is a major concern for India particularly with respect to its energy security dependence upon the region.

China: The Saudi–Chinese relations have grown manifold in recent times. China has started to emerge as a major global player because of its economic strides and soft strategic presence in many parts of the world. It has emerged as a main competitor for India in the Persian Gulf because of the overlapping trajectories of interests particularly with Iran and Saudi Arabia. On the other hand, Saudi Arabia has looked to diversify its dependence on outside powers and considers China as a major international player. Bilateral trade has grown manifold between the two countries and China has emerged as Saudi Arabia's largest trading partner accounting for US$73 billion during 2012–13.[85] Notwithstanding the growing trade and commerce, the Saudi–Chinese relations face numerous challenges. China is equally interested in Iran and maintains commercial ties and friendly relations. In fact, together with Russia, China has emerged as a major strategic player working towards bringing an end to Iranian isolation as well as in countering Saudi moves in Syria. Moreover, China neither has the desire nor the capability to replace American military presence in the region, which is critically important for Saudi security.[86] India's options are limited when it comes to Chinese presence in the region. On the bilateral front, it has to compete with China in terms of trade and energy imports but at the regional front it needs to cooperate with China in the case of receding American presence.

Pakistan: Pakistan and Saudi Arabia have maintained 'brotherly' relations based on their Islamic heritage since 1947.[87] This had remained a major roadblock for Indo-Saudi relations in the past. However, the situation changed with changing global dynamics as both Saudi Arabia and Indian recognized each other's importance and economic potential of bilateral relations. The Saudi decision in 2012 to extradite a number of terror suspects to India despite Pakistani reservations is seen by commentator as significant change.[88] This situation has started to look different in 2013. With the interim Iranian nuclear deal, Saudi Arabia has begun to look at Pakistan as a counterforce against Iran. Reports have emerged that Saudi Arabia might try to procure nuclear weapons from Pakistan.[89] Moreover, many commentators have highlighted the intricate relations between the two that encompass their domestic and external concerns.[90] Given the fast-changing situation in the Middle East and Saudi policy to counterweight Iran and receding US influence, India needs to keep the Pakistani angle in mind while devising a policy towards the region.

Iran: The interim nuclear deal between Iran and world powers concluded in Geneva in November has disturbed Saudi Arabia as it competes with Iran for regional dominance. The two share deep-seated suspicion towards each other due to political, ethnic and sectarian differences. Saudi Arabia has become increasingly suspicious and uneasy with

Iran's alleged nuclear ambitions leading to speculations that the kingdom might try to procure nuclear weapons in the eventuality of an Iranian rapprochement with the West. Moreover, Saudi Arabia has accused Iran of trying to incite Shias in Bahrain and in its Eastern Province since the outbreak of Arab Spring. The Kingdom sees it as an Iranian design to destabilize the Arab countries in the Gulf region that would enhance Iran's strategic position. India, however, looks at Iran as an important regional player which is closer home and has overlapping interests when it comes to Afghanistan. With the growing likelihood of American withdrawal from Afghanistan by December 2014 without putting in place a stable and strong Afghanistan, Iranian importance in the region would increase manifold.[91]

Israel: Israel is another important regional player that has good relations with India. However, Saudi Arabia and Israel do not share diplomatic ties as the former does not recognize the latter as a legitimate state because of historical reasons. The situation does not seem to alter anytime soon despite renewed American efforts at finding a resolution to the Israeli-Palestinian conflict. Despite antagonistic relations, Israel and Saudi Arabia found themselves on the same page over the Iranian nuclear issue and evoked speculations about their possible cooperation to counter Iran. Although Israel does not directly affect India's relations with Saudi Arabia, India's policy towards the region will need to balance the contrary forces with respect to its interests.

Challenges

There are numerous macro- and micro-level challenges pertaining to India's relations with Saudi Arabia. At the macro level, the most important aspect is to take the bilateral engagements beyond trade and commerce. Defence and security cooperation have made some strides but the two would need to improve political and cultural exchanges to realize the vision of 'strategic partnership'. There are several aspects that need more attention particularly, with respect to each other's engagements with regional adversaries. India has been able to balance its bilateral relations with multiple regional actors, such Iran, Israel and Saudi Arabia, but as engagements get deeper India would need to tread a fine line on issue basis. There are several differences with Saudi Arabia on regional issues such as the Syrian problem, turmoil in Egypt, Iranian nuclear issue and Israeli-Palestinian conflict. Additionally, Saudi engagements in Afghanistan and Pakistan have harmed Indian interests and compromised on its security which needs to be taken up with Saudi Arabia.

The two developing economies can further enhance their strategic relations by taking confidence-building measures at the micro level. For example, despite robust economic relations, there are scopes for further improving bilateral trade. Investments in each other economies in emerging areas would be beneficial and help deepen the engagements. India needs to increase people-to-people contacts with Saudi Arabia through non-traditional means such as youth exchange programme, educational exchanges and cultural activities. India needs to think about Saudi market and find mechanism for skill development for workers going to Saudi Arabia. Labour outflow is an important area; India now has an agreement on domestic workers and it would be important that an agreement covering all workers is signed. It needs to streamline the means and processes at internal level, taking measures so as to avoid frivolous recruitments that lead to exploitation. The Ministry of Overseas Indian Affairs (MOIA) has taken steps to educate workers, seeking emigration for work, of the pitfalls and problems they might face. However, it still reaches very few of those who seek work abroad particularly in rural areas.

Another important challenge is to monitor the funding of Islamic seminaries in India that have contributed in perpetuating educational backwardness among India Muslims.[92] A number of such seminaries seek private funding from Saudi Arabia and other Arab countries which helps them in sustaining the system.[93] Arguably, some motivated and disgruntled elements have used these channels to finance radical behaviour including violent activities.[94] It is, however, a sensitive issue among Indian Muslims as well as can ruffle Saudi feathers. Therefore, the issue needs to be taken up with Saudi Arabia in a manner to avoid any repercussions. Since internal security has become a concern for Saudis as well, it is important that this issue is used to build confidence and streamline the process of seeking foreign funds for seminaries. More importantly, India needs to monitor these funding and act firmly when necessary.

CONCLUSION

The year 2013 proved to be another good year in Indo-Saudi bilateral relations as the Indian External Affairs Minister visited the Kingdom and India succeeded in signing a labour agreement. The continued cooperation in the area of defence and security and prospects for intelligence sharing were major diplomatic achievements. Trade and commerce continued to flourish and two-way investments got a boost during the year while energy imports from Saudi Arabia witnessed increase. Another important achievement on part of India was its reaction and response to the *Nitaqat* issue. Initial concerns regarding impact on Indian workers proved to be misguided as the impact remains limited due to proactive role played by the Indian authorities and the Indian mission in Riyadh. A smooth Hajj with large Indian participation during 2013 indicated strong relations. Moreover, India tried to attract Saudi tourists and investments through roadshows in various cities in the Kingdom, which should help attract business as well as casual tourists. However, there is still a need to strengthen the ties and think beyond traditional measures and look for innovative means to engage with the Kingdom that will attract investments as well as go a long way in realizing the vision of 'strategic partnership'. A proactive engagement remains by and large missing, which requires attention of the authorities as infinite possibilities remain unachieved in Indo-Saudi relations.

NOTES

1. For a through reading, see Joseph Kéchichian, *Legal and Political Reforms in Saudi Arabia* (London: Routledge, 2013); Madawi al-Rasheed, *A History of Saudi Arabia* (Cambridge: Cambridge University Press, 2010); Sarah Yizraeli, *Politics and Society in Saudi Arabia: The Crucial Years of Development, 1960–1982* (London: Hurst and Company, 2012).
2. 'Saudi Arabia Religious Police Chief Announces New Curbs', *BBC News*, 3 October 2012, available at: http://www.bbc.co.uk/news/world-middle-east-19819791/.
3. Frank Gardner, 'London Olympics 2012: Saudis Allow Women to Compete', *BBC News*, 24 June 2012, available at: http://www.bbc.co.uk/news/world-middle-east-18571193/.
4. Saudi Woman's Weblog, 'Loujain Al Hathloul', 9 November 2013, available at: http://saudiwoman.me/2013/11/09/loujain-al-hathloul/.

5. Eman al-Nafjan, 'Saudi Women Drivers Not Deterred by Arrest', *Al-Monitor*, 1 November 2013, available at: www.al-monitor.com/pulse/originals/2013/11/saudi-arabia-women-driving-campaign.html/.

6. Fouziya Khan, 'First Female Law Firm Opened in Jeddah', *Arab News*, 3 January 2014, available at: http://www.arabnews.com/news/502791/.

7. Amnesty International, 'Saudi Arabia Punishes Two Activists for Voicing Opinion', 11 March 2013, available at: http://www.amnesty.org/en/news/saudi-arabia-punishes-two-activists-voicing-opinion-2013-03-11/.

8. Ibid.

9. Abdullah Al Dahlan and Badr Al Shahry, 'Court Convicts Oyouni and Huweider to Ten Months Prison and Two Years Travel Ban', *Al-Hayat* [Arabic Daily], 16 June 2013, available at: http://alhayat.com/Details/524187/.

10. Manal al-Sharif, 'Conviction of Wajeha Al-Huweider and Fawziya Al-Oyouni', 16 June 2013, available at: www.manal-alsharif.com/.

11. Suad Abu-Dayyeh, 'Saudi Activists Wajeha Al-Huweider and Fawzia Al-Oyouni Jailed for Trying to Help Starving Women', *The Independent*, 15 July 2013, available at: http://blogs.independent.co.uk/2013/07/15/saudi-activists-wajeha-al-huwaider-and-fawzia-al-oyouni-jailed-for-trying-to-help-starving-woman/.

12. 'Appeal Court Confirms District Court's Conviction of Oyouni and Huweider to Ten Months Prison and Two Years Travel Ban', 26 September 2013, available at: www.saudiwomenrights.wordpress.com/.

13. Toby Matthiesen, 'A "Saudi Spring?": The Shi'a Protest Movement in the Eastern Province 2011–2012', *The Middle East Journal*, 2012, Vol. 66, No. 4, pp. 628–59.

14. Prince Muhammad bin Faisal who was Governor of Eastern Province since 1985 was replaced by Prince Saud bin Nayef in January 2013 allegedly because of his failure in handling the protests.

15. The seat was vacated due to the death of Prince Sattam who had succeeded Prince Salman after his elevation as Defence Minister upon the death of Crown Prince Sultan. Khalid is son of Bandar, the oldest surviving son of Abdulaziz bin Abdulrahman al-Saud who had lost out to Sultan in 1982 in the line of succession. He had lobbied since then to place his sons in plum position in the government.

16. 'The Kingdom Takes a Historic and Unprecedented Stand to Refuse UNSC Seat', *Al-Riyadh* [Arabic Daily], 19 October 2013, available at: http://www.alriyadh.com/2013/10/19/article876690.html/.

17. See Robert F. Worth, 'Saudi Arabia Rejects U.N. Security Council Seat in Protest Move', *The New York Times*, 18 October 2013, available at: http://www.nytimes.com/2013/10/19/world/middleeast/saudi-arabia-rejects-security-council-seat.html?_r=0/.

18. For example, see Mutlaq Saud al-Mutery, 'Nothing New in Saudi Stand', *Al-Riyadh* [Arabic Daily], 21 October 2013, available at: http://www.alriyadh.com/2013/10/21/article877255.html/.

19. For example, see Jamil al-Ziyabi, 'The "Great Satan" Succeeds ... and Gulf disappears!' *Al-Hayat* [Arabic Daily], 25 November 2013, available at: www.alhayat.com/OpinionsDetails/575545/.

20. Abdel Aziz Aluwaisheg, 'Saudi Budget 2014 and Economic Performance', *Arab News*, 29 December 2013, available at: http://www.arabnews.com/news/500101/.

21. Fahad Alturki, 'Saudi Arabia's 2014 Budget' *Jadwa Investment*, Riyadh, 23 December 2013, available at: www.jadwa.com/.

22. 'Recent Economic Developments and Highlights of Fiscal Years 1434/1435 (2013) and 1435/1436 (2014)', *Press Release*, Ministry of Finance, KSA, 23 December 2013, available at: http://www.mof.gov.sa/English/DownloadsCenter/Budget/Statement%20Details%20(PDF).pdf/.

23. 'Recent Economic Developments and Highlights of Fiscal Years 1433/1434 (2012) and 1434/1435 (2013)', *Press Release*, Ministry of Finance, KSA, 23 December 2012, available at: http://www.mof.gov.sa/English/DownloadsCenter/Budget/Statement%20by%20the%20Ministry%20of%20Finance%202013%20Final.pdf/.

24. 'Recent Economic Developments and Highlights of Fiscal Years 1434/1435 (2013) and 1435/1436 (2014)'.

25. Ibid.

26. Central Department of Statistics & Information, Kingdom of Saudi Arabia, available at: http://www.cdsi.gov.sa/english/index.php?option=com_docman&task=cat_view&gid=85&Itemid=162/.

27. 'Saudi Arabia's Strong Growth Offers Chance to Tackle Job Challenge', *International Monetary Fund*, 24 July 2013, available at: http://www.imf.org/external/pubs/ft/survey/so/2013/car072413a.htm/.

28. King Saud visited India in 1955 which was reciprocated by Prime Minister Jawaharlal Nehru in 1956. Twenty-six years later, Prime Minister Indira Gandhi visited Saudi Arabia in 1982. For details, see Prithvi Ram Mudiam, *India and the Middle East* (London: British Academy Press, 1994).

29. For the details of official Indian statements during the visit, including the Riyadh Declaration, see Sonia Roy, 'Prime Minister Manmohan Singh in Saudi Arabia, 27 February–1 March 2010', *India Speaks-Special Issue*, No. 4–S, 8 March 2010, Middle East Institute, New Delhi, available at: http://mei.org.in/front/cms/resourcesDetail.php?id=MTcz&cid=MTM=/.

30. 'Visit of External Affairs Minister to Saudi Arabia, May 25–26, 2013', *Press Release*, Minister of External Affairs, New Delhi, 20 May 2013, available at: http://www.mea.gov.in/outoging-visit-detail.htm?21725/Visit+of+External+Affairs+Minister+to+Saudi+Arabia+May+2526+2013/.

31. Siraj Wahab, 'Salman Khurshid: Nitaqat Issue Has Been Completely Misunderstood', *Arab News*, 27 May 2013, available at: http://www.arabnews.com/news/453027/.

32. Ibid.

218 MD. MUDDASSIR QUAMAR

33. 'Opening Statement by External Affairs Minister at Joint Press Conference with Foreign Minister of Kingdom of Saudi Arabia, in Jeddah', *Speeches and Statements*, Ministry of External Affairs, New Delhi, 25 May 2013, available at: http://www.mea.gov.in/Speeches-Statements. htm?dtl/21748/Opening+Statement+by+External+Affairs+Minister+at+J oint+Press+Conference+with+Foreign+Minister+of+Kingdom+of+Saudi +Arabia+in+Jeddah/.
34. 'India–Saudi Bilateral Relations', Embassy of India, Kingdom of Saudi Arabia, Riyadh, January 2014, available at: http://www.indianembassy.org.sa/ Content.aspx?ID=849&PID=690/.
35. Ibid.
36. 'Chidambaram Leaves on a Two-day Visit to Saudi Arabia', *The Times of India*, 27 January 2014, available at: http://articles.timesofindia.indiatimes. com/2014-01-27/india/46683817_1_india-saudi-arabia-saudi-companies-p-chidambaram/.
37. 'Crown Prince's February India Visit to Promote Business Links', *Arab News*, 28 January 2014, available at: http://www.arabnews.com/print/.
38. 'India–Saudi Bilateral Relations'.
39. 'India, Saudi Arabia to Ink Labour Cooperation Agreement', *Business Standard*, 31 December 2013, available at: www.business-standard.com/article/ printer-friendly-version?article_id=113123100852_1/.
40. 'India–Saudi Bilateral Relations'.
41. Ibid.
42. 'Factsheet on FDI', Department of Industrial Policy and Promotion, New Delhi, available at: www.dipcc.nic.in/.
43. Ibid.
44. Ibid.
45. Farah Naaz Gauri, 'Indo-Saudi Trade Relations', *Arabian Journal of Business and Management Review*, 2013, Vol. 1, No.2, pp. 45–57; 'India–Saudi Arabia Economic Relations', *Federation of Indian Chambers of Commerce and Industry*, available at: http://www.ficci.com/international/75148/Project_docs/India-Saudi-Economic—Relations.pdf/.
46. Gauri, 'Indo-Saudi Trade Relations'.
47. 'India–Saudi Bilateral Relations'.
48. 'Growing Indo-Saudi Ties', *Saudi Gazette*, Jeddah, 1 February 2014, available at: http://www.saudigazette.com.sa/index.cfm?method=home.regcon &contentid=20140201194318/.
49. P. K. Abdul Ghafour, 'KSA Offers India $ 625 Bn Investment Opportunities', *Arab News*, Riyadh, 8 March 2013, available at: http://www.arabnews. com/saudi-arabia/ksa-offers-india-625-bn-investment-opportunities/.
50. 'The Finance Minister P. Chidambaram Returns Home after His Successful Two Day Visit of Saudi Arabia ...', *Press Information Bureau*, New Delhi, 29 January 2014, available at: http://pib.nic.in/newsite/PrintRelease. aspx?relid=102831/.

51. 'Tata Motors-owned JLR Mulls Plant in Saudi Arabia, Signs Letter of Intent', *The Economic Times*, 11 December 2012, available at: http://articles.economictimes.indiatimes.com/2012-12-11/news/35749480_1_chief-executive-ralf-speth-jlr-jaguar-land-rover/.
52. 'SABIC Opens $100m Technology Centre in Bangalore', *The Economic Times*, 2 December 2013, available at: http://articles.economictimes.indiatimes.com/2013-12-02/news/44657406_1_sabic-saudi-basic-industries-corporation-technology-and-innovation/.
53. Sun-Joo Ahn and Dagmar Graczyk, *Understanding Energy Challenges in India: Policies, Players and Issues* (Paris: International Energy Agency, 2012).
54. 'Demand Continues to be Driven by the BRICS', *Global Energy Statistical Yearbook 2013*, available at: http://yearbook.enerdata.net/#analyse/. Other sources claim it is the fourth largest consumer after China, the US and Russia, for example, see Victor Mallet, 'India's Reliance on Imported Energy Threatens Long-term Recovery', *Financial Times*, 12 September 2013, available at: http://www.ft.com/cms/s/0/c20792e2-1b84-11e3-b678-00144feab7de.html#axzz2t69yYVXn/.
55. 'The Finance Minister P. Chidambaram Returns Home after His Successful Two Day Visit of Saudi Arabia ...'.
56. 'First Meeting of India–Saudi Arabia Joint Committee on Defence Co-operation', *Press Information Bureau*, New Delhi, 10 September 2012, available at: http://pib.nic.in/newsite/erelease.aspx?relid=87674/.
57. 'Opening Statement by External Affairs Minister at Joint Press Conference with Foreign Minister of Kingdom of Saudi Arabia, in Jeddah'.
58. Ibid.
59. Wahab, 'Salman Khurshid'.
60. Indrani Bagchi, 'Can India Take on a Bigger Role in the Persian Gulf?', *The Times of India*, 14 December 2013, available at: http://timesofindia.indiatimes.com/india/Can-India-take-on-a-bigger-role-in-the-Persian-Gulf/articleshow/27363253.cms/.
61. Ibid.
62. 'Vast Indian Community behind Flourishing Indo-Saudi Relations', *The Times of India*, 26 January 2012, available at: http://articles.timesofindia.indiatimes.com/2012-01-26/middle-east-news/30666095_1_indo-saudi-indian-consulate-saudi-arabian/.
63. 'To Boost Tourism India Likely to Sign MoU with Saudi Arabia', *Holiday Home Times*, 16 January 2012, available at: www.holidayhometimes.com/traveler-and-tourism/boost-tourism-india-sign-mou-saudi-arabia1673.html/.
64. 'Indian Cultural Week Celebration in KSA from 3rd to 7th November 2012', *Press Release*, Embassy of India, Kingdom of Saudi Arabia, Riyadh, available at: http://www.indianembassy.org.sa/Content.aspx?ID=854/.
65. 'Visit of the Saudi Indian Youth Forum', *Connect*, Special Issue, May 2012, available at: http://youngindians.net/img/documents/SaudiIndianYouthForum.pdf/.

66. 'India–Saudi Bilateral Relations'.
67. K. P. M. Basheer, 'At 28 Lakh, There Are More Indians in Saudi Arabia Than Estimated', *Business Line*, 6 November 2013, available at: http://www.thehindubusinessline.com/news/international/at-28-lakh-there-are-more-indians-in-saudi-arabia-than-estimated/article5322421.ece/.
68. *Annual Report 2012–13*, MOIA, available at: http://moia.gov.in/writereaddata/pdf/Annual_Report_2012-2013.pdf/.
69. 'Gulf Indians Send Home $29.7bn in Remittances', *Arab News*, 26 August 2013, available at: www.arabnews.com/news/462525/; MOIA, *Annual Report 2012–13*.
70. 'One Woman, Two Organisations among Diaspora Awardees', *Overseas Indian*, 9 January 2013, available at: http://overseasindian.in/2013/jan/news/20130903.shtml/.
71. 'Exploitation of Indian Workers in Gulf Has Come Down: Minister', *Overseas Indian*, 8 January 2014, available at: http://overseasindian.in/2014/jan/news/20141001-0151057.shtml/.
72. Atul Aneja, 'India–Saudi Arabia Joint Working Group to Mitigate Nitaqat Fallout', *The Hindu*, 29 April 2013, available at: www.thehindu.com/news/international/world/indiasaudi-arabia-joint-group-to-mitigate-nitaqat-fallout/article4663427.ece/.
73. 'India–Saudi Bilateral Relations'.
74. 'Saudi Arabia Seeks to Allay Fears in India over New Labour Law', *The Hindu*, 21 November 2013, available at: http://www.thehindu.com/news/national/saudi-arabia-seeks-to-allay-fears-in-india-over-new-labour-law/article5375913.ece?homepage=true/.
75. Atul Aneja, 'Over a Million Indian Secure their Stay ahead of Saudi Deadline', *The Hindu*, 11 April 2013, available at: www.thehindu.com/news/international/world/over-a-million-indians-secure-their-stay-ahead-of-saudi-deadline/article5309909.ece?homepage=true/.
76. Wahab, 'Salman Khurshid'.
77. 'India–Saudi Bilateral Relations'.
78. For a thorough reading of the US presence in the Persian Gulf and strategic relations with Saudi Arabia, see David E. Long, *The United States and Saudi Arabia: Ambivalent Allies* (Boulder: Westview Press, 1985); Rachel Bronson, *Thicker Than Oil: America's Uneasy Partnership with Saudi Arabia* (New York: Oxford University Press, 2006); F. Gregory Gause III, *Oil Monarchies: Domestic and Security Challenges in the Arab Gulf States* (Washington, D.C.: Council on Foreign Relations, 1994); and Robert J. Pauly, *US Foreign Policy and the Persian Gulf: Safeguarding American Interests through Selective Multilateralism* (London: Ashgate, 2005).
79. 'Morsi's Fall in Egypt Comforts Saudis, Disconcerts Qatar', *Ahram Online*, 11 July 2013, available at: http://english.ahram.org.eg/NewsContent/1/64/76273/Egypt/Politics-/Morsis-fall-in-Egypt-comforts-Saudis,-disconcerts-.aspx/.

80. Jennifer Epstein, 'Obama "Deeply Concerned" by Egyptian Military's Removal of Morsi', *Politico*, 3 July 2013, available at: http://www.politico.com/politico44/2013/07/obama-deeply-concerned-by-egyptian-militarys-removal-167603.html/.

81. Madawi al-Rasheed, 'Saudi Arabia Pushes toward Military Strike in Syria', *Al-Monitor*, 2 September 2013, available at: http://www.al-monitor.com/pulse/originals/2013/09/saudi-arabia-pushes-us-toward-military-strike-in-syria.html/.

82. Michael R. Gordon, 'U.S. and Russia Reach Deal to Destroy Syria's Chemical Arms', *The New York Times*, 14 September 2013, available at: http://www.nytimes.com/2013/09/15/world/middleeast/syria-talks.html?pagewanted=all/.

83. Robert F. Worth, 'Saudi Arabia Rejects U.N. Security Council Seat in Protest Move', *The New York Times*, 18 October 2013, available at: http://www.nytimes.com/2013/10/19/world/middleeast/saudi-arabia-rejects-security-council-seat.html/.

84. Robert F. Worth, 'U.S. and Saudis in Growing Rift as Power Shifts', *The New York Times*, 25 November 2013, available at: http://www.nytimes.com/2013/11/26/world/middleeast/us-and-saudis-in-growing-rift-as-power-shifts.html?nl=tod aysheadlines&emc=edit_th_20131126&_r=1&pag%E2%80%A6&/.

85. 'Saudi–Chinese Trade Increases by 14 Percent', *Asharq Al-Awsat*, 20 November 2013, available at: http://www.aawsat.net/2013/11/article55323012/.

86. Daniel Wagner, 'Is the U.S. Losing Saudi Arabia to China?' *The World Post*, 10 February 2014, available at: http://www.huffingtonpost.com/daniel-wagner/is-the-us-losing-saudi-ar_b_4176729.html/.

87. Mujtaba Rizvi, 'Pak-Saudi Relations: An Example of Entente Cordiale', *Pakistan Horizon*, 1981, Vol. 34, No 1, pp. 81–92.

88. For details, see P. R. Kumaraswamy (ed.), *Persian Gulf 2013: India's Relations with the Region* (New Delhi: SAGE, 2014); Tom Wright, 'Saudi Arabia Uses India to Balance Pakistan', *The Wall Street Journal*, 23 October 2012, available at: http://blogs.wsj.com/indiarealtime/2012/10/23/saudi-arabia-uses-india-to-balance-pakistan/; and Stephen Tankel, 'Pakistan's Sticky Wicket: The India–Saudi Link', Foreign Policy, 30 July 2012, available at: http://southasia.foreignpolicy.com/posts/2012/07/30/pakistans_sticky_wicket_the_india_saudi_link/.

89. Mark Urban, 'Saudi Nuclear Weapons "On Order" from Pakistan', *BBC News*, 6 November 2013, available at: http://www.bbc.co.uk/news/world-middle-east-24823846/.

90. Madawi al-Rasheed, 'Saudi Strategy Includes Alliance with Pakistan', *Al-Monitor*, 8 January 2014, available at: http://www.al-monitor.com/pulse/originals/2014/01/saudi-pakistan-investment-alliance-cooperation-military.html/.

91. Harsh V. Pant, 'Contradictions Live in Iran–India's Tangled Web', *The Japan Times*, 28 May 2013, available at: www.japantimes.co.jp/opinion/2013/05/28/

commentary/contradictions-live-in-iran-indias-tangled-web/#.UbROS-cziSp/.

92. D. Bandyopadhyay, 'Madrasa Education and the Condition of Indian Muslims', *Economic and Political Weekly*, 20–26 April 2002, Vol. 37, No. 16, pp. 1481–84.

93. See Yoginder Sikand, *Bastions of Believers: Madrasas and Islamic Education in India* (New Delhi: Penguin Books, 2005), pp. 117–18.

94. See Stephen Tankel, *Jihadist Violence: The Indian Threat* (Washington: Wilson Center, 2013).

9

UAE

Jatung Raja Philemon Chiru

Key Information

Area: 83,600 sq km; **Population:** 5,628,805 (2014 est.); **Native:** 19 per cent; **Expats:** 81 per cent; **Youth:** 13.7 per cent; **Population growth rate:** 2.71 per cent; **Life expectancy at birth:** 77.09 years; **Major population groups:** Emirati 19 per cent, other Arab and Iranian 23 per cent, South Asian 50 per cent, other expatriates (includes Westerners and East Asians) 8 per cent; **Religious groups:** Sunni 80 per cent, Shia 16 per cent, others 4 per cent; **GDP:** US$269.8 billion; **Per capita income:** US$29,900; **Foreign trade:** US$618.5 billion; **Oil reserves:** 97.8 million bbl (2013); **Gas reserves:** 6.089 trillion m³; **Ruling family:** Federation of Sheikhdoms; **Ruler:** President Khalifa bin Zayed al-Nahyan (since 3 November 2004), **Crown Prince:** Not Nominated; **National Day:** 2 December; **Defence budget:** 3.14 per cent of GDP; **HDI rank:** 41; **Literacy rate:** 77.9 per cent; **UN education index:** 0.686; **Gender inequality index:** 0.241; **Labour force:** 4.588 million; **Unemployment rate:** 2.4 per cent; **External debt:** US$167.9 billion (December 2013); **Sovereign wealth fund:** US$975 billion; **Infant mortality rate:** 10.92 deaths out of 1,000; **Last national census:** 2005; **Parliament:** 40-member Federal National Council; **Last parliament election:** 24 September 2011; **Number of Indians:** more than 2.6 million; **Last Indian prime minister to visit:** Indira Gandhi, May 1981.

Sources: CIA, *The World Factbook*, available at: https://www.cia.gov/library/publications/the-world-factbook/; *UN Human Development Report*, Statistics, available at: http://hdr.undp.org/en/statistics/; United States Commission on Religious Freedom, US Department of State; *Annual Report 2013*; *Briefs on Foreign Relations*, Ministry of External Affairs, Government of India and Centre for Arms Control and Proliferation (Washington, D.C.). *Note:* All figures for 2013.

As a major economic player and India's largest trading partner, the United Arab Emirates (UAE) is one of the most important countries in the Persian Gulf region. The UAE has managed to weather not only the global economic meltdown but also the regional upheaval in the form of the Arab Spring. During 2013, however, the country witnessed some rumblings over its human rights situation. Though a close ally of the US, the UAE has been quick to embrace the Iranian rapprochement with the West over the nuclear controversy and the conclusion of the interim Geneva agreement in November. During 2013, India and the UAE continued their engagements in areas of mutual interest. While trade remains the most important aspect of bilateral relations, 2013 witnessed increased cooperation in other areas.

DOMESTIC DEVELOPMENTS

Political developments during 2013 had been quite satisfactory for the UAE, though there were a few incidents which fuelled tensions within the country. The overall positive developments could be seen in economics, and social and cultural empowerments. According to a report issued by the World Economic Forum, the country ranked third in terms of high confidence in political leadership among 148 countries worldwide.[1] This was because of its achievements during 2013, and the credit was given to the leadership of the president, Sheikh Khalifa bin Zayed al-Nahyan. Besides this, it ranked 14th worldwide in the UN happiness and satisfaction survey.[2] During this year, the country's president pledged to improve the educational standards, and provide adequate housing and world-class health care services.

However, during the early 2013, the wave of uprisings in other parts of the Middle East or the Arab Spring seemed to have engulfed the UAE. Although this did not brew into a major crisis, there were alleged attempts to overthrow the ruling government. In this regard, around 70 activists were accused of causing disturbances and were sent for trials.[3] The detained activists were believed to be tortured and this raised major concerns. Around this time, there were also calls for election of all the members of the 40-member parliament, and to give full legislative and regulatory powers to the Federal National Council. Many who were part of such activities called for 'full judicial independence, the retreat of the security state and standard human rights'.[4]

In June, the Supreme Court announced long prison terms of 15 years for about 70 activists who were trying to topple the regime. This coincided with the Egyptian President Mohammed Morsi facing the fiercest protests, resulting in his overthrow by the military in July. According to a report, the defendants were believed to be the members of a secret organization, widely understood to be the Islamist group, al-Islah.[5] This crisis not only disturbed the political establishment but also raised several questions regarding human rights and freedom of media.

In the words of a political analyst,

> I worry that a democratic transition in this period for a state like the UAE would put us in the throes of reactionary conservatism, probably for the next 30 or 40 years. I look at what is happening in Egypt and other places, and I wonder, do I need that kind of transition?[6]

Apart from the above developments, no other major political event troubled the country. The year ended with the celebration of the UAE's 42nd National Day, and Sheikh Khalifa reaffirmed his commitment to the enhancement of human dignity, social justice and a decent life as pillars of society and fundamental rights guaranteed by the constitution and protected by an independent and fair judiciary.[7]

The UAE contains almost 6 per cent of the world's proven oil reserves and 3.3 per cent of global gas reserves, with most of the crude being found in Abu Dhabi. Its oil production was estimated to be approximately 2.65 million barrels per day in 2012.[8]

Before oil was discovered, the Emirati economy was based on fishing and pearl industry. It was only after the discovery of oil that the society and economy transformed. Abu Dhabi is the most preeminent emirate and its national hydrocarbon revenue is highest in the GCC. It has a per capita GDP of US$82,000, more than double the UAE average. In Dubai, another emirate, the production of hydrocarbon has been reduced significantly after 1990. To meet this gap, the UAE has emphasized its infrastructural development in order to diversify its economy and develop trade and manufacturing. As a result, it has a development comparable to Abu Dhabi.[9] It has succeeded in attracting foreign investments in construction projects (the Burj Khalifa skyscraper which is the world's current tallest man-made structure) and futuristic land reclamation projects such as the Palm Islands.[10] Among the rest of the emirates, Sharjah and Ajman based their economy on the rents of the residence workers, whereas the rest three emirates are subsidized by the federal government.

The economic freedom score of the UAE is 71.4 and it is the 28th freest country according to the 2014 economic freedom index. Its score is 0.3 point higher than last year, which is the result of improvements in several sectors such as labour freedom, business freedom, and monetary freedom which cover up the declines in control of government spending and freedom from corruption. It does not levy income tax or federal-level corporate tax on its citizens. In some emirates, different corporate taxes exist for certain business activities. The overall tax on citizens is quite low at 6.1 per cent of the economy.[11]

After the financial crash and Arab uprising, this country was facing trouble to curb spending. The UAE is attempting to overcome this by diversifying the economy. It opened the Khalifa Port in 2012 which was built at a cost of US$7.1 billion, and presently it is constructing the world's largest aluminium smelter and a financial free zone.[12]

The UAE has been steadily enhancing its armed forces with purchases of large defence equipments. The country has over 2,000 Armoured Infantry Fighting Vehicles (AIFVs) that have been either delivered or are in the process of being delivered.[13] During 2013, major announcements were made by Abu Dhabi for purchases of various defence items. In February, it signed defence contracts worth US$1.4 billion, mainly for 750 mine-resistant, ambush-protected, all-terrain vehicles from Oshkosh Corp.[14] Along with these, the UAE armed forces agreed to buy numbers of Predator drones, or unmanned aerial vehicles (UAVs), from privately-owned US firm, General Atomics worth approximately US$196 million.[15] This became necessary due to the UAE's inability to manufacture such systems domestically.

In 2013, the UAE alone accounted for about 4.9 per cent of global arms imports, making it the world's fourth-largest defence importer.[16] Its defence budget shot up from US$8.1 billion in 2008 to US$9.2 billion in 2012. This was primarily for the purchase of systems such as Thermal High Altitude Area Defence (THAAD) missile defence systems, Apache fighter helicopters, and F-16 fighter aircraft from the

US. Furthermore, major American defence firms such as Lockheed Martin participated in the Dubai Air Show held in November. There were reports of this firm securing a contract from the UAE, worth billions of dollar, to produce elements of the THAAD Weapons System.[17] Towards the end of 2013, Lockheed Martin was very hopeful of replacing the current fleet of C-130H Hercules and L-100 transports with the new-generation C-130Js, and also hopeful for the sale of F-16 fighter jets.[18] According to a report, the defence budget for the UAE has been expected to grow from US$9.6 billion in 2013 to US$11.4 billion in 2017.[19]

Besides the UAE's relations with the major Western countries, few developments pertaining to its approach towards other Middle Eastern countries could also be seen during 2013. The two most important events were it reaching out to the crisis-ridden Syria and the visit of its leaders to Iran.

With the escalation of the Syrian crisis, Abu Dhabi provided humanitarian aid worth US$83.53 million during 2012–13.[20] The UAE also coordinated with Saudi Arabia and pledged US$900 million to help fund humanitarian efforts for the Syrians affected by the conflict.[21] It was one of the first countries to respond to the ongoing Syrian crisis. Abu Dhabi also reaffirmed its 'firm support for the UN's efforts to resolve the Syrian crisis and to alleviate the suffering of the Syrian people, as well as its efforts in support of peace negotiations'.[22] In this regard, Foreign Minister Abdullah bin Zayed al-Nahyan met UN Secretary-General Ban Ki-Moon in September.

The UAE's relations with the not-so-friendly Iran also witnessed some positive developments during 2013. An initial common ground for them was found when both Abu Dhabi and Tehran called for a political solution to end the ongoing Syrian crisis. This was announced during the meeting between Iranian Deputy Foreign Minister for Arab and African Affairs Hossein Amir-Abdollahian and Emirati Deputy Foreign Minister Tariq Ahmad al-Heidan, in Tehran in October.[23] Both the countries discussed the need to jointly fight rising radicalism, insecurity and instability in the Middle East. In a rare gesture, the UAE and Iran called for regional cooperation to preserve Gulf security.

The warming of relations between the two timed with Iran's rapprochement with the US and other Western countries. The UAE welcomed the interim nuclear agreement between Iran and the West, concluded in Geneva in November. A few important visits took place thereafter. In November, after many years, Foreign Minister of the UAE visited Tehran and met with his Iranian counterpart Mohammad Javad Zarif and also the newly elected Iranian President Hassan Rouhani.[24] Leaders from both the countries discussed issues of mutual concern. In a quick succession, the Iranian Foreign Minister visited the UAE in December and met with the Prime Minister Sheikh Mohammed bin Rashid al-Maktoum.[25] The minister also met the Iranian citizens living in the UAE. The highlight of this visit was the acceptance of the invitation by the President of the UAE to visit Iran.

These developments indicate the UAE's urge to forge better relations with different countries in the Persian Gulf and to work together to maintain regional security and stability.

BILATERAL RELATIONS

The year 2013 saw the deepening of the cordial and friendly centuries-old bilateral ties. India's political, economic, defence and cultural ties flourished with the high-level bilateral visits and people-to-people contacts. Important agreements were signed by the two countries. Various discussions and consultations were held to address a number of issues and concerns that directly or indirectly affected the interests of the two nations.

Political Relations

The strong bilateral bonds were enhanced by mutual political visits, exchanges, dialogues and agreements. However, there were no presidential or prime ministerial visits during the period. The highest political visit from India was paid by the External Affairs Minister Salman Khurshid on 13 March during which he met the Abu Dhabi Crown Prince and Deputy Supreme Commander of the UAE Armed Forces General Mohammad Bin Zayed al-Nahyan, Foreign Minister Abdullah Bin Zayed al-Nahyan, and other senior officials.[26] They '... reviewed the existing cooperation between the two sides and emphasized on the importance of continuous coordination and consultation between the two friendly countries ... exchanged views on a number of issues of mutual interest', and 'tackled the latest regional and international developments'.[27] A reciprocal visit by the UAE Foreign Minister Sheikh Abdullah took place in December, during which he met with the National Security Advisor and discussed 'boosting prospects of joint cooperation, stressing the importance of expanding avenues of joint investment, particularly in areas of economy, trade, and renewable energy'.[28]

There were several ministerial-level visits from India. In January, the Minister of State for External Affairs, E. Ahamed went to the UAE and held talks primarily on amnesty granted by the UAE government to the expatriates and workers who were staying illegally.[29] Later that month, the UAE's Minister of Foreign Trade, Lubna Bint Khalid al-Qasimi participated in the Partnership Summit 2013—Global Partnerships for Enduring Growth—held in Agra.[30] Minister for Commerce, Industry and Textile, Anand Sharma led a delegation to the first meeting of the India–UAE High Level Task Force on Investments (HLTFI) which was held in Abu Dhabi on 18 February and was co-chaired by Hamed bin Zayed al-Nahyan, Chairman of the Abu Dhabi Crown Prince Court.[31] In March, Finance Minister P. Chidambaram visited and inaugurated Bank of Baroda's 100th global branch in Dubai.[32] He again took a one-day trip to the UAE on 26 May to promote bilateral ties,[33] held meetings with Finance Minister Hamdan bin Rashid al-Maktoum and Crown Prince of Abu Dhabi Mohammed bin Zayed al-Nahyan and with Managing Director of Abu Dhabi Investment Authority (ADIA) Hamed bin Zayed al-Nahyan, and sought more investments in India's infrastructure and corporate sectors.[34]

Minister of Overseas Indian Affairs Vayalar Ravi visited the UAE in April[35] to take part in the third edition of the global meet of the Overseas Indian Cultural Congress (OICC) at the Indian Social and Cultural Centre (ISCC) held at Abu Dhabi.[36] He paid a second visit in October to inaugurate the Second Employers' Conference held at Dubai that was jointly organized by the Ministry of Overseas Indian Affairs (MOIA) and the India Centre for Migration (ICM).[37] Minister of Civil Aviation Ajit Singh inaugurated the Global Convention on Business Excellence held at Dubai in May.[38] Apart from high profile visits, there were some important bilateral agreements signed between the two countries. The first one was the Memorandum of Understanding (MoU) on Air Services signed on 24 April at Abu Dhabi.[39] The other one was the Bilateral Investment Promotion and Protection Agreement (BIPA) which was inked on 12 December.[40]

Apart from warm relations between the two nations, India and the UAE have also set up various institutional structures and task forces to provide a platform for discussions, exchange of ideas and knowledge, and addressing and redressing grievances for the smooth conduct of bilateral ties. Talks and meetings are regularly held at various government-to-government levels on consular, foreign office, economic, technical, investment, security, defence, manpower, etc. The India–UAE HLTFI meeting took place on 18 February (Abu Dhabi); the meeting of Joint Committee on Security Matters (JCSM) took place on 18 March (Abu Dhabi) and the meeting of Joint Committee on Consular Matters took place on 17 and 18 June (New Delhi).[41]

Economic Relations

The prime driving force behind the overall India–UAE bilateral ties are trade, economic and commercial ties. It involves bilateral government contracts and dealings as well as public and private investors in different capacities. Another important fact is that though most of the bilateral trade is conducted by sea routes, air traffic between the two nations is relatively high. The frequency of 700 flights per week is set to increase with the signing of an MoU on Air Services in April and the number of seats is expected to go from 13,330 per week to 24,330 immediately and to 37,130 by the winter of 2014 and to 50,000 per week by the winter of 2015.[42]

A small nation, with just over nine million inhabitants, the UAE has emerged as India's largest trading partner since 2008–09; dropping to a second place after China only in 2011–12; and regaining the top position in 2012–13 with almost US$1 billion excess trade as against China (Table 9.1). Though there has been an increase in the bilateral trade from 2011–12 to 2012–13, the total margin of trade has decreased. The increase in total volume of trade from 2010–11 to 2011–12 was US$6.1 billion, but that from 2011–12 to 2012–13 was only US$2.8 billion (Table 9.2 and Figure 9.1). India's negative balance of trade has further increased more than three-fold from US$0.8 billion in 2011–12

Table 9.1
India's Five Largest Trading Partners in 2012–13 (in US$ Million)

Country	Exports	Imports	Total trade	Trade balance
United Arab Emirates	36,316.65	39,138.36	75,455.01	–2,821.72
China	13,534.88	52,248.33	65,783.21	–38,713.45
United States	36,155.22	25,204.73	61,359.95	10,950.4
Saudi Arabia	9,785.78	33,998.11	43,783.89	–24,212.33
Switzerland	1,117.28	32,166.54	33,283.82	–31,049.25

Source: Adapted from Directorate General of Foreign Trade, New Delhi, available at: www.dgft.gov.in/.

Table 9.2
India–UAE Bilateral Trade (in US$ Million)

	2009–10	2010–11	2011–12	2012–13
India's exports to the UAE	23,970.40	33,822.39	35,925.52	36,316.65
India's imports from the UAE	19,499.10	32,753.16	36,756.32	39,138.36
Total bilateral trade	43,649.50	66,575.55	72,681.84	75,455.01
Share of the UAE in total trade	9.31	10.72	9.14	9.54

Source: Adapted from Directorate General of Foreign Trade, New Delhi, available at: www.dgft.gov.in/.

to US$2.8 billion in 2012–13 (Table 9.1). Moreover, the UAE continued to be India's largest export destination in 2012–13 but the US is rapidly catching up. Importantly, India's trade with the UAE is diverse and unlike other countries in the Persian Gulf it is not dominated by energy, which accounted for only 8.26 per cent of the bilateral trade in 2012–13 (Table 9.3 and Figure 9.2).

As the UAE became India's largest trading partner, India had also become the former's favourite export destination for its manufactured goods. India's export and import items from and to the UAE are diverse and distributed more evenly, than with rest of the Gulf countries. India mainly exports petroleum products, precious metals, stones, gems and jewellery, minerals, food items (cereals, sugar, fruits and vegetables, tea, meat and seafood), textiles (garments, apparel, synthetic fibre, cotton,

Figure 9.1
India–UAE Bilateral Trade

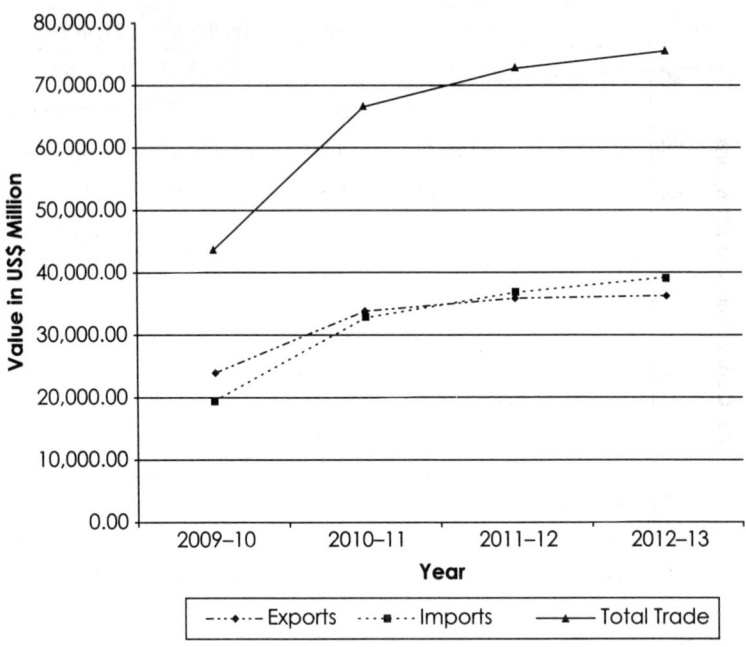

Source: Adapted from Directorate General of Foreign Trade, New Delhi, available at: www.dgft.gov.in/.

Table 9.3
Share of Oil in India's Imports from the UAE (in US$ Million)

Year	Oil imports from the UAE	Total oil imports	UAE share in total oil imports	Imports from the UAE	Per cent of oil in imports from the UAE
2009–10	6,443.36	96,321.16	6.69	19,499.10	33.04
2010–11	9,398.23	115,929.02	8.11	32,753.16	28.69
2011–12	15,102.54	172,753.92	8.74	36.756.32	40.79
2012–13	14,984.64	181,344.67	8.26	39,138.36	38.29

Source: Adapted from Directorate General of Foreign Trade, New Delhi, available at: www.dgft.gov.in/.

Figure 9.2
Share of Oil in India's Imports from the UAE

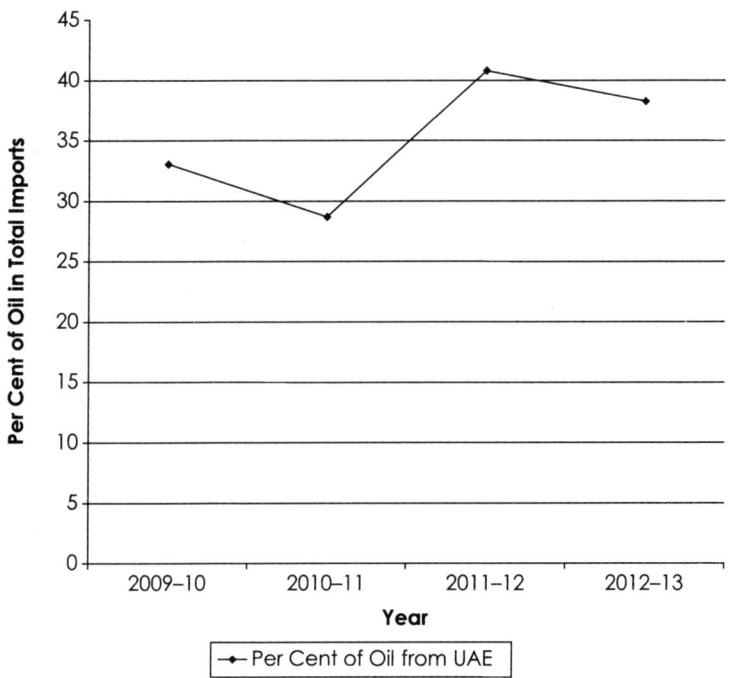

Source: Adapted from Directorate General of Foreign Trade, New Delhi, available at: www.dgft.gov.in/.

yarn) and engineering and machinery products and chemicals to the UAE. It imports petroleum and petroleum products, precious metals, stones, gems and jewellery, minerals, chemicals, wood and wood products from the UAE.[43]

Bilateral investments, both from the public and private sectors, are an important part of its economic ties. India is one of the 'top investors in the UAE as nearly 26,500 companies from the subcontinent operate in the second largest Arab economy, with an estimated combined investment of around US$52 billion'.[44] Though this assessment might be slightly exaggerated, the accessibility to world-class infrastructural facilities and provisions of huge tax breaks have attracted Indian investors

and companies in service sectors like Information Technology, manufacturing, education, entertainment and others. In addition, Abu Dhabi
and Dubai have emerged as the hub of international trade and finance
in the region. Further, Dubai is considered the re-export centre which
the Indian trading and business community has utilized to enhance and
widen their reach within the Persian Gulf nations and beyond.

Many Free Trade Zones (FTZ) created by the UAE such as the Abu
Dhabi Industrial City, Hamiriya Free Trade Zone, Jebel Ali Free Trade
Zone, Ajman and RAK Fujairah Free Trade Zones had seen significant
investments from Indian companies. There is a large presence of Indian
companies, operating through joint ventures or in Special Economic
Zones (SEZs), in cement, building materials, textiles, engineering
products, consumer electronics, tourism, hospitality, catering, health,
retail, education, retail, construction, entertainment, etc. Some highly
recognizable names of Indian companies in the UAE are: Ashok Leyland,
Taj Group of Hotels, EMKE Group, Al-Fara'a, J. K. Cement, Mahindra,
Dabur, Zuari Agro Chemicals, Tata Power, Essar Steel Processing and
Distribution (ESPD), Apollo Tyres, Larson and Toubro, Dodsal, Punj
Lloyd, Infrastructure Leasing & Financial Services Limited (IL&FS), Zee
Entertainment, Birla Institute of Technology and Science (BITS) Pilani,
Manipal University, Mahatma Gandhi University, Pune University, S. P.
Jain School of Global Management, etc.[45]

India as one of the fastest growing economies in the world with a
huge potential for growth and high returns, had attracted investments
from the UAE in areas like infrastructure, communications, energy, IT,
Government bonds and other sectors. With India liberalizing some key
sectors of its economy, particularly in real estate, housing, construction,
retail, communications, petroleum and natural gas, aviation, etc., opportunities for foreign investors are opening up rapidly. Public and private
investors from the UAE are taking a note of these changes.

The UAE has invested about US$8 billion in India, of which US$2.65
billion is in the form of foreign direct investment (FDI) and it is the
10th largest source of FDI in India[46] and the rest is in portfolio and
other types of investments. The five main preferred destinations for UAE
investments are: power (15 per cent), metallurgical industries (12 per
cent), construction development (11 per cent), services sector (10 per
cent), and computer software and hardware (5 per cent).[47] To look into

new avenues for bilateral investment, India–UAE HLTFI was brought into existence in May 2012 with the first meeting of the task force held at Abu Dhabi on 18 February. At the meeting, an agreement 'was reached between the two countries on the format and structure of future discussions, and the meeting decided to establish sub-committees in areas such as infrastructure, energy, investment and trade, manufacturing and technology, aviation and transport for investment purposes'[48] to sort out outstanding issues. The UAE also undertook to invest US$2 billion initially in infrastructure projects, 'support and work for the establishment of strategic oil reserves in India,' and 'agreed in principle to put in place a bilateral investment promotion and protection agreement and expedite its conclusion'.[49]

In April, Jet Airways and Etihad signed a deal by which the latter would invest US$379 million and acquire a 24 per cent stake in Jet Airways.[50] Several bilateral visits, meetings and discussions took place between India and the UAE to promote investment, solve outstanding issues, and chalk out agreements. In December, during the visit of Foreign Minister Zayed al-Nahyan to India, the two signed BIPA, 'that seeks to accelerate fresh capital inflows from the Emirates and provide a thrust to stalled projects'.[51]

Energy Relations

Although energy constitutes a small portion of bilateral trade, the UAE contributes nearly 8 per cent of India's energy imports (Table 9.4). Moreover, it amounts to 14 per cent of India's energy imports from the Persian Gulf (Table 9.4). Diminishing oil reserves will continue to limit energy imports but there are possibilities of India exporting finished petroleum products to the UAE.

Defence and Security Relations

Defence and security continued to be an important part of the bilateral ties, although it remained less impressive than the political and economic relations. In defence and security, the national interests of the two countries converge on three broad themes. First is securing sea routes and maintaining an open and safe Sea Lines of Communication (SLOC)—mainly against piracy—where a major chunk of bilateral trade

Table 9.4
India's Energy Imports from the UAE (in US$ Million)

	2009–10	2010–11	2011–12	2012–13
India's energy imports from the UAE	6,443.36	9,398.23	15,102.54	14,984.64
India's total energy imports	96,321.12	115,929.02	172,753.92	181,344.67
Total energy imports from Persian Gulf	55,904.14	66,688.4	105,056.26	105,859.15
Share in total energy imports (in per cent)	6.69	8.11	8.74	8.26
Share in energy imports from Persian Gulf (in per cent)	11.53	14.09	14.38	14.16

Source: Adapted from Directorate General of Foreign Trade, New Delhi, available at: www.dgft.gov.in/.

is conducted. Second, there is a need for an enhanced and closer cooperation in combating terrorism and organized crimes, such as weapons trafficking, drug smuggling, human trafficking, money laundering, etc. Third is the untapped potential for further cooperation and growth in areas such as research, development and production of military equipments, joint training and exercises, military medical services, defence industry, humanitarian and peace-keeping operations, etc. In recent years, improvement in the bilateral defence relationship had been witnessed 'notably in the field of defence training and supply of defence inventory, besides regular exchange programmes'.[52]

The idea of a defence cooperation was mulled as far back as the 1990s. However, nothing concrete materialized until June 2003 when India and the UAE signed an MoU of Defence Cooperation,[53] and agreed to set up Joint Defence Cooperation Committee (JDCC) as a forum for strategic dialogue between the two countries. The last meeting of the JDCC took place in 2012.[54] Further, India has regularly participated in the International Defence Exhibition and Conference (IDEX) held in Abu Dhabi in alternate years. In the 2013 edition of the IDEX-NAVDEX (Naval Exhibition), which was held from 17 to 21 February, the Indian participation comprised of a three-member delegation led by Lt. Gen. Naresh Chandra Marwah, Chief of Integrated Defence Staff (CIDS) to the Chairman Chiefs of Staff Committee (CISC), 10 Indian Companies and the Indian Coast Guard Ship (ICGS) *Samudra Prahari*.[55] As a sign of growing importance of its defence cooperation with the UAE, India for the first time appointed Group Captain K. Premkumar as defence attaché in its embassy in the UAE on 4 March.[56]

Maritime cooperation between the two nations has also increased dramatically since the inauguration of the India–UAE Naval Staff Talks in January 2007. This results from the growing necessity to expand interaction and training of naval personnel to effectively tackle piracy and from a shared interest in securing the sea lanes for energy and other trades. The visit paid by a delegation led by India's Chief of Naval Staff (CNS) Admiral Devendra Kumar Joshi during 16–19 April, where he held talks with the Chief of the UAE Naval Forces, Rear Admiral Ebrahim Salem Mohammad al-Musharrakh and other UAE Naval officials at Abu Dhabi, highlighted the growing ties between the two navies.[57] Other Indian Navy officers in the delegation were Captain Vinay Kalia, Naval Adviser to CNS and Flag Lieutenant TP Singh, Staff Officer to CNS.[58] Apart from reinforcing bilateral defence ties and enhancing maritime security,[59] the goodwill visits and joint exercises between the navies of India and the UAE continued. On 15 September, four Indian Naval Ships (INS), namely, destroyer *INS Mysore*, missile frigates *INS Tarkash* and *INS Tabar* and tanker *INS Aditya,* docked at Dubai's Port Rashid.[60] On a goodwill visit, headed by Rear Admiral Anil Kumar Chawla, the Flag Officer Commanding Western Fleet,[61] Indian naval ships held joint exercises and manoeuvres with five UAE vessels.[62]

In order to tackle various security concerns such as terrorism, smuggling and other activities, India and the UAE signed the Agreement on Security Cooperation on 23 November 2011.[63] To streamline regular dialogues on security matters, a Joint Committee on Security Matters (JCSM) was established in 2012 with the first meeting being held at Abu Dhabi on 18 March 2013.[64] India's security cooperation with the UAE has been fruitful particularly with respect to terrorism. Reflecting on the cooperation and assistance provided by the UAE to Indian intelligence agencies, one analyst observed: 'The arrests of wanted terrorists like … Syed Zabiuddin Ansari … Abdul Karim Tunda and … Yasin Bhatkal, wouldn't have been possible …' without close cooperation with the UAE.[65]

Cultural Relations

The India–UAE cultural ties date back thousands of years, which began mainly through trade and commerce. Today, there are about 2.6 million[66] Indian expatriates and migrant workers in the UAE constituting more than 30 per cent of the total UAE resident population. The presence of a large migrant community is a big factor behind the strong India–UAE cultural relations. Indian culture expressed through dance, music and festivals is popular not only among the Indian expatriates but also among migrant workers from other countries and the local UAE population. For example, languages like Hindi and Malayalam, spoken by majority of Indian migrant workers have been found to influence the local Arabic dialects.

India and the UAE have signed many agreements since 1975 to promote cultural interactions, people-to-people contact and cultural exchanges at various levels between the two countries. The cultural departments of the Indian government and the UAE have cooperated to conduct cultural exchange programmes and hold other events to promote each others' culture in the past. The UAE's Ministry of Culture and Abu Dhabi Authority for Culture and Heritage (ADACH) has provided invaluable help in organizing cultural events, Indian film festivals, painting exhibitions, etc. Ketab and Kalima, institutions affiliated to ADACH had been instrumental in translating some of the prominent Indian works into Arabic.

In a significant move, the Indian Council of Cultural Relations (ICCR) opened an Indian Cultural Centre (ICC) in the Indian Embassy at Abu Dhabi in December 2009. The cultural centre or the cultural wing of the Indian Embassy has been actively holding events such as cultural festivals, seminars, talks, exhibitions, handicraft shows, poetry reading sessions, etc. It also holds yoga and Hindi classes for expatriates and local citizens. The cultural wing strives to maintain contact with students, teachers, academicians, prominent personalities, etc., among the expatriates and native population.[67] In March 2013, talks were given by

Shehnaz Hussain, an entrepreneur and a prominent Indian personality in the fashion industry.[68]

In the UAE, non-Muslims are free to practice their religion, and there are 35 Christian churches built on land donated by the ruling families of the various emirates.[69] However, there are no Buddhist temples. A Sikh temple shares a building with one of the two existing Hindu temples. Buddhists, Hindus and Sikhs conduct religious ceremonies in private homes, generally without interference.[70] However, there have been instances of government acting against non-UAE Shia Muslims because of their perceived support for Iran, Syrian President Bashar al-Assad, Lebanese Hezbollah or the Shia opposition in Bahrain.[71]

Migration

Emigration to the UAE has been continuing since times immemorial. These migrations were mostly for trade and commercial reasons. Following the oil boom of the 1970s and especially after 2000, many Indians were attracted to the UAE by jobs opportunities in the infrastructure and construction development works. Thus, most of the emigrants from India go to the UAE for economic reasons and were semi-skilled and unskilled labourers. Though this has changed in recent years with the increasing number of white-collared Indians going to the UAE, the majority of Indian migrant workers heading for the UAE still comprised unskilled and semi-skilled labourers. The majority of Indian workers do not settle in the UAE but return to India as most of them go on a time-bound work visa or work permit or on a contract basis for fixed number of years. The UAE had been the preferred destination for migrant workers after Saudi Arabia; a total number of 141,138 persons emigrated for work in 2012. Traditionally, most of the migrant workers were from the southern states of Kerala, Tamil Nadu and Andhra Pradesh. However, in the past few years, states like Bihar, Uttar Pradesh and West Bengal had counted for a significant number of semi-skilled or unskilled Indian emigrants to the UAE.[72] According to the *International Migration Report 2013*, published by the UN Secretariat's Economic and Social Affairs Division, migration from India to the UAE was ranked fifth for the year 2010–13 and second for the years 2000–10.[73] Thus, in 2013, the total number of Indians in the UAE was estimated to be 2.9 million.[74]

Migrant Indian workers in the UAE have faced a number of challenges and problems. Though the UAE has labour laws and is party to various international labour laws, these are often violated, causing physical and mental hardships to the Indian workers. The UAE Labour Law and its amended version [previously known as Federal Law No. (8) of 1980][75] is also lenient towards infractions by the employers. According to the Ministry of Overseas Indian Affairs, 'Overseas Indian workers face a number of risks. The nature of risks includes high costs of migration, non/delayed/under payment of salaries, poor living and working conditions, physical abuse, fraudulent recruitment practices, difficulties in resettlement on return, financial insecurity, and vulnerability against emergencies.'[76] This is true for the condition of Indian migrants in the UAE in particular and the Gulf States in general.[77]

In November 2010, before President Pratibha D. Patil visited the UAE, the Human Rights Watch urged her to use her visit to

> ... address the systemic abuse of migrant workers in the United Arab Emirates and press for urgent labour reforms ... [and] ... outline abuses frequently faced by Indians and other migrant workers employed in low-wage jobs in the UAE, such as unpaid wages, indebtedness from recruitment fees that create conditions of forced labour, confiscation of passports, hazardous working conditions, and, at times, physical abuse.[78]

Exploitative working conditions, non-payment and underpayment of wages and other forms of abuses have compounded the problem for many Indian migrant workers leading to a high suicide rate among Indians in the UAE.[79] Other causes that have driven many Indian expatriates to commit suicide are financial problems owing to inadequate payment of wages, reduced social support, increasing financial demands and insensitive attitudes of families back home in India.[80]

External Players

Of the three external players under discussion here, India has good relations with only the US. With China and Pakistan, India has outstanding unresolved issues which had and could on occasions come to the surface creating tensions in bilateral relationship. The UAE, unlike India, has friendly ties with all the three countries. In times to come, these three countries would have a significant influence on the India–UAE ties.

The US: The US–UAE strategic partnership is based on two broad paradigms: security and defence cooperation, and oil and energy supply. The strategic security alliance dates back to 1971 when the UAE became independent and the US provided security to the ruling regime from internal and external threats. The alliance was further broadened in 1994 with the signing of the US–UAE Defence Cooperation Agreement which was primarily aimed at containing the influence of Iran and providing stability to the region. The 11 September 2001 terrorist attacks in the US opened a new chapter in the US–UAE strategic partnership when the two began to further strengthen their counter-terrorism efforts. At present, apart from providing security to the regime, the security and defence relations between the two countries had diversified into stationing of US troops at al-Dhafra air base, use of Jebel Ali port by the US Navy, training of UAE military by the US, supply and the purchase of US-made weapons and weapon-systems, etc. For example, in April, an agreement was reached to sell warplanes and other weapons worth about US$5 billion to the UAE.[81]

The second factor driving the US–UAE ties is energy and trade. Though the US had imported 1.217 billion barrels of crude oil and other petroleum products in 2012,[82] which is a small quantity compared to the US's total energy imports,[83] cooperation with the US is essential for maintaining stability in the region and for an uninterrupted supply of energy especially through the Strait of Hormuz. The US–UAE bilateral trade in 2013 reached US$26.9 billion, a growth of over 8.5 per cent from 2012.[84] In 2013, the US exports to the UAE was US$24.61 billion which was more than its exports to other key regional trade partners, including Saudi Arabia (US$18.99 billion), Israel (US$13.73 billion), Turkey (US$17.1 billion) and Egypt (US$5.22 billion). With such voluminous trade, the UAE remains the top US export destination in Middle East North Africa (MENA).[85]

In 2013, the US and the UAE also shared common concerns and interests, working closely on a number of regional issues. Foremost is Iran's nuclear programme, which according to most Gulf States, is a threat to the stability of the region. The UAE supported the sanctions imposed on Iran by the West and the US. The other important concern for the UAE is Iran's continued occupation of the three Islands, namely, Abu Musa, the greater and lesser Tunbs and other Iranian ambitions in the region. During his speech in the UN General Assembly on 28 September, the

UAE's Foreign Minister Abdullah Bin Zayed al-Nahyan asked Iran to end its 'continued occupation' of the Islands. The US and the UAE also cooperated on the Syrian issue by extending financial support to the rebels in their struggle against Bashar al-Assad's regime.[86]

China: In their bilateral relationship, the UAE and China has mainly focused on trade and commerce, and energy and strategic cooperation. China, as a fast growing economy based on exports is eyeing to improve its trade ties with the UAE. For China, the UAE is an important export destination as the latter positioned itself as a financial and commercial hub in the region. Thus, nearly 70 per cent of China's export to the UAE is re-routed to other countries in the region and even to Africa and Europe. Since 2007, China has been the UAE's largest trading partner after India.[87] In 2012, bilateral trade between the two countries stood at US$40.42 billion; from January to June 2013, trade grossed US$21.435 billion.[88]

Energy is another important factor behind China courting and seeking closer ties with the UAE. China is one of the largest energy importing nations in the world. At present, though China imports a minimal quantity of crude oil and other petroleum products from the UAE, this is expected to increase in the coming years. Energy security remains one of China's main concerns at present. In 2012, China imported 3 per cent[89] of its total energy needs from the UAE, which is about 9.82 million barrels per day.[90] China was keen on oil exploration projects in the UAE with an objective of diversifying its energy sources.[91]

China is also seeking to enhance its strategic and security ties with the UAE. With a view to play a more active security role in the Persian Gulf, both agreed upon a strategic cooperation in 2012 whereby they would cooperate in 'law-enforcement security, anti-terrorism and crackdowns on crime ... to establish safe and long-term cooperation mechanism and realize intelligence exchange and ... to reinforce military exchanges of visits, conduct exchanges between military colleges, and to strengthen cooperation in such aspects as personnel training, technical equipment, military industry and military trade'.[92]

Pakistan: Pakistan and the UAE have cordial political, economic and cultural ties. Among the high level visits, the UAE President Sheikh

Khalifa Bin Zayed al-Nahyan visited Pakistan in December and met Prime Minister Nawaz Sharif and held talks on 'bilateral relations, and ways to strengthen them in all fields for the mutual benefit of both countries ... exchanged views on recent developments on the regional and international level, as well as issues of mutual concern'.[93] They also expressed 'satisfaction with the current state of bilateral relations and the progress made in cooperation in various areas, which is reflected in the strong ties between the two friendly peoples'.[94] The UAE is Pakistan's biggest trading partner with bilateral trade touching US$10 billion in 2013, an increase from US$7.6 billion in 2012.[95] In November, the two countries held the UAE–Pakistan 11th Joint Ministerial Commission Meeting and agreed to establish Joint Trade Council to 'enhance economic cooperation'.[96] The UAE is also involved in many welfare projects in Pakistan like road and bridge construction and other infrastructural projects, especially through Project to Assist Pakistan, with US$300 million already been spent.[97]

In security, defence and strategic cooperation, Pakistan had provided training and equipment to the UAE armed forces after the Gulf state gained independence in 1971. There have been robust defence and security ties between Pakistan and the UAE since the two nations signed a defence cooperation agreement in 2006.[98] They have also cooperating on counter-terrorism since the launch of US's war of terror campaign. Similarly, the UAE and Pakistan have shared a strong cultural and religious relation. With about 1.25 million Pakistani emigrants in the UAE, they form the largest expatriate community after Indians.[99]

Issues and Challenges

India and the UAE have close and warm bilateral relations. However, there are some issues and problems that need addressing to smoothen and further enhance the bilateral ties. Most importantly, India needs to improve investment atmosphere and opportunities if it is desirous of attracting more FDI from the UAE. As a rich nation with more than US$600 billion sovereign wealth fund, the current investments from the UAE in India which stand around US$8 billion, is rather minuscule. Red tapes and delays should be minimized and FDI needs to be handled at a faster pace. In addition, some UAE companies such as Etisalat, Taqa,

DP World and Emaar doing business in India have faced problems over their investment plans in India.[100] The signing of India–UAE BIPA seems to be a step forward in the right direction.

Another source of irritation in bilateral ties is the treatment of Indian migrant workers in the UAE. Indian workers have faced a lot of abuses and exploitations from their UAE employers in contravention of the UAE and international labour laws.[101] The two governments have put in place mechanisms to tackle this particular problem but such cases will need a sensitive handling and stricter punishments for violators by the UAE authorities. Somewhat similar to this issue is the fact that many Indians overstay or stay illegally in the UAE. The UAE's Interior Ministry gave a two months amnesty beginning from 4 December 2012 to 3 February 2013, for illegal foreign residents to leave the UAE. By the end of this period, more than 3,000 Indians availed the amnesty.

It is of common interest to India and the UAE to strengthen their efforts at tackling terrorism and organized crimes. In the past, it has been known that criminals wanted by the law in India for terrorism or other organized crimes take refuge in the UAE. Though India and the UAE have agreements on security and extradition, stepping up cooperation would benefit both countries. Further, it is necessary to keep a close look out against extremist ideology and anti-Indian elements especially from Pakistan and to prevent them from using the UAE soil for carrying out subversive activities against India.

As India's largest trading partner with a long history of friendly ties, a closer attention should be paid to the UAE. For instance, no Indian Prime Minister has visited the UAE since 1981 when the then Prime Minister Indira Gandhi toured the UAE. India's Prime Minister Manmohan Singh was scheduled to visit the UAE in March[102] or August 2013.[103] The March visit was cancelled citing 'logistics and scheduling' problem.[104] In fact, according to India's External Affairs Minister Salman Khurshid, the visit was aborted due to insistence from the UAE that the two countries sign BIPA at the earliest.[105] However, no explanation was offered for the cancelation of the August visit.

Issues, problems and challenges aside, there are huge opportunities that India and the UAE can seize and tap into for their interest. With the UAE diversifying its economy into various areas, India could provide assistance in agriculture, land and natural resource management, food security, green energy, etc. India is a leading nation in information technology, education, biotechnology, medicine and space science which could help the UAE. There also exists huge and attractive investment opportunities in India, particularly in infrastructure development projects which the UAE could utilize.

CONCLUSION

During 2013, the India–UAE relations continued to grow and warm ties flourished. Secondary level political visits took place and economic and commercial ties reached new heights with the bilateral trade touching US$75 billion. Relations remained free of major irritants and no regional or international actors were able to bring about a major shift. Treatment of Indian workers is gaining greater media attention but could remain a problem if left unresolved.

NOTES

1. '2013 Was an Outstanding Year for the UAE and Sheikh Khalifa', *The National (Abu Dhabi)*, 1 January 2014, available at: http://www.thenational.ae/uae/government/2013-was-an-outstanding-year-for-the-uae-and-sheikh-khalifa/.
2. Ibid.
3. 'The UAE's Bizarre, Political Trial of 94 Activists', *The Guardian (London)*, 6 March 2013, available at: http://www.theguardian.com/commentis-free/2013/mar/06/uae-trial-94-activists/.
4. Ibid.
5. Michael Peel and Camilla Hall, 'Scores of Emiratis Jailed after Coup Plot Trial in Abu Dhabi', *The Financial Times*, 2 July 2013, available at: http://www.ft.com/intl/cms/s/0/379fc630-e2ed-11e2-9bb2-00144feabdc0.html#axzz2twHASNV9/.
6. Ben Hubbard, 'Emirates Balk at Activism in Region Hit by Uprisings', *The New York Times*, 8 June 2013, available at: http://www.nytimes.com/2013/06/09/world/middleeast/emirates-balk-at-activism-in-region-hit-by-uprisings.html?pagewanted=all&_r=0/.
7. 'UAE Marks 42nd National Day as Union Gets More Competitive and Dynamic', *Emirates 24/7 News*, 1 December 2013, available at: http://www.emirates247.com/news/government/uae-marks-42nd-national-day-as-union-gets-more-competitive-and-dynamic-2013-12-01-1.529751/.

8. Joanne Bladd, 'UAE Economy Back on Track', *Gulf Business*, 12 October 2013, available at: http://gulfbusiness.com/2013/10/uae-economy-back-on-track/#.UwfBOaKZjIU/.

9. UAE Economic Insight, QNB, available at: http://www.qnb.com.qa/cs/Sate llite?blobcol=urldata&blobheader=application%2Fpdf&blobkey=id&blobt able=MungoBlobs&blobwhere=1355486404313&ssbinary=true/.

10. 'United Arab Emirates Profile', *BBC News*, 26 October 2013, available at: http://www.bbc.co.uk/news/world-middle-east-14703998/.

11. 'United Arab Emirates, 2014 Index of Economic Freedom', *The Heritage Foundation*, available at: http://www.heritage.org/index/country/unitedar abemirates/.

12. Joanne Bladd, 'UAE Economy Back on Track', *Gulf Business*, 12 October 2013, available at: http://gulfbusiness.com/2013/10/uae-economy-back-on-track/#.UwfBOaKZjIU/.

13. 'IDEX 2013—UAE Fighting Vehicles', *Military Technology*, 13 February 2013, available at: http://www.miltechmag.com/2013/02/idex-2013-uae-fighting-vehicles.html/.

14. 'UAE Signs $1.4 Billion Defence Contracts, Including Drones', *Reuters*, 18 February 2013, available at: http://www.reuters.com/article/2013/02/18/ us-emirates-drones-idUSBRE91H0AY20130218/.

15. Ibid.

16. 'UAE Is Expected to Spend US$52.5 bn on Defence during 2013–2017', *Aerospace and Defence News*, 22 February 2013, available at: http://www. asdnews.com/news-47799/UAE_is_Expected_to_Spend_US$52.5bn_on_ Defense_during_2013-2017.htm/.

17. 'Lockheed Martin Receives $3.9 Billion THAAD Production Contract', *News Releases*, Lockheed Martin, 23 September 2013, available at: http:// www.lockheedmartin.com/us/news/press-releases/2013/september/mfc-092313-lm-receives-thaad.html/.

18. Tom Arnold, 'Lockheed Martin Hoping for F-16 Fighter Jet Deal with UAE', *The National (Abu Dhabi)*, 19 November 2013, available at: http://www.the-national.ae/business/industry-insights/aviation/lockheed-martin-hoping-for-f-16-fighter-jet-deal-with-uae/.

19. 'UAE is Expected to Spend US$52.5 bn on Defence during 2013–2017', *Aerospace and Defence News*.

20. 'AED 306.8 Million of UAE Aid to Syria Crisis over the Last Two Years', *MICAD News*, United Arab Emirates Ministry of International Cooperation and Development', 14 January 2014, available at: http://www.micad.gov. ae/En/MediaCenter/OCFANews/Pages/AED3068millionofUAEaidtoSyri acrisisoverthelasttwoyears.aspx/.

21. 'Saudi Arabia, Kuwait, UAE Pledge $900 mln for Syrians at Donors Conference', *Al Arabiya News*, 30 January 2013, available at: http://english.alara biya.net/articles/2013/01/30/263374.html/.

22. 'UAE Reaffirms Support to UN Role in Syria Crisis', *Khaleej Times*, 27 September 2013, available at: http://www.khaleejtimes.com/kt-article-display-1.asp?xfile=data/government/2013/September/government_September80.xml&section=government/.

23. 'Iran, UAE Urge Political Solution to Syria Crisis', *Press TV (Iran)*, 22 October 2013, available at: http://www.presstv.com/detail/2013/10/22/330770/iran-uae-urge-syria-political-solution/.

24. 'UAE Foreign Minister Arrives on Rare Iran Visit', *The Daily Star (Beirut)*, 28 November 2013, available at: http://www.dailystar.com.lb/News/Middle-East/2013/Nov-28/239235-uae-foreign-minister-arrives-on-rare-iran-visit.ashx#axzz2u2bGdcKz/.

25. 'Iran's Foreign Minister Arrives in UAE, Meets with PM', *Alalam (Iran)*, 4 December 2013, available at: http://en.alalam.ir/news/1541304/.

26. 'India–UAE Relations', Embassy of India, United Arab Emirates, available at: http://indembassyuae.org/political.html/.

27. 'Mohammad Receives Indian Foreign Minister', *Gulf News*, 13 March 2013, available at: http://gulfnews.com/news/gulf/uae/government/mohammad-receives-indian-foreign-minister-1.1158063/.

28. 'Abdullah bin Zayed Meets with his Indian Counterpart To Review Bilateral Ties', *Gulf News*, 12 December 2013, available at: http://gulfnews.com/business/economy/abdullah-bin-zayed-meets-with-his-indian-counterpart-to-review-bilateral-ties-1.1266510/.

29. 'India–UAE Relations', Embassy of India, United Arab Emirates.

30. 'Lubna Takes Part in "Partnership Summit 2013" in India', *Khaleej Times*, 27 January 2013, available at: http://www.khaleejtimes.com/kt-article-display-1.asp?xfile=data/uaebusiness/2013/January/uaebusiness_January374.xml&section=uaebusiness/.

31. 'UAE–India Task Force on Investments Meet in Abu Dhabi', *Gulf News*, 19 February 2013, available at: http://gulfnews.com/business/economy/uae-india-task-force-on-investments-meet-in-abu-dhabi-1.1148208/.

32. 'Chidambaram Opens Bank of Baroda's 100th Branch in Dubai', *The Economic Times*, 29 March 2013, available at: http://articles.economictimes.indiatimes.com/2013-03-29/news/38125463_1_difc-dubai-international-finance-centre-uae/.

33. 'Chidambaram in UAE, Holds Bilateral Talks', *Business Standard*, 27 May 2013, available at: http://www.thehindubusinessline.com/news/chidambaram-to-visit-dubai-tomorrow-to-woo-investments/article4750017.ece/.

34. 'Chidambaram Urges UAE Investment in Infrastructure Sector', *The Times of India*, 26 May 2013, available at: http://articles.timesofindia.indiatimes.com/2013-05-26/india-business/39537965_1_infrastructure-sector-p-chidambaram-uae-investment/.

35. 'India–UAE Relations', Embassy of India, United Arab Emirates.

36. Binsal Abdul Kader, 'Meeting of Global Non-Resident Indians with Kerala Ministers in Abu Dhabi', *Gulf News*, 11 April 2013, available at: http://gulfnews.com/news/gulf/uae/society/meeting-of-global-non-resident-indians-with-kerala-ministers-in-abu-dhabi-1.1169531/; For further details on OICC, see http://www.oiccabudhabi.com/.

37. '2nd Overseas Employers' Conference, Dubai, UAE—October 27–28, 2013', NRI Commission, Government of Goa, available at: http://www.nri.goa.gov.in/oeconferance.html/; Also see, 'Summary/Preliminary Report of the Employers' Conference 2013, Dubai', Ministry of Overseas Indian Affairs, New Delhi, available at: http://moia.gov.in/writereaddata/pdf/Employers_Conference_2013_Summary_Report_ICM.pdf/.

38. 'India–UAE Relations', Embassy of India, United Arab Emirates.

39. 'India and UAE Sign MoU on Air Services', *Press Release*, Press Information Bureau, New Delhi, 24 April 2013, available at: http://www.pib.nic.in/newsite/erelease.aspx?relid=95006/.

40. 'Bilateral Investment Promotion and Protection Agreement (BIPPA) Signed between India and Government of UAE to Boost Investment Flows between the Two Countries', *Press Release*, Press Information Bureau, New Delhi, 12 December 2013, available at: http://pib.nic.in/newsite/erelease.aspx?relid=101573/.

41. 'India–UAE Relations', Embassy of India, United Arab Emirates.

42. 'India–UAE Economic and Commercial Relations', Embassy of India, United Arab Emirates, available at: http://indembassyuae.org/Com_bilateral.html/.

43. Ibid.

44. '$52 bn Indian Investments in UAE', *Emirates 24/7*, 19 August 2013, available at: http://www.emirates247.com/business/economy-finance/52bn-indian-investment-in-uae-2013-08-19-1.518074/.

45. 'India–UAE Economic and Commercial Relations', Embassy of India, United Arab Emirates.

46. 'Fact Sheet on Foreign Direct Investment (FDI)', Department of Industrial Policy and Promotion, Ministry of Commerce and Industry, New Delhi, p. 2, 6, available at: http://dipp.nic.in/English/Publications/FDI_Statistics/2013/india_FDI_December2013.pdf/.

47. 'India–UAE Economic and Commercial Relations', Embassy of India, United Arab Emirates.

48. Ibid.

49. K. R. Srivats, 'UAE Commits $2 Billion Initial Investment in India Infrastructure Sector', *The Hindu*, 18 February 2013, available at: http://www.thehindubusinessline.com/industry-and-economy/uae-commits-2-billion-initial-investment-in-indian-infrastructure-sector/article4427922.ece/.

50. 'All You Need to Know About Jet-Etihad Deal', *Business Standard*, 20 November 2013, available at: http://www.business-standard.com/article/

companies/all-you-need-to-know-about-jet-etihad-deal-113112000302_1. html/.

51. 'India, UAE Ink Investment Pact', *Business Standard*, 13 December 2013, available at: http://www.business-standard.com/article/economy-policy/india-uae-ink-investment-pact-113121200641_1.html/.
52. 'India–UAE Relations', Embassy of India, United Arab Emirates.
53. 'India, UAE Sign Defence Cooperation Pact', *The Times of India*, 1 July 2003, available at: http://articles.timesofindia.indiatimes.com/2003-07-01/india/27205796_1_defence-cooperation-defence-industry-subir-dutta/.
54. 'India–UAE Relations', Embassy of India, United Arab Emirates.
55. Ibid.; and Ramesh Mathew, 'Anti-Pollution Ship Comes Calling', *The Gulf Times*, 25 February 2013, available at: http://www.gulf-times.com/qatar/178/details/343428/anti-pollution-ship-comes-calling/.
56. 'India–UAE Relations', Embassy of India, United Arab Emirates. Until March 2013, the Defence Advisor of the Defence Wing at Indian Embassy in Oman was additionally handling defence charges for the UAE. However, the UAE has had a defence attaché at its New Delhi Embassy since August 1998. For more details, see: http://uaeembassy-newdelhi.com/military_attache_office_information.asp/.
57. Binsal Abdul Kader, 'Indian Expatriates' Contributions Support UAE–India Ties, Indian Navy Chief Says', *Gulf News*, 17 April 2013, available at: http://gulfnews.com/news/gulf/uae/general/indian-expatriates-contributions-support-uae-india-ties-indian-navy-chief-says-1.1171654/.
58. 'India–UAE Relations', Embassy of India, United Arab Emirates.
59. The two navies are cooperating in anti-piracy operations in the Gulf of Aden and Horn of Africa region.
60. Ramola Talwar Badam, 'UAE and Indian Warships to Take Part in Joint Exercises', *The National (Abu Dhabi)*, 16 September 2013, available at: http://www.thenational.ae/news/uae-news/uae-and-indian-warships-to-take-part-in-joint-exercises/.
61. Shafaat Shahbandari, 'UAE, Indian Navies Enhance Cooperation', *Gulf News*, 16 September 2013, available at: http://gulfnews.com/news/gulf/uae/government/uae-indian-navies-enhance-cooperation-1.1231707/.
62. Muaz Shabandri, 'Indian Navy will Support Anti-Piracy Operations', *Khaleej Times*, 17 September 2013, http://www.khaleejtimes.com/kt-article-display-1.asp?xfile=data/nationgeneral/2013/September/nationgeneral_September109.xml&section=nationgeneral/.
63. 'India, UAE Step up Security Cooperation', *The Hindu*, 24 September 2011, available at: http://www.thehindu.com/news/national/india-uae-step-up-security-cooperation/article2653594.ece/.
64. 'India–UAE Relations', Embassy of India, United Arab Emirates.
65. 'India PM to Visit UAE', *StratPost*, 23 September 2013, available at: http://www.stratpost.com/indian-pm-to-visit-uae/.

66. 'India–UAE Relations', Embassy of India, United Arab Emirates.
67. 'Cultural Wing', Embassy of India, United Arab Emirates, Abu Dhabi, available at: http://indembassyuae.org/culturalwing.html/.
68. 'India–UAE Relations' Embassy of India, United Arab Emirates.
69. Kenneth Katzman, 'The United Arab Emirates (UAE): Issues for U.S. Policy', *Congressional Research Service*, 24 February 2014, p. 10, available at: http://www.fas.org/sgp/crs/mideast/RS21852.pdf/.
70. Ibid.
71. Ibid.
72. *Annual Report 2012–13*, MOIA, pp. 54–55, available at: http://moia.gov.in/writereaddata/pdf/Annual_Report_2012-2013.pdf/.
73. 'International Migration Report 2013', *UNDESA*, p. 6, available at: http://esa.un.org/unmigration/documents%5Cworldmigration%5C2013%5CFull_Document_final.pdf/.
74. 'International Migration 2013: Migrants by Origin and Destination', *UNDESA*, p. 4, available at: http://esa.un.org/unmigration/documents/PF_South-South_migration_2013.pdf/.
75. For more details see: 'U.A.E. Labour Law', Ministry of Labour, United Arab Emirates, Abu Dhabi, available at: http://www.mol.gov.ae/newcontrolpanel2010/Attachments/21062012/labour%20law%20no.8%20year%201980.pdf/.
76. *Annual Report 2012–13*, MOIA, p. 24.
77. For example see: 'Indian Migrant Workers Return Home with Horror Tales from UAE', *The Times of India*, 13 February 2013, available at: http://timesofindia.indiatimes.com/nri/middle-east-news/Indian-migrant-workers-return-home-with-horror-tales-from-UAE/articleshow/18473461.cms/.
78. Human Rights Watch, 'India/UAE: Use Visit to Raise Migrant Worker Issue', 22 November 2010, available at: http://www.hrw.org/news/2010/11/22/indiauae-use-visit-raise-migrant-worker-issue/.
79. Emirate Centre for Human Rights, 'Migrant Workers in the United Arab Emirates (UAE)', p. 2, available at: http://www.echr.org.uk/wp-content/uploads/2012/07/ECHR-Report-on-Migrant-Workers-in-the-UAE.pdf/.
80. National Confederation of Human Rights Organization, 'Suicide Tendency High Among Troubled Expats', available at: http://www.nchro.org/index.php?option=com_content&view=article&id=617:suicide-tendency-high-among-troubled-expats&catid=35:migrant-workers-migrant-workers&Itemid=18/; Also see, Shveta Pathak, '72 Indians Committed Suicide so far this Year', *Gulf News*, 12 December 2013, available at: http://gulfnews.com/news/gulf/uae/society/72-indians-committed-suicide-so-far-this-year-1.1118103/.
81. Thom Shankar, 'U.S. Arms Deal with Israel and 2 Arab Nations is near', *The New York Times*, 18 April 2013, http://www.nytimes.com/2013/04/19/world/middleeast/us-selling-arms-to-israel-saudi-arabia-and-emirates.html?_r=0/.

UAE 251

82. 'U.S. Imports by Country of Origin', *US Energy Information Administration*, available at: http://www.eia.gov/dnav/pet/pet_move_impcus_a2_nus_ep00_im0_mbbl_a.htm/.
83. Total U.S. Crude oil and Products from all sources is 3,878.852 billion barrels in 2012.
84. 'U.S.–U.A.E. Trade Reaches Record $26.9 billion in 2013', *U.S.–U.A.E Business Council*, 6 February 2014, available at: http://usuaebusiness.org/2014/02/u-s-u-a-e-trade-reaches-record-26-9-billion/.
85. For a detailed trade figures between US and UAE, see, 'Trade in Goods with United Arab Emirates', Foreign Trade, United States Census Bureau, U.S. Department of Commerce, available at: http://www.census.gov/foreign-trade/balance/c5200.html/.
86. Katzman, 'The United Arab Emirates (UAE)'.
87. 'The UAE and China: A Strategic Partnership', *The Emirates Center for Strategic Studies and Research,* 26 January 2012, available at: http://www.ecssr.ac.ae/ECSSR/print/ft.jsp?lang=en&ftId=/FeatureTopic/ECSSR/FeatureTopic_1500.xml/.
88. 'UAE–China Trade up 14 Per cent in H1, 2013', *UAE Interact*, 11 December 2013, available at: http://www.uaeinteract.com/docs/UAE-China_trade_up_14_percent_in_H1,_2013_/58774.htm/.
89. Kang Wu, 'Energy Security in China: Role of Oil and Gas in the Global Context', June 2013, p. 17, available at: http://www.esi.nus.edu.sg/docs/event/kang-wu-presentation-at-esi-june-2013.pdf?sfvrsn=0/.
90. 'Oil Market Report', *International Energy Agency*, 13 February 2013, available at: http://omrpublic.iea.org/currentissues/fullpub.pdf/.
91. April Yee, 'China and Abu Dhabi Keen on Oil Exploration Partnership', *The National (Abu Dhabi)*, 16 June 2012, available at: http://www.thenational.ae/business/industry-insights/energy/china-and-abu-dhabi-keen-on-oil-exploration-partnership/.
92. 'China, UAE Issue Joint Statement on Establishing Strategic Partnership', *Xinhua News*, 17 January 2012, available at: http://news.xinhuanet.com/english/china/2012-01/17/c_122598697.htm/.
93. 'UAE President Meets Pakistan Prime Minister', *Gulf News*, 31 December 2013, available at: http://gulfnews.com/news/gulf/uae/government/uae-president-meets-pakistan-prime-minister-1.1272576/.
94. 'Shaikh Khalifa All Praise for UAE–Pakistan Relations', *Khaleej Times*, 12 January 2014, available at: http://khaleejtimes.com/nation/inside.asp?xfile=/data/government/2014/January/government_January54.xml&section=government/.
95. M. Aftab, 'UAE–Pakistan Trade to Expand', *Khaleej Times*, 25 November 2013, available at: http://www.khaleejtimes.com/biz/inside.asp?xfile=/data/opinionanalysis/2013/November/opinionanalysis_November22.xml&section=opinionanalysis/.

96. 'Pakistan, UAE Agree to Establish Joint Trade Council', *The Nation (Pakistan)*, 8 November 2013, http://www.nation.com.pk/business/08-Nov-2013/pakistan-uae-agree-to-establish-joint-trade-council/.

97. 'UAE's Welfare Projects in Pakistan Top One Billion Dirhams', *The News (Pakistan)*, 1 January 2014, available at: http://www.thenews.com.pk/Todays-News-13-27664-UAEs-welfare-projects-in-Pakistan-top-one-billion-dirhams/.

98. Sehar Kamran, *Pak–Gulf Defence and Security Cooperation*, Centre for Pakistan and Gulf Studies, January 2013, pp. 3–5, available at: http://cpakgulf.org/documents/Pak-Gulf-Security-Ties-final.pdf/.

99. Ahmad Tauqir, 'Relations with UAE Immensely Important to Pakistan: PM', *Pakistan Today*, 31 December 2013, available at: http://www.pakistantoday.com.pk/2013/12/31/national/relations-with-uae-immensely-important-to-pakistan-pm/.

100. 'UAE Investor's Legal Interests Will Be Protected: Sharma Assures UAE Minister of Economy', *Press Release*, Press Information Bureau, New Delhi, 28 January 2014, available at: http://pib.nic.in/newsite/PrintRelease.aspx?relid=102793.

101. Ali Al Youha and Froilan T. Malit Jr., 'Labour Migration in the United Arab Emirates: Challenges and Responses', *Feature*, Migration Policy Institute, 18 September 2013, available at: http://www.migrationpolicy.org/article/labor-migration-united-arab-emirates-challenges-and-responses/.

102. Preeti Kanna, 'India PM Linked to First UAE Visit in 30 Years', *The National (Abu Dhabi)*, 25 February 2013, available at: http://www.thenational.ae/news/uae-news/politics/india-pm-linked-to-first-uae-visit-in-30-years/.

103. Andy Sambidge, 'Indian PM Plans First UAE Visit for 32 Years', *Arabian Business*, 5 April 2013, available at: http://www.arabianbusiness.com/indian-pm-plans-first-uae-visit-for-32-years-496738.html/.

104. 'Indian PM's UAE Visit Cancelled', *Khaleej Times*, 13 March 2013, available at: http://www.khaleejtimes.com/nation/inside.asp?xfile=/data/nationgeneral/2013/March/nationgeneral_March250.xml&section=nationgeneral/.

105. Rohini Singh, 'UAE Insistence on Signing BIPA Treaty First Put off PM's Visit: Salman Khurshid', *The Economic Times*, 26 March 2013, available at: http://articles.economictimes.indiatimes.com/2013-03-26/news/38040700_1_uae-bipa-etisalat-db/.

10

Yemen

Dipanwita Chakravortty

Key Information

Area: 527,968 sq km; **Population:** 26,052,966 (2014 est.); **Native:** NA; **Expats:** NA; **Youth:** 21.1 per cent; **Population growth rate:** 2.72 per cent; **Life expectancy at birth:** 64.83 years; **Major population groups:** NA; **Religious groups:** Sunni (Shafi), Shia (Zaydi), small number of Jews, Christian and Hindus; **GDP:** US$61.63 billion; **Per capita income:** US$2,500; **Foreign trade:** US$17.66 billion; **Oil reserves:** 2.88 billion bbl (2013); **Gas reserves:** 478.5 billion m³; **Ruling party:** General People's Congress; **Ruler:** President Abd Rabbuh Mansur Hadi (since 25 February 2012); **National Day:** 22 May; **Defence budget:** 6.6 per cent of GDP; **HDI rank:** 160; **Literacy rate:** 63.9 per cent; **UN education index:** 0.311; **Gender inequality index:** 0.747; **Labour force:** 7.1 million; **Unemployment rate:** 35 per cent; **External debt:** US$7.806 billion (December 2013); **Sovereign wealth fund:** NA; **Infant mortality rate:** 50.41 deaths out of 1,000; **Last national census:** 2004; **Parliament:** 111-member nominated Shura Council, 301-member elected House of Representative; **Last parliament election:** 27 April 2003; **Number of Indians:** 100,000; **Last Indian prime minister to visit:** none since 1947.

Sources: CIA, *The World Factbook*, available at: https://www.cia.gov/library/publications/the-world-factbook/; *UN Human Development Report*, Statistics, available at: http://hdr.undp.org/en/statistics/; *United States Commission on Religious Freedom*, US Department of State; *Annual Report 2013*; *Briefs on Foreign Relations*, Ministry of External Affairs, Government of India and Centre for Arms Control and Proliferation (Washington, D.C.). *Note:* All figures for 2013.

Political turbulence continues to rock Yemen despite Abd Rabbuh Mansur Hadi replacing Ali Abdullah Saleh as President on 27 September 2012. While popular protests have receded, debates over the future of the country and its federal arrangement continue. Sectarian violence, especially between Houthis—a Zaidi Shia group—and Salafists, has been on the decline in 2013. Efforts towards drafting a new constitution that guarantees the right to cede were met with strong opposition. Indeed, part of the present problems in Yemen can be traced to the troubled unification of North and South Yemen carried out under the leadership of Saleh on 22 May 1990. Despite these uncertainties and domestic difficulties, Indo-Yemeni relations improved in 2013, including a considerable increase in India's imports.

DOMESTIC DEVELOPMENTS

After months of violent protests and foot dragging, on 27 February 2012, President Ali Abdullah Saleh ceded power under an accord brokered by Gulf Cooperation Council (GCC) and backed by the United Nations Security Council (UNSC), the US and the European Union (EU). In a key concession, Saleh was granted immunity for political crimes committed during his 33-year long regime. Acting President Mansur Hadi took over the reins for a two-year transition period.[1] As per the GCC-brokered deal, President Hadi called for a National Dialogue Conference (NDC) to commence from September 2012 aimed at bringing together all political and sectarian factions and draft a new constitution.[2]

The composition of the NDC led to continued clashes between various groups, such as the Houthis, who refused to participate. On 28 November 2012, the final seat allocation was declared by UN Secretary General's Special Advisor on Yemen Jamal Benomar. The membership gave 50 per cent of seats to Yemenis from the south, 30 per cent to women and 20 per cent to youth (Table 10.1 and Figure 10.1).[3] Additionally, 62 seats were allocated to President Hadi to fill in the gaps and add figures from the community as well as other groups representing religious minorities, handicaps, artists, displaced persons, emigrants, businessmen, new parties, academics and religious leaders.[4]

In early January 2013, the preparatory committee of the National Dialogue submitted its final report to President Hadi.[5] On 18 March,

Table 10.1
Composition of the National Dialogue Conference (NDC) in Yeman

Entity	Number
GPC and alliance	112
Islah	50
Yemeni Socialist Party	37
Nasserite Party	30
Four seats each for the five political parties currently in the government, namely Arab Socialist Ba'ath Party, Yemeni Unionist Party, Popular Union Forces, National Council, Al-Haq party	20
Hirak (Southern Movement)	85
Houthis	35
Independent Youth	40
Women other than those represented in the political entities	40
Civil Societies	40
Rashad Party (Salafi)	7
Justice and Construction	7
Other groups and social figures (appointed by President Hadi)	62
Total	565

Source: Adapted from *Yemen Times*, 29 November 2012.

under the supervision of UNSC, the NDC started its first plenary session. Nine working groups, namely on Southern Issue, Sa'ada Issue, National Issue and Transitional Justice, State Building, Good Governance, Military/Security, Special Entities, Rights/Freedom and Development were formed. The working group on southern issue was given the task of building north–south relations while the group on Sa'ada issue was tasked with defusing the sectarian tension in the Northern Yemeni governorate of Sa'ada.[6] Other working groups were based on more general issues pertaining to different aspects of the new constitution.

Based on the first plenary session, President Hadi on 10 April issued a decree to reorganize the armed forces of Yemen in support of the goals and objectives of the NDC. The decrees included the disbanding of the Republican Guard led by Brig. Gen. Ahmed Ali Abdullah Saleh—son of former President Ali Abdullah Saleh—as well as the appointment of

Figure 10.1
Composition of the National Dialogue Conference in Yemen

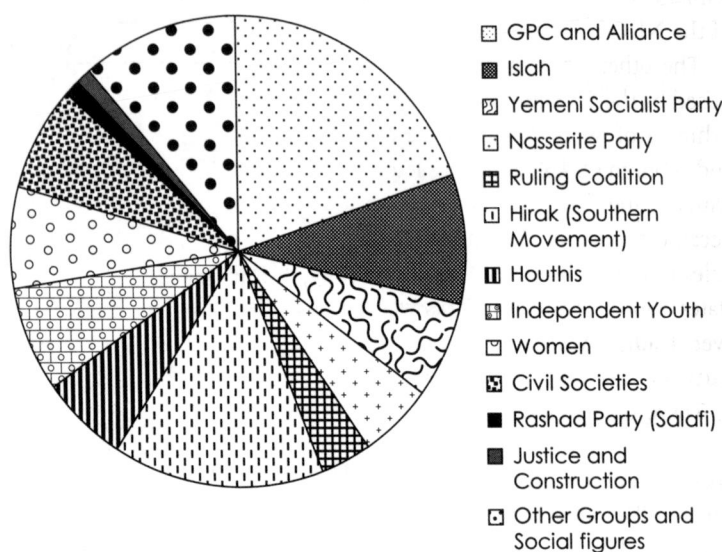

GPC and Alliance

Islah

Yemeni Socialist Party

Nasserite Party

Ruling Coalition

Hirak (Southern Movement)

Houthis

Independent Youth

Women

Civil Societies

Rashad Party (Salafi)

Justice and Construction

Other Groups and Social figures

Source: Adapted from *Yemen Times*, 29 November 2012.

a new Chief-of-Staff of the Central Security Forces replacing Brig. Gen. Yahya Mohammed Abdullah Saleh, a nephew of the former president.[7]

The second plenary session started on 8 June and lasted for a month with reports submitted by groups on Rights/Freedoms, Special Entities, Good Governance, Defence/Security, Development and Transitional Justice. The working groups on the Southern issue and the Sa'ada issue failed to reach a compromise on unifying the northern and southern parts of Yemen.[8] The lack of progress in these working groups prompted a new committee to be set up known as the Consensus Committee to look into issues that were not resolved, especially the Southern issue.

By September, a large number of the NDC members withdrew from the talks which included Mohammad Ali Ahmed, a prominent southern leader who was heading the working group on the Southern question, and other members of the Southern movement due to the lack of tangible solutions. This led to the split of the Southern movement with Ahmed blaming the NDC for ignoring the plight of the Southern Yeminis since 1990s. Another Southern Movement wing led by Yassin

Makkawi and Mohammad Ali al-Shaddadi condemned the withdrawal while asserting that Southern movement would continue to be a part of the NDC.[9] The other issue that caused a roadblock was the federal plan proposed by the Socialist Party and the Houthis. The plan calls for the establishment of two to five separate regions that would have equal political and economic rights. This has led to the establishment of 8+8 committee with equal members from the North and South.[10] The number of regions became a bone of contention between several power blocs. Al-Hirak's delegation proposed a federal Yemen that encompasses only two federal states, North and South. This was backed by the Socialist Party. However, Hadi, along with the General People's Congress and the Al-Islah Party, has been pressing for four or five federal states.[11]

These divisions in the NDC delayed the start of the third and final plenary which was scheduled to start in the first week of September. The opening ceremony eventually took place on 8 October. The Houthis and Hiraak NDC members boycotted it, citing lack of a reparation fund for victims of the wars waged against rebels in Sa'ada and disagreements over the federal structure of the state. Members of the General National Congress also withdrew from the transitional justice and good-governance working groups, citing disagreements over immunity and political participation of officials of the former regime.[12] On 27 November, a trust fund was set up as an attempt to bring back members of the Southern movement and the Houthis. The trust fund, worth US$350 million contributed by Qatar, is for compensating southern Yemenis who were unfairly dismissed from public service posts or whose land was confiscated following the 1994 civil war.[13] The NDC continued until 27 January 2014 with the adoption of a document that pledged a multi-regional federal system.[14]

Progress was made on Yemen's external issues. On 27 January, a 15-member UNSC headed by the UK and Morocco met with President Hadi, parliamentarians, civil society and GCC members. This was the first UNSC mission to Yemen in five years and the mission pledged its support to the NDC and the political transition process.[15] On 7 March, the fifth ministerial-level meeting of the Friends of Yemen was held in London, hosted by the UK and co-chaired by Saudi Arabia and Yemen. It was attended by 39 countries including India. On 25 September, the sixth ministerial-level meeting of the Friends of Yemen was held in New York.

Earlier in September 2012, the fourth meeting had pledged US$7.9 billion.[16] The World Bank also launched six new projects for Yemen to generate employment and to restore basic services in the country.[17]

The year 2013 also saw Yemen embroiled in increasing tribal strife and violence. Clashes between the Houthis and Salafists in northern Yemen have led to the death of more than a hundred people and wounding of more than 500 civilians.[18] The Shia–Sunni clash between the tribals of north Yemen spilled over to other parts of the country. Several tribes in South Yemen called for attacks against Shias or Houthis as they were seen as 'legitimate targets'.[19] Violence in Yemen worsened partly due to the involvement of Iran and Saudi Arabia. On 27 January, the Yemeni coast guard—in coordination with the US Navy—intercepted a ship carrying missiles and rockets allegedly sent by Iran towards undermining the transition process. Following a request from the UNSC, the Panel of Experts that monitors compliance with the UN sanctions regime[20] arrived in Sana'a on 22 February to investigate the incident. The panel confirmed the involvement of Iran in the arms cache.[21] Additionally, on 2 May, Yemeni coast guard intercepted a boat carrying 20,000 Turkish-made pistols. Saudi Arabia, on the other hand, has started providing jets to the American programme of drone attacks against al-Qaeda in Yemen.[22]

The number of terrorist attacks increased during 2013. Yemen-based al-Qaeda in the Arabian Peninsula (AQAP) conducted dozens of deadly bombings and other attacks on Yemeni security targets especially in the south-eastern Hadramawt province and southern province of Lahij.[23] On 24 May, al-Qaeda militants seized control of villages near the city of Al-Mukalla, the capital of Hadramawt. In May, there were a number of kidnappings of foreigners and humanitarian workers, including International Committee of the Red Cross (ICRC) employees, by tribesmen.[24] On 25 August, a Yemeni air force bus was bombed, killing six people and wounding 26 in Sa'naa.[25] On 5 December, a suicide-bomber attacked Yemen's defence ministry, which killed 52 people, including foreign medical staff, and wounded 167 people.[26]

The AQAP also sent series of video threats to the US embassy and to embassies of some European countries. In January, it offered three kilograms of gold worth US$160,000 for anyone who kills the US ambassador to Yemen, Gerald Feierstein. The group said it would pay 5 million Yemeni Riyals to anyone who kills an American soldier inside Yemen.[27] In August, Britain, Germany, France and the US closed down their embassies and other official missions for a week following the threats from suspected al-Qaeda leaders.[28]

Another issue that affected Yemen was the massive influx of refugees from Africa, especially Somalia. As a signatory to the 1951 Refugee Convention and its 1967 Protocol, Yemen acts as a transit country for the flow of asylum seekers, migrants and refugees. In mid-2013, over 240,000 refugees arrived in Yemen, majority of who were Somalis. By August, more than 1,200 Syrians refugees were living in Yemen.[29] Domestically, the number of internally displaced persons (IDPs) stood at over 306,000 in July and the vast majority then were from the northern governorates. Sectarian violence in Al-Baidha and Dhamar Governorates led to displacement of 8,000 people in the latter part of the year.[30]

As a result of political and sectarian turmoil, the economy of Yemen continued to suffer. The country slipped into recession in 2011–12, with GDP shrinking by 12.7 per cent but in 2012–13, there was a growth of 2.4 per cent which stabilized the trade.[31] Even though, the imports were higher than exports, there was a significant improvement in the overall trade. Inflation reduced from 25.5 per cent in 2011 to 10.1 per cent in 2013. By February, the currency stabilized around 215 Yemeni Riyals to the US dollar; it had dropped to 243 Yemeni Riyals in 2011.[32] Despite certain economic stability, the living conditions continued to deteriorate. Prospects for local production of goods became worse. In 2013, 90 per cent of goods used in Yemen were imported.[33] Growing unemployment, increasing inflation, food insecurity and rising levels of malnutrition further pushed down the economy. Almost half of the population lacked sufficient food supplies and more than half had no access to safe water and basic sanitation.[34]

BILATERAL RELATIONS

India and Yemen share historical ties that can be dated back to the Roman Empire as the port of Aden was a gateway to the Arab world and Europe for the Indian traders while Yemeni traders came to India to trade horses and weapons in exchange of spices. In 1839, Aden became part of the British Empire and was administered by the Bombay Presidency. Several families came from Aden and settled down in South India, especially near Hyderabad. Some of India's Bohra, Kachchi and Khoja communities migrated and settled in Aden.

Discovery of oil in South Yemen in the late 1950s sparked oil trade and created opportunities for emigration of many Indians as labourers. India was quick to recognize the Republic of Yemen in May 1990, marking the unification of Yemen Arab Republic and People's Democratic Republic of Yemen. Since January 2011, Ali Abdullah Saleh who was the President of the Republic of Yemen since 1990 faced nationwide protests. The uprising not only affected the political structure of the state but also its economy. Rise of terrorism and sectarian violence also had a negative impact on the economic growth. These factors affected Yemen's relations with the outside world, including India. Though there were several economic setbacks, such as terror attacks on oil pipelines and continuous civil unrest, there were a few encouraging signs in the bilateral relations.

Political Relations

The year 2013 saw several key developments in the political relations between the two countries. On 3 March, Foreign Minister of Yemen Abu Bakr al-Qirbi met the Indian ambassador Ausaf Sayeed and discussed bilateral relations between the two countries. They discussed India's participation in the meeting of Friends of Yemen held in London on 7 March.[35]

The Eighth Session of the India–Yemen Joint Committee for Economic, Scientific and Technical Cooperation (JCM) took place in New Delhi during 11–12 March. The Indian delegation was led by Sanjay Singh, Secretary (East), while the Yemeni side was led by the Deputy Minister of Planning and International Cooperation Omer Abdulaziz Abdulghani. Both the sides emphasized on age old people-to-people contacts and agreed to further strengthen them through new ventures in education, training, culture, health, hydrocarbons, agriculture, fertilizers, trade, investment and security. Abdulghani also called on External Affairs Minister Salman Khurshid and Minister of State E. Ahamed. The two sides signed a Cultural Exchange Programme for 2013–15.[36]

On 29 May, Indian Ambassador to Yemen met Mohammed Saeed al-Saadi, Minister of Planning and International Cooperation (MoPIC), and both sides reviewed ongoing bilateral cooperation towards implementing decisions taken during the Eighth India–Yemen Joint Committee. Saeed also met Mohammad al-Ashabi, Director General, Asia and Australia Desk in the Ministry of Foreign Affairs, and discussed the Joint Committee report.[37]

On 12 August, Amrit Lugun was appointed as the Indian ambassador to Yemen.[38] On 12 December, he met Abu-Bakr Abdullah Al-Qirbi, Foreign Minister of Yemen, and presented his credentials.[39] In November, Joint Secretary of the Ministry of External Affairs of India Mridul Kumar visited Yemen to hand over US$1.8 million worth of humanitarian grants in the form of wheat to the World Food Programme (WFP) in Yemen. This assistance was part of India's commitment to Friends of Yemen group. Previously, in 2012, India had provided US$2 million worth of rice as humanitarian grant. The WFP Representative and Country Director Bishow Parajuli and Yemeni Minister for Planning and International Cooperation Mohammed Saeed al-Sa'adi welcomed the Indian assistance that would support 121,300 Yemenis for a period of six months.[40]

A Memorandum of Understanding (MoU) was signed between the two countries during a visit by India's Chief Election Commissioner (CEC) V. S. Sampath on 23 December. He had been invited by Judge Mohammed Hussain al-Hakimi, President of the Supreme Commission for Elections and Referendum (SCER) of Yemen. The CEC also extended an invitation to the SCER President to send a delegation to India to witness the general elections in India scheduled for April–May 2014. Further, he expressed the willingness of Election Commission of India to support Yemen through various electoral process based on India's long experience. He also met President Mansur Hadi and discussed bilateral cooperation in the field of election management and cooperation between the two countries.[41]

Economic Relations

The year 2013 witnessed a degree of stability in Yemeni economy after two years of turmoil. Its total external trade significantly increased, while inflation rates declined, currency stabilized and interest rates were slashed to minimum. More importantly, huge foreign aid helped to stabilize the economy. The bilateral trade between India and Yemen saw substantial increase. India's exports to Yemen, which stood at US$514.10 million in 2010–11, had increased to US$730.62 million in 2011–12, and double to reach US$1.47 billion in 2012–13 (Table 10.2 and Figure 10.2). The 102 per cent increase in India's exports to Yemen came after a gap of nearly five years.[42] India's imports from Yemen decreased marginally in comparison to 2011–12; it stood at

US$970.72 million in 2011–12 and decreased to US$958.92 million in 2012–13 (Table 10.2 and Figure 10.2). Though Yemen's share in India's total oil imports is marginal at 0.52 per cent, it constitutes nearly 98 per cent of imports from Yemen (Table 10.3 and Figure 10.3). The bilateral trade reached US$2.43 billion in 2012–13, an increase of

Table 10.2
India–Yemen Bilateral Trade (in US$ Million)

	2009–10	2010–11	2011–12	2012–13
India's exports to Yemen	727.39	514.10	730.62	1,477.27
India's imports from Yemen	1,575.55	1,743.90	970.72	958.92
Total bilateral trade	2,302.95	2,258.00	1,701.34	2,436.19
Share of Yemen in India's total trade	0.49	0.36	0.21	0.31

Source: Adapted from Directorate General of Foreign Trade, available at: http://dgft.gov.in/.

Figure 10.2
India–Yemen Bilateral Trade

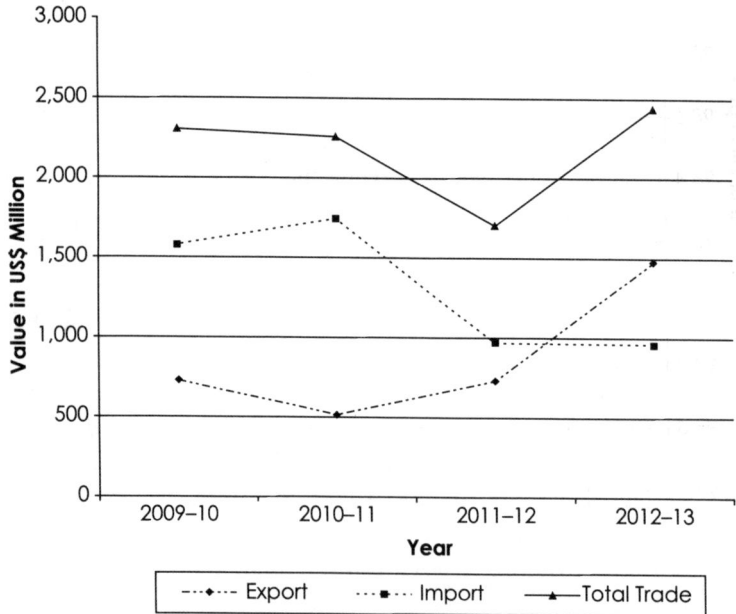

Source: Adapted from Directorate General of Foreign Trade, New Delhi, available at: www.dgft.gov.in/.

Table 10.3
Share of Oil in India's Imports from Yemen (in US$ Million)

Year	Oil imports from Yemen	Total oil imports	Yemen's share in total oil imports	Imports from Yemen	Per cent of oil in imports from Yemen
2009–10	1,563.15	96,321.16	1.62	1,575.55	99.21
2010–11	1,722.95	115,929.02	1.49	1,743.90	98.80
2011–12	955.26	172,753.92	0.55	970.72	98.11
2012–13	942.00	181,344.67	0.52	958.92	98.24

Source: Adapted from Directorate General of Foreign Trade, available at: www.dgft.gov.in/.

Figure 10.3
Share of Oil in India's Imports from Yemen

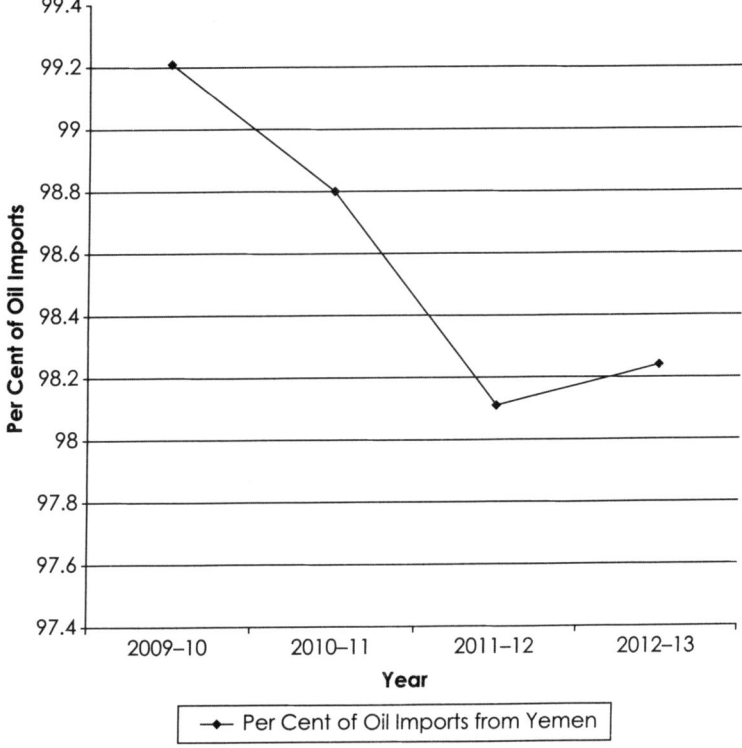

Source: Adapted from Directorate General of Foreign Trade, New Delhi, available at: www.dgft.gov.in/.

43.19 per cent. In terms of its share in India's overall foreign trade, it was 0.47 per cent in 2010–11, 0.20 per cent in 2011–12 and 0.31 per cent in 2012–13.

Both took notable steps to improve economic relations. A high-level Yemeni business delegation led by Ahmed Salem Shammakh, Chairman of the Yemen–India Business Council (YIBC), visited India from 14 to 16 March to participate in the Indian Engineering Sourcing Show held in Mumbai. The delegation included several leading Yemeni entrepreneurs and senior officials of the Federation of Yemen's Chambers of Commerce and Industry and the Ministry of Trade and Industry.[43]

On 2 April, India issued a notification whereby Yemen became a beneficiary under India's Duty Free Tariff Preference (DFTP) Scheme for the Least Developed Countries. The DFTP Scheme grants duty free access on 94 per cent of India's total tariff lines. This scheme would provide preferential market access to Yemeni exports to India, as well as encourage manufacturing sector in Yemen. In 2013, Yemen was added as new market under Market Linked Focus Product Scheme (MLFPS).[44]

On 17 June, Indian Embassy organized a seminar titled Enhancing Potential Business Partnerships in Yemen, in collaboration with Sana'a Chamber of Commerce and Industry. It was preceded by an India Catalogue Show. Omar Abdulaziz Abdulghani, Deputy Minister, Ministry of Planning and International Cooperation, was the keynote speaker.[45] A two-member delegation from Jaguar Overseas Limited visited Yemen during 2–4 March and had discussions with Shawky Hayel Saeed, Governor of Taiz, and several leading business groups in Yemen.[46]

Energy Relations

Due to continuous sectarian violence and attacks against oil pipelines, the overall oil export from Yemen has declined during the past two years. In 2013, there were 41 attacks against oil pipelines out of which 38 took place in Marib governorate, two in Shabwa and one in Hadramawt governorates. Blockage of oil wells, prevention of access to the pipelines for repairs, clashes with oil pipeline guards, theft of oil and use of bombs to explode pipelines resulted in the loss of more than US$310 million in revenue (100,000 barrels monthly) due to production halts from March 2011 to the end of 2013. During 2013, Yemen earned about US$2.25 billion in total revenues from oil exports, which is about US$750 million less compared to same period in 2012. It also exported 5 million barrels less in 2013 than it did in 2012.[47]

More than 98 per cent of India's imports from Yemen are oil related and they declined during 2012–13. In 2011–12, the imports stood at US$955.26 million and marginally came down to US$942 million in 2012–13. Though the total energy import of India from Persian Gulf region has increased, the share of energy import from Yemen decreased from 0.91 per cent to 0.89 per cent (Table 10.4).

Apart from traditional energy trade, India and Yemen also took steps in the renewable energy sector. A two-member delegation from Waaree Group, one of India's business groups in the field of renewable energy, visited Yemen from 18 to 20 February and installed a solar water pumping system in Hodeida.[48] A three-member delegation from the Nagarjuna Group visited Yemen from 8 to 10 February at the invitation of the General Investments Authority (GIA) to discuss a proposal for setting up a gas-based urea plant in Balhaf worth US$1.3 billion. The delegation had meetings with Muhammad Salim Basindwa, Prime Minister of Yemen, Saad al-Din Ali Bin Talib, Minister of Industry and Trade, Ahmed

Table 10.4
India's Energy Imports from Yemen (in US$ Million)

	2009–10	2010–11	2011–12	2012–13
India's energy imports from Yemen	1,563.15	1,722.95	955.26	942.00
India's total energy imports	96,321.12	115,929.02	172,753.92	181,344.67
Total energy imports from Persian Gulf	55,904.14	66,688.40	105,056.26	105,859.15
Share in total energy imports (in per cent)	1.62	1.49	0.55	0.52
Share in energy imports from Persian Gulf (in per cent)	2.80	2.58	0.91	0.89

Source: Adapted from Directorate General of Foreign Trade, available at: http://dgft.gov.in/.

Darees, Minister of Oil and Minerals, and Yahya Mohsen, Chairman of General Investment Authority.[49] A business delegation from GMR Group led by its President Ashis Basu visited Sana'a from 30 June to 3 July to explore opportunities in the power and infrastructure sectors. The delegation met Saleh Sumea, Minister of Electricity, and senior officials of different ministries.[50] These visits opened up future avenues of investment and cooperation between the two countries.

Cultural Relations

In 2013, the cultural relations between the two countries got strengthened with the signing of the Cultural Exchange Programme (2013–15). It was signed on the sidelines of the Eighth India–Yemen Joint Committee Meeting by Sangita Gairola, Secretary, Ministry of Culture, and Omar Abdulaziz Abdul Ghani, Deputy Minister of Planning and International Cooperation of Yemen. According to the agreement, the number of scholarships given by Indian Council of Cultural Relations (ICCR) was increased from 36 to 54.[51] The agreement also offered Ayush Scholarship in traditional forms of medicine such as Ayurveda, Unani, Siddha and Homeopathy.

Apart from the Cultural Exchange Programme, several steps were taken to forge close people-to-people contacts. A new online visa processing was inaugurated on 7 February.[52] On 5 March, Padma Bhushan awardee Saroj Ghose, former Director General of the National Council of Science Museums (NCSM), India, and Abdulaziz M.S. al-Ariqi, Chairman of the National Science Museum, Yemen, met to discuss sourcing exhibits from India for the proposed National Science Museum in Sana'a.[53] Later in the month, the Ambassador of India called on Abdul Hafed Noaman, Minister of Technical Education and Vocational Training, to review the ongoing bilateral cooperation in the field of technical education and vocational training between the two countries.[54] As per the Cultural Exchange Programme (2013–15), India has agreed to a Yemeni proposal for setting up of three vocational training centres and two information and communication technology centres in Yemen.

On 20 May, Hisham Sharaf, Yemen's Minister of Higher Education, and Indian Ambassador Ausaf Sayeed discussed the implementation of the Educational Exchange Programme (EEP) signed between India and Yemen in April 2012.[55] Sayeed also called on the Yemeni Minister of

Religious Endowments and Guidance, Hamoud Muhammed Ou'bad, for the conservation of Indian heritage sites in Aden.[56] On 22 June, Indian officials met Yemen's Minister of Human Rights Hooria Mashhour and discussed bilateral cooperation in the field of human rights.[57] India has extended the facility of training and capacity building under the Indian Technical and Economic Cooperation (ITEC) programme to officials of the Human Rights Ministry in Yemen.

There is a marginal presence of Indian nationals in Yemen, estimated to be around 14,000 in 2010 which declined to an estimated 5,000 by June 2011 following political instability. In 2013, there has been a slight increase in the number, though only 6,000 are registered with the Embassy.[58] Expatriate workers often face problems, including in practising their faith. Although the Constitution provides for freedom of religion, there are restrictions on religious proselytization except for Islam. Muslims are prohibited to convert to other faiths while public practice of other faith can invite trouble. Moreover, attacks on religious and sectarian minorities have increased with the rise of al-Qaeda. According to the *International Religious Freedom Report for 2012*, many South Asians, including Indians, are subjected to harsh imposition of Islamic law by the members of al-Qaeda and its affiliate Ansar al-Sharia. There have been reports on forced prayers and harassment of women; some expats complained of being forced to pray five times a day at mosques while women were harassed on the streets or at work about their dresses.[59]

External Players

The US: In the past couple of years, relations between the US and Yemen have been dominated by two issues, namely drone attacks and economic assistance. Under President Saleh, bilateral relations were an extension of Saleh's desire to befriend the US. However, Yemen's lax policy towards the militants of AQAP as well as its apathy towards the rise of new terror outfits considerably strained the relations. As part of its Yemen Strategic Plan of 2002, the US deployed drone attacks in Yemen against suspected militants and terrorists. In 2013, there were 16 confirmed and 17 possible drone attacks which were a sharp decrease from the previous year with 36 confirmed and 70 possible drone attacks. Between 71 and 99 people were killed in 2013 due to these attacks out of whom 23 were identified as civilians.[60] AQAP's deputy commander Said Ali al-Shihri was killed on 24 January after being wounded during a drone strike in northern Yemen.[61]

In 2013, the US committed US$256 million in assistance to Yemen, in addition to US$356 million allocated in 2012. The monetary assistance was divided into several packages, US$39 million was earmarked for political transition and successful completion of the NDC, US$221 million for humanitarian assistance such as food packages and medicines, US$100 million for improving education and creating jobs and US$247 million for counter-terrorism capacity building.[62] Apart from financial assistance, several Yemeni leaders were given technical education on topics such as women and youth leadership, interfaith dialogue, university administration, disability rights, water resource management and small business development.

China: In 2013, China and Yemen's bilateral relations reached new heights and on 28 January, Chinese Vice Foreign Minister Zhai Jun visited Yemen and met Prime Minister Salim Basindwa. They discussed China's role and support to the transitional government in Yemen. During the visit, an agreement was signed under which China would provide medical equipments and furniture worth US$5 million for the Yemeni-Chinese Friendship Hospital. The agreement was signed by Minister of Planning and International Cooperation Mohammed al-Sa'adi and Chinese Ambassador to Yemen Chang Hwa.[63] Chinese Vice Foreign Minister Zhai Jun met Foreign Minister Abu Bakr al-Qirbi and announced that China would reduce 95 per cent of the custom duties on Yemeni products.[64]

President Mansur Hadi visited China during 12–15 November and met Chinese President Xi Jinping, Premier Li Keqiang and Chairman of the National Committee of the Chinese People's Political Consultative Conference (CPPCC) Yu Zhengsheng. Both sides exchanged views on further deepening and developing the relations.[65] During the visit, China vowed to provide monetary as well as technical aid to Yemen to pursue economic development. President Xi further added that he was encouraging more qualified Chinese enterprises to invest in Yemen and hoped that Yemen would provide a secure environment for Chinese firms and staff.[66] Premier Li Keqiang assured President Hadi that China would build two power plants in Yemen with total output capacity of 5,000 megawatts and expand Yemen's main container ports.[67]

Apart from economic ties, both the countries made strides on defence ties. On 23 September, Yemeni Defence Minister Muhammad Nasir Ahmad visited China and met Xu Qiliang, Vice Chairman of China's Central Military Commission. Xu Qiliang assured Muhammad Nasir Ahmad of bilateral military cooperation as well as common training programmes.[68]

To improve people-to-people contact, the Chinese embassy in Yemen started new scholarships and technical programmes for Yemeni youth. On 25 December, Ambassador Chang Hua met Basaleem, Director General of Yemen State Television, for introducing Chinese television programmes in Yemen State Television. He said that broadcasting Chinese television programmes would help 'introduce China's time-honoured history, profound culture, beautiful natural scenery as well as achievements in economic and social development to Yemeni people'.[69]

Pakistan: Pakistan has friendly political, economic, cultural and people-to-people relations with Yemen. The Pakistani expatriate population in Yemen is around 700. As members of the Organization of Islamic Cooperation (OIC), they supported each other on various issues. On 29 September, Special Assistant to the Prime Minister on Foreign Affairs Tariq Fatemi expressed support to the NDC, which according to him was 'aimed at peace and security in Yemen and at normalization of the situation'.[70]

Pakistan and Yemen regularly exchange ministerial-level meetings to evaluate their economic and trade relations. In 2010, they commenced discussion to establish Yemeni-Pakistani Business Council which would have equal number of investors from both the countries.[71] In 2011–12, Pakistan's export to Yemen was US$7,103 million which increased to US$9,018 million in 2012–13. Majority of the export was in rice which was worth US$5,660 in 2012–13, an increase from US$4,845 million in 2011–12. Hydrocarbons are the major component in Pakistan's imports from Yemen but during the past two years Pakistan's imports have reduced drastically.[72]

One of the most important issues faced by both the countries is constant US drone attacks on their territory. These attacks are an intrusion to their territorial integrity and sovereignty and were responsible for destroying infrastructure and economic capabilities. Several villages and surrounding farms have been destroyed due to these attacks. This has made the economy of both the countries vulnerable to increasing fluctuations due to lack of stable local produce. Yemen and Pakistan have not only individually condemned these drone attacks but have also come together in the OIC to take a strong position against the violation of their territories by the US.[73]

Challenges

With the conclusion of the NDC in February 2014, Yemen has stepped into a new threshold of reconstructing and stabilizing the country. With approximately 1,400 recommendations made in the final report, it has become imperative for Yemen's leaders to translate these into meaningful action and to incorporate the main principles in the new Constitution. At this point of time, Yemen requires the support of other countries not only financially but also in providing technical assistance in the reconstruction of the nation. India has the potential to play a crucial role in this. Most of the Indians living in Yemen comprise nurses, hospital staff, university professors, professionals, and skilled and semi-skilled workers. The medical personnel and hospital staff form the dominant group and their number exceeds 2,000 out of the 6,000 registered with the embassy.[74] Apart from the Indian diaspora in Yemen, India also financially assists through the Friends of Yemen group which has started various programmes, such as small industries to increase employment in Yemen. However, there is a scope for larger Indian involvement in assisting Yemen by building schools, hospitals, roads and other basic amenities that would provide structural assistance to the violence-stricken nation.

Sectarian violence has been one of the main reasons for the shattering economy in Yemen. As a neutral yet mutually respected nation, India has the potential to engage with various factions in Yemen and establish confidence-building mechanisms through Track II dialogues. India can also diversify its exports to Yemen to bolster the failing economy of Yemen. These potential options will help in building sustainable bilateral relations.

CONCLUSION

The year 2013 proved to be a fruitful year for India–Yemen bilateral relations. Politically, the successful completion of the Eight Session of the India–Yemen Joint Committee for Economic, Scientific and Technical Cooperation was an important milestone in the bilateral relation. The most important visit was by India's CEC. Economic relations witnessed growth in total trade even though the energy import from Yemen declined. India's exports to Yemen doubled and an important step was the inclusion of Yemen as a beneficiary under India's Duty Free Tariff Preference Scheme for the Least Developed Countries. The Cultural Exchange Programme (2013–15) was signed which increased the number of scholarships provided by ICCR. Even though Yemen is still grappling with political instability, the strengthening bilateral ties not only provide Yemen with a helping hand but also give India a foothold in the region.

NOTES

1. 'Yemen', *UNSC Report, March 2012*, available at: http://www.securitycouncilreport.org/monthly-forecast/2012-03/lookup_c_glKWLeMTIsG_b_7996437.php/.
2. 'Yemen', *UNSC Report, July 2012*, available at: http://www.securitycouncilreport.org/monthly-forecast/2012-07/lookup_c_glKWLeMTIsG_b_8192003.php/.
3. 'Yemeni Parties Reach Agreement Paving Way for Holding of National Dialogue—UN Envoy', UN News Centre, 28 November 2012, available at: http://www.un.org/apps/news/story.asp/www.wmo.int/story.asp?NewsID=43627&Cr=yemen&Cr1=#.UwrPZfmSw/.
4. 'National Dialogue Conference's Share Distribution Decided', *Yemen Times*, 29 November 2012, available at: http://www.yementimes.com/en/1629/news/1666/National-Dialogue-Conference%E2%80%99s-share-distribution-decided.htm/.
5. 'Yemen President Announces Preparatory Committee for National Dialogue', *Istanbul Forum Supporting Dialogue*, available at: http://www.ifdyemen.com/?fid=307&lang=en/.
6. National Dialogue Conference, Yemen, available at: http://www.ndc.ye/default.aspx/.

7. 'Yemen', *UNSC Report, June 2013*, available at: http://www.securitycouncil-report.org/monthly-forecast/2013-06/yemen_5.php/.
8. 'Yemen', *UNSC Report, September 2013*, available at: http://www.security-councilreport.org/monthly-forecast/2013-09/yemen_6.php/.
9. Abubakr al-Shamahi, 'All Talk at Yemen's National Dialogue', *The Majalla*, 25 December 2013, available at: http://www.majalla.com/eng/2013/12/article55247584/.
10. Ibid.
11. 'Yemen's National Dialogue Is Running out of Time', *Al-Monitor*, 27 October 2013, available at: http://www.al-monitor.com/pulse/politics/2013/12/yemen-national-dialogue-conference-disputes-delays.html#/.
12. Ibid.
13. 'Yemen', *UNSC Report, January 2014*, available at: http://www.securitycouncilreport.org/monthly-forecast/2014-01/yemen_8.php/.
14. Ali Ibrahim Al-Moshki, 'National Dialogue Conference Concludes', *Yemen Times*, 28 January 2014, available at: http://www.yementimes.com/en/1750/news/3398/National-Dialogue-Conference-concludes.htm/.
15. 'Yemen', *UNSC Report, February 2013*, available at: http://www.security-councilreport.org/monthly-forecast/2013-02/yemen_3.php/.
16. The World Bank, 'Friends of Yemen Committed to Support Next Stage of Yemen Transition', *Press Release*, 25 September 2013, available at: http://www.worldbank.org/en/news/press-release/2013/09/25/friends-of-yemen-committed-support-next-stage-yemen-transition/.
17. Ibid.
18. Farea al-Muslimi, 'Yemen's Democratic Transition Marred by Its Two Warring Sects', *Al-Monitor*, 4 June 2013, available at: http://www.al-monitor.com/pulse/originals/2013/06/sectarian-tensions-yemen-regional-powers.html#ixzz2uLUE0oOb/.
19. 'Four People Killed in Sectarian Violence in North Yemen', *Reuters*, 30 October 2013, available at: http://www.reuters.com/article/2013/10/30/us-yemen-violence-idUSBRE99T0T820131030/.
20. For the text of the resolution, see Security Council Committee for Resolution 1737, United Nations, available at: https://www.un.org/sc/committees/1737/.
21. 'Yemen', *UNSC Report, June 2013*.
22. Ibid.
23. Human Rights Watch, *World Report 2013: Yemen*, available at: http://www.hrw.org/world-report/2013/country-chapters/yemen?page=2/.
24. 'Yemen', *UNSC Report, June 2013*.
25. 'Six Killed in Bomb Attack on Yemen Air Force Bus', *The Telegraph (London)*, 25 August 2013, available at: http://www.telegraph.co.uk/news/world-news/middleeast/yemen/10264869/Six-killed-in-bomb-attack-on-Yemen-air-force-bus.html/.

26. Mohammed Ghobari, 'Suicide Bomber, Gunmen Kill 52 at Yemeni Defense Ministry', *Reuters*, 5 December 2013, available at: http://www.reuters.com/article/2013/12/05/us-yemen-explosion-idUSBRE9B406520131205/.

27. 'Al Qaeda Offers Gold Bounty for the Life of US Ambassador in Yemen', *The Telegraph*, 1 January 2013, available at: http://www.telegraph.co.uk/news/worldnews/middleeast/yemen/9772220/Al-Qaeda-offers-gold-bounty-for-the-life-of-US-ambassador-in-Yemen.html/.

28. Raf Sanchez, 'Western Embassies Closed in Yemen Following Al-Qaeda Warning', *The Telegraph*, 5 August 2013, available at: http://www.telegraph.co.uk/news/worldnews/middleeast/yemen/10224085/Western-embassies-closed-in-Yemen-following-al-Qaeda-warning.html/.

29. '2014 UNHCR Country Operations Profile—Yemen,' *United Nations High Commissioner for Refugees*, available at: http://www.unhcr.org/pages/49e486ba6.html/.

30. Ibid.

31. The World Bank, 'Yemen Overview', available at: http://www.worldbank.org/en/country/yemen/overview/.

32. Mohammed Ghobari, 'Yemen Economy Starts to Recover from Political Crisis', *Reuters*, 13 February 2013, available at: http://www.reuters.com/article/2013/02/13/yemen-economy-idUSL5N0BC21S20130213/.

33. 'Yemen', *UNSC Report, January 2014.*

34. Ibid.

35. 'Yemen India Discuss Bilateral Relations', *Yemen News Agency*, 3 March 2013, available at: http://sabanews.net/en/news300607.htm/.

36. 'Eight India–Yemen Joint Committee Meeting', *Press Release*, Ministry of External Affairs, New Delhi, 13 March 2013, available at: http://www.mea.gov.in/press-releases.htm?dtl/21355/Eight+IndiaYemen+Joint+Committee+Meeting/.

37. 'Ambassador Calls on Minister of Planning & International Cooperation', Embassy of India, Sana'a, 29 May 2013, available at: http://www.eoisanaa.org/newsfeed.xml/.

38. 'Shri Amrit Lugun Appointed as the Next Ambassador of India to Republic of Yemen', *Press Release*, Ministry of External Affairs, New Delhi, 12 August 2013, available at: http://www.mea.gov.in/press-releases.htm?dtl/22055/Shri+Amrit+Lugun+appointed+as+the+next+Ambassador+of+India+to+Republic+of+Yemen/.

39. 'Ambassador Shri Amrit Lugun Met Dr. Abu-Bakr Abdullah Al-Qirbi, Foreign Minister of Yemen on 12 December 2013', Embassy of India, Sana'a, 12 December 2013, available at: http://www.eoisanaa.org/newsfeed.xml/.

40. 'WFP Receives a Contribution from India in Support of Yemen's Poorest Households', *World Food Programme*, 21 November 2013, available at: http://www.wfp.org/news/news-release/wfp-receives-contribution-india-support-yemen%E2%80%99s-poorest-households/.

41. 'Election Commission Signs MoU with Yemen', *The Hindu*, 24 December 2013, available at: http://www.thehindu.com/news/international/world/election-commission-signs-mou-with-yemen/article5497494.ece/.
42. 'India's Exports to Yemen Increase by 102%', Embassy of India, Sana'a, 9 July 2013, available at: http://www.eoisanaa.org/newsfeed.xml/.
43. 'Leading Yemeni Businessmen to Participate in IESS 2013', Embassy of India, Sana'a, 14 March 2013, available at: http://www.eoisanaa.org/newsfeed.xml/.
44. 'Highlights of Annual Supplement 2013–2014', Directorate General of Foreign Trade, Ministry for Commerce, Industry and Textiles, New Delhi, 18 April 2013, available at: http://dgftcom.nic.in/exim/2000/Highlights1314E.pdf/.
45. 'Indian Catalogue Show and Seminar Organised in the Sana'a Chamber of Commerce', Embassy of India, *Sana'a*, 17 June 2013, available at: http://www.eoisanaa.org/newsfeed.xml/.
46. 'Indian Company Explores Opportunities in Taiz Governorate', Embassy of India, Sana'a, 4 March 2013, available at: http://www.eoisanaa.org/newsfeed.xml/.
47. Ali Ibrahim Al-Moshki, '2013 Oil Pipeline Sabotage Chronology', *Yemen Times*, 28 January 2014, available at: http://www.yementimes.com/en/1750/report/3397/2013-Oil-pipeline-sabotage-chro%ADnology.htm/.
48. 'Waaree Delegation Visits Yemen', Embassy of India, Sana'a, 20 February 2013, available at: http://www.eoisanaa.org/newsfeed.xml/.
49. 'Nagarjuna Delegation Visits Yemen', Embassy of India, Sana'a, 10 February 2013, available at: http://www.eoisanaa.org/newsfeed.xml/.
50. 'GMR Delegation Visits Yemen', Embassy of India, Sana'a, 3 July 2013, available at: http://www.eoisanaa.org/newsfeed.xml/.
51. 'India and Yemen Signed Cultural Exchange Programme', Embassy of India, Sana'a, 16 March 2013, available at: http://www.eoisanaa.org/newsfeed.xml/.
52. 'Indian Embassy in Sana'a Launches Online Visa Issuance System', *Yemen Fox*, 7 February 2013, available at: http://yemenfox.net/news_details.php?sid=5732/.
53. 'Proposal for Exhibits for the National Science Museum Discussed', Embassy of India, Sana'a, 5 March 2013, available at: http://www.eoisanaa.org/newsfeed.xml/.
54. 'India–Yemen Sides Discuss Cooperation in the Field of Technical Education & Vocational Training', Embassy of India, Sana'a, 30 March 2013, available at: http://www.eoisanaa.org/newsfeed.xml/.
55. 'Yemen, India Discuss Cooperation in the Field of Higher Education', Embassy of India, Sana'a, 20 May 2013, available at: http://www.eoisanaa.org/newsfeed.xml/.
56. 'Conservation of Indian heritage sites in Aden Discussed', Embassy of India, Sana'a, 10 June 2013, available at: http://www.eoisanaa.org/newsfeed.xml/.

57. 'India, Yemen Discuss Cooperation in the Field of Human Rights', Embassy of India, Sana'a, 22 June 2013, available at: http://www.eoisanaa.org/news-feed.xml/.

58. 'Indian Diaspora in Yemen', Embassy of India, Sana'a, available at: http://eoisanaa.org/indian-diaspora-in-yemen/.

59. *International Religious Freedom Report for 2012*, US Department of State, available at: http://www.state.gov/j/drl/rls/irf/religiousfreedom/index.htm#wrapper/.

60. 'Yemen: Reported US Covert Actions 2013', *The Bureau of Investigative Journalism*, available at: http://www.thebureauinvestigates.com/2013/01/03/yemen-reported-us-covert-actions-2013/.

61. 'Yemen', *UNSC Report, February 2013*.

62. 'U.S. Relations with Yemen', US Department of State, 28 August 2013, available at: http://www.state.gov/r/pa/ei/bgn/35836.htm/.

63. 'Yemen, China Sign US$5 Million Agreement, Discuss Aid for Dialogue', *Yemen Fox*, 29 January 2013, available at: http://www.yemenfox.net/news_details.php?sid=5659/; see also 'Chinese Vice Foreign Minister Zhai Jun Meets Yemen's President Abd-Rabbu Mansour Hadi', Ministry of Foreign Affairs of the People's Republic of China, Beijing, 29 January 2013, available at: http://www.fmprc.gov.cn/eng/wjb/zzjg/xybfs/gjlb/2908/2910/t1010208.shtml/.

64. 'China Cuts 95% of Yemeni Exports Customs Duties', *Yemen News Agency*, 28 January 2013, available at: http://www.sabanews.net/en/news296611.htm/.

65. 'Ambassador to Yemen Chang Hua Gives Exclusive Interview to Yemeni Al-Thawra', Ministry of Foreign Affairs of the People's Republic of China, Beijing, 11 December 2013, available at: http://www.fmprc.gov.cn/eng/wjb/zwjg/zwbd/t1109359.shtml/.

66. 'Xi Vows Aid for Yemen to Develop its Economy', *China Daily*, 14 November 2013, available at: http://usa.chinadaily.com.cn/epaper/2013-11/14/content_17104818.htm/.

67. 'China to Build Power Plants in Yemen, Expand Ports', *Reuters*, 16 November 2013, available at: http://www.reuters.com/article/2013/11/16/us-yemen-china-power-idUSBRE9AF05A20131116/.

68. 'China, Yemen Vow to Strengthen Military Ties', *People's Daily*, 23 September 2013, available at: http://english.peopledaily.com.cn/90786/8407411.html/.

69. 'Ambassador to Yemen Chang Hua Meets with Basaleem, Director General of Yemen State Television', Ministry of Foreign Affairs of the People's Republic of China, Beijing, 25 December 2013, available at: http://www.mfa.gov.cn/eng/wjb/zwjg/zwbd/t1114325.shtml/.

70. 'Pakistan Expresses Support for the Government of Yemen', Ministry of Foreign Affairs, Government of Pakistan, Islamabad, 29 September 2013, available at: http://www.mofa.gov.pk/pr-details.php?prID=1482/.

71. 'Yemen, Pakistan Emphasize Trade Relations' Development', *Pakistan Defence*, 29 December 2010, available at: http://defence.pk/threads/yemen-pakistan-emphasize-trade-relations-development.86662/.
72. 'Trade Statistics, 2013', Ministry of Commerce, Government of Pakistan, Islamabad, available at: http://www.commerce.gov.pk/?page_id=7/.
73. M. A. Niazi, 'Extraordinary OIC Summit Ahead', *The Nation (Pakistan)*, 27 July 2012, available at: http://www.nation.com.pk/columns/27-Jul-2012/extraordinary-oic-summit-ahead/.
74. 'Indian Diaspora in Yemen', Embassy of India, Sana'a, available at: http://eoisanaa.org/indian-diaspora-in-yemen/.

11

Gulf Cooperation Council (GCC)

Priyanka Mittal

India has a history of close economic and cultural relations with the Gulf Cooperation Council (GCC) countries. It now commands an increasingly important role in the Gulf region with its growing trade relations and expatriate population. The GCC is a consortium of six nations, namely, Bahrain, Kuwait, Oman, Qatar, Saudi Arabia and the United Arab Emirates (UAE) and the Persian Gulf region is the source of roughly two-thirds of India's oil and gas imports and is the largest trading region accounting for over 26 per cent of India's global trade.[1] Therefore, the Gulf region holds a premium stake and is of prime importance for India's security, peace, progress and stability, especially when it is home to about 6 million Indians expatriates.[2]

INTERNAL DEVELOPMENTS

After the Arab Uprisings, the nature and the conduct of the GCC states has been undergoing an important change, if not transformation. The Syrian civil war and the West's interim nuclear deal with Iran in November 2013 have changed the dynamics of the region. Despite the GCC welcoming the interim Iranian nuclear deal with P5+1,[3] there are major concerns in Saudi Arabia over its Shia majority neighbour. While Oman has chosen to take a different line, the UAE, Qatar, Kuwait and Bahrain are on the same page with Saudi Arabia on Iran. On the other hand, there are problems between Saudi Arabia–the UAE and Qatar over the latter's support to the Muslim Brotherhood. Even though Arab Spring has forced the GCC leaders to look for a cohesive approach towards strengthening GCC Union, things have not moved in the expected direction. The initiative first outlined in December 2011 has failed to take off. Understanding the implications of the changing Gulf region confrontations, Omani Foreign Minister Youssef bin Alawi, in December, bluntly declared his country's opposition to the Saudi proposal to transform GCC into a political union.[4] He expressed Omani reservation against involvement in any of the major clashes with Iran which would lead to armed confrontations as it would be harmful to Oman's development and growth.

Security has emerged as an important concern for the GCC monarchies. In September, Kuwait's Interior Ministry Undersecretary Ghazy al-Omar told Kuwaiti News Agency (KUNA) that the GCC states have reached 'a full agreement' on measures to be taken against all terrorist organizations. The position demanded GCC countries to be more stringent about the policies and positions against the terrorist organizations.[5] GCC countries are working towards counter-proliferation and strategic trade control activities. SIPRI, in conjunction with the UAE and the German Federal Office of Economics and Export Control (BAFA), organized a counter-proliferation and strategic trade control course for export licensing, customs and law enforcement officials belonging to GCC member-states.[6]

During the 34th annual summit of GCC held in Kuwait, it was agreed that the UAE would host the Gulf Academy for Strategic and Security Studies,[7] a regional think tank devoted to studying common security threats to the region. The GCC countries underscored their commitment for deeper military, economic and political cooperation among the member states. The summit approved the setting up of an EU-style political and economic union with a joint GCC military command.[8] In order to strengthen internal ties, the GCC countries are planning to launch a European-style Schengen visa by mid-2014 to allow Gulf-based expats and foreign businessmen to move easily across the borders of the bloc.[9]

The shifting political landscape due to rising protests and clashes in Bahrain has prompted the need for reform by other ruling families. The

Saudi incursion into Bahrain in 2011, dwindling Bahraini oil reserves and unsuccessful attempts to create a Gulf Union in 2012 are reminders of the limitations of Saudi efforts vis-à-vis Iran.[10] Concerns over protests in Bahrain have forced the wealthier Gulf States to pledge US$10 billion in aid to Bahrain over the next 10 years. This money was expected to start flowing in 2013 and 2014, further reviving the economy and providing stability to the monarchy. In February, the UAE granted US$2.5 billion to Manama, to finance projects in housing, electricity, water, infrastructure and social services. In April, the Kuwait Fund for Arab Economic Development approved US$1.3 billion for funding a raft of development schemes in Bahrain.[11]

Although the cultural and historical ties among the GCC countries are strong, internal cleavages and ruptures are beginning to surface.

BILATERAL RELATIONS

The Gulf region is India's extended neighbourhood with sea-borne trade that has helped in building prosperity in both the regions. India's two-way trade with the GCC countries had grown to more than US$159 billion in 2012–13 (Table 11.1). India received over US$30 billion of remittances in 2012 from the GCC countries.[12] This year GCC still remains the largest source of remittances to India, accounting for 37 per cent of the total remitted amount.[13] Today, the GCC is India's largest regional trading partner.[14]

The 'Look East' policy of the Gulf States and the 'Look West' policy of India have spurred strong economic and business ties. To promote cross-border investments, several joint initiatives and country specific investments have taken place between India and GCC. These country specific funds focus on channelizing cross border investments into specific sector projects. The India–GCC bilateral trade increased at a Compound Annual Growth Rate (CAGR) of 14.8 per cent to US$159.1 billion during 2009–13 (Table 11.1 and Figure 11.1). During this period, trade flows from GCC to India expanded at a CAGR of 16.1 per cent to US$108.1 billion, while trade from India to GCC rose at a CAGR of 12.3 per cent to US$51.1 billion (Table 11.1 and Figure 11.1). Growth in bilateral trade was driven by numerous agreements and by India's

Table 11.1
India–GCC Bilateral Trade (in US$ Million)

Country	2009–10	2010–11	2011–12	2012–13
Bahrain	753.07	1,293.08	1,345.97	1,268.13
Kuwait	9,031.95	12,169.65	17,621.05	17,649.21
Oman	4,532.82	5,088.55	4,668.08	4,609.21
Qatar	5,185.49	7,195.27	13,724.30	16,380.26
Saudi Arabia	21,004.57	25,069.68	37,501.00	43,783.89
UAE	43,469.50	66,575.55	72,681.84	75,455.01
Total trade with GCC	83,977.40	117,391.78	147,542.24	159,145.71
India's total trade	467,124.31	620,905.32	795,283.41	791,137.33
Share in total trade	17.98	18.91	18.32	20.12

Source: Adapted from Directorate General of Foreign Trade, New Delhi, available at: www.dgft.gov.in/.

Figure 11.1
India–GCC Bilateral Trade

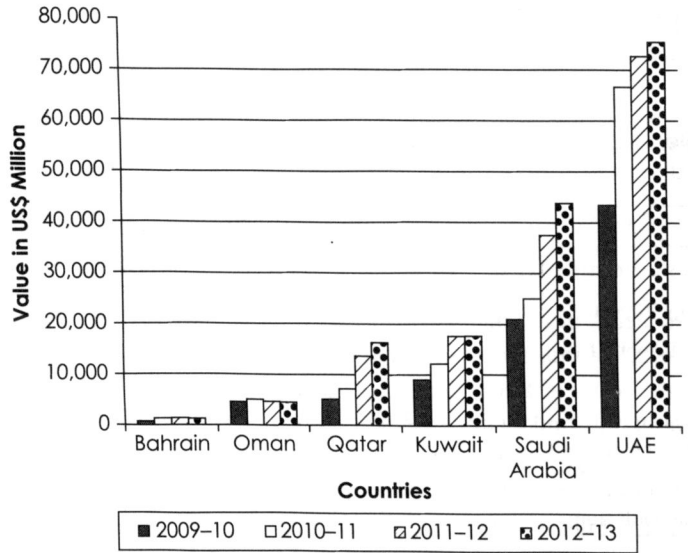

Source: Adapted from Directorate General of Foreign Trade, New Delhi, available at: www.dgft.gov.in/.

increasing oil imports.[15] During 2012–13, India imported nearly US$76 billion worth of oil from GCC countries that contributed to nearly 41.93 per cent of India's total oil imports (Table 11.2 and Figure 11.2). Besides oil, nearly 100 categories of products are exported annually from GCC to India.

The FDI outflows from India to GCC and vice versa have lately witnessed an uptrend, indicating higher coordination. The sectors that have attracted investments include manufacturing, real estate and construction, financial services, ICT, and agriculture and allied activities. The cumulative FDI outflows from India to the GCC region during 2008–13 stood at US$8.4 billion, registering a CAGR of 3.8 per cent. Meanwhile, the cumulative FDI outflows from GCC to India during 2008–13 stood at US$2.2 billion, registering a CAGR of 2.8 per cent.[16] The sectors that attracted most investments include power, construction, services, and metallurgical industries.

In September, a ministerial level meeting was held at the headquarters of the GCC's mission in New York between India and GCC. The Indian delegation was led by Minister for External Affairs Salman Khurshid and the GCC delegation was headed by Bahrain's Minister of Foreign Affairs Khalid Bin Ahmed Bin Mohammad al-Khalifa. The meeting stressed the need for strengthening and developing better cooperative relations to achieve common interests.[17] Both sides have been keen on strengthening

Table 11.2
India's Energy Imports from GCC (in US$ Million)

	2009–10	2010–11	2011–12	2012–13
India's total energy imports	96,321.12	115,929.02	172,753.92	181,344.67
Energy imports from GCC	36,997.63	46,632.91	73,510.80	76,034.70
Total imports from Persian Gulf	55,904.14	66,688.4	105,056.26	105,859.15
GCC share in total imports (in per cent)	38.41	40.23	42.55	41.93
GCC share in imports from Persian Gulf (in per cent)	66.18	69.93	69.97	71.83

Source: Adapted from Directorate General of Foreign Trade, New Delhi, available at: www.dgft.gov.in/.

Figure 11.2
India's Energy Imports from GCC

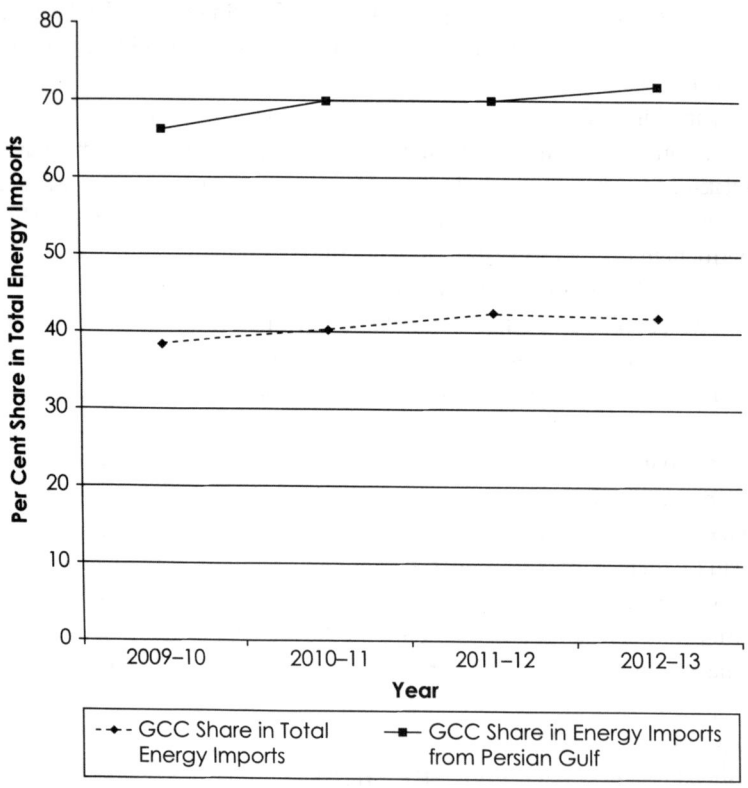

Source: Adapted from Directorate General of Foreign Trade, New Delhi, available at: www.dgft.gov.in/.

their existing military ties since four Indian naval ships arrived in the region for a goodwill visit.[18]

Minister of External Affairs Salman Khurshid represented India at the International Institute for Strategic Studies (IISS) Manama Dialogue, which is devoted to 'International Interests in Middle East Security and Non-Proliferation', held in December.[19] The Minister identified the Gulf region as a source of potential investment for India. In addition to a demand for favourable investments in India, Khurshid also referred to the bilateral partnership in counter-terrorism, anti-piracy, money laundering, weapon of mass destruction (WMD) proliferation and disarmament and joint defence exercise.[20]

India has a three-dimensional policy towards the Gulf. The first dimension talks about its long-term strategic relation with the Gulf and in this, has been pushing for partnership in energy-based sector. Therefore, efforts and policy changes are being made to transform these relationships from a buyer–seller one to a more broad-based one, with equity partnership in oil production, joint ventures in oil exploration, petrochemical complexes and fertilizer plants, and with partnership in strategic reserves storage facility that is being built in India.[21]

The second dimension talks about the investment and economic cooperation where strong impetus is given for the cross-sector FDI initiatives. While FDI investment from the Gulf countries into India stands modestly at around US$3 billion from April 2000 to August 2013, the portfolio investment figure is higher. Sovereign Wealth Funds of the Gulf countries can be a game changer for infrastructure investments in India, which would add a stable and profitable element to the portfolio of assets held by them. Bilateral cooperation in the field of higher education, skill development, agriculture, tourism, health care, power and infrastructure projects can add heft to the existing trade ties, which, for too long, has centred on oil. The last dimension talks about defence and security cooperation which includes joint military exercises, protection of Sea Lines of Communications (SLOCs) and fighting sea piracy. Already the Indian Ocean hosts the world's most significant SLOCs and as such plays a pivotal role in the global economy, in particular for the past 20 years.

India is pursuing a Free Trade Agreement (FTA) with the GCC, but over the years the dialogue has lost directions. India sought the help of Kuwaiti Prime Minister Jaber bin al-Sabah during his visit in November[22] and underlined the need for an early conclusion of the FTA agreement with GCC.[23] However, there is a strong need to revitalize institutionalized interaction between both sides. The India–GCC Industrial Conference (IGIC), an initiative aimed at fostering economic opportunities, which was started back in 2004, lost its momentum mid-way as the fourth GCC–India Industrial Conference, scheduled to be held in Jeddah, Saudi Arabia from 19 to 21 February, got postponed.

External Players

GCC countries have globalized their approach towards major key players and its relations with the US, China and Pakistan that have a bearing upon India–GCC relations. With the changing global pragmatism, GCC countries have realized the need to have their own multi-operational and multi-directional planks.

The US: The US has a deep strategic engagement with the GCC countries rooted in energy and defence. However, the changing regional dynamics have raised opportunities for other countries particularly India and China to deepen their relations with the GCC countries. This has been recognized by the GCC states that have tried to deepen their ties with the external world. However, as the US pivots towards Asia, there looms the possibility of GCC losing its strategic prominence in the region. The expected shale oil boom in the US might impact the energy trade and importance of GCC countries.[24] Thus, there is a rising concern among the GCC countries over the competition emerging in world energy market.

Last year, GCC confronted the US policies over Syria and Iran because it feared rising cross-sectarian tension impacting peace and stability of the region. At the same time, GCC and the US share strong defence ties irrespective of the tensed dialogue. At Manama, the US Defence Secretary Chuck Hagel attempted to dismiss such notions. As the US withdraws from Iraq and Afghanistan, he said, Washington remained deeply invested in the Middle East region, in trying to develop a 'new strategic agility'.[25] According to a strategic analyst, the US and GCC share three types of relations—a strategic relation, a military-to-military relation and a political relation.[26] During 2013, the US–GCC relation faced few challenges particularly because of the US policy towards Syria and the interim nuclear deal between Iran and the six global powers. Saudi Arabia that looks at Iran as a regional rival resented the deal and has been critical of the US's unwillingness to intervene in the Syrian crisis.[27] Hence, the dynamics of relationship is changing between Saudi Arabia and the US on account of the Syrian crisis and the nuclear deal between Iran and the US. This resulted in Saudi Arabia advising the Gulf region to stick together in order to maintain security apparatus.[28]

China: China poses a strong competition to India's interests in the Gulf region. Both China and India emerged as trade beneficiaries with the GCC countries and their relations are based on strong energy exchanges. China imports over 6 million barrels per day (bpd), and more than one-third comes from the GCC countries.[29] With the growing energy and other consumption needs of China and India, the GCC is extremely interested in the Indian Ocean security. Oman's plans to develop a huge oil storage hub at Ras Markaz on the Wusta Coast has sparked provisional interest from a number of countries like China, India and fellow members of the GCC.[30] The GCC has been continuing its strategic dialogues with China.[31] India needs to be watchful of the Chinese engagement with the GCC countries as it has huge stakes in the region.

Pakistan: Pakistan has a long history of friendly relations with the GCC countries but ironically the focus of Pakistan's foreign policy has always been the US. The current GCC trade with Pakistan stands at US$59 billion, which is expected to reach US$200 billion by 2015.[32] India has the world's second largest Muslim population and the world's second largest Shia population. The Islamic factor plays a very significant role in India's relations with the Gulf region and in Pakistan's close association with the UAE. Saudi Arabia occupies a place of geostrategic importance for India. Most of these countries were on Pakistan's side, especially over Kashmir at Organisation of Islamic Cooperation (OIC).[33] After India, Pakistan has the largest expatriate population in the GCC countries. Pakistani workers sent US$5.98 billion as remittances during 2012 which amounted to a 9.8 per cent share of the total remittances.[34] Pakistan has been supporting the Gulf countries in the field of defence and security, science and technology, and provides trained manpower to various fields. Pakistan, being the sixth largest army of the world and a sole nuclear Muslim state, proposed the setting up of a formal 'security bloc' to combat any external or internal security threats. Thus, the existing Peninsula Shield in the GCC would be further strengthened and streamlined.[35] However, the Indian engagement with the GCC does not need to be blurred by Pakistan. It needs to bank on the interest of the GCC states, and 'overcome its Pakistan obsession while engaging with the region'.[36]

CONCLUSION

The GCC countries need to instil a larger degree of confidence in the Indian market and its capabilities. Establishing a competent investment authority in all GCC nations, efforts to encourage small and medium enterprises (SMEs) investments and easing visa restrictions would foster India–GCC relations. Other areas of bilateral cooperation, such as in higher education, skill development, agriculture, tourism, health care, power and infrastructure projects, can add heft to the existing trade ties, that have been for too long centred on oil. Defence and security is another area where the two can benefit through mutual cooperation. The GCC countries have been trying to diversify their economies by promoting strong investments in the non-oil sector which has attracted huge investments. However, the problem of non-skilled local labour force, GCC's strict policies towards expatriate and migrant population and several protectionist policies for high-cost European and Asian producers make foreign investment unfavourable in the GCC countries. Other shortcomings that investors face are the inadequate disclosures on investment regulations and economic policies, procedural hurdles and economic vulnerabilities resulting from an over-reliance on the oil and gas sector.

NOTES

1. 'Official Visit of External Affairs Minister to the Kingdom of Bahrain', *Press Release*, Ministry of External Affairs, New Delhi, 6 December 2013, available at: http://www.mea.gov.in/press-releases.htm?dtl/22590/Official+visit +of+External+Affairs+Minister+to+the+Kingdom+of+Bahrain/.
2. Indian Diaspora, Ministry of Overseas Indian Affairs, available at: http://moia.gov.in/accessories.aspx?aid=11/.
3. Dahlia Kholaif, 'GCC States Hope Iran Deal Will End Tension', *Al Jazeera*, 12 December 2013, available at: http://www.aljazeera.com/news/middleeast/2013/12/gcc-states-hope-iran-deal-will-end-tension-20131210191314641802.html/.
4. 'Omani Rejection of GCC Union Adds Insult to Injury for Saudi Arabia', *Al-Monitor*, 28 November 2013, available at: http://www.al-monitor.com/pulse/originals/2013/12/oman-rejects-gcc-union-insults-saudi-arabia.html#/.

5. 'GCC Agrees on Measures against Terrorist Organisations', *Gulf News*, 14 February 2014, available at: http://gulfnews.com/news/gulf/saudi-arabia/gcc-agrees-on-measures-against-terrorist-organisations-1.1231461/.

6. 'SIPRI Conducts First Counter-Proliferation and Strategic Trade Controls Course', *Stockholm International Peace Research Institute (SIPRI)*, 25 January 2013, available at: http://www.sipri.org/events/activities/sipri-conducts-first-counter-proliferation-and-strategic-trade-controls-course/.

7. 'GCC Elects UAE to Host Defence Think Tank to Combat Common Security Threats', *The National*, 11 December 2013, available at: http://www.thenational.ae/world/middle-east/gcc-elects-uae-to-host-defence-think-tank-to-combat-common-security-threats/.

8. 'GCC Nations Step Closer to an EU-style Union with Joint Military Command Plan', *The National*, 10 December 2013, available at: http://www.thenational.ae/world/middle-east/gcc-nations-step-closer-to-an-eu-style-union-with-joint-military-command-plan/.

9. 'Single GCC Visa Likely by mid-2014: Report', *Times of Oman*, 23 December 2013, available at: http://www.timesofoman.com/News/Article-27339.aspx/.

10. Ulrichsen Coates Kristian, 'Bahrain's Uprising: Regional Dimensions and International Consequences', *Stability: International Journal of Security and Development,* 2013, Vol. 2, No. 1, pp. 1–12, available at: http://www.stabilityjournal.org/article/view/sta.be/58.

11. 'Bahrain: The Long Road Ahead', *Gulf Business*, 26 August 2013, available at: http://gulfbusiness.com/2013/08/bahrain-the-long-road-ahead/#.Uv4G-Dyo8Ib8/.

12. Shane McGinley, 'Revealed: Where Gulf Expats Sent Remittance in 2012', *arabianbusiness.com*, 13 May 2013, available at: http://www.arabianbusiness.com/revealed-where-gulf-expats-sent-remittance-in-2012-501232.html/.

13. 'GCC Again India's Top Remittance Source', *The National*, 11 December 2013, available at: http://www.thenational.ae/business/industry-insights/economics/gcc-again-indias-top-remittance-source/.

14. 'FTA Talks between India, Gulf Council to Resume Soon', *The Financial Express*, 16 February 2014, available at: http://www.financialexpress.com/news/FTA-talks-between-India—Gulf-council-to-resume-soon/1191211/.

15. 'GCC as an Investment Destination', *Alpen Capital*, 5 November 2013, available at: http://www.alpencapital.com/news-article-2013-nov.htm/.

16. Ibid.

17. 'GCC Seeks Stronger Ties with India', *Gulf News*, 26 September 2013, available at: http://gulfnews.com/news/gulf/saudi-arabia/gcc-seeks-stronger-ties-with-india-1.1235848/.

18. 'India "Keen to Strengthen Defence Ties with GCC"', *Making Waves*, National Maritime Foundation, New Delhi, 16 September 2013, available at: http://www.maritimeindia.org/sites/all/files/MW_91_September_2013.pdf/.

19. 'Address by Minister for External Affairs on "International Interests in Middle East Security and Non-Proliferation" at IISS Manama Dialogue', Ministry

of External Affairs, New Delhi, 8 December 2013, available at: http://www.
mea.gov.in/Speeches-statements.htm?dtl/22592/Address+by+Minister+for
+External+Affairs+on+International+Interests+in+Middle+East+Security+a
nd+NonProliferation+at+IISS+Manama+Dialogue/.

20. 'India Keen to Work with GCC in Fighting Piracy', *Gulf Daily News*, 16
     February 2014, available at: http://www.gulf-daily-news.com/NewsDetails.
     aspx?storyid=366448/.

21. 'Address by Minister for External Affairs on "International Interests in Mid-
     dle East Security and Non-Proliferation" at IISS Manama Dialogue', Ministry
     of External Affairs.

22. 'Kuwaiti Prime Minister arrives in Four-Day State Visit', *DNA*, 7 November
     2013, available at: http://www.dnaindia.com/india/report-kuwaiti-prime-
     minister-arrives-on-four-day-state-visit-1915245/.

23. 'Support Early Conclusion of FTA with GCC: India to Kuwait', *The Eco-
     nomic Times*, 8 November 2013, available at: http://articles.economictimes.
     indiatimes.com/2013-11-08/news/43822238_1_india-and-gcc-early-con-
     clusion-economic-cooperation/.

24. 'US Shale Boom Could Impact GCC in Long-term', *Gulf Business*, 24
     November 2014, available at: http://gulfbusiness.com/2013/11/us-shale-
     boom-can-impact-gcc-in-long-term/#.UvtD6Co8Ib8/.

25. 'Can India Take on a Bigger Role in the Persian Gulf?' *The Times of India*,
     14 December 2013, available at: http://articles.timesofindia.indiatimes.
     com/2013-12-14/india/45189622_1_bippa-uae-india/.

26. 'Despite Tensions, US–GCC Military Relations Strong', *Defense News*,
     10 November 2013, available at: http://www.defensenews.com/article/
     20131110/DEFREG02/311100004/Despite-Tensions-US-GCC-Military-
     Relations-Strong/.

27. 'Omani Rejection of GCC Union Adds Insult to Injury for Saudi Arabia', *Al-
     Monitor*, 28 November 2013, available at: http://www.al-monitor.com/pulse/
     originals/2013/12/oman-rejects-gcc-union-insults-saudi-arabia.html#/.

28. 'Stick Together for Security, Saudi Arabia Warns GCC', *The National*, 9
     December 2013, available at: http://www.thenational.ae/world/middle-east/
     stick-together-for-security-saudi-arabia-warns-gcc/.

29. 'GCC–Asia Growing Interdependence Seen on US Oil Self-reliance', *Saudi
     Gazette*, 16 February 2014, available at: http://www.saudigazette.com.sa/
     index.cfm?method=home.regcon&contentid=20131022184284/.

30. 'GCC, China and India Evince Interest in Oman Crude Oil Park', *Cerebral
     Business Research*, 23 October 2013, available at: http://www.cerebralbusi-
     ness.com/KnowledgeBase/News/GCC-China-and-India-evince-interest-in-
     Oman-Crude-Oil-Park-200179.htm/.

31. 'The GCC turns East', *Arab News*, 17 February 2014, available at: http://
     www.arabnews.com/gcc-turns-east/.

32. 'Future of Palk–Gulf Relations', *Pakistan Observer*, 16 May 2013, available
     at: http://pakobserver.net/201305/16/detailnews.asp?id=206918/.

33. 'Can India Take on a Bigger Role in Persian Gulf?' *The Times of India*, 14 December 2013, available at: http://articles.timesofindia.indiatimes.com/2013-12-14/india/45189622_1_bippa-uae-india/.
34. 'Asia–GCC Relations: Growing Interdependence', *Al Arabiya News*, 18 June 2013, available at: http://english.alarabiya.net/en/special-reports/bridging-the-gulf/2013/06/18/Asia-GCC-relations-Growing-interdependence.html/.
35. 'Pakistan Proposes Common Military Bloc to GCC', *Economic Affairs*, October 2013, available at: http://economicaffairs.com.pk/today/pakistan-proposes-common-military-bloc-to-gcc/.
36. C. Raja Mohan, 'Bridging the Gulf', *The Indian Express*, 25 February 2014, available at: http://indianexpress.com/article/opinion/columns/bridging-the-gulf/.

12

Policy Options for India

MEI@ND

1. **Engage Politically:** Political contacts between India and the Persian Gulf countries dwindled considerably during 2013. There were no state visits from India to the region and from the region only the Prime Minister of Kuwait visited India in November. Indeed, since the outbreak of popular protests in the Arab world, there have been no state visits from India. Even the Foreign Minister-level engagements have reduced. Such political indifference to a region of considerable importance does not bode well for India as a responsible international actor.

2. **Generation Next:** The leadership in a number of countries is in the midst of a generational transition. Hence, it is essential for the Indian missions in the region to diversify their engagements and contacts and move beyond, but without ignoring, the immediate Arab leadership. Tamim al-Thani, the new Emir of Qatar, became the Crown Prince in August 2003 and has never visited India. The uncertainty over the line of succession in Saudi Arabia should enable India to reach out to a number of groups, factions and potential successors in al-Saud. The same holds true for Oman, where the line of succession is not defined.

3. **Recognize Regional Tensions:** There are growing tensions in the Persian Gulf; while the traditional Arab-Persian tensions are growing, there are also new tensions emerging among the Arab countries. Not long ago, the GCC was seeking to expand by

including Jordan and Morocco. But in recent months, internal divisions within the GCC have emerged over Qatari actions and its position on some sensitive issues. Taking sides in the Arab–Persian or intra-Arab divide is not an option for India; but it would not be able to stay indifferent to the growing tensions in the region. Anticipating a nuanced approach to these tensions is imperative.

4. **Recognize Internal Cleavages:** In a political sense, the wider Middle East, especially the Gulf region, is in a flux. The popular protests in many Arab countries have highlighted the growing trust deficiency between the ruler and the ruled, and the widening popular discontent and disapproval of regimes. India and its elites need to recognize competing political and social forces in various countries. Without appearing to be patronizing in their approach, those Indians interested in the Persian Gulf must recognize, understand and closely follow various internal fault-lines and cleavages, and also the minority groups that exist in the region and their sociopolitical function and importance.

5. **Managing the US:** A number of American actions towards the Persian Gulf have come under public criticism and closer scrutiny. The exclusion of Saudi Arabia (and also Israel) from the Geneva agreement was not well received. The surprising refusal of Saudi Arabia to take up its non-permanent seat in the UN Security Council was attributed to its displeasure over some of the American policies, especially towards its engagement with Iran. India would have to learn to manage the fallout resulting from the growing tensions between the US and Saudi Arabia.

6. **Rise of Conservatism:** The Arab Spring has not only highlighted the political power of the Islamists but also witnessed a resurgence of conservative elements in some Gulf countries. While King Abdullah has been trying to modernize Saudi Arabia and limit the influence of the cleric, Qatar is moving in the opposite direction. The new Emir Tamim al-Thani is viewed as more conservative than his father. Recognizing this growing conservatism and its impact on the region is important.

7. **Iranian Puzzle:** Iran would continue to be a major concern for India. While the Geneva deal has relaxed one form of tension,

it has also highlighted Arab concerns vis-à-vis Iran as well as the US. Until a permanent arrangement over the nuclear issue is concluded, India will not be able to pursue its energy security interests with the Islamic Republic. Moreover, without finding a permanent settlement with regard to the payment mechanism India should not enter into any major energy deals with Iran.

8. **Security Engagement:** Without appearing to be intrusive, India should expand its military and security contacts with the Gulf region. The problems of sea piracy, protection of sea lanes of communication, and terrorism should motivate India to engage with the Arab countries and Iran in furtherance of its interests.

9. **Prepare for Arabization:** For a long time, the oil-rich Arab Gulf countries have been seeking increased employment opportunities for their citizens over the expatriates. While the progress has been slow, the Arab Spring and economic hardships have intensified the calls for the Arabization of the workforce. As highlighted by the Nitaqat policy pursued by Saudi Arabia, India would be adversely affected by this Arabization process. India would have to prepare itself for a gradual decrease in the flow of Indians to the Persian Gulf and also for its economic consequences at home.

10. **Re-focus Bilateral Trade:** India's economic relations with the Gulf are dominated by oil and gas imports and are highly skewed in the favour of the Persian Gulf region. Growing energy imports also contribute to widening trade deficit and have intensified India's payment problems with Iran. Hence, India should seek to bring down the trade deficit with the Persian Gulf by increasing or expanding its exports to the region. The excessive domination of oil, in some cases over 90 per cent of India's imports, does not augur well for the stable economic relationship.

11. **Labour Exploitation:** Media has been highlighting the grow-ing instances of labour-related problems in the Gulf countries, including non-payment, harsh living and working conditions, non-availability of religious rights, confiscation of passports, travel restrictions, sexual harassments and other forms of exploitation. The presence of the Indian expatriate community is a voluntary process and there are limitations on what the government could or should do. At the same time, improving and strengthening labour

agreements with the Gulf countries and stricter law enforcements against exploitative labour contractors would considerably reduce such instances. Some of the labour agreements are narrow and, especially, do not include domestic workers. Blacklisting of Indian as well as the Arab employment firms and travel agents over workers' treatment could be an effective deterrent strategy.

12. **Inaccurate Data:** Official figures regarding the number of Indian expatriates in the Gulf region are nothing more than estimates. The number of expatriate workers who seek Emigration Clearance is the only reliable data on the subject. With the likelihood of large-scale returnees from Gulf, resulting from the Arabization of the workforce, India would have to urgently start building a more accurate data base.

13. **Nomenclature:** Etymologically, the name 'India' is a foreign construct. If that name is adopted for self-identity, the region must also be recognized by its historic and widely accepted international names, namely Middle East and the Persian Gulf. Middle East is a term of self-identity for the region. Like other geographic terms, such as the Arabian Sea, the Indian Ocean and the South China Sea, the expression Persian Gulf does not denote Iranian ownership of the said waters.

About the Editor and Contributors

EDITOR

P. R. Kumaraswamy teaches contemporary Middle East at Jawaharlal Nehru University, New Delhi, and is the Honorary Director of Middle East Institute, New Delhi (MEI@ND).

He was a Research Fellow at the Harry S. Truman Research Institute for the Advancement of Peace, the Hebrew University of Jerusalem (1991–99). Ever since joining JNU in September 1999, he has been researching, teaching and writing on various aspects of contemporary Middle East. His works include *India's Israel Policy, A to Z of Arab-Israeli Conflict* and *Persian Gulf 2013*.

CONTRIBUTORS

Dipanwita Chakravortty is a doctoral candidate at the Centre for West Asian Studies, School of International Studies, Jawaharlal Nehru University, New Delhi.

Jatung Raja Philemon Chiru is a doctoral candidate at the Centre for West Asian Studies, School of International Studies, Jawaharlal Nehru University, New Delhi.

Melissa M. Cyrill is pursuing her MPhil from Centre for West Asian Studies, School of International Studies, Jawaharlal Nehru University, New Delhi.

Priyanka Mittal is pursuing her MPhil from Centre for West Asian Studies, School of International Studies, Jawaharlal Nehru University, New Delhi.

Alvite Singh Ningthoujam is a doctoral candidate at the Centre for West Asian Studies, School of International Studies, Jawaharlal Nehru University, New Delhi.

Md. Muddassir Quamar is a doctoral candidate at the Centre for West Asian Studies, School of International Studies, Jawaharlal Nehru University, New Delhi.

Paulami Sanyal is a doctoral candidate at the Centre for West Asian Studies, School of International Studies, Jawaharlal Nehru University, New Delhi.

Anjani Kumar Singh is a doctoral candidate at the Centre for West Asian Studies, School of International Studies, Jawaharlal Nehru University, New Delhi.

Manjari Singh is a doctoral candidate at the Centre for West Asian Studies, School of International Studies, Jawaharlal Nehru University, New Delhi.

Marimuthu Ulaganathan is a doctoral candidate at the Centre for West Asian Studies, School of International Studies, Jawaharlal Nehru University, New Delhi.

About MEI@ND

Middle East Institute (MEI) is a forward-looking, policy-oriented non-governmental research institution striving for academic openness. Non-partisan, non-nationalistic and non-ideological, the MEI has no agenda of its own. Its aim is to facilitate a professional and comprehensive understanding of the Middle East.

We at MEI intend to do so by actively engaging with all regional actors and great powers with stakes in the region. The MEI functions as a forum for debate, dialogue and discourse concerning the Middle East.

The MEI is India-based but not Indo-centric.

Index

Abu Dhabi, 146, 225, 227
Abu Dhabi Authority for Culture and
    Heritage (ADACH), 238
Abu Dhabi Industrial City, 234
Abu Dhabi Investment Authority
    (ADIA), 229
Aditya (fleet tanker), 150
Afghanistan, 61–62, 76, 111, 168
Agility Logistics, 128
Ahamed, E., 8, 43, 125, 149, 198–99,
    229, 260
Ahluwalia, Montek Singh, 125, 129
Ahmadinejad, Mahmoud, 2, 55–56, 61
Ajman Free Trade Zone, UAE, 234
Alghanim Group of Kuwait, 128
al-Islah, 225
Al Jazeera network, 4, 32n7, 181–82
Al-Khobar, 194
al-Maktoum, Sheikh Mohammed bin
    Rashid, 228
al-Maliki, Nouri, 101–2, 109
Al-Nahrain Center for Strategic
    Studies, Baghdad, 103
A Look towards the Sky (Hadi
    Mohaqqeq), 75
al-Qaeda, 100, 169, 258, 267
al-Qaeda in the Arabian Peninsula
    (AQAP), 258, 267–68
al Qaida in Iraq (AQI), 110
Anglican Church, 123
Annan, Kofi, 62
Ansari, M. Hamid, 7, 63, 124
Antony, A. K., 76, 198, 207

Apache fighter helicopters, 226
Arabian Gate Expo, 154
Arabization, 30
Arabization of labour force, 1
Arab League, 2
Arab News, 207
Arab–Persian tensions, 1
Arab Spring, 119–20, 144, 169, 193,
    211, 213, 224
Armenian Orthodox Church, 123
Armoured Infantry Fighting Vehicles
    (AIFVs), UAE, 226
Asian Regional Forum, 7
Associated Chambers of
    Commerce and Industry of India
    (ASSOCHAM), 124, 128, 177
Azad, Ghulam Nabi, 198

Bahonar, Mohammad Reza, 56
Bahrain
    bilateral relations
        cultural relations, 46
        economic relations, 41–45
        energy relations, 45
        political relations, 40–41
    domestic developments, 35–40
    India ties with, 49
    key information on, 34
    relations with external player,
        46–48
Bahraini India Society, 46
Bahrain Independent Commission of
    Inquiry (BICI), 35

Bahrain–India Exhibition and Conference, Manama, 43–44
Bahrain International Investment Park (BIIP), 38
Bahrain International Technology Exhibition (BITEX), 40
Bahrain National Guard, 48
Bait Al Falaj, 150
balance of plant (BOP), 107
Baloch community, Oman, 158
Balochzehi, Samiyeh, 57
Barzani, Masoud, 101
Bashar al-Assad, 4
Bharatiya Janata Party (BJP), 61
Bharat Oman Refineries Limited (BORL), 153
Biden, Joseph, 109
Biduns, 122
Bilateral Investment Promotion and Protection Agreement (BIPA) between India and UAE, 230
bilateral trade
  India–Bahrain, 42–43
  India–GCC, 280
  India–Iran, 64–65
  India–Iraq, 105
  India–Kuwait, 125–29
  India–Oman, 151
  India–Qatar, 174–75
  India–Saudi Arabia, 200–201
  India–UAE, 231–32
  India–Yemen, 261–62
Brahimi, Syria Lakhdar, 125
Brazil, Russia, India, China and South Africa (BRICS), 7
British Petroleum (BP), 160
Bureau of Indian Standards (BIS), 62
Burj Khalifa skyscraper, 225–26

California Public Employees' Retirement System (CalPERS), 70–71
Capital Markets Authority of Kuwait, 128

Central Board of Secondary Education (CBSE), 132, 156
Central Military Commission, China, 269
Centre for Middle East Studies, 31
Centre for Strategic and International Studies (CSIS), 167
Chabahar–Faraj–Bam railway, 68
Chabahar port, 61–62, 69, 79
Chamber of Commerce for Iran Trade Promotion (CCITP), 68
Chemical and Allied Export Promotion Council of India (CAPEXIL), 177
Chennai International Film Festival (CIFF), 75
Chennai Petroleum Corporation Limited (CPCL), 72
Chidambaram, P., 61, 173, 177, 185, 206
Chief Election Commissioner (CEC), 261
Chief of Integrated Defence Staff (CIDS), 237
Chief of Naval Staff (CNS), 237
China–Kuwait Cooperation Forum, 135
Chinese People's Political Consultative Conference (CPPCC), 268
cinema role in bridging cooperation between Iran and India, 75
Clinton, Hillary, 8
Communist Party of India (Marxist) (CPI-M), 61
compound annual growth rate (CAGR), 279, 281
Comptroller and Auditor General of India, 149
Confederation of Indian Industry (CII), 43, 124, 128
Conference on Disarmament, 63
Congress, 7
Coptic Orthodox Church, 123

Council of Scientific and Industrial Research, 131
Crown Prince Nayef (1934–2012), 3
Crown Princes Sultan (1928–2011), 3
Cultural Exchange Programme for 2013–15, 260, 266, 271
Cultural Fairs Institute, Iran, 75

Defence Security Cooperation Agency, 134
Delhi-Mumbai Industrial Corridor (DMIC), 204
Department of Economic Affairs (DEA), India, 74
Directorate General of Foreign Trade, India, 31
diwaniyas, 120
Diyanat, 81
Doha Trade Exhibition, 177
Doha Tribeca Film Festival, Doha, 179
Dragon Mart, 182
Dubai Air Show, 227
Duty Free Tariff Preference (DFTP) Scheme of India, 264, 271

Economic Development Board (EDB) report, 38
Educational Exchange Programme (EEP) signed between India and Yemen, 266
Emigration Check Required (ECR), 26–28
energy imports by India, 17–18, 45, 71, 129, 156, 178, 205, 236, 265, 281–82
Energy Insurance Pool (EIP) fund, 72
Energy Management Exhibition, Bahrain, 39–40
energy share in total foreign trade, India, 22–23
Engineering Export Promotion Council (EEPC), 70
Engineering, Procurement and Construction (EPC), 153

enhanced oil recovery (ECR) techniques, 148
Enhancing Potential Business Partnerships seminar, Yemen, 264
Etihad, 235
European Union, 6
European Union (EU), 254
Euros, 63
expatriate Indian community in Saudi Arabia, 208–9
expatriate population size in Saudi Arabia, 29
exports, Persian Gulf share in India, 12–13

F-16 fighter aircraft, 226
Federal National Council, UAE, 224
Federation of Andhra Pradesh Chamber of Commerce and Industry (FAPCCI), 68, 70
Federation of Indian Chambers of Commerce and Industry (FICCI), 70, 124, 128–29, 177
FIFA World Cup (2022), 171
foreign direct investment (FDI), 38, 203, 234, 243, 281, 283
foreign policy of Iran, changes during 2013, 59
Foreign Service Institute (FSI), 124
Fotros, 60
Free Officers Revolution of 1952, 2
free trade agreement (FTA), 283
Free Trade Zones (FTZ) in UAE, 234

G-8, 7
Gandhi, Indira, 102
General Investments Authority (GIA), 265
Geneva nuclear deal, 2, 30, 60, 78, 212
German Federal Office of Economics and Export Control (BAFA), 278
Global Convention on Business Excellence, Dubai, 229

Global Investment House, 128
Guardian Council, 56
Guardian, The, 180
Gujarat Narmada Valley Fertilisers
  and Chemicals (GNFC), 68
Gujarat State Fertilisers and
  Chemicals Limited (GSFCL), 68
Gujral, I. K., 102
Gulf Cooperation Council (GCC), 6,
  35, 37–38, 46–47, 59, 125, 134,
  144, 146, 173, 208–9, 225, 254,
  286
  bilateral relations with India,
    279–83, 286
  internal developments in, 277–79
  relations with external players,
    284–85

Guru Nanak, 76

Hafiz, 196
Hajj pilgrimage, 197, 199, 210
Hamiriya Free Trade Zone, UAE, 234
Hindustan Petroleum Corporation
  Limited (HPCL), 71–72
Hongkong and Shanghai Banking
  Corporation (HSBC), 121, 159–60
Houthis, 254–58
Human Rights Watch, 122, 132, 171,
  240
hydrocarbon resources/sector, 100,
  125, 144, 147–48, 173, 178

Incredible India, 131
India and Persian Gulf, relationship
  between, 7–30
India-Arab Cultural Centre at Jamia
  Millia Islamia, New Delhi, 208
India Centre for Migration (ICM),
  229
India–GCC Free Trade Agreement,
  125
India–GCC Industrial Conference
  (IGIC), 283

India–Israel Joint Working Group
  (JWG) on counter-terrorism, 80
Indian Business and Professional
  Network (IBPN), 179–80
Indian Coast Guard Ship (ICGS), 237
Indian Community Benevolent Forum
  (ICBF), 179
Indian Council of Cultural Relations
  (ICCR), 109, 238, 266, 271
Indian Cultural Centre (ICC), 179,
  238
Indian Cultural Centre, Tehran, 75
Indian Cultural Week, Riyadh, 208
Indian Engineering Sourcing Show,
  Mumbai, 264
Indian Medical Association, 180
Indian Naval Ships (INS), 237
Indian Ocean Naval Symposium
  (IONS), 130
Indian Ocean Rim Association for
  Regional Cooperation (IOR-ARC),
  148
Indian Oil Corporation (IOC), 73
Indian Social and Cultural Centre
  (ISCC), Abu Dhabi, 229
Indian Technical and Economic
  Cooperation (ITEC), 109, 267
Indian Technical and Economic
  Cooperation Day, 156
Indian Union Muslim League (IUML),
  8
India–Oman Joint Investment Fund
  (IOJIF), 154
India–Oman Strategic Consultative
  Group (IOSCG), 149
India–UAE High Level Task Force on
  Investments (HLTFI), 229–30, 235
India–Yemen Joint Committee for
  Economic, Scientific and Technical
  Cooperation (JCM), 260, 271
Indo–Iranian Joint Commission
  meeting, 69
Indo–Qatar Labour agreement of
  1985, 185

Indsil Group, 154
Institute for Defence Studies and
    Analyses, Delhi, 103
Institute of Chartered Accountants,
    180
Institution of Engineers (India), 180
internally displaced persons (IDPs),
    259
International Atomic Energy Agency
    (IAEA), 63, 77
International Committee of the Red
    Cross (ICRC), 258
International Defence Exhibition and
    Conference (IDEX), Abu Dhabi, 236
International Design Week, Bahrain,
    40
International Film Festival of Kerala
    (IFFK), 75
International Humanitarian Pledging
    Conference on Syria, 125
International Institute for Strategic
    Studies (IISS), 282
International Migration Report 2013,
    239
International Monetary Fund (IMF),
    196
International Religious Freedom
    Report for 2012, 267
International Trade Union
    Confederation (ITUC), 170,
    180–81
investments by Saudi Arabia in India,
    203–4
Iran
    attracted global attention in 2013,
        55
    bilateral relations
        cultural relations, 75–76
        defence relations, 76
        economic relations, 64–70
        energy relations, 70–74
        political relations, 60–64
    challenges and problems before,
        80–81
    domestic developments, 55–60
    key information on, 54
    relations with external players,
        76–80
    US postures with, 55
Iranian Offshore Oil Company
    (IOOC), 72
Iranian Revolutionary Guard Corps
    (IRGC), 81
Iran–Pakistan–India (IPI) gas
    pipeline, 62
Iran–Pakistan (IP) pipeline project,
    79–80
Iran Tea Association (ITA), 67
Iraq
    challenges before, 111–12
    domestic developments, 100–102
    hydrocarbon resources
        concentrated in Shia areas, 100
    key information on, 99
    prospects in, 111–12
    registered refugees from Syria to,
        102
    relations with external players,
        109–11
    relations with India
        economic, 104–5
        energy trade, 106–7
        political, 102–3
        security cooperation, 103
        sociocultural ties, 107–9
    US-led invasion of 2003, 100
Islamic State of Iraq and the Levant
    (ISIL), 100
Israel, 55, 60, 78, 210
    American spat and disagreements,
        5
    bilateral relations
        with Iran, 80
        with Saudi Arabia, 213
    –Palestinian peace process, 182

Jaipur International Film Festival, 75
Jawaharlal Nehru ports, 69

Jebel Ali Free Trade Zone, UAE, 234
Jet Airways, 235
Jewish Israel, 3
Jiabao, Wen, 182
Jindal Steel and Power Ltd. (JSPL), 153
Joint Business Council (JBC), 150
Joint Commission Meeting (JCM), 150
Joint Committee on Security Matters (JCSM), 237
Joint Defence Cooperation Committee (JDCC), 236

kafala (sponsorship) system, 132–33, 171
KAPICO Group, 128
Karat, Prakash, 61
Kavakebian, Mostafa, 56
KCIC, 128
Kerala employed as workers in Saudi Arabia, 30
Kerry, John, 157, 182
KGA Group, 128
Khazzan tight gas project, 160
Khurshid, Salman, 8, 61–62, 75, 102–3, 125, 198, 207, 209, 228, 244, 282–83
Ki-Moon, Ban, 227
KIPCO, 128
KLJ Organic Limited, 177
Krishna, S. M., 198
Kumar, Meira, 61
Kurdish Regional Government (KRG), 101
Kuwait, 12, 37, 48, 72, 109, 118–21–23, 131–37. See also Arab Spring
  bans foreign ownership of its resources, 121
  bilateral relations with India, 136–37
  cultural, 129–30
  defence, 129
  economic, 125–29
  energy, 129
  political, 123–25
  relations with external players, 133–35
  singed contract with HSBC, 121
  unrecognized Christian groups, 123
  voting rights in, 120
Kuwait Diplomatic Institute (KDI), 124
Kuwait Finance House, 128
Kuwaiti News Agency (KUNA), 278
Kuwait Institute for Scientific Research (KISR), 131
Kuwait Investment Authority (KIA), 121, 128–29
Kuwait Petroleum Corporation, 121

labour migration, 26
Ladakh International Film Festival (LIFF), 75
Lankarani, Kamran Baqeri, 56
Life Insurance Corporation, 153
Liquefied Natural Gas (LNG), 39, 71, 178–79, 184
London Olympic Games, 192

Majlis al-Shura, 193
Manama Dialogue, 37, 46
Mangalore Refinery and Petrochemicals Limited (MRPL), 71–73
Market Linked Focus Product Scheme (MLFPS), 264
matams, 37
Mecca, 76
Menon, Shivshankar, 61, 198
Middle East, 1, 4–6, 8, 30–31
Middle East and North Africa (MENA), 38, 241
Middle East Institute at New Delhi (MEI@ND), 31

Middle East Peace Initiative
  Scholarship programme by the US,
  157
migrant workers from India 26,
  131–33, 170, 239–40
Ministry of External Affairs (MEA), 8
Ministry of Overseas Indian Affairs
  (MOIA), 26–27, 199, 209, 214,
  229, 240
Mishra, Brajesh, 63
Moily, Veerappa M., 79–80, 102, 130
Morsi, Mohammed, 1–2, 225
Mubarak, Hosni, 1–2
Mukherjee, Pranab, 61, 124, 173
Muscat, 74, 144–45, 149, 153–56,
  159
Muscat International Folklore
  Festival, 156
Muscat Overseas Group, 154
Muslim brotherhood, 1, 4, 32n3, 181
Mutawwa (Commission for the
  Promotion of Virtue and Prevention
  of Vice), 192

Nair, T. K. A., 199
Naseem Al Bahr, 150
National Audit Court (NAC), 39
National Book Trust (NBT), 75
National Commodity and Derivatives
  Exchange (NCDEX), 154
National Consensus Dialogue,
  initiative of Bahrain government, 35
National Council of Educational
  Research and Training (NCERT),
  136
National Council of Science Museums
  (NCSM), India, 266
National Dialogue Conference (NDC),
  Yemen, 254–57, 268, 270
National Evangelical (Protestant)
  Church, 123
National Iranian Gas Exports
  Company (NIGEC), 74

National Iranian Oil Corp (NIOC), 72
National Iranian Tanker Company
  (NITC), 71
National Science Museum, Yemen,
  266
National Security Bureau of Kuwait,
  124
National Security Council Secretariat
  of India, 124
NATO, 181
Netanyahu, Benjamin, 5
New India Assurance Company, 153
ninth Formula One Grand Prix,
  Bahrain, 39
Nitaqat policy introduction by Saudi
  Arabia, 30, 33n17, 192–93, 196,
  199, 209
non-Muslims in UAE, 239
non-UAE Shia Muslims, 239
NSG, 77
Nuclear Non-Proliferation Treaty
  (NPT), 77

Obama, Barack, 5, 59, 133
oil
  imports by India, 44, 65–66,
    107–8, 127, 152, 175–76, 206,
    232–33, 263
  Persian Gulf share, 24
  production of Iraq, 106
  products share in exports, India,
    21–22
  -related exports to Iran by India,
    19–20
  reserves, 24, 35
Oil and Gas Journal, 122
Oil and Natural Gas Corp (ONGC),
  71–72, 106
Oil Industry Development Board
  (OIDB), 74
Oman, 10, 16, 27, 30, 48, 74
  bilaterial relations with India, 160
  cultural relations, 155–56

economic relations, 150–55
energy relations, 155
political and defence relations,
    149–50
domestic developments in, 144–147
key information on, 143
relations with external players,
    157–60
Oman Electricity Transmission Co.
    (OETC), 153
Omani Chamber of Commerce and
    Industry (OCCI), 155, 158
Oman India Fertilizer Company
    (OMIFCO), 153
Organization of Islamic Cooperation
    (OIC), 269–70, 285
Organization of Petroleum Exporting
    Countries (OPEC), 101, 121
Overseas Indian Cultural Congress
    (OICC), 229

Pakistan, 62
bilateral relations with
    Bahrain, 47–48
    Iran, 79–80
    Iraq, 111
    Saudi Arabia, 212
Partitioned Neutral Zone (PNZ), 122
Patil, Pratibha D., 240
People's Democratic Republic of
    Yemen, 260
Persian Gulf Series, 31
Petroleum Contracts and Licensing
    Directorate (PCLD), Iraq, 106
Petroleum Development Oman
    (PDO), 153
Pharmaceutical Export Promotion
    Council of India (Pharmexcil),
    66–67
policy options for India, 290–93
post-Tahrir Square democratic
    experiment, Egypt, 1
Pravasi Bhartiya Divas (PBD), India,
    209

Presidential elections in 2013, Iran,
    57–58
protection and indemnity (P&I), 73
Protection of Society from Acts of
    Terrorism 2006, Bahrain, 36
Public Authority for Investment
    Promotion of Export Development
    (PAIPED), 149, 154
Public Authority for Manpower
    (PAM), Kuwait, 133
Puppet Theatre Group, The, 75

Qader cruise missile, 60
Qatar, 3, 48
bilateral relations with India, 185
    cultural relations, 179–81
    economic relations, 174–77
    energy relations, 178–79
    political relations, 173–74
challenges before, 184–85
diplomatic involvement in region
    trouble zones, 4
domestic developments in, 167–72
key information on, 166
opportunities in, 184–85
problems in, 184–85
relations with external players,
    181–84
rivalry and tensions between Saudi
    Arabia and, 6
Qatari Business Association, 177
Qatar Industrial Manufacturing
    Company (QIMC), 177
Qatar Investment Authority (QIA),
    172
Qatar Solar Technologies (QSTec),
    183
Queen Elizabeth, 159

Ra'ad 85, 60
Rashtriya Chemicals and Fertilisers
    (RCF), 68
Reddy, S. Jaipal, 198
Religious Freedom Report, 171

Reluctant Fundamentalis, The (Mira Nair), 179
Reserve Bank of India (RBI), 67, 69, 74
Riyadh, 2–3, 5
Rouhani, Hassan, 2, 7, 55–56, 59, 63, 157, 228
Royal Navy of Oman Vessels (RNOV), 150
Royal Omani Navy, 150
rupee-payment mechanism, 67–68

Sakina International Trading Company, 136
Salafists, 254, 258
Sampath, V. S., 261
Samudra Prahari, 237
Saudi Arabia
    bilateral relations with India, 197
        cultural relations, 207–10
        defence relations, 206–7
        economic relations, 200–204
        energy relations, 205–6
        political relations, 198–200
    challenges before, 213–14
    domestic developments in, 192–96
    expatriate population size in (*see* expatriate population size in Saudi Arabia)
    failures, 4–5
    key information on, 191
    Nitaqat policy introduction by (*see* Nitaqat policy introduction by Saudi Arabia)
    relations with Bahrain, 48
    relations with external players, 2010–13
    tensions with the US, 5
    uncertainty over American commitments, 5
Saudi Arabian General Investment Authority (SAGIA), 204
Saudi Civil and Political Rights Association (ACPRA), 194

sea lines of communication (SLOC), 207, 235–36, 283
sectarian violence, 101, 254, 259–60, 264, 270
Securities and Exchange Board of India, 128
Sharif, Nawaz, 111, 184, 243
Sharma, Anand, 104
Shia
    in Bahrain, 34, 213
    counterpart, 37
    in Iran, 54
    in Saudi Arabia, 191
Shinde, Sushil Kumar, 103
Shura Council, 36
Singh, Ajit, 229
Singh, Manmohan, 7, 63, 106, 124, 197–98
Singh, Rajnath, 61
Singh, Sujatha, 64
SIPRI, 278
small and medium enterprises (SMEs), 147, 177, 286
Sohar Free Zone, 154
Soltanieh, Ali Asghar, 77
Special Economic Zones (SEZs), 234
Sridevi Nrithyalaya, 156
State Audit Institution of Oman, 149
State Bank of India, 153
succession uncertainties, 1
Suddenly, Zinat (Navid Nikkhah Azad), 75
Sultan Qaboos, 144, 146, 155, 157
Sunni minority in central Iraq, 100
Sunni mosques, 37
Sunni Muslim, 37, 123
Supreme Commission for Elections and Referendum (SCER) of Yemen, 261
Syrian conflict, 2
Syrian crisis, 62, 101

Talabani, Jalal, 100
Tehran, 7, 55, 59–60, 62, 64, 68–70, 73, 75, 227

Tehran Chamber of Commerce,
Industries, Mines and Agriculture,
70
terrorist organization, 1, 4, 278
terror/terrorism, 6, 36, 61, 197, 199,
207, 212, 236–37, 241, 243–44,
260, 267, 292
Tharoor, Shashi, 198
Thermal High Altitude Area Defence
(THAAD) missile defence system,
157, 226–27
trade balance with India's trading
partners, 14
trade deficit–oil import linkages,
India, 15–16
Travelling Lens, The (Shreekant
Somany), 131
Tunisia progress towards
constitutional processes, 1

UN General Assembly, 59, 184,
241–42
UN Human Development Report
2013, 145
United Arab Emirates (UAE), 10–11,
27, 48, 112, 147
bilateral relations with India, 245
cultural relations, 238–39
defence and security relations,
235–38
economic relations, 230–35
energy relations, 235
political relations, 228–30
domestic developments in, 224–28
issues and challenges before,
243–45
key information on, 223
migration from India, 239–40
relations with external players,
241–43
United Nations Security Council
(UNSC), 41, 195, 254
Iraq reiterated support to India
candidature in, 103

Resolution 2118, 2, 5
Saudi Arabia refused to take non-
permanent seat, 211
United Progressive Alliance (UPA)
government, 7
unmanned aerial vehicles (UAVs),
60, 226
US Central Command (CENTCOM),
181–82

Vahanvati, G. E., 199

weapon of mass destruction (WMD),
283
World Bank, 30, 169
World Food Programme (WFP),
Yemen, 261
World Islamic Banking Conference,
Bahrain, 39
World Trade Organization (WTO),
69

Yemen, 6–7, 10, 18, 27, 147, 157
bilateral relations with India, 259,
271
cultural relations, 266–67
economic relations, 261–64
energy relations, 264–66
political relations, 260–61
challenges before, 270
domestic developments in,
254–59
key information on, 253
progress towards constitutional
processes, 1
relations with external players,
267–70
Yemen Arab Republic, 260
Yemeni–Chinese Friendship Hospital,
268
Yemen–India Business Council
(YIBC), 264, 269
Yemen State Television, 269
Yemen Strategic Plan of 2002, 267